FIELD GUIDE TO
Wisconsin Streams

FIELD GUIDE TO
Wisconsin Streams

PLANTS
FISHES
INVERTEBRATES
AMPHIBIANS
AND REPTILES

Michael A. Miller, Katie Songer, and Ron Dolen

THE UNIVERSITY OF WISCONSIN PRESS

the waters run
THE CURRENT FUND

The University of Wisconsin Press
1930 Monroe Street, 3rd Floor
Madison, Wisconsin 53711-2059
uwpress.wisc.edu

3 Henrietta Street
London WC2E 8LU, England
eurospanbookstore.com

Printed in the United States of America

Library of Congress Cataloging-in-Publication Data
Miller, Michael A. (Ecologist), author.
Field guide to Wisconsin streams : plants, fishes, invertebrates, amphibians, and reptiles /
Michael A. Miller, Katie Songer, and Ron Dolen.
pages cm
Includes bibliographical references and index.
ISBN 978-0-299-29454-0 (pbk. : alk. paper)
1. Stream plants—Wisconsin—Identification. 2. Stream animals—Wisconsin—Identification.
3. Stream ecology—Wisconsin. I. Songer, Katie, author. II. Dolen, Ron, author. III. Title.
QH105.W6M55 2014
577.6'409775—dc23
2013017555

Field Guide Sections

PLANTS
(page 21)

Green and leafy;
usually rooted

INVERTEBRATES
(page 87)

Spineless; usually with
body segments and an
exoskeleton or shell

CRAYFISHES
(page 133)

Large invertebrate with
two big claws and a
broad flipper

MUSSELS AND CLAMS
Class Bivalvia
(page 141)

Two shells enclosing
a soft body

FISHES
(page 166)

Fins and gills;
usually with scales

AMPHIBIANS
Frogs and salamanders
(page 251)

Thin, moist skin;
four legs

REPTILES
(page 260)

Scaly, dry skin;
usually terrestrial

CONTENTS

PREFACE

This book is the product of the combined efforts of many ecologists and biologists from the Wisconsin Department of Natural Resources (DNR), the University of Wisconsin, and various other agencies. Many of those who contributed to the project have spent years and even decades developing the expertise and materials that they contributed.

Mike Miller initiated the creation of this field guide and directed Katie Songer and Ron Dolen to work on it. Songer, with much assistance from Dolen, organized and managed the project. Together, Songer and Dolen authored initial drafts of the sections on invertebrates and fishes, authored the sections on plants (Dolen) and crayfishes (Songer), provided major edits to all sections, selected and/or acquired most images, and created all distribution maps and supplemental materials. Miller authored the general introduction, the final draft of the invertebrate section, and the introduction to the fish section.

We would like to thank several people in particular on whom we relied for either their authorship, major contributions in the form of publications (listed in the references), or both. These are Rebecca Christoffel and Bob Hay (authors and major contributors, amphibians and reptiles); Lisie Kitchel (author, mussels); John Lyons (author and major contributor, fishes); the late George C. Becker, author of *Fishes of Wisconsin* (major contributor, fishes); William R. Bouchard (major contributor, invertebrates); Horton H. Hobbs III and the late Joan P. Jass (major contributors, crayfishes); and Paul Skawinski (major contributor, plants).

Over the course of the project, we called upon various experts in graphic design and publishing. Their help was instrumental in developing a book format that would be pleasing and easy to use. In particular, we would like to thank Michelle Voss, Karl Scheidegger, and Julie A. Schroeder for their input on design and Gary Casper, Jill Rosenberg, and William A. Smith for their assistance with the creation of distribution maps.

In addition to authors and editors, this book was reviewed by dozens of people, a few of whom performed extensive reviews. These are Jeff Dimick (invertebrates), Susan Knight (plants), Michelle Nault (plants), and Paul Skawinski (plants). We greatly appreciate their taking the time to so thoroughly improve the quality of this book. Finally, we thank Russ Rasmussen and Todd Ambs for giving permission to go ahead with the project and thank Susan Sylvester, Greg Searle, Ryan Raab, Tim Asplund, and Mari Nord for providing administrative support.

The following is a list of all other contributors who spent time reviewing and assisting with the guide. Sincere thanks to all.

Thomas Boos (woody plants)
Gary Casper (amphibians, reptiles)
Rebecca Christoffel (amphibians, reptiles)
Robert DuBois (invertebrates)
Robert Freckmann (plants)
Jen Hauxwell (plants)
Bob Hay (amphibians, reptiles)
Laura Herman (plants)
Horton H. Hobbs III (crayfishes)
Joan P. Jass (crayfishes)

Heather Kaarakka (mussels)
Kelly Kearns (plants)
Jim Klosiewski (fishes)
Jim Kreitlow (fishes)
Gina Laliberte (plants)
Heidi Langrehr (plants)
Laura MacFarland (plants)
Marty Melchior (woody plants)
Alison Mikulyuk (plants)
Matt Mitro (fishes)

Aaron Nelson (fishes)   Kris Stepenuck (invertebrates)
Bobbi Peckarsky (invertebrates)   Pat Trochlell (woody plants)
Craig Roesler (crayfishes)   Scott Van Egeren (crayfishes, mussels)
Karl Scheidegger (fishes)   Dreux Watermolen (invertebrates)
Kurt Schmude (invertebrates)   Sandy Wickman (plants)
Mike Sorge (fishes)   Catherine Woodward (woody plants)

A complete list of illustration credits precedes the index at the end of the book.

FIELD GUIDE TO
Wisconsin Streams

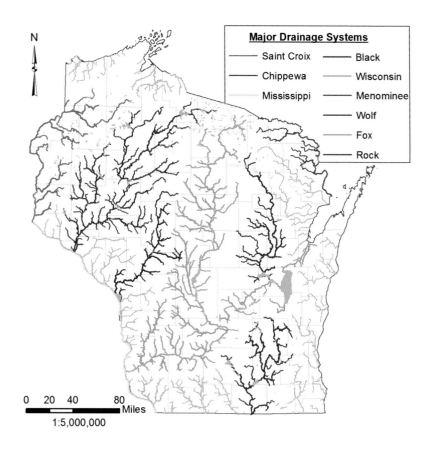

N

Major Drainage Systems

—— Saint Croix   —— Black
—— Chippewa   —— Wisconsin
—— Mississippi   —— Menominee
                    —— Wolf
                    —— Fox
                    —— Rock

0   20   40   80
                Miles
1:5,000,000

Introduction

In Nature's infinite book of secrecy, a little I can read.

—*William Shakespeare*

Streams are magical places for those who explore them. This guide represents the collective knowledge of dozens of technical experts who are passionate about Wisconsin's aquatic resources. It is our strong desire to pass this knowledge and passion on to the readers of this book. Although Wisconsin is a water-rich state, we need to be water-wise. The more we know about streams, their inhabitants, and what affects them, the more we'll appreciate and treasure these vital resources and better manage them for current and future generations.

Introduction

Wisconsin is defined by water, bounded by Lakes Michigan and Superior and the Mississippi River. Even the name Wisconsin is thought to have originated from the Ojibwe name for the Wisconsin River.

Wisconsin has an estimated 1.2 quadrillion gallons of groundwater, enough to cover the entire state with ten feet of water; however, it is not evenly distributed across the state and some areas are experiencing shortages. On the land's surface, there are 15,000 lakes, 5.2 million acres of wetlands, and 22,000 perennial streams and rivers. If all of Wisconsin's streams and rivers were placed end to end, they would measure 42,000 miles long, enough to encircle the planet over one and a half times. If we include Wisconsin's *ephemeral* streams (streams that flow only at certain times of the year), the number of stream miles more than doubles to an estimated length of 86,000 miles.

Satellite image of Wisconsin in autumn. Lakes Superior and Michigan form part of Wisconsin's northern and eastern borders, and the Mississippi River is visible in the west.

Introduction

From a global perspective, streams and rivers make up a very small fraction of the earth's water. Oceans contain approximately 96 percent of the planet's total water volume, glaciers 1.7 percent, groundwater 1.7 percent, lakes 0.013 percent, and the atmosphere 0.001 percent. Streams and rivers account for only about 0.0002 percent.

Clean water is essential for life, and while water is seen by many as free and limitless, in reality it is a finite resource that needs to be managed wisely. Protecting aquatic resources requires an understanding of natural and human-influenced factors that affect our streams. Even though Wisconsin is seemingly awash in water, streams are a limited, vulnerable resource greatly influenced by their surrounding environments; many external factors affect their physical, chemical, and biological conditions. These factors—from geological events to human land use—are described in the following text.

Watersheds

To understand how streams are connected to their surrounding landscape, it is important to understand the concept of watersheds. *Watershed*, *drainage basin*, and *catchment* are all terms used to describe an area of land that collects water from rainfall and snowmelt. Watersheds are defined by changes in landscape elevation, with hills and ridges separating one watershed from another. These elevation changes may be a few feet or thousands of feet depending upon watershed size and location. Typically, there is an outlet stream or river draining each watershed.

Streams have branching, tree-like flow paths that efficiently drain water from the land. This branching pattern can be seen on a sidewalk at our feet at the start of a rainstorm or in a photograph of the Mississippi River from space. Small streams join together, creating increasingly larger streams and rivers, analogous to the many small branches and fewer large limbs and, ultimately, the trunk of a tree. One common method used by scientists to define stream size based on a hierarchy of branching is called *Strahler's stream order*. In this system, the smallest headwater streams are called *first order streams*, and when two first order streams join, they create a *second order stream*. (When two streams of different orders join, the resulting order is the highest order number of the two streams—for example, if a first and second order stream join, the stream remains a second order stream.)

There are many more small streams in the state than large ones. Wisconsin has an estimated 14,700 first order perennial streams, 5,300 second order, 1,900 third order, 550 fourth order, and 150

Maple Dale Creek, a first order stream in Vernon County. This small stream is outlined by marsh marigolds and sedges growing along its banks.

The Bad River, a sixth order river in Ashland County, flowing into Lake Superior.

fifth or higher order streams. In Wisconsin, streams generally become too deep to wade somewhere between fourth and fifth order. The Mississippi River along the Wisconsin border is a ninth order river, and it eventually becomes a tenth order river before entering the Gulf of Mexico. This field guide generally deals with the ecology of *wadeable* streams, streams shallow enough to safely wade (up to chest level) during most of the year.

Watersheds vary in size. A watershed for a headwater stream may be less than a square mile in area, whereas the Wisconsin River watershed is over 12,000 square miles and is comprised of hundreds of smaller catchments. Typically, watersheds are nested within one another: the outlet stream of one watershed flows into another stream, forming increasingly larger watersheds. As the land area of a watershed increases, the numbers of tributaries and the total stream miles within the watershed increase, as does the stream order of the stream draining the watershed.

Glaciation

Many of Wisconsin's most prominent landscape features, including streams, are influenced by glaciers or the absence of glaciation. Glacial land formations strongly influence the distribution and characteristics of streams in the state by altering topography and affecting the composition, distribution, and depths of soil deposits.

Over the last 2.5 million years, the earth has had periods of warming and cooling; cooling periods resulted in the formation of glaciers that covered much of the higher latitudes and altitudes of both the Northern and Southern Hemispheres. The last glacial period in North America began about 100,000 years ago and is referred to as the Wisconsin Glaciation, so named because the glacier's influence on the landscape was extensively studied in this state. The glacier that formed in North America is referred to as the Laurentide Ice Sheet. It covered much of what is now Canada and Greenland and extended far south into areas of what are now Wisconsin, Iowa, Illinois, and Indiana. At its greatest extent, the Laurentide Ice Sheet is estimated to have been a 2-mile-thick layer of ice and snow, with the thickest area in northern Canada. This glacier advanced and receded many times. Its southernmost advance into Wisconsin is thought to have occurred 30,000 years ago, finally receding from the state about 11,000 years ago.

Introduction

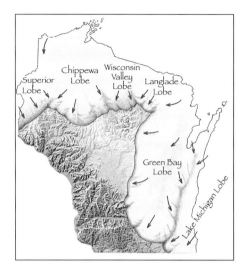

The Laurentide Ice Sheet, Wisconsin's most recent glacier.

As glaciers advance, they grind the earth's surface, flattening hilltops and mountain ranges and gathering the fragmented rock and soil in their path. This debris, called *glacial till* or *drift*, accumulates on the leading edge and along the sides of lobes of the advancing ice sheet. As glaciers melt, the accumulated rock and soil is left behind, piled up in *moraines* along the edges of the melting glacier. While overall, glaciers have smoothed much of Wisconsin's land surface, the glacial till left by retreating glaciers has also had the localized effect of increasing topographic relief and altering surficial soil composition in significant portions of the state.

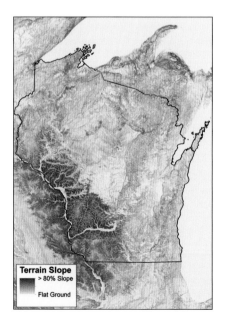

Varying terrain slope in Wisconsin denoted by color shading, and cold and coolwater streams (in blue).

Introduction

Variation in land elevation, soil, and bedrock types strongly influence whether Wisconsin's streams are primarily fed by surface runoff or by groundwater discharge. Groundwater-dominated streams are predominantly found in areas of Wisconsin where rainwater and snowmelt can infiltrate the water table at higher elevations on valley slopes and ridgetops and then discharge to streams via springs, hillside seeps, wetlands, and the streambeds themselves in the valley bottoms. Groundwater tends to have a more constant flow volume than surface runoff and is referred to as a stream's *baseflow*. Groundwater in Wisconsin flows out of the earth at approximately 53 degrees Fahrenheit year-round. As a result, groundwater-dominated streams have a relatively narrow and stable water temperature range, cooler than the ambient air temperature throughout the summer and warmer than the air in winter. Streams in areas with less topographic variability generally receive less groundwater and more surface runoff.

Soil and bedrock permeability also strongly influences surface water infiltration and groundwater flow and discharge to streams. Glacial tills comprised mainly of rock, gravel, and sand are relatively porous soils that promote surface water infiltration and groundwater movement. In contrast, areas with clay-rich, less porous soils inhibit water infiltration and groundwater discharge to streams. Similarly, sedimentary bedrock types such as sandstone and limestone, which are relatively porous and prone to weathering and fracturing, will facilitate groundwater recharge and movement compared to volcanic rock such as granite, which is less porous and inhibits water movement. Land use and development can also significantly alter the proportions of groundwater and surface water that contribute to a stream's flow volume. Watersheds with greater proportions of impervious surfaces like blacktop and concrete have greater surface runoff and less groundwater infiltration, and thus a higher proportion of stream flow coming from surface runoff.

Southwestern Wisconsin was not covered by ice or glacial drift during the most recent glacial periods, so it is called the Driftless Area. Absent the grinding forces of glaciers, the Driftless Area has relatively deep and steeply sloped valleys with greater changes in topographic relief compared to most other areas of Wisconsin. Similar to steeply sloped glacial moraines, the significant elevation changes in the Driftless Area promote rain and snowmelt infiltration at higher elevations along the valley slopes and ridgetops and subsequently significant discharge of groundwater into streams in the valley bottoms.

Wisconsin's cold-, cool-,
and warmwater streams.

——— Cold Water
——— Cool Water
——— Warm Water

The Physical Features of Streams

Three major habitat types are found in streams: pools, riffles, and runs. *Pools* are areas where the water depth is greater and the water velocity is lower relative to other stream habitats. A number of fish species prefer pools because there is more living space and the deeper water provides protection from avian predators such as kingfishers and great blue herons. Fish also seek the lower water velocities of pools, particularly in winter, when these cold-blooded animals are less active and need to conserve energy by avoiding strong currents. The lower water velocities of pools often result in sediment settling out of the water column and being deposited on the bottom of the pool, known as the *benthic* zone. This fine benthic substrate and low water velocity form a preferred habitat for many invertebrate species such as midge larvae, aquatic worms, and burrowing mayflies.

Riffles are relatively shallow, fast-flowing areas where the water flows turbulently over boulders, rocks, and coarse gravel. The turbulent flow helps aerate the water and keep the streambed free of sand and silt. This sediment-free environment is a preferred habitat for many aquatic insect larvae and other invertebrate species that live in the *interstitial* spaces between the rocks and gravel or that graze on the algae growing on the rocks. The greatest species diversity and highest density of invertebrates are usually found in riffles. Many small fish species and young fish also rely on the crevices between the rocks as key habitat. Fishes such as trouts, suckers, and darters will lay their eggs among the rocks and gravel in this well-oxygenated environment. Fish also feed on the invertebrates that are abundant in the riffles or position themselves immediately downstream to feed on riffle invertebrates as they drift downstream.

A *run* (also referred to as a *glide*) is a habitat type intermediate between pools and riffles. Runs tend to be shallower than pools and deeper than riffles, often with water velocities greater than those of pools but less than those of riffles. In general, runs have relatively uniform water depth and velocity with little turbulence. Water velocities in runs are often sufficient to maintain a streambed free of silt and provide interstitial habitat for large numbers of invertebrates. The number of fish species and their population densities tend to be lower in runs relative to riffle and pool habitats.

Restoration of the Pecatonica River riparian corridor in Dane County: creating gently sloping streambanks and reducing channel incision.

Introduction

Streambanks and adjacent *riparian corridors* are also very important habitat for the functioning of streams and are a good indicator of watershed health. In Wisconsin, steep, eroded streambanks are often a result of poor land management. Steep banks frequently indicate upland erosion that has deposited soil in lowlands along streams, sometimes up to 10 or more feet thick. This deposition cuts off streams from their natural floodplain and from riparian plants and other biota. The steep banks alter stream flow and flooding dynamics, promoting further erosion in the stream. Eroded streambanks greatly reduce the quality of habitat at the land-water interface—in a healthy watershed, this interface (*ecotone*) typically supports more animal species than either the upland habitat or the stream itself. Stream habitat restoration projects often include removing topsoil along stream riparian corridors to slope the streambanks and thereby reconnect streams with their floodplain.

In general, the slope (*gradient*) of a stream is steeper at its headwater than farther down its course because many streams begin at the base of hillsides. This change in gradient influences a number of physical characteristics of streams, including water velocity (which also influences whether the streambed will be comprised of coarse material such as boulders, rock, and gravel or finer materials such as sand and silt) and stream meander (*sinuosity*).

Water naturally has a meandering flow path regardless of whether it is confined in a stream channel or (like the Gulf Stream) flows through the open ocean. Stream slope and size (volume) influence the degree of a stream's meander; more steeply sloped headwater streams will generally be straighter than larger, lower-gradient streams. Meandering, in turn, influences where erosion and sediment deposition take place within a stream channel. The outside edges of stream bends are typically where the most erosion takes place, often creating deeper pool habitat along those reaches. The inside edges of stream bends are where sediment tends to be deposited and where the water is typically the shallowest. In natural conditions, a stream or river will move through this process of erosion and deposition, continually carving into the outsides of bends and building up the inside banks.

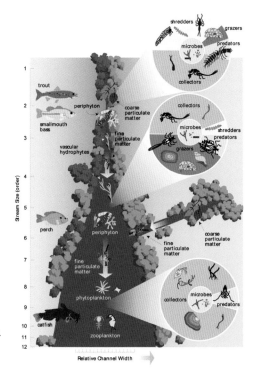

The river continuum concept, illustrated.

Introduction

The River Continuum Concept

From the origin of a stream to where it flows into another body of water, there are natural and predictable changes in its physical, chemical, and biological characteristics. This ecological principle of predictable change is referred to as the *river continuum concept*.

Streams increase in size along their course as they receive additional groundwater inputs or surface runoff or as they are fed by tributary streams, lakes, or wetlands. This increased water volume usually results in a widening of the stream channel, increasing the stream's surface area. As water flows along the earth's surface, it is influenced by ambient air temperature and solar radiation; larger streams with more surface area and surface water inputs thus generally have more variable daily and seasonal water temperatures than groundwater-fed headwater streams.

In addition to water temperature, energy inputs also change along a stream's course. Both terrestrial and aquatic food chains rely on sunlight as the primary source of energy through photosynthesis, which enables plant growth. Since headwater streams are relatively narrow and often shaded by vegetation, the most important energy source tends to be organic matter in the form of leaves and grasses that fall or wash into streams in autumn. These leaves and grasses are colonized by bacteria and fungi and become a rich food source eaten by aquatic insects such as crane fly and stonefly larvae and crustaceans such as scuds and aquatic sow bugs. These animals are referred to as *shredders*, since they shred leaves and consume the smaller pieces. Shredders tend to dominate the invertebrate community in headwater streams, and much of the shredded leaf matter and feces of the shredders washes downstream and is fed upon by other invertebrates, which in turn are eaten by animals higher up the food chain such as predatory invertebrates and fish.

As a stream increases in volume and width, more sunlight reaches the streambed. This results in a greater proportion of a stream's energy coming directly from photosynthesis occurring within the stream (versus plant matter washing into the stream). Microscopic algae—diatoms and green and brown algae, collectively called *periphyton*—cover virtually all surfaces of the streambed that receive sunlight and produce organic matter through photosynthesis. Larvae of insects such as some mayfly and caddisfly species "graze" this plant growth from surfaces of the streambed; grazers are thus more common than shredders in larger streams, and they too are fed upon by predators higher up the food chain.

Fish populations also change as streams increase in size. Small, groundwater-dominated streams tend to have only a few fish species such as sculpin and trout, which require cool, highly oxygenated water. Headwater streams that are dominated by surface runoff similarly have few species, though these tend to be disturbance-tolerant fishes such as brook sticklebacks and fathead and other minnow species. These fishes can live in harsh environments where water volume, temperature, clarity, and dissolved oxygen concentrations can vary dramatically over the course of the day, season, or year.

Fish inhabiting small streams tend to be relatively small in size and feed primarily on aquatic and terrestrial invertebrates. Farther downstream, as streams increase in size, the numbers of fish species and the overall amount of their biomass increase dramatically, as fish are able to occupy more types and greater volumes of habitat and have available to them a greater number of food types. Fish in larger streams feed not only on invertebrates but also on other fish, or they may be omnivorous and feed on algae, animals, or detritus.

The Impacts of Poor Land Management

The streams of [the Midwest] have undoubtedly changed much in character since the country has become so thickly settled. . . . I have been informed that many streams, formerly deep and narrow, and abounding in pickerel, bass and catfishes, have since grown wide and shallow, while the water in them varies greatly in the different seasons, and they are inhabited only by bullheads, suckers, and a few minnows.

—*Seth Meek, 1892*

Wisconsin's watersheds and streams are strongly influenced by both historic and current land use. Seth Meek was a naturalist who spent some of his life in Iowa and occasionally visited Wisconsin during his explorations of nature. Judging from his quote, over a century ago people were already starting to make the link between changes in land use and human population growth and the impacts

Introduction

of these changes on aquatic resources—a lesson that seemingly needs to be relearned by each subsequent generation.

Prior to the arrival of Europeans in the Upper Midwest, the Wisconsin landscape was covered with forests, wetlands, oak savannas, and grasslands. When European settlers arrived in the early 1800s, they rapidly altered the land cover by clear-cutting the pine forests of northern Wisconsin and harvesting the hardwood forests in the western part of the state. Over the next fifty years, much of the state was deforested, quickly altering watersheds and their streams. Trees were also removed from central and southern Wisconsin's natural land cover, and the prairies were plowed for crop production. Plowing steep slopes and removing native vegetation that had held topsoil in place for thousands of years resulted in horrific soil erosion problems. Millions of tons of topsoil that once covered hillsides flowed into the valleys after each rainstorm, filling valley bottoms and streams with many feet of topsoil. In 1933 the first federal soil conservation project in the country was started in Coon Valley in western Wisconsin because of the tremendous erosion problems occurring in this region.

Upland and cropland soil erosion problems have, to a large extent, been reduced in Wisconsin. Yet thousands of stream miles are still greatly impacted by a legacy of poor land management and upland soil movement into the valleys. Streams naturally flow out of their banks onto their floodplain during spring runoff or intense rainstorms to accommodate the additional volume of water. The floodplain helps disperse the floodwaters and decrease the water's velocity and accompanying erosive forces. In addition, floodplains often harbor rich reserves of wildlife and habitat. However, in areas of high historic soil erosion, the deposition of a thick layer of topsoil in the valleys results in stream channels that are cut (*incised*) deeply into the earth, with high, vertical-walled banks. Many streams have

Logging the pine forests of N. Wisconsin, ca. 1860.

Gully erosion in Coon Valley, Wisconsin, ca. 1900. A person on horseback can be seen in the center of the photograph.

11

eroded down over decades through 10 or more feet of deposited topsoil to the presettlement streambeds. Deeply incised streams are less able to flow up onto the floodplain during high flows. As a result, the erosive forces of snowmelt runoff and stormflows are not dampened, and extensive erosion or undercutting and collapse of the steep, incised streambanks often occurs.

Major Determinants of Stream Health

There are five major factors that influence stream quality, and each of these factors is strongly influenced by watershed land use. These factors are (1) the *quantity* of water in a stream and how it changes over time, (2) water *quality*, (3) *habitat* within streams and along stream corridors, (4) the *food chain*, and (5) stream *connectivity*.

Water Quantity

Hydrology is the study of water, especially the movement of water in the atmosphere, across the land surface, and underground. Human activities such as agriculture and suburban and urban development can significantly alter stream hydrology, including effects on the quantity of water within a stream. For example, decreasing the amount of perennial vegetation within a watershed reduces the amount of rainfall intercepted by the vegetation. Plants use rainfall and return it directly to the atmosphere via evaporation off the surfaces of the plants or through *transpiration* (water vapor lost from the pores in plant stems and leaves during photosynthesis). With less perennial vegetation in a watershed, a higher proportion of rainfall can reach the streams, thereby increasing the volume of water in the streams and erosion potential.

A watershed's permeability has another significant impact on stream hydrology and water quantity. Urbanized watersheds have higher proportions of impervious surfaces such as concrete, asphalt, and rooftops, resulting in less rainfall and snowmelt entering the ground and more precipitation flowing directly overland and into streams. Urban streams thus typically have much greater water volumes

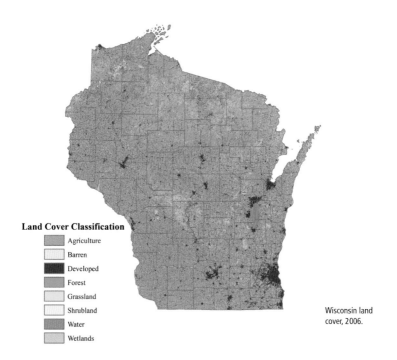

Land Cover Classification

- Agriculture
- Barren
- Developed
- Forest
- Grassland
- Shrubland
- Water
- Wetlands

Wisconsin land cover, 2006.

Introduction

Wisconsin population density, 2011.

and velocities during storm events as water quickly reaches the stream channel via storm drains and direct overland flow. At the same time, groundwater recharge is reduced in urban areas, creating surface runoff-dominated streams that have lower baseflows during dry periods (since they receive lesser amounts of groundwater discharge). This stark difference in flow volume means that stormflows in urban streams often result in increased streambank erosion, creating wide stream channels that are shallow during periods with little rainfall. These wide, shallow channels have less deep-water habitat, which is important to many aquatic plants, fish, and other aquatic and terrestrial animals.

Water Quality

Water quality includes factors such as temperature and turbidity as well as dissolved oxygen, nutrient, and pollutant concentrations. Polluted runoff from agricultural and urban lands and discharges from industrial and municipal water treatment plants reduce water quality by adding sediment, nutrients, toxics, organic materials, and pathogens to surface and ground waters. Inputs of phosphorus from manure and chemical fertilizers cause an excess of nutrients in streams, which often results in eutrophication—excessive aquatic plant growth, algal blooms, and, consequently, large daily fluctuations in dissolved oxygen concentrations.

By volume, soil is the greatest pollutant entering streams both in Wisconsin and nationally. While soil may seem innocuous, sediment covers important stream-bottom habitat, increases water turbidity, and delivers particulate-bound nutrients, toxics, and pathogens to surface waters. Sediment in the water column also leads to increased water temperatures because the soil particles in the water absorb solar energy. In turn, warming and eutrophication of surface waters reduces the concentration of dissolved oxygen, an important regulator of aquatic life and a key indicator of stream health.

Riparian and In-Stream Habitat

Aquatic plants, coarse woody debris, terrestrial vegetation that overhangs streams, undercut streambanks, and diverse streambeds composed of rocks of varying sizes are all critical in-stream habitats for a number of invertebrate and vertebrate animals. Many invertebrate species need stable rock or woody substrate to cling to or hide under, and both invertebrates and fish need pockets of reduced water velocity where they can rest and hide.

There are a myriad of changes that can degrade stream habitat. Loss of streamside vegetation reduces habitat quantity and quality. Increased surface runoff (e.g., through urbanization) results in higher water velocities that erode streambanks, also reducing riparian habitat quality. Straightening (*channelization*) of meandering stream channels reduces the diversity of aquatic and terrestrial habitat.

As mentioned, sedimentation is the single most important factor degrading in-stream habitat for invertebrates and fish; sediment covers diverse stream-bottom habitat with a uniform layer of sand or silt and fills in critical interstitial habitat, greatly reducing species diversity, populations, and stream productivity. It smothers animals living in or clinging to the streambed, and the unstable, shifting bottom sediment also inhibits the establishment of rooted aquatic plants.

Introduction

The Food Chain

Headwater streams generally have a more intimate relationship with the land than larger streams. Small streams receive a greater proportion of their energy from streamside vegetation that falls or washes into the water in autumn and, as a result, are more strongly influenced by poor riparian land management. Removal of streamside trees and shrubs can significantly reduce populations of aquatic insects and other stream-bottom invertebrates that depend on plant material as a primary food source and, in turn, can reduce populations of animals higher up the food chain such as fish that rely on the invertebrates for food.

Elevated nutrient concentrations in streams can also affect the food chain. Excess nutrients often promote the growth of filamentous algae, which displaces more desirable microscopic plants on which many aquatic invertebrate species feed.

The food chain can be affected from the top of the chain as well as the bottom. Game fishes such as trouts and bass are very sensitive to changes in water quality and stream habitat. When the populations of these top predators decline, the food chain often becomes unbalanced, resulting in less desirable fish species predominating. The common carp is an example of a fish species that flourishes in degraded environments with few predators. Carp degrade stream habitat by uprooting aquatic plants and further reduce water quality by stirring up bottom sediment that releases additional nutrients, increases water turbidity and temperature, and ultimately reduces dissolved oxygen concentrations.

Connectivity

Connectivity refers to the pathways and movement of water, energy, and organisms in streams. Under natural conditions, energy flows downstream in the form of organic matter, such as plant leaves, algae, and aquatic invertebrates. This energy flow delivers food to organisms throughout the stream system. For many animal species, both upstream and downstream movement is important and influences ecosystem stability and productivity. Depending upon the animal and its life stage, the need for stream connectivity can range from a few feet to many miles.

However, Wisconsin has nearly 4,800 dams and over 80,000 roadway crossings over streams. While it has long been recognized that dams fragment rivers, only recently have the impacts of culverts and bridge crossings begun to be assessed. Dams, culverts, and some bridges fragment streams and are barriers to energy flow and the movement of aquatic, amphibious, and terrestrial animals. Reduced connectivity can result in lower stream productivity if animals cannot reach habitats that are seasonally important or essential to certain life stages, such as overwintering habitats, summer feeding grounds, and spawning, nesting, or nursery habitats. For instance, most aquatic invertebrates and fishes produce large numbers of offspring that normally disperse in order to reduce competition and take advantage of available habitat.

As the amount of undeveloped land in Wisconsin decreases, stream corridors become increasingly important movement pathways for a number of amphibious and terrestrial species as well. If culverts are too narrow or too long, water depths too shallow, or velocities too great, roadway stream crossings can become barriers to animal movement. Many mammal, reptile, and amphibian species will often try and go around these stream corridor barriers by crawling up onto roadways; too often, they end up being struck by vehicles.

Streams as Communities of Life

Wisconsin's abundant streams are among the most beautiful, delicate, and fascinating features of the landscape. We have described how streams are intimately connected to the land, influenced by both ancient glacial forces and current human impacts. Streams are complex environments where physical, chemical, and biological processes interact to contribute to their overall ecological condition. The plants and animals that live in and along streams are the proverbial "canaries in a coal mine" and tell us much about the health of both our aquatic environments and terrestrial world. This overview of stream ecology provides a backdrop for better understanding the lives and ecological roles of the plants and animals described throughout this book.

How to Use This Guide

Organization

This book is organized into seven sections: plants, invertebrates, crayfishes, mussels and clams, fishes, amphibians, and reptiles. Each section contains descriptions of organisms or groups of organisms found in and along streams. Organization of the guide is based partly on *taxonomy*, the scientific system that arranges biota into a hierarchy of evolutionary relationships. From broad to specific, the main taxonomic levels are kingdom, phylum, class, order, family, genus, and species. Most plants and animals in the book are described at the species level, but some are described at the family level or at higher taxonomic levels. In these cases, such as with most invertebrates, distinguishing between different species would be difficult without the help of a microscope or detailed taxonomic keys.

The organization of the book differs slightly among sections. When deciding how to organize a field guide, there are several factors to keep in mind:

1. *Consistency and ease of use*. As much as possible, it's desirable to be consistent in organization throughout the book so that readers can become familiar with the system and find things easily.
2. *Scientific accuracy*. Common names can vary regionally, but each species has only one scientific name worldwide (although these sometimes change). Due to such variations, organizing species by common name can lead to confusion, even though the common name is more familiar to many readers. In addition, it's important to place plants and animals in scientifically accurate categories. For example, while freshwater sponges may appear similar to plants, they are actually invertebrates and should be placed in that section.
3. *Usefulness for identification*. When examining a specimen in the field, we often wonder, "Is it what I think it is, or is it something that looks similar?" It's helpful to place similar-looking organisms near each other in the book, preferably on the same page, but this can interfere with the needs for consistency and accuracy.

With all these factors in mind, most sections of this guide are organized as follows. First, the biotic descriptions are placed in groups based on similarity, usually by scientific family. This often places similar-looking organisms near to each other because plants or animals that are more closely related often (but not always) look similar. Within their groups, the biota are then arranged alphabetically by scientific (Latin) name—the name found in *italics* in each description. Although many readers will not know the scientific names and may need to hunt a little (use the index!), this arrangement also helps to place similar-looking things near each other for comparison.

Finally, the groups themselves (families, etc.) are organized alphabetically by *common* rather than scientific name. For example, fishes are alphabetized by family: lampreys, minnows, pikes, sunfishes, and so on; invertebrates are alphabetized by taxonomic order: caddisflies, mayflies, stoneflies, and so on. This organization of groups helps laypeople, who usually do not know scientific names, to find the correct section quickly.

This system isn't perfect and varies by section. For example, one invertebrate category is "non-insects," a catchall for snails, planarians, mites, and many other groups. And because there are almost as many plant families as there are plant species in the guide, we grouped plants by habitat rather than by family. Below are some more details on the variations within the sections and the reasons behind them.

Plants

There are so many species of stream-related plants in Wisconsin that we could not include all of them in the guide. Instead, we chose plants most *commonly* found in and along streams and added other *important* plants such as invasive or endangered/threatened species. The plant section contains 105 descriptions of different species or groups. These plants belong to so many different families that, unlike most other sections of the guide, we organized this section by habitat (terrestrial, emergent, floating-leaf, free-floating, submersed) instead of family.

Invertebrates

We included those fifty-five groups of invertebrates most commonly found in and along Wisconsin streams. Invertebrates cannot usually be identified to the species level in the field, so in this guide they are instead described to the level at which they can be field-identified. The section is first divided into insects and noninsects. Insects are then described at the family level, and families of insects are grouped at the order level: caddisflies, mayflies, stoneflies, and so on. Noninsects are often only identifiable to the class level in the field, so some descriptions are at that level.

Crayfishes

Crayfishes are invertebrates, but they have been placed in their own section because they can be identified to the species level. Their species identification is important to stream management because invasives such as the rusty and red swamp crayfishes have the potential to do great damage to stream ecosystems. All of Wisconsin's eight crayfishes are included.

Mussels and Clams

Like crayfishes, mussels and clams are invertebrates but have been placed in their own section of the guide. There are fifty species of native mussel and over forty species of native clam in Wisconsin, many of which are endangered or threatened. There are also a few invasive mussels and clams. Since they can be identified to the species level in the field, we have included all of them here. Because many taxonomic differences are not easily visible in the field, we have organized them by overall shape and other features such as texture.

Fishes

The fish section includes all 116 species of fishes that are known to be found in Wisconsin streams. These are described at the species level and are grouped by family.

Amphibians

The amphibian section includes the seven frog and two salamander species that are found in Wisconsin streams. They are described at the species level and grouped by order (frogs vs. salamanders), then by family.

Reptiles

The reptile section includes the two snake and six turtle species most commonly found in Wisconsin streams. They are described at the species level and are grouped by order (snakes vs. turtles), then by family.

Species Descriptions

Each description, whether of a species or a group, contains several key features. These are illustrated on page 17 in a sample species description:

COMMON NAME
Scientific name (formerly *Former scientific name*)

STATUS

DESCRIPTION: Description, in basic terms, of species, using bold to highlight features that are most useful for distinguishing this species from look-alikes.

LOOK-ALIKES: List of common names of similar species (including *Scientific name of each species not described elsewhere in the guide*)—brief description of each species not described elsewhere in the guide.

NOTES: The notes section describes where the species is found in Wisconsin. It also describes what type of habitat it prefers, as well as other interesting things such as what it likes to eat, when it blooms if it's a plant, when it breeds if it's a fish, and so on.

Common Name

Common name is listed first; we selected the most prevalently used common name in Wisconsin. If several common names may be used for a species (or group), additional names are listed in parentheses.

Scientific Name

Scientific name is listed beneath the common name in *italics*. Keep in mind that although we have tried to use the most up-to-date scientific names and classification for each entry, taxonomy is constantly being revised. Former scientific names that are relatively recent and well known are given in parentheses.

Status

Some species have a special status, which is listed beneath the names. A species' status may change over time. The following is a list of possible statuses and their definitions in this guide:

- *Endangered*: Refers to species that are endangered in the state of Wisconsin. Describes any species whose continued existence as a viable component of this state's wild animals or wild plants is determined by the state Department of Natural Resources to be in jeopardy on the basis of scientific evidence.
- *State and Federally Endangered*: Refers to species that are endangered in both Wisconsin and nationwide. *Federally Endangered* describes any species that is in danger of extinction throughout all or a significant portion of its range, other than insects determined to be pests whose protection would present a risk to humans.
- *Threatened*: Refers to species that are threatened in the state of Wisconsin. Describes any species that appears likely, within the foreseeable future, on the basis of scientific evidence to become endangered in the state of Wisconsin.
- *State and Federally Threatened*: Refers to species that are threatened in both Wisconsin and nationwide. *Federally Threatened* describes any species that is likely to become an endangered species within the foreseeable future throughout all or a significant portion of its range.
- *Special Concern*: A Wisconsin designation that describes a species about which some problem of abundance or distribution is suspected but not yet proven. The main purpose of this category is to focus attention on certain species before they become threatened or endangered in the state.
- *Invasive*: Describes any species or "variety" that is not native to Wisconsin and that causes or is likely to cause economic or environmental harm or harm to human health. Invasive species may be further classified as prohibited or restricted species. With a few exceptions, it is illegal in Wisconsin to transport, transfer, or introduce a prohibited or restricted species without a permit. It is also illegal to possess prohibited species.
  - *Invasive—Prohibited*: Describes a nonnative species that is not currently found in Wisconsin or that is present only as small infestations but that, if introduced into the state, is likely to cause significant harm.

- *Invasive—Restricted*: Describes a nonnative species that is already well established in Wisconsin and is known to cause, or have the potential to cause, significant harm.
- *Do Not Touch*: A label for species that may be painful or harmful to touch. (Not comprehensive; some animals not marked *Do Not Touch* may be harmful if provoked, and some plants not labeled *Do Not Touch* may be harmful if swallowed.)

Description

The description contains key traits for identification. Traits in bold will be especially helpful in distinguishing the species from look-alikes.

Look-Alikes

Before drawing conclusions about the identity of a specimen, it's important to consider potential look-alikes. If look-alikes are not on nearby pages, use the guide's index to find and compare them with your specimen. Look-alikes are usually listed in alphabetical order by common name. When a look-alike is not described elsewhere in the field guide, its scientific name is also given in parentheses along with a brief summary of its traits that differ from the species being described. (Scientific names are also listed for a few insect look-alikes in cases where the insect might be better known by its scientific rather than its common name.)

Notes

Notes include descriptions of where the species is likely to be found in the state, its habitat, feeding, and reproductive habits, and other interesting traits.

Distribution Map

The map shows (in red) where the species is known to be found in the state, even in sparse numbers. If the species is found statewide, the entire map is red. These distribution maps were generated mainly using survey data coupled with the best professional judgment of biologists.

Photographs

When possible, we included photos that were helpful for identification purposes. Arrows point to key features useful for identifying the organism.

Line Drawings

Since photos of individuals can vary in quality, more generalized line drawings are a useful supplement. Arrows, when included, highlight key features useful for identification.

What to Do if You Find an Invasive Species

Invasive species are one of the biggest threats to stream ecosystems and are easiest to manage when detected early. If you encounter an invasive species and you think you may be the first to notice it in your area, you might help stop its spread by reporting it to the Wisconsin Department of Natural Resources.

To report an invasive species, send an email to invasive.species@wisconsin.gov. Include a digital photo of the species and detailed location information with your email. To report a violation of invasive species regulations, contact the DNR Aquatic Invasive Species Education Specialist.

For more detailed reporting information and to find out how to deliver specimens to your local DNR office, visit the Wisconsin DNR's reporting page. Go to www.dnr.wi.gov and type the keywords "reporting invasives."

Plants

AQUATIC PLANTS (*continued*)

 | Submersed plants with alternate, thin leaves (page 69) | Aquatic; most of leaves below the water surface; submersed leaves alternate and thin

 | Submersed plants with alternate, broad leaves (page 75) | Aquatic; most of leaves below the water surface; submersed leaves alternate and broad

 | Submersed plants with finely divided leaves (page 79) | Aquatic; most of leaves below the water surface; submersed leaves finely divided

 | Algae (page 85) | Aquatic; often stringy, in floating mats or attached to objects; do not have roots, leaves, or stems

From delicate pondweeds to towering trees, hundreds of plant species play critical roles in Wisconsin's streams. Plants are the foundation of stream communities, providing food, oxygen, and habitat for wildlife. They are also often the easiest organisms to identify because they tend to be stationary. This section includes those plants most commonly found in or near streams, as well as threatened and invasive species that affect stream management.

Plant species composition—and thus that of the entire ecosystem—gradually changes as you move toward deeper water. Large willows in the riparian area, for instance, might give way to arrowheads emerging on the shoreline and wild celery waving gently along the stream bottom. We hope this field guide provides a starting point for appreciating the role of plants in Wisconsin's streams, helping you get your feet wet along the way.

Identification

Despite being easy to "catch," plants can be difficult to tell apart—especially underwater. When identifying a plant it is helpful to focus on habitat. Where is the plant growing: on land or in water? If in water, is it emerging above the surface or submersed underwater?

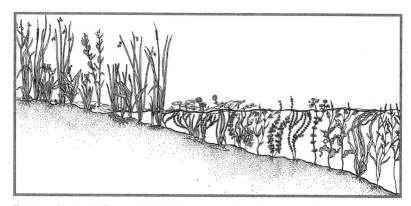

Plant communities transition from terrestrial plants to distinct types of aquatic plants: emergent, floating-leaf, and submersed plants. Free-floating plants can appear in any location on the water surface, although they are usually in quiet areas.

Because location is one of the simplest ways to sort plants, this section of the book is organized according to habitat. The section is divided into *terrestrial* plants, which grow mainly on dry land, and *aquatic* plants, which grow mainly in water. Aquatic plants are then arranged into four groups: emergent, free-floating, floating-leaf, and submersed (see page 40 for more detail). These differences do not necessarily reflect taxonomic differences, because the same family or genus of plants can include species from various habitats.

After considering location, turn your attention to plants' flowers and leaves. Flowers differ widely from species to species and, if present, can be helpful for identification. When possible we have included flower descriptions and the time of year when they bloom, as well as fruit descriptions (see "Life Cycle" below).

Another useful trait for identification is *leaf arrangement*, or the placement of leaves on the plant. Leaves may be *alternate* (placed singly along the stem), *opposite* (in pairs along the stem), *whorled* (in groups of three or more along the stem), or entirely *basal* (growing only from the plant base).

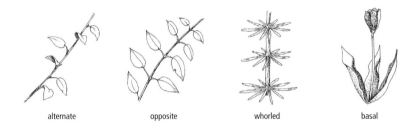

alternate   opposite   whorled   basal

Leaf shape and leaf type are also important for identification. Leaf shape may be broad (round, heart-shaped, triangular, oval); narrow (lance-like or linear); compound (many leaflets) or simple (one blade, as in most species); lobed or divided; with toothed, serrated, or smooth edges; and so on.

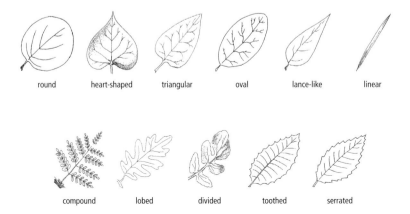

round   heart-shaped   triangular   oval   lance-like   linear

compound   lobed   divided   toothed   serrated

In aquatic plants, leaf type may be *emergent* (held above the water), *floating* (atop the water surface), or *submersed* (beneath the surface). Some plants, such as pondweeds, have multiple types of leaves.

emergent leaves

floating leaves (*upper*) and
submersed leaves (*lower*)

Note that a plant species can look very different in a lake versus a stream. Though most pictured specimens in this section are from lakes, plants growing in streams are generally "streamlined," with thinner, more elongated leaves.

Life Cycle

Most plants reproduce by flowering in a regular yearly cycle. With many exceptions, seeds germinate in spring, flowers bloom between late spring and early fall, and flowers become seed-bearing fruits by summer or fall. For *annual* plants, this life cycle takes place in a single year, whereas *perennial* plants reproduce for multiple years except possibly their first season.

As the reproductive headquarters of a plant, flowers contain one or both types of sexual structures: male parts (*stamens*, which contain pollen) and female parts (*pistils*, which contain ovaries). Most flowers use sweet-smelling nectar and colorful petals to attract pollinators like bees and birds to transfer pollen to the pistils. However, some flowers achieve the same goal by using foul smells to attract flies or only have dull-colored petals because they are wind-pollinated. Thus, there is great diversity of flowers in the plant kingdom, and the beauty of each flower is in the eye of the pollinator.

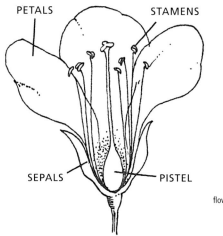

PETALS STAMENS

SEPALS PISTEL

flower anatomy

Flowers are held on floral stalks and grow as a single flower or in arrangements of multiple flowers, such as *spikes* or *umbels*. These floral traits are all useful for identification.

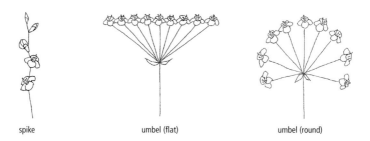

spike   umbel (flat)   umbel (round)

Many aquatic plants can reproduce *vegetatively*, or asexually, without flowers. Rather than using seeds, vegetative reproduction occurs through fragmentation or budding from vegetative tissue, such as *winter buds* (thickened shoot tips), *tubers* (thickened parts of roots), or *rhizomes* (modified underground stems that grow outward to produce new plants). The presence or absence of these structures can help distinguish between species.

rhizome   tuber   winter bud

Ecological Notes

Plants are interdependent and critical to the wildlife of aquatic ecosystems. As primary producers, plants use chlorophyll to absorb sunlight and drive photosynthesis, which provides sugars and oxygen that become the building blocks for the aquatic food web of bacteria, plankton, macroinvertebrates, fish, amphibians, reptiles, mammals, and birds. Plant structures themselves are also critical to stream life. Macroinvertebrates attached to plants provide a key food source for fish and birds. Fish hide in "weed beds" to find prey, avoid predatory fish, or spawn. Waterfowl use leaves, stems, seeds, and tubers for food and shelter, particularly during migration.

Aquatic plants can also *improve* water quality and habitat in myriad ways. Plants are a major source of dissolved oxygen, a critical gas for sensitive organisms like trout and stoneflies. Plants dampen the effects of human pollution by filtering excess nutrients and toxics from the water column and by stabilizing soft sediment, improving bank habitat and water quality. A strong community of native plants can even prevent the establishment of invasive species such as purple loosestrife and Eurasian water-milfoil. Invasive species homogenize ecosystems, outcompeting native species and reducing the ecosystem services of the plant community.

TERRESTRIAL PLANTS

Terrestrial plants are plants that grow with their roots in dry ground all or most of the year. Terrestrial plants that grow along streambanks are called *riparian* plants.

Riparian plants influence streams in a variety of ways. They provide shade that helps lower water temperatures. Their root networks can hold streambanks in place and reduce erosion. They provide valuable habitat for mammals, birds, reptiles, and amphibians and for adult aquatic insects emerging from streams for metamorphosis. Streamside plants also drop fruits, flowers, leaves, and other plant parts into the water, delivering nutrients to the aquatic food web.

In this section, we have included some of the most common terrestrial plants found on streambanks, as well as a few important invasives and look-alikes.

WOODY PLANTS

Woody plants are trees, shrubs, and vines that have hard stems composed of wood. Trees and shrubs are an important component of Wisconsin's riparian areas and streams, providing bank stabilization and habitat for stream biota. Large woody debris—whole trees and branches that fall into the stream—create complex in-stream habitat for fish, cover from predators, refuges from floods, attachment sites for aquatic insects, and habitat for turtles and waterfowl. In forested headwaters, fallen leaves and fruits provide an important food source for stream invertebrates, which in turn are consumed by animals higher in the food web, especially fish.

In many cases, however, woody plants can be more detrimental than beneficial to streams. The composition of woody plants has changed over time in Wisconsin. In the southern part of the state, what was once prairie or savanna has given way to more dense woody plant growth due to the absence of fire and of wild grazers (e.g., bison). In riparian areas, fire-intolerant trees such as boxelder can hinder the establishment of restored prairie and savanna by shading and inhibiting the growth of grasses and other herbaceous plants. In forested riparian areas, invasive species such as buckthorn, honeysuckle, and black locust can completely dominate streambanks, outcompeting other plants and potentially destabilizing banks.

To improve stream ecosystem health, government, nonprofit, and private organizations have collaborated over the past few decades to restore more than 5,000 stream miles in the Upper Midwest. The primary goals of restoration projects are (1) to improve fish habitat, (2) to provide fish passage, (3) to restore natural channel form, and (4) to reduce excessive bank erosion. To achieve these goals, restoration projects manage woody plants on a site-by-site basis, removing aggressive and invasive species and/or planting other woody species to stabilize the streambank.

Here we describe fifteen woody plants commonly found along Wisconsin's streams. Along with leaf shape, leaf arrangement, and other characteristics used to identify most plants, there are a few additional features specifically useful for identifying woody plants: leaf scars (marks left behind by fallen leaves), buds, and bark.

BOXELDER
Acer negundo (Aceraceae)

DESCRIPTION: Tree 12–20 m tall, usually with multiple trunks. Branches green or purple with a light waxy coating that can be wiped off; leaf scars U-shaped and meet in the middle at a point; buds often with white hairs. Leaves opposite, compound (divided into 3–7 leaflets), with a few large teeth. Winged fruit hanging in pairs at an acute angle, emerging September–October.

LOOK-ALIKES: Ash. Poison ivy (*Toxicodendron radicans*)—vine or shrub; leaves similarly shaped to boxelder's but alternate and shiny.

NOTES: Boxelder is common statewide, especially in S. Wisconsin. It is found near riparian areas, wetlands, and roadsides. Although native, it is an aggressive colonizer, growing quickly and crowding out other native species at disturbed open sites. The management of boxelder—along with buckthorn and honeysuckle—is one of the most common steps to restoring prairie and savanna streams in Wisconsin. However, boxelder does provide habitat for wildlife and can compete with more aggressive, nonnative invasive species such as reed canary grass (*Phalaris arundinacea*).

SILVER MAPLE
Acer saccharinum (Aceraceae)

DESCRIPTION: Tree 12–24 m tall, often with multiple trunks. Bark light gray with thin vertical plates that are shaggy on older trees. Leaves opposite, divided deeply into 5 lobes, coarsely toothed, with light silvery underside. Fruit hanging in pairs of flattened, elongate seeds with long wings, forming a right angle or V-shape, falling May–June.

LOOK-ALIKES: Red maple (*A. rubrum*)—leaves divided more shallowly into 3 lobes and doubly serrate, with serrations more angular; bark very similar to silver maple's; associated with swamps more than streams. Sugar maple (*A. saccharum*)—common to abundant statewide; leaves pointed with fewer serrations, divided more shallowly; fruit hanging in pairs of round, plump seeds with small wings, forming a U-shape. Black maple (*A. nigrum*)—very similar to sugar maple but uncommon; leaves shallowly 3-lobed, untoothed, slightly hairy stalk and underside, with stipule and overlapping basal lobes on blade; associated with floodplains and bottomlands, especially in S.W. Wisconsin.

NOTES: Silver maple is common statewide except in N. Wisconsin, where it is found sporadically. Silver maple is found along streams, lakes, and wetlands, particularly in forested floodplains. Its root system stabilizes streambanks. Because it is adapted to wet, oxygen-poor soil, it also grows well as a planting in paved urban areas and is a common street tree.

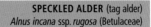

SPECKLED ALDER (tag alder)
Alnus incana ssp. *rugosa* (Betulaceae)

DESCRIPTION: Small tree or shrub up to 10 m tall. Leaves alternate, doubly serrated, oval, often pale beneath. Twigs speckled with white lenticels on gray or reddish-brown bark. Flowers on 2 types of conspicuous clusters (catkins): small woody, cone-like catkins (female) and large, loose, stalked catkins (male), blooming March–May but persistent through most of the year.

LOOK-ALIKES: Yellow birch. European alder (*A. glutinosa*)—invasive; leaf tip indented instead of pointed; frequently found in saturated or low-lying areas in urban/suburban areas. Witch-hazel (*Hamamelis virginiana*)—leaves with rounded teeth and asymmetric base; zigzag twigs with brown, taco-shaped buds; in dry forests, usually in S. Wisconsin.

NOTES: Speckled alder is common statewide, especially in N. Wisconsin. It is mostly found in dense thickets along small streams but is also found near lakes, wetlands, and roadsides. Speckled alder provides an important food source for white-tailed deer and beavers and is also effective at fixing nitrogen in the soil.

YELLOW BIRCH
Betula alleghaniensis (Betulaceae)

DESCRIPTION: Tree up to 25 m tall. Bark reddish brown when young, becoming purplish or grayish with age, with horizontal lenticels, and peeling into thin papery strips (unlike wide strips of other birches). Branches often have a slight minty aroma and taste when scratched. Leaves alternate, doubly serrated, often attached in pairs to short shoots. Tiny, hairy, 3-lobed fruit bracts resemble "chicken-feet," dropping from late fall through winter.

LOOK-ALIKES: White birch (*B. papyrifera*)—bark white; branches without minty aroma; fruit bracts with 2 lobes pointed outward; leaves often attached to short shoots in whorls of 3; distributed in a variety of sites, including along streams. River birch (*B. nigra*)— branches without minty aroma; bark peeling in irregular large plates; leaves irregular but often Christmas tree–shaped; smooth bracts; found in riparian floodplains.

NOTES: Yellow birch is found statewide but is most common in N. Wisconsin. It is associated with floodplains, streams, lakes, and swamps, as well as upland forests. Yellow birch often grows from the nutrient-rich remains and stumps of fallen trees, called "nurse logs," which can decompose to leave a striking root system raised above the ground.

DOGWOOD
Cornus spp. (Cornaceae)

DESCRIPTION: Shrub 1–5 m tall (1 species is a tree up to 10 m tall). Leaves opposite, untoothed, with arcing parallel veins and sometimes a long tip. When a leaf is pulled gently apart, thin white strings keep the veins connected (compare with buckthorn, page 31). Flowers small, white, blooming May–July. Fruit white or blue.

Gray dogwood (*C. racemosa*)—smooth gray bark; spreading clonally. Red-osier dogwood (*C. stolonifera*)—bright red bark; twigs with white pith. Silky dogwood (*C. amomum*)—red, purple, or gray bark with white fissures and silky pubescence; twigs with brown pith; blue fruit. Alternate-leaved dogwood (*C. alternifolia*)—alternate leaves; blue fruit; the only dogwood that is a tree.

LOOK-ALIKES: Buckthorn.

NOTES: Dogwood is common statewide, usually preferring wet habitats along streams, lakes, swamps, roadsides, and moist forests. Birds eat and disperse its fruits, and humans often plant it as an ornamental. Dogwoods provide a dense root system and are commonly used in bank stabilization projects.

red-osier dogwood

red-osier dogwood

red-osier dogwood

GREEN ASH
Fraxinus pennsylvanica (Oleaceae)

DESCRIPTION: Tree up to 20 m tall. Bark hard with small, spongy, interwoven ridges, somewhat resembling a fishing net. Branches and leafstalks fuzzy when young. Buds resemble chocolate chips. Leaves opposite, compound, usually with 5–7 leaflets, small serrations, and short stalks. Bud scars are half-moon-shaped. Fruit winged, slender, straight, pointed, hanging in unpaired clusters.

LOOK-ALIKES: Black ash (*F. nigra*)—leaves serrated, 7–11 leaflets without stalks; bark with spongy ridges; broad fruit; associated with swamps. White ash (*F. americana*)—usually found in dry upland areas, with 5–9 leaflets; bud scars U-shaped. Blue ash (*F. quadrangulata*)—threatened; leaves serrated, leaflets stalked; branches 4-sided with ridges; rare and only associated with calcareous soils restricted to S.E. Wisconsin.

NOTES: Green ash is common statewide. It is associated with riparian floodplains and lakeshores, only found occasionally in upland areas. Because it is adapted to wet, oxygen-poor soil, it also grows well as a planting in paved urban areas and is a common street tree.

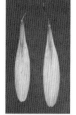

Tatarian honeysuckle

EURASIAN BUSH HONEYSUCKLE
Lonicera × bella, L. maackii, L. morrowii,
and *L. tatarica* (Caprifoliaceae)

INVASIVE—RESTRICTED

DESCRIPTION: Shrub 1–5 m tall. Twigs thin, delicate-looking, and often hollow in cross section. Leaves opposite, untoothed, oval-shaped, and often pointed. Flowers 5-petaled (often tubular), white to pink, in pairs at leaf bases, blooming May–June. Berries small, red, in pairs July–September.

Showy bush honeysuckle (*L.* × *bella*)—invasive—restricted; pink flowers. Amur honeysuckle (*L. maackii*)—invasive—restricted/prohibited (prohibited in N. Wisconsin); tall (up to 5 m); leaves with long tip; persistent berries. Asian fly honeysuckle (*L. morrowii*)—invasive—restricted; white flowers. Tatarian honeysuckle (*L. tatarica*)—invasive—restricted; white to pink flowers.

Tatarian honeysuckle

LOOK-ALIKES: Buckthorn, viburnum. Native honeysuckles: American fly honeysuckle (*L. canadensis*)—native; small shrub with relatively large leaves; flowers sometimes with purple or red hue. Mountain honeysuckle (*L. dioica*)—native; short viny shrub (<1.5 m tall); flowers orange, yellow, or purple. Northern bush honeysuckle (*Diervilla lonicera*)—native; flowers funnel-shaped with yellow to red petals in clusters of 3–7 flowers; fruit is a capsule of seeds.

showy bush honeysuckle

NOTES: These species of honeysuckle are common statewide. All are related and similar in appearance and behavior (showy bush honeysuckle is actually a hybrid of Tatarian honeysuckle and Asian fly honeysuckle). They are found in disturbed areas and can tolerate wet conditions, such as floodplain forests associated with buckthorn. As ornamental and aggressive invaders, they can form dense stands that crowd out native species. Honeysuckle is removed from stream restoration sites, usually by a combination of physical removal and chemical spraying of stumps.

EASTERN COTTONWOOD
Populus deltoides (Salicaceae)

DESCRIPTION: Tree up to 25 m tall. Thick bark with flat-topped, interwoven ridges and deep fissures. Bud large, pointy, and sticky. Leaves alternate, triangular, pointy, with flat base and rounded (wavy) teeth. Flowers cottony, hanging in long clusters, blooming April–May.

LOOK-ALIKES: Trembling aspen (*P. tremuloides*)—leaves round and small; bark white to yellow, becoming less smooth with age. Big-toothed aspen (*P. grandidentata*)—leaves egg-shaped; bark white to yellow, becoming less smooth with age; found in upland areas.

NOTES: Eastern cottonwood is common in S. Wisconsin but sporadic elsewhere. It is found in disturbed, open, wet sites on river floodplains, lakeshores, and wet fields. Its flowers are wind-pollinated. Like willow, it resprouts from cuttings, grows quickly, and stabilizes soil in areas that flood frequently, such as streambanks. It can quickly colonize disturbed wet sites.

SWAMP WHITE OAK
Quercus bicolor (Fagaceae)

DESCRIPTION: Tree up to 20 m tall. Bark relatively thick, with ridges. Leaves alternate, shallowly lobed, untoothed, with narrow base, pale and velvety beneath. Twigs shaggy. Acorns usually in pairs, with long stalk and a slightly hairy cap.

LOOK-ALIKES: Bur oak (*Q. macrocarpa*)—gnarled appearance; bark very thick, ropey; twigs corky; leaves divided at middle, having a "thin waist"; acorn with a hairy, deep cap and short stalk; associated with both wet bottomland forests and dry savannas. Other oaks (*Quercus* spp., especially white [*Q. alba*], red [*Q. rubra*], and black [*Q. velutina*])—associated with savannas or upland forests.

NOTES: Swamp white oak is uncommon in S. Wisconsin, where it is restricted to poorly drained floodplains and bottomlands, especially along the Wisconsin River. Its acorns are eaten and dispersed by wildlife, especially birds and squirrels. Swamp white oak root systems can provide excellent streambank stabilization.

BUCKTHORN
Rhamnus carthartica, Rhamnus frangula (Rhamnaceae)

INVASIVE—RESTRICTED

DESCRIPTION: Shrub or tree up to 6 m tall. Branches often with thorny tips. Leaves nearly opposite (*subopposite*), opposite, or alternate, finely serrated, and usually with fewer than 5 pairs that arc toward the leaf tip. When a leaf is pulled gently apart, it breaks cleanly (compare with dogwood, page 29). Flowers small, in clusters blooming May–June. Fruit blue-black, emerging in late summer.

Common buckthorn (*R. carthartica*)—leaves often subopposite, dull green, with rounded teeth and 3–5 pairs of arcing veins. Glossy buckthorn (*F. alnus*)—leaves alternate, shiny, untoothed, with 8–9 pairs of nonarcing veins; branches without thorny tips.

LOOK-ALIKES: Dogwood. Alder buckthorn (*R. alnifolia*)—native; small shrub (up to 1 m tall); leaves alternate with small, rounded teeth and 5–7 pairs of nonarcing veins; branches without thorny tips.

common buckthorn

NOTES: Buckthorn is common statewide. It is found in forest understories, riparian areas, floodplains, lakeshores, and urban areas. This plant is highly aggressive, outcompeting native plants and taking over disturbed wetland areas. Birds spread buckthorn seeds by eating its fruits. When possible, buckthorn is removed from stream restoration sites, usually by a combination of physical removal and chemical spraying of stumps.

common buckthorn   glossy buckthorn

31

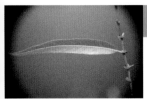

BLACK WILLOW
Salix nigra (Salicaceae)

DESCRIPTION: Tree up to 15 m tall, often with multiple, irregular trunks. Bark shaggy with interwoven ridges. Leaves alternate, linear to lance-shaped, and pointed, with tiny serrations. Leaf stipules partly surround stem near leaf base.

LOOK-ALIKES: Sandbar willow (*S. interior*)—shrub with many stems; leaves similar to black willow except with widely spaced serrations and no conspicuous stipules; found in high densities along streambanks. Crack willow (*S. fragilis*)—very similar to black willow but with leaves dark green above, whitened underneath, with coarse teeth. Weeping willow (*S. babylonica*)—leaves similar to sandbar willow; ornamental species with a "weeping" form of drooping branches; established near many streams and lakes. Pussy willow

(*S. discolor*)—shrub; leaves oval; flowers white, downy; usually near swamps.

NOTES: Black willow is common in S. Wisconsin and sporadic in N. Wisconsin. It is found along streams, lakes, swamps, and roadsides, usually in open areas. Like eastern cottonwood, it resprouts from cuttings and establishes quickly. Black willow is tolerant of flooding and has dense root systems that provide excellent bank stabilization.

ELDERBERRY
Sambucus spp. (Adoxaceae, formerly Caprifoliaceae)

DESCRIPTION: Shrub up to 4 m tall. Branches tan or gray with warty lenticels. Leaves opposite, compound (with 7–11 leaflets), and serrated. Flowers small, white, in large clusters. Fruit dark purple or red.

Common elderberry (*S. nigra* ssp. *canadensis*)—branch cross section white; flat-topped clusters of flowers blooming April–May; fruit dark purple; more common in S. Wisconsin. Red elderberry (*S. racemosa*)—branch cross section dark brown; pyramidal clusters of flowers blooming June–July; fruit red and poisonous (DO NOT EAT); more common in N. Wisconsin.

common elderberry

LOOK-ALIKES: Ash.

NOTES: Elderberry is common statewide. It is found along riparian areas, lakeshores, wooded edges, and wetlands. Wildlife, especially birds, eat its fruits and disperse the seeds widely. The fruit of common elderberry can be used by humans for jams, pies, and wines, but its seeds and vegetative parts are poisonous.

red elderberry

STEEPLEBUSH
Spiraea tomentosa (Rosaceae)

DESCRIPTION: Erect shrub 60–110 cm tall. Leaves alternate, oval to lance-shaped; leaf undersides pale with felt-like hairs; leaf edges finely toothed. Flowers pink with 5 petals, tiny (to 3 mm wide), in a large, conical set of spikes (to 13 cm tall), blooming July–September.

LOOK-ALIKES: Purple and swamp loosestrifes.

NOTES: Steeplebush is common statewide. It is found in riparian areas, bogs, and meadows, in full to partial sun, on sand or loamy substrate.

AMERICAN BASSWOOD
Tilia americana (Malvaceae, formerly Tiliaceae)

DESCRIPTION: Tree up to 40 m tall, forming multiple trunks with a "root collar" of small stems at the base. Bark with parallel, flat-topped ridges. Buds lopsided, round, smooth, and reddish-colored. Leaves alternate, toothed, asymmetrically heart-shaped, with an especially lopsided base. Flowers small, yellowish white, 5-petaled, growing in clusters attached to the middle of a leafy bract, blooming June–July. Fruits are tan, pea-like nuts.

LOOK-ALIKES: Elms. Eastern redbud (*Cercis canadensis*)—leaves widely heart-shaped with smooth edges; pink flowers.

NOTES: Basswood is common statewide. It is shade tolerant and found in moist forests associated with sugar maple, bottomlands, and recent clearings and along streams and lakes. The root systems of basswoods stabilize streambanks.

AMERICAN ELM
Ulmus americana (Ulmaceae)

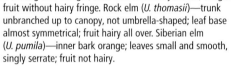

DESCRIPTION: Tree up to 30 m tall and umbrella-shaped. Bark thick with interlacing ridges; bark red and white striped in cross section. Leaves alternate, doubly serrate, slightly rough above, with a lopsided base and veins that rarely fork. Flowers in small hanging clusters, blooming March–April. Fruit winged with a hairy fringe and a notch, appearing in May.

LOOK-ALIKES: Slippery elm (*U. rubra*)—leaves often rough both above and below, with some veins forking near margin; inner bark uniformly brown; winged

fruit without hairy fringe. Rock elm (*U. thomasii*)—trunk unbranched up to canopy, not umbrella-shaped; leaf base almost symmetrical; fruit hairy all over. Siberian elm (*U. pumila*)—inner bark orange; leaves small and smooth, singly serrate; fruit not hairy.

NOTES: American elm is common statewide. It is found in moist floodplain forests, swamps, roadsides, and open disturbed sites. It is susceptible to Dutch elm disease, but as an aggressive colonizing species it is still well established. In riparian areas it develops a widespread shallow rooting system that stabilizes streambanks.

highbush cranberry

VIBURNUM (arrowwood)
Viburnum spp. (Adoxaceae, formerly Caprifoliaceae)

nannyberry

DESCRIPTION: Shrub or small tree up to 7 m tall. Leaves opposite, often toothed, and sometimes lobed. Flowers small, white, in clusters, blooming May–June. Fruit small, fleshy, emerging in September.

Nannyberry (*V. lentago*)—long, velvety, pointy buds without bud scales, resembling a "witch's finger"; 4–7 m tall; leaves oval, toothed, pointed, on a slightly winged stalk; fruit blue-black.

Highbush cranberry (*V. opulus* ssp. *americanum*)—up to 4 m tall; leaves 3-lobed, nearly maple-shaped, toothed; fruit red. Mapleleaf viburnum (*V. acerifolium*) and downy arrowwood (*V. rafinesqueanum*)—usually found in upland oak forests.

nannyberry

highbush cranberry

LOOK-ALIKES: Red maple (*Acer rubrum*)—tree; leaves doubly serrated. Buckthorn, honeysuckle.

NOTES: Viburnum is common statewide, particularly in S. Wisconsin. It is found in moist soils near streams, lakes, swamps, and roadsides. Wildlife, especially birds, eat its fruits, which can also be used by humans to make jam.

highbush cranberry

nannyberry

HERBACEOUS PLANTS

NODDING BEGGAR-TICKS
Bidens cernua (Asteraceae)

DESCRIPTION: Erect, 10–100 cm tall. Leaves opposite, lance-shaped, undivided, coarsely toothed, stalkless. Flowers yellow, 3–5 cm wide, with petal-like rays 1 cm long. Leafy bracts underneath flower usually longer than flower's center disk. Flowers borne in large, loose, stalked clusters, often "nodding" with age, blooming August–October. Seed with 2–4 barbs.

LOOK-ALIKES: Other beggar-ticks (*Bidens* spp.)—sometimes submersed and have divided leaves.

seed

NOTES: Nodding beggar-ticks are common statewide. They are found in wet meadows and marshes and along the shores of streams and lakes. Seeds and leaves provide food for terrestrial invertebrates such as caterpillars, birds such as ducks, and mammals such as rabbits.

FIREWEED
Chamerion angustifolium
(formerly *Epilobium angustifolium*; Onagraceae)

DESCRIPTION: Erect, 60–180 cm tall, growing alone or in clumps. Stems usually single. Leaves alternate, lance-shaped, crowded along stem, toothed, stalkless. Flowers pink, purple, or blue with 4 petals, long stigmas, 2–4 cm wide. Individual flowers on long stalks, widely spaced along a long spike, blooming June–August. Fruit capsule long and pointy.

LOOK-ALIKES: False dragonhead, prairie blazing star, purple loosestrife, and swamp loosestrife. Dame's rocket (*Hesperis matronalis*)—invasive—restricted; flowers white, pink, or purple, on short stalks, in loose spike at the top of the stem.

NOTES: Fireweed is common statewide. It is found in riparian areas, moist forests, and clearings. Seed germination is stimulated by fire.

fruit
capsule

35

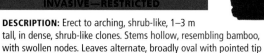

JAPANESE KNOTWEED
Fallopia japonica var. *japonica*
(formerly *Polygonum cuspidatum*; Polygonaceae)

INVASIVE—RESTRICTED

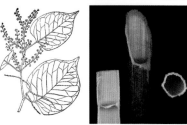

DESCRIPTION: Erect to arching, shrub-like, 1–3 m tall, in dense, shrub-like clones. Stems hollow, resembling bamboo, with swollen nodes. Leaves alternate, broadly oval with pointed tip and flat base (10–23 cm long, 7–13 cm wide); young leaves heart-shaped. Leaves lighter on underside, upper side feels like fine sandpaper. Flowers small, greenish white, growing from leaf axils in branched clusters 7.5–15 cm tall, blooming in late summer.

LOOK-ALIKES: Giant knotweed (*F. sachalinensis*)—invasive—prohibited; larger, heart-shaped leaves to 30 cm long. Mile-a-minute vine (*Persicaria perfoliata*)—invasive—prohibited; smaller, triangular leaves.

NOTES: Japanese knotweed is distributed sporadically statewide—except in N.W. Wisconsin—and its distribution is spreading in some areas. It is found in riparian corridors, wetlands, grasslands, woods, and disturbed sunny areas. Part of its success probably lies in its tolerance of a variety of conditions, such as high temperatures, shade, salinity, flooding, and drought. It tends to outcompete other plants and reduce wildlife habitat.

JAPANESE HOP
Humulus japonicus (Cannabaceae)

**INVASIVE—
PROHIBITED/RESTRICTED**

DESCRIPTION: Vine, climbing clockwise, sometimes forming dense stands. Stem and leafstalks rough with downward-pointing hairs. Leaves opposite, palmately divided into 5–9 lobes (upper leaves sometimes 3–5 lobes), 5–13 cm long, serrated, with stalks as long or longer than leaves. Flowers dull green with 5 petals, in spikes to 2 cm long, blooming July–October.

LOOK-ALIKES: Common hop (*H. lupulus*)—leaves usually 3-lobed, with shorter leafstalk. Virginia creeper (*Parthenocissus quinquefolia*)—woody vine with tendrils; leaves with 5 fully separated lobes.

NOTES: Japanese hop is found in S.W. Wisconsin; its distribution is currently limited, but it is spreading rapidly along a few rivers. It is prohibited in all Wisconsin counties except Crawford and Grant, where it has a restricted status. It is found in riparian areas, floodplains, lakeshores, and disturbed areas such as roadsides in full sun to shade; it prefers moist substrate. This plant can be aggressive, outcompeting native plants and taking over wetland areas. Although it cannot survive Wisconsin's cold winters, new seeds can sprout each spring to maintain its establishment in an area.

JEWELWEED
Impatiens capensis and *I. pallida* (Balsaminaceae)

DESCRIPTION: Erect, 60–180 cm tall. Stems often branched near top, with clear fluid inside. Leaves alternate, undivided with subtle toothing, soft, on long stalks. Flowers pale yellow (*I. pallida*) to orange (*I. capensis*) with 5 parts (appearing 3-parted), 2–3 cm long with a tubular shape and a curved spur extending from the back of the flower. Flowers drooping from stalks, arranged in broad, spreading clusters from leaf axils, blooming July–September. Fruit long and narrow, bursts open when touched.

LOOK-ALIKES: None in wadeable streams.

NOTES: Jewelweed is common statewide, preferring to grow in moist areas such as forests. It is especially abundant in partially sunny edge places, such as alongside roads or streambanks. The clear fluid inside the stems and leaves of jewelweed can be used as a remedy for stinging nettle or poison ivy; simply mash stems and leaves and rub the fluid over the affected area. From August to September the ripe fruits burst open explosively when touched, hurling seeds up to a meter or more.

PRAIRIE BLAZING STAR (thick-spike gayfeather)
Liatris pycnostachya (Asteraceae)

DESCRIPTION: Erect, 60–120 cm tall. Stem leafy, hairy. Leaves alternate, lance-shaped, thin (11–22 cm long, 0.4–1.3 cm wide), abundant; upper leaves much smaller than lower. Flower heads pink, appearing like "powder puffs," with many thin petals, stalkless, densely arranged along spike, blooming July–September.

LOOK-ALIKES: Fireweed, purple loosestrife, and swamp loosestrife. Dense gayfeather (*L. spicata*)—special concern; stems usually smooth; flower heads longer and more widely spaced; usually found in prairies, not near flowing water. Rough blazing star (*L. aspera*)—flower heads broad, widely spaced on spike.

NOTES: Prairie blazing star is common in S. Wisconsin and rare in the north. It is found in riparian areas and meadows, in full sun, on sandy to loamy substrate. Its flowers and seeds provide food for terrestrial invertebrates such as caterpillars; its leaves, roots, and other plant parts provide food for terrestrial rodents, deer, and livestock.

leaf

WILD PARSNIP
Pastinaca sativa (Apiaceae)

DO NOT TOUCH!

INVASIVE—RESTRICTED

DESCRIPTION: Erect, 30–150 cm tall. Stem flat, with ridges. Leaves alternate, pinnately divided into 5–15 broad, separate, stalkless leaflets 5–10 cm long. Leafstalks long on lower leaves, shorter on upper leaves. Flowers yellow with 5 parts, small, arranged in broad umbels 10–20 cm wide, blooming June–July.

LOOK-ALIKES: Cow parsnip (*Heracleum sphondylium* ssp. *montanum*)—taller (90–300 cm tall); flowers white.

NOTES: DO NOT TOUCH. Wild parsnip is one of Wisconsin's most hazardous plants. Touching sap from a damaged part of the plant can cause severe photo-dermatitis, in which the skin blisters when exposed to sunlight as if from a third-degree burn. Blisters can persist for weeks and cause scarring. Wild parsnip is common in most of Wisconsin except the northwest. It is found in edge areas such as roadsides and in fields and pastures. An aggressive invader, it can form dense stands that crowd out native species.

FALSE DRAGONHEAD (obedient plant)
Physostegia virginiana (Lamiaceae)

DESCRIPTION: Erect, 50–150 cm tall, growing from rhizomes. Stem square, smooth, often forking near top. Leaves opposite, lance-shaped, usually toothed and stalkless. Flowers violet-pink, tubular, 5-parted (petals fused: 2 petals on upper lip, 3 on lower lip), 1.5–3.5 cm long, in large spikes 5–15 cm tall, blooming August–October.

LOOK-ALIKES: Fireweed and blue vervain.

NOTES: False dragonhead is common statewide except in N. Wisconsin. It is found in riparian areas, woods, and fields, in full to partial sun, on sandy or loamy substrate. It is popularly cultivated.

NETTLES
Urticaceae spp.

DO NOT TOUCH!

DESCRIPTION: Erect, usually 40–100 cm tall (except stinging nettle). Stem usually unbranched. Leaves usually opposite (except Canadian wood-nettle—alternate), oval to lance-shaped, coarsely toothed. Flowers tiny, cream-colored with 4 petals, in long clusters from axils of upper leaves, blooming June–September.

Small-spike false nettle (*Boehmeria cylindrica*)—no stinging hairs. Leaves opposite, long-stalked; flowers blooming August–September.

Canadian wood-nettle (*Laportea canadensis*)—stinging hairs on stem and leaves. Leaves alternate, broadly oval-shaped, with long stalks; female flowers in upper leaf axils and male clusters in lower leaf axils, blooming July–August.

stinging nettle

Stinging nettle (*Urtica dioica*)—stinging hairs on stem and leaves. Up to 180 cm tall; leaves opposite, with short stalks; flowers blooming June–September.

LOOK-ALIKES: Mints (Lamiaceae spp.)—stems square; no stinging hairs.

small-spike false nettle

Canadian wood-nettle

NOTES: AVOID TOUCHING—2 species, stinging and Canadian wood-nettles, have tiny hairs that sting to the touch. The sting lasts several minutes but can be alleviated with the clear fluid from the crushed stems and leaves of jewelweed, which often grows nearby. Nettles are common statewide, with stinging nettle especially common in disturbed sites. They prefer moist areas such as forests, although stinging nettle may also be found in dry areas. Nettles are often found along streambanks and can form dense stands.

BLUE VERVAIN
Verbena hastata (Verbenaceae)

DESCRIPTION: Erect, 40–120 cm tall. Stem square, hairy, forking near top of plant. Leaves opposite, lance-shaped (to 18 cm long), mostly undivided but occasionally with 3 lobes, coarsely toothed, stalked. Flowers violet blue, tiny (3–6 mm wide), with 5 petals, crowded along thin spikes 20 cm tall; only a few flowers bloom at a time from July to October.

LOOK-ALIKES: False dragonhead, purple loosestrife, and swamp loosestrife.

NOTES: Blue vervain is common statewide. It is found in riparian areas, meadows, and fields, in full sun, on sandy or loamy substrate.

39

AQUATIC PLANTS

Aquatic plants are plants that grow in water or saturated soil for a significant part of the year. They play many crucial roles in streams, such as providing cover for fish and providing food and habitat for invertebrates. Certain aquatic plants are invasive and can aggressively choke out native species. However, oftentimes the sight of aquatic plants—a bed of pondweeds billowing in the current, a field of water lilies in a quiet pool—is a sign of a healthy stream ecosystem.

There are many types of aquatic plants:

Emergent: leaves extending *above* the water surface;
Free-floating: without roots;
Floating-leaf: rooted, with leaves floating *on* or just above the water surface;
Submersed: rooted, with leaves growing only *below* the water surface.

Note that many plants combine two different growth forms. For example, pondweeds may have both floating and submersed leaves. We have placed each plant in the category that best characterizes it (e.g., pondweeds are placed in the "submersed" category because most of their leaves are usually underwater).

EMERGENT PLANTS

Emergent plants are rooted in the ground and have leaves that extend above the water surface. This section is divided into two parts: emergent plants with narrow leaves and emergent plants with broad leaves.

Emergent Plants with Narrow Leaves

Narrow-leaved emergent plants fall into two categories: grass-like plants (*graminoids*) and non-grass-like plants (*forbs*). (Both graminoids and forbs are *herbs*, or nonwoody plants.) Whereas grass-like plants produce tiny flowers, forbs are known for their larger, more colorful flowers. However, many forbs are found in streams without flowers and may be mistaken for graminoids.

Grass-like plants may be grasses (Poaceae), sedges (Cyperaceae), or rushes (Juncaceae). Many grass-like species, particularly sedges, can be very difficult to tell apart, and this guide only describes a few species, so be aware that many other graminoid species are also present in Wisconsin streams. Understanding the differences between the three graminoid families can be helpful for identification. Here are their general characteristics:

Grasses (Poaceae)—Stems hollow, round in cross section (or sometimes flattened), with joints. Leaves are flat, *two-ranked* (growing along the stem in two primary rows). Leaf sheath open (not fused around the stem). *Ligule* (a thin outgrowth between the leaf and the leafstalk) is present. Tiny flowers are scale-covered florets without petals, arranged in flattened, sharp, zigzagging spikelets. Floret scales (*lemma* and *palea*) are important for identification.

Sedges (Cyperaceae)—Stems solid or pithy (filled-in), usually triangular in cross section (sometimes round or square), without joints. Leaves are grooved or folded and may be *basal* (originating from the base of the plant), reduced to sheaths at the base of the stem, or *three-ranked* (growing along the stem in three primary rows). Leaf sheath is closed (fused around the stem). Ligule is absent. Tiny flowers are scale-covered florets without petals on small, distinct heads and are often necessary for identification. Note that bulrushes and spike-rushes are not truly rushes but instead are in the sedge family.

Rushes (Juncaceae)—Stems are solid or pithy (filled in), mostly round. Leaves are basal or alternate along the stem. Leaf shape is variable: round, flat, rolled inward in cross section, or reduced to sheaths at the base of the stem. Leaf sheath is closed (fused around stem). Tiny flowers appear to have six papery tan petals (actually three petals and three sepals). Fruit is a capsule with numerous seeds and is usually important for identification.

FLOWERING-RUSH
Butomus umbellatus (Butomaceae)

DESCRIPTION: Emergent or sometimes submersed forb forming dense stands. Stem thin, 0.3–1.5 m tall. Leaves growing from rhizomes, erect or floating, triangular in cross section, linear (to 1 m long, 0.5–1 cm wide), without central band. Flowers pink to white, appearing to have 3 or 6 petals, 2–2.5 cm wide, on thin stalks in round umbel, blooming June–August. Submersed form with only limp floating leaves and no flowers.

LOOK-ALIKES: Arrowheads, bur-reeds, and wild celery.

NOTES: Flowering-rush is found sporadically in E. and N. Wisconsin, sometimes locally established. It is found along lake shorelines and in stream backwaters, marshes, and quiet water that is shallow to 2 m deep. It may provide waterfowl habitat but also may outcompete native plants. It is originally from Africa and Eurasia.

BRISTLY SEDGE (bottle brush sedge)
Carex comosa (Cyperaceae)

DESCRIPTION: Emergent or semiaquatic sedge to 1 m tall, growing from rhizomes. Leaves with W-shaped cross section, 6–15 mm wide. Flower spikes cylindrical, green, and bristly, resembling a bottle brush. Fruit with long, 2-parted beak.

LOOK-ALIKES: Bur-reeds and sedges (especially *Carex* spp.).

NOTES: Bristly sedge is common statewide. It is found in marshes, lakes, ponds, and streams in dense clusters on banks or in very shallow water. It stabilizes shorelines, and its nutlets provide food for waterfowl.

cross section   fruit

CREEPING SPIKE-RUSH
Eleocharis palustris (Cyperaceae)

DESCRIPTION: Emergent sedge (not a rush), 0.1–1 m tall, with similar shape to a long, burning match. Stems 0.5–3 mm thick, solitary or in small groups, emerging from rhizomes. Leaves appear absent (sheaths at stem bases). Single spikelet atop each stem brown, pointed, wider than stem, and 5–25 mm long. Flower scales 2–4.5 mm.

LOOK-ALIKES: Needle spike-rush (when emergent); water horsetail. Bald spike-rush (*E. erythropoda*)—common; very similar except for mature fruit. Robbins' spike-rush (*E. robbinsii*)—special concern; emergent stems bluntly 3-angled, submersed leaves thread-like. Brown-fruited rush (*Juncus pelocarpus*)—outer leaves cup inner leaves; stem with faint horizontal lines.

NOTES: Creeping spike-rush is common statewide, especially in N. Wisconsin. It is found in marshes, ditches, and wet meadows, from shorelines to water 2 m deep on firm substrate. It provides streambanks with a buffer from wave erosion and stabilizes sediment, as well as providing cover and food for waterfowl and muskrats.

WATER HORSETAIL
Equisetum fluviatile (Equisetaceae)

DESCRIPTION: Emergent herb. Stems distinctively jointed, sometimes branching at nodes. Stems stiff, hollow, up to 1 m tall, ridged. Central cavity very large. Leaves reduced to 15–20 small, pointed, dark teeth encircling each jointed node, 1.5–3 mm long. Flowers absent.

LOOK-ALIKES: Other horsetails (*Equisetum* spp.)—smaller central cavity; teeth appear different. Rushes (Juncaceae spp.) and sedges (Cyperaceae spp.)—unjointed stems. Grasses (Poaceae spp.)—flowers present.

NOTES: Water horsetail is common statewide. It is found in lakes, ponds, and marshes and along streams in water up to 1 m deep. It provides food for waterfowl, especially geese, as well as for moose. It reproduces by spores, not flowers.

NORTHERN MANA GRASS
Glyceria borealis (Poaceae)

DESCRIPTION: Emergent grass up to 1 m tall, growing in clusters. Emergent leaves narrow (2–5 mm wide), with leaf sheath wrapping completely around stem. Floating leaves (when present) flexible, finely hairy, and waxy. Flowers arranged in thin spike with branches (8–12 cm long) composed of several linear spikelets (1–2 cm long). Florets with outer scales (*lemmas*) 3–4 cm long, rounded, strongly ridged, with thin, brittle edges and tips. Blooming in midsummer.

LOOK-ALIKES: Other manna grasses (*Glyceria* spp.)—spikelets ovate, <1 cm long, often laterally compressed. Also bur-reeds, irises, and wild rice.

NOTES: Northern manna grass is common statewide. It is found along lakes and marshes in water up to 1 m deep. It provides spawning habitat for fish and food for many ducks. Its fruits provide food for mammals, and its leaves are eaten by muskrats and deer.

northern blue flag

southern blue flag

IRISES
Iris spp. (Iridaceae)

northern blue flag

DESCRIPTION: Emergent or terrestrial forb up to 1 m tall, emerging from rhizomes. Leaves erect, basal, in flat, fan-like arrangement. Leaf blade sword-like and V-shaped in cross section (0.5–5 cm wide). Distinct flowers, appearing 6-petaled, purple, blue, or yellow, large (6–8 cm wide), blooming May–July.
  Northern blue flag (*I. versicolor*)—common in N. and central Wisconsin; flowers blue to purple, sometimes with small, greenish-yellow spot at base of outer "petals," unopened flower with 3 sides. Southern blue flag (*I. virginica*)—common except in very N. Wisconsin; flowers bright blue with yellow, hairy area at base of outer "petals." Yellow iris (*I. pseudacorus*)—invasive; flowers yellow and held below leaves, unopened flower with 6 sides, blooming May–June.

LOOK-ALIKES: Bur-reeds, cattails, manna grasses (*Glyceria* spp.), and wild rice. Sweet-flag (*Acorus calamus*)—leaves with wavy margin and midrib not centered.

NOTES: Irises are common statewide. They are found along streambanks and in wetlands, lakes, and ponds, in quiet water >1 m deep, on sandy or loamy substrate. They provide food and cover for waterfowl and other wildlife and are adapted for bee pollination. The rhizomes and rootstocks of irises are poisonous.

southern blue flag

yellow iris

43

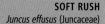

SOFT RUSH
Juncus effusus (Juncaceae)

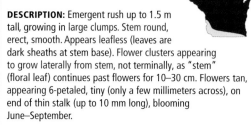

DESCRIPTION: Emergent rush up to 1.5 m tall, growing in large clumps. Stem round, erect, smooth. Appears leafless (leaves are dark sheaths at stem base). Flower clusters appearing to grow laterally from stem, not terminally, as "stem" (floral leaf) continues past flowers for 10–30 cm. Flowers tan, appearing 6-petaled, tiny (only a few millimeters across), on end of thin stalk (up to 10 mm long), blooming June–September.

LOOK-ALIKES: Other rushes (Juncaceae spp.)— stems single or in loose clumps or having terminal flowers and leaf blades. Bulrushes (in Cyperaceae family)—sedge characteristics; flowers without petals.

NOTES: Soft rush is common statewide, especially in N. Wisconsin. It is found in wetlands and shallow waters. It provides habitat for fish. Its seeds provide food, its stem clumps provide shelter for birds, and its stems and leaves are eaten by muskrats.

REED CANARY GRASS
Phalaris arundinacea (Poaceae)

INVASIVE

DESCRIPTION: Emergent wetland grass 0.5–1.5 m tall, forming dense stands from rhizomes. Stem thick, erect, hollow. Leaves narrow (10–20 cm long, 1–2 cm wide), rough-textured, gray-green. Ligule at leaf base transparent, paper-like, 3–8 mm long. Clusters of flower spikelets (4–6 mm long) blooming May–June, green to purple, turning tan in late summer.

LOOK-ALIKES: Bluejoint grass (*Calamagrostis canadensis*)—flower spikelets in loose clusters; nodes bluish. Orchard grass (*Dactylis glomerata*)—spikelets in distinct, smaller bunches. Phragmites.

NOTES: Reed canary grass is abundant statewide. It is found on the shores of lakes and streams, in meadows, marshes, and floodplain forests, and on disturbed wet ground. It prefers water up to 0.5 m deep and full sun, but it may persist in shade. Although it is an aggressive invasive plant, it is sometimes planted for erosion control or livestock forage. As of 2012 it had not yet been designated restricted or prohibited by the Wisconsin Department of Natural Resources, but in the future this status may change.

PHRAGMITES (common reed, giant reed)
Phragmites australis (Poaceae)

INVASIVE—RESTRICTED

DESCRIPTION: Emergent wetland grass, 1–5 m tall, growing in dense clones from rhizomes. Stems thick, erect, hollow. Leaves long, flat, broadly narrow (to 75 cm long, 1–3 cm wide), gray-green. Ligule with short hairs at leaf base. Large clusters of flower spikelets resembling feather dusters, 10–15 mm long, with silky hairs and 3–7 florets, blooming July–September, grayish purple, turning tan in fall.

LOOK-ALIKES: Native subspecies of phragmites (known as *P. australis americana*)—uncommon; stands less dense; stems turn reddish brown; leaf sheaths loose; sparse flower clusters blooming July–August. Reed canary grass.

NOTES: Phragmites ("frag-MY-tees") is common statewide, especially near the Great Lakes. It is found on shorelines, especially near wetlands and in sunny disturbed areas, in water <2 m deep. Although there is a native subspecies, the Eurasian subspecies is invasive: dense stands impair navigation and out-compete native vegetation. Phragmites provides little food or shelter to wildlife, although it is eaten by muskrats.

HARD-STEM BULRUSH
Schoenoplectus acutus (Cyperaceae)

DESCRIPTION: Semiaquatic, emergent sedge (not a rush) that can grow in large colonies from rhizomes. Stem erect, firm, round, 1–3 m tall, 0.5–1 cm wide, spongy with small air chambers that cannot be easily crushed with fingers, usually olive green. Appears leafless: leaves are sheaths at stem base. Flower clusters open, stiff (not drooping) near top of stem; "stem" (floral leaf) continues slightly beyond flowers. Florets without petals; floret scales gray-brown with red flecks and fringed edges, 3–4 mm long.

LOOK-ALIKES: Soft-stem bulrush.

NOTES: Hard-stem bulrush is common in N. and E. Wisconsin. It is found in marshes, lakes, and streams, in water up to at least 2 m deep, on firm substrate. It provides habitat for invertebrates and fish and cover and food for birds and muskrats.

SOFT-STEM BULRUSH
Schoenoplectus tabernaemontani (Cyperaceae)

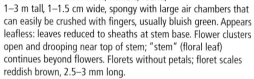

DESCRIPTION: Semiaquatic, emergent sedge (not a rush) that can grow in large colonies from rhizomes. Stem erect, flexible, round, 1–3 m tall, 1–1.5 cm wide, spongy with large air chambers that can easily be crushed with fingers, usually bluish green. Appears leafless: leaves reduced to sheaths at stem base. Flower clusters open and drooping near top of stem; "stem" (floral leaf) continues beyond flowers. Florets without petals; floret scales reddish brown, 2.5–3 mm long.

LOOK-ALIKES: Hard-stem bulrush. Common three-square and river bulrushes (*Bolboschoenus fluviatilis*, *Schoenoplectus pungens*)—triangular stems. Rushes (Juncaceae spp.)—tiny, petaled flowers.

NOTES: Soft-stem bulrush is common statewide. It is found in marshes, in quiet water to depths of 2 m, on mucky substrate. It provides habitat for invertebrates and fish and cover and food for birds and muskrats.

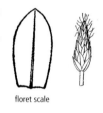

floret scale

common bur-reed

floating-leaf bur-reed

BUR-REEDS
Sparganium spp. (Typhaceae)

DESCRIPTION: Emergent or floating grass-like forb. Leaves long, narrow (<1.5 m long). Leaf veins appear as net-like pattern in light. Flower stalk often zigzags, inflorescence green to white, spherical, fuzzy, blooming June–July. Fruits clustered in spiky green-brown balls or "heads."

Emergent bur-reeds—leaves erect, spongy, with cross section resembling flattened triangle, and a conspicuous keel (fleshy ridge); floating leaves flat (if present); somewhat tolerant of pollution: Common bur-reed (*S. eurycarpum*)—most common; stem triangular; leaves large (6–12 mm wide) and keeled; fruit pyramid-shaped, clustered in round fruit heads wide (2.5 cm), with 2 stigmas (all other bur-reeds with thin fruit having 1 stigma). Eastern bur-reed (*S. americanum*)—leaves flat, not stiff; fruit cluster heads 1.5–2.5 cm wide. Narrow-leaf bur-reed (*S. emersum*)—leaves erect or floating (only species that often has both); leaves 6–12 mm wide, often keeled, flat except for triangular base, and much taller than unbranched flowering stalk. Shining bur-reed (*S. androcladum*)—leaves up to 0.8 m tall, keeled to triangular; fruit 2–3 cm wide, with stalk sometimes branched. Northern bur-reed (*S. glomeratum*)—threatened; only in N.W. Wisconsin; leaves erect or floating, flat, not stiff; up to 0.8 m tall.

Floating bur-reeds—leaves floating, flat; mostly in N. Wisconsin; sensitive to pollution: Floating-leaf bur-reed (*S. fluctuans*)—floating leaves flat, wide (5–9 mm); flower stalk branched with 2–4 fruit heads 1.5–2 cm wide. Narrow-leaf bur-reed (*S. angustifolium*)— floating leaves narrow (2–5 mm wide), with rounded backs; flower stalk unbranched; fruit heads 1.5–1.8 cm wide. Small bur-reed (*S. natans*)— smallest bur-reed in region;

cross section of emergent leaf (*above*; often appearing more flattened than in photo)

leaves thin (2–7 mm wide), flat, long, floating or erect; fruit heads only 1–1.2 cm wide.

LOOK-ALIKES: Cattails, flowering-rush, irises, manna grasses (*Glyceria* spp.), sedges (*Carex* spp.), wild celery, and wild rice.

NOTES: Bur-reeds are found statewide and are common to rare, depending on the species. They are found in marshes and along shores of streams, ponds, and lakes, in water up to 1 m deep. They are often associated with high nutrient levels and are tolerant of high turbidity. Bur-reeds help to stabilize sediment. They provide nesting habitat for waterfowl—which also eat their fruit—and are grazed by deer and muskrats.

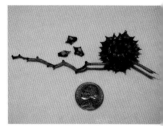

CATTAILS
Typha spp. (Typhaceae)

DESCRIPTION: Emergent, grass-like forb. Leaves basal, lance-shaped, long (to >1 m tall), in circular arrangement. Flower spike brown, cylindrical, resembling a hotdog, blooming May–July. Male spike disappears after pollination above persistent female spike.

Broad-leaved cattail (*T. latifolia*)—leaves 10–23 mm wide and pale green, nearly flat in cross section; no gap between male and female flower spikes. Narrow-leaved cattail (*T. angustifolia*)—invasive—restricted; leaves 5–11 mm wide and dark green; back rounded; small bare gap between male and female flower spikes. Hybrid cattail (*Typha × glauca* Godr.)—invasive—restricted; leaves 6–15 mm wide; small bare gap between male and female flower spikes.

LOOK-ALIKES: Bur-reeds, irises, manna grasses (*Glyceria* spp.), and wild rice.

NOTES: Cattails are common statewide. They are found along lakeshores and in marshes, river backwaters, and ditches, in water up to 1 m deep and in full sun. Cattails are tolerant of moderate fluctuations in water levels and high nutrient levels. They provide habitat for invertebrates and fish, food for birds, and they also provide the basis for the diet and habitat of muskrats, which can help to prevent the domination of cattails.

narrow-leaved
cattail

broad-leaved
cattail

northern wild rice

southern wild rice

NORTHERN AND SOUTHERN WILD RICE
Zizania palustris and *Z. aquatica* (Poaceae)

DESCRIPTION: Emergent grasses around 3 m tall, growing as single stems or in small clusters. Leaves flat, wide, pointed, with lengthwise veins and open leaf sheaths (not wrapping completely around stem). Early floating leaves long, narrow, smooth, pointed, from at least May to June. Flower clusters large (10–60 cm long), at ends of stalks, all spikelets round with single flowers. Female spikelets above, densely arranged, with long erect bristles, resembling a thin broom. Male spikelets dangle loosely below on side branches. Blooming June–September.

Northern wild rice (*Z. palustris*)—mostly in N. Wisconsin, often along lakes. Usually <3 m tall. Leaves 0.3–3 cm wide. Female spikelets flattened, 1.5–2 mm wide. Southern wild rice (*Z. aquatica*)—mostly in S. Wisconsin, often along rivers; usually taller (often >3 m tall); leaves larger (1–5 cm wide); female spikelet thin, <1.5 mm wide.

LOOK-ALIKES: In early floating-leaf stage, similar to bur-reeds and manna grasses (*Glyceria* spp.), also cattails and irises.

NOTES: Northern wild rice is typically found in N. Wisconsin, while southern wild rice is found in S. and central Wisconsin, but their ranges overlap, and there is much variation within populations. Both species are found in lakes, streams, and rivers, in water up to 1 m deep, usually on sand, silt, or mucky substrate. Wild rice prefers moderate to high pH and is sensitive to water level fluctuations. It provides food and habitat for birds and muskrats, and its grains are edible by humans after being processed.

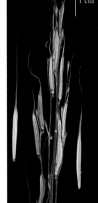

1 cm

male   female
spikelet   spikelet

49

Emergent Plants with Broad Leaves

WILD CALLA (marsh calla, water arum)
Calla palustris (Araceae)

DESCRIPTION: Emergent, 13–25 cm tall. Leaves heart-shaped, 5–10 cm wide, with pointed tips and parallel veins. Leafstalks thick, 5–20 cm long, growing from fleshy rhizomes. Floral leaf resembling a large white flower petal, with 2–5 cm long flower spike inside, blooming in June. Fruits are red berries clustered atop a stalk.

LOOK-ALIKES: Pickerelweed.

NOTES: Wild calla is common in N. Wisconsin and less common in S. Wisconsin. It is found in bogs and cold, shallow water in mucky substrate. Its berries are eaten by many species, and its rhizomes and leaves are eaten by muskrats.

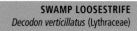

SWAMP LOOSESTRIFE
Decodon verticillatus (Lythraceae)

DESCRIPTION: Emergent, often tangled, from rhizomes. Stems angled, arching (often rerooting at tips), up to several meters long, thick, spongy, woody at base. Leaves opposite or in whorls of 3–4, lance-shaped (5–15 cm long, 1–4 cm wide). Flowers magenta to pink with 5 slightly crinkled, long petals (10–15 mm), bunched in the top leaf axils, with long stamens, blooming August–September.

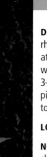

LOOK-ALIKES: See purple loosestrife's look-alikes, page 51.

NOTES: Swamp loosestrife is found sporadically statewide. It grows in shallow water, in muck or peat. Its fruits provide food for waterfowl, and it sometimes provides food and habitat for muskrats.

PURPLE LOOSESTRIFE
Lythrum salicaria (Lythraceae)

INVASIVE—RESTRICTED

DESCRIPTION: Emergent wetland forb in dense, bushy stands, 0.5–1.5 m tall. Stems square to many-sided, stiff, and upright, growing from woody roots. Leaves usually opposite (though sometimes whorled above), lance-shaped, stalkless, 3.5–11.5 cm long, finely hairy, with smooth edges. Flowers magenta to pink with 5–7 narrow, crinkled petals, 1.3–2.5 cm wide, closely arranged in leaf axils on long spikes (10–40 cm long), blooming July–September.

LOOK-ALIKES: Blue vervain, fireweed, prairie blazing star, steeplebush, and swamp loosestrife. Cultivated purple loosestrife (*L. virgatum*)—leaves smooth (not hairy); more flowers in each leaf axil. Wing-angled loosestrife (*L. alatum*)—single flowers at leaf axils with shorter petals.

NOTES: Purple loosestrife is common statewide. It is found on streambanks and shorelines and in floodplains, wetlands, and disturbed sites such as ditches. Originally from Eurasia, it is a nuisance species that disturbs native plants, wildlife habitat, and boats.

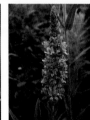

FORGET-ME-NOT
Myosotis scorpioides (Boraginaceae)

INVASIVE

DESCRIPTION: Emergent, 10–60 cm tall. Stems hairy, creeping. Leaves alternate, 2.5–8 cm long, 7–20 mm wide, hairy, stalkless, and evergreen in ponds. Flowers small (0.6–1 cm wide), blue with yellow center and 5 petals, borne in branched cluster. Flowers tubular, with petals shorter than the tube. Blooming June–September.

LOOK-ALIKES: Watercress and water speedwell.

NOTES: Forget-me-not is found statewide and is abundant in many local areas where it is found. It grows in streams, springs, and ponds in shallow water or along banks. As of 2012, forget-me-not had not yet been designated restricted or prohibited by the Wisconsin Department of Natural Resources, though in the future its status may change.

WATERCRESS
Nasturtium officinale (Rorippa nasturtium-aquaticum; Brassicaceae)

INVASIVE

DESCRIPTION: Emergent, 10–20 cm tall, forming large tangled beds. Stems textured, trailing, up to several meters long, often with scattered rooting from lower nodes. Leaves wintergreen, subdivided into 3–9 rounded leaflets, with terminal leaflet as the largest; whole leaf 4–12 cm long, including leaflets; young leaves simple, not compound. Flowers white with 4 petals, small (5 mm wide), in clusters at the end of shoots, blooming May–October. Fruit a thin pod (1–2.5 cm long) containing coarse seeds.

LOOK-ALIKES: Forget-me-not. Bittercress (*Cardamine* spp.)—not in large beds; stems and seeds smooth; lower nodes of stems without scattered roots.

NOTES: Watercress is found sporadically statewide and is locally abundant. It grows in streams and most springs, in sun with cold, clear water on soft or gravelly substrate. Its leaves provide food for fish, waterfowl, deer, and muskrats and are also edible to humans if found in unpolluted water. Watercress can be evergreen year-round and can grow densely, impeding water flow and outcompeting native plants. It is originally from Eurasia and Africa; as of 2012 it had not yet been designated restricted or prohibited by the Wisconsin Department of Natural Resources, but in the future its status may change.

PICKERELWEED
Pontederia cordata (Pontederiaceae)

DESCRIPTION: Emergent, 0.3–1 m tall, often forming large colonies from rhizomes. Leaves heart-shaped, glossy, firm, on tall, air-filled stalks. Leaf veins fine, parallel, and all terminating at single upper leaf tip. Flowers purplish blue, small (1.3 cm wide), clustered in single spike (5–15 cm long), blooming June–August. Submersed form of plant with ribbon-like leaves.

LOOK-ALIKES: Arrowheads and wild calla. Water plantains (*Alisma* spp.)—leaves with prominent veins and cross-venation; flowers with 3 petals in widely branching clusters.

NOTES: Pickerelweed is common statewide, especially in N. and W. Wisconsin. It is found in shallow waters up to 2 m deep, often on muddy substrate. Its flowering stalks provide habitat to insects, its roots and leaves provide habitat for fish, and its fruits provide food for waterfowl and muskrats.

ARROWHEADS
Sagittaria spp. (Alismataceae)

DESCRIPTION: Emergent, 15 cm–1.2 m tall. Leaves highly variable (arrowhead-shaped, spoon-shaped, or grass-shaped). Submersed leaves narrow and pointed (if present). Flower stalks with whorls of white flowers (2–3 cm wide) with 3 petals and 3 leafy bracts (4–15 mm long) below each whorl. Lower flowers produce a round head of individual nutlets with pointy beaks. Blooming in midsummer.

Common arrowhead (*S. latifolia*)—leaves arrow-shaped, forming "A" shape (5–40 cm long, 0.5–25 cm wide). Leaves palmately veined, with veins terminating at 3 separate lobe tips. Nutlet beak at right angle. Arum-leaved arrowhead (*S. cuneata*)—lower lobes shorter than upper lobe, with long leafy bracts (10–40 mm) underneath flowers. Often also with floating, arrowhead-shaped leaves. Nutlet beak small and upright (not angled). Midwestern arrowhead (*S. brevirostra*)—angled flower stalks, long leafy bracts (14–40 mm) underneath flowers, and nutlet beak longer and more erect than *S. cuneata*. Grass-leaved arrowhead (*S. graminea*) and stiff arrowheads (*S. rigida*)—leaves narrow, long, often appearing like spoons or lances, though very rarely arrowhead-shaped. Nutlet beak angled.

LOOK-ALIKES: Pickerelweed; also flowering-rush and wild celery.

NOTES: Arrowheads are common statewide. They are found in streams, ponds, lakes, and marshes, in water 5 cm–1 m deep, often in muddy or organic substrate. They are tolerant of pollution. They provide habitat for young fish; their tubers and fruits provide food for waterfowl; and their tubers and leaves provide food for mammals such as muskrats and beavers.

common
arrowhead

common
arrowhead

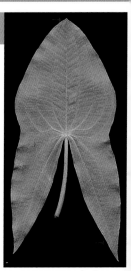

common arrowhead

grass-leaved arrowhead

midwestern arrowhead

stiff arrowhead

WATER SPEEDWELL
Veronica anagallis-aquatica (Plantaginaceae)

DESCRIPTION: Emergent or submersed, 10–25 cm tall, often forming large beds. Stems trailing or erect, 1–3 m long, smooth, often rooting from lower nodes. Leaves opposite, oblong to lance-shaped, 2–10 cm long, stalkless, usually wrapping around stem at leaf base. Flowers light blue or white with 4 petals, small (6–8 mm), in clusters on flower stalks that curve from upper leaf axils. Flowers tubular with petal lobes longer than tube. Blooming June–October.

LOOK-ALIKES: Forget-me-not; submersed form may be confused with clasping-leaf pondweed.

NOTES: Water speedwell is common in E. Wisconsin. It is found in the water or on the shores of cold streams and ditches.

FREE-FLOATING PLANTS

Free-floating plants are not rooted in the ground and float freely on the water surface, drifting with the wind and current. Their roots dangle directly into the water as they float. They are most common in quiet water because they are quickly carried out of areas with fast currents. They might be found in pools or backwaters of streams or in wetland areas.

EUROPEAN FROGBIT
Hydrocharis morsus-ranae (Hydrocharitaceae)

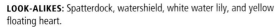
INVASIVE—PROHIBITED

DESCRIPTION: Free-floating, in thick mats not attached to substrate. Roots 7–20 cm long, unbranched and dangling freely. Leaves in broad rosettes. Leaves heart-shaped, small (<6.5 cm wide), thick, with spongy purplish undersides. Leaves on elongated stalks (4–6 cm long). Flower white with yellow center and 3 petals, 1.5 cm wide. Resembles miniature white water lily.

LOOK-ALIKES: Spatterdock, watershield, white water lily, and yellow floating heart.

NOTES: European frogbit is not yet known to be present in Wisconsin but is found in New York, Vermont, Quebec, and Ontario. It grows in the quiet water of medium to large rivers, ponds, lake edges, and marshes. It is a nuisance species that can form dense floating mats, disturbing fish, birds, and boats.

SMALL DUCKWEED
Lemna minor (Araceae)

DESCRIPTION: Free-floating, growing individually or in colonies. Root single and long, dangling below. Leaves round to oval-shaped, tiny (2–6 mm long, 1.5–4 mm wide). No stalks.

LOOK-ALIKES: Large duckweed, forked duckweed. Winter bud duckweed (*L. turionifera*)—leaves in multilobed clusters and forming dark green or brown, starch-filled winter buds in fall. Common watermeal (*Wolffia columbiana*)—rootless, smaller (0.3–1.4 mm), with rounded surface.

NOTES: Small duckweed is common statewide. It is found on the surface of quiet, often eutrophic water. It provides cover for invertebrates and fish and is a very important food source for many ducks and geese. Broad mats of small duckweed can reduce mosquito breeding and nutrient concentrations in the water.

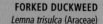

FORKED DUCKWEED
Lemna trisulca (Araceae)

DESCRIPTION: Free-floating, often in mats. Root single and dangling below. Leaves oar-shaped, flattened, small, with long stalks (4–16 mm long). Flowers tiny and rare.

LOOK-ALIKES: Other duckweeds.

NOTES: Forked duckweed is common statewide. It is found below the surface of quiet, often nutrient-rich water. It provides cover for invertebrates and fish and food for waterfowl.

LARGE DUCKWEED
Spirodela polyrrhiza (Araceae)

DESCRIPTION: Free-floating, often in dense mats. Roots many (5–12), dangling below. Leaves irregularly oval-shaped with multiple lobes. Largest duckweed (3–10 mm long, 2.5–8 mm wide). Leaves green above, often magenta below. No stalks.

LOOK-ALIKES: Other duckweeds and common watermeal (see small duckweed look-alikes, page 55).

NOTES: Large duckweed is common statewide. It is found on the surface of ponds, lakes, and streams in quiet, often nutrient-rich water. It provides cover for invertebrates and fish and is an important food source for waterfowl, muskrats, and fish.

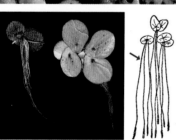

FLOATING-LEAF PLANTS

Floating-leaf plants are rooted in the ground and have leaves that float on the water surface. Some floating-leaf plants' leaves are actually held just above the water surface, making them resemble emergent plants at times. Two examples are American lotus and yellow pond lily. However, these plants most resemble truly floating-leaf plants such as spatterdock, so all are placed together in the floating-leaf section.

Many submersed and emergent plants also have leaves that float on the water surface. This section includes mainly plants whose primary or only leaves are floating leaves.

WATERSHIELD (water target)
Brasenia schreberi (Cabombaceae)

DESCRIPTION: Leaves floating, football-shaped, with faint bull's-eye in center where leafstalks attach; green above and purple below. Submersed parts of plant often covered with clear gel. Flower held above water, dull purple to pink, 2 cm wide, appearing to have 6 to 8 petals, and blooming June–August.

LOOK-ALIKES: European frogbit, white water lily, and yellow floating heart.

NOTES: Watershield is common in N. Wisconsin and common to uncommon in the rest of the state. It is found in lakes and ponds, in soft water <2 m deep on mucky substrate. It provides habitat for invertebrates and fish, and its fruits, leaves, and stems provide food for waterfowl.

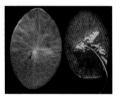

AMERICAN LOTUS (American lotus-lily)
Nelumbo lutea (Nelumbonaceae)

DESCRIPTION: Leaves mostly held up to 1 m above water surface. Leaves round, very large (30–70 cm wide), with bluish hue, no notch, and

waxy upper surface. Leafstalks attached to center of leaves, forming a funnel shape. Flower held above the water, creamy yellow, large (15–25 cm wide), with many petals surrounding a yellow central structure that resembles a shower nozzle. Fruit flat-topped, conical, and green, with brown acorn-like seeds.

LOOK-ALIKES: White water lily.

NOTES: American lotus is common in W. Wisconsin on Mississippi River backwaters; it is rare on inland waters. It is also found in ponds and lakes, preferring quiet water <1 m deep, and is tolerant of moderate turbidity. It provides habitat for fish, its fruits provide food for waterfowl, and its rhizomes provide food for mammals such as beavers. The seeds of American lotus may still sprout after two hundred years of dormancy.

YELLOW POND LILY
Nuphar advena (Nymphaeaceae)

SPECIAL CONCERN

DESCRIPTION: Leaves mostly held above water surface, at various angles. Connected to thick rhizomes (see spatterdock illustration, page 59). Leaves thinly heart-shaped, 20–40 cm long, with somewhat pointed lobes and triangular notch. Leafstalk round. Flower yellow (sometimes green at base), spherical, 3–5 cm wide, appearing to have 5–6 petals around central yellow-green disk. Held above water and blooming June–August.

LOOK-ALIKES: Small yellow pond lily, spatterdock, white water lily, and yellow floating heart.

NOTES: Yellow pond lily is found in south-central Wisconsin and is rare. It grows in ponds and streams in quiet water to 2 m deep, often on soft substrate. It provides habitat for invertebrates and fish; its fruits provide food for waterfowl; its rhizomes, leaves, flowers, and stems provide food for mammals such as deer. It also contains tannins used for dying and tanning.

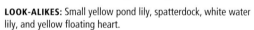

SMALL YELLOW POND LILY
(yellow pond lily)
Nuphar microphylla (Nymphaeaceae)

DESCRIPTION: Leaves both floating and submersed. Leafstalks flat on upper side. Leaves small (3.5–10 cm long), deeply notched (notch ≥⅔ length of leaf). Flower yellow with red central disk, small (≤2 cm wide), usually appearing to have 5 petals. Blooming June–August.

LOOK-ALIKES: Spatterdock, yellow pond lily, and yellow floating heart.

NOTES: Small yellow pond lily is found in N. Wisconsin, where it is locally common. It grows in lakes, ponds, and quiet streams.

SPATTERDOCK (bullhead pond lily)
Nuphar variegata (Nymphaeaceae)

DESCRIPTION: Leaves mostly floating. Connected to thick rhizomes with leaf and flower scars; rhizomes may float to water surface. Leaves thinly heart-shaped, large (10–25 cm long), thinly notched, with rounded parallel or overlapping lobes. Leaf notch ≤½ length of the leaf. Leafstalks flattened and slightly winged (see illustration). Flower yellow (sometimes red at base), spherical, 2.5–5 cm wide, appearing to have 5–6 petals around the yellow central disk. Held above water and blooming June–August.

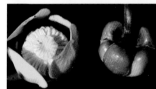

LOOK-ALIKES: European frogbit, small yellow pond lily, white water lily, yellow floating heart, and yellow pond lily.

NOTES: Spatterdock is common statewide. It is found in streams and ponds, in quiet water <2 m deep, often on soft substrate. Its leaves provide habitat for invertebrates and fish; its fruits provide food for waterfowl; its leaves and stems provide food for deer; and its rhizomes provide food for other mammals.

FLOATING-LEAF PLANTS

WHITE WATER LILY
Nymphaea odorata (Nymphaeaceae)

DESCRIPTION: Leaves mostly floating. Leaves round (10–30 cm wide), narrowly notched, sometimes purple below. Leafstalks round with 4 large air passages, growing from large rhizomes. Flower large (7–20 cm wide), sweet-smelling, white with yellow center and numerous petals, often floating on water surface.

LOOK-ALIKES: American lotus, European frogbit, spatterdock, watershield, yellow floating heart, and yellow pond lily.

NOTES: White water lily is common statewide. It is found in streams, ponds, and lakes, in quiet water up to 2 m deep, on various sediment types. It tolerates low nutrient conditions by growing smaller leaves. It provides habitat for fish; its fruits provide food for waterfowl; and its rhizomes provide food for mammals such as muskrats. It is often cultivated.

YELLOW FLOATING HEART
Nymphoides peltata (Menyanthaceae)

INVASIVE—PROHIBITED

DESCRIPTION: Stems long, branching, 2.5 mm thick. Leaves mostly floating, opposite, roundly heart-shaped, thinly notched, unequal (5–15 cm diameter), with wavy edges and purple undersides. Flower yellow, 2.5–3.5 cm wide, with 5 fringed petals and 1–5 flowers on each stalk. Fruit capsule 2.5 cm long, with many small barbed seeds.

LOOK-ALIKES: European frogbit, small yellow pond lily, spatterdock, watershield, white water lily, and yellow pond lily.

NOTES: Yellow floating heart has been found in private ponds around Madison, Milwaukee, and Marinette; it is not yet known in the natural waters of the state. It is found in lakes and ponds in quiet water <4 m deep, often in mud. Originally from Eurasia, it is a nuisance species: dense mats impede native plants and recreation and reduce dissolved oxygen levels. It spreads quickly and can overwinter.

WATER SMARTWEED
Persicaria amphibia (Polygonaceae)

DESCRIPTION: Aquatic or terrestrial, 0.3–1.5 m tall. Stems with swollen nodes. Floating leaves alternate, elliptical, with rounded tips. Terrestrial and emergent leaves pointed and hairy. Flowers pink, tiny (5 mm wide), appearing to have 5 petals, in terminal spike 2–15 cm long. Blooming June–September.

LOOK-ALIKES: Floating-leaf, long-leaf, and large-leaf pondweeds.

NOTES: Water smartweed is common statewide. It is found in wet meadows, lakes, and backwaters, in quiet water <2 m deep, on various substrates. It provides habitat for invertebrates and fish, and its seeds provide food for muskrats, deer, and waterfowl, especially during migration.

WATER CHESTNUT
Trapa natans (Lythraceae)

INVASIVE—PROHIBITED

DESCRIPTION: Floating or submersed leaves, sometimes forming dense mats. Floating leaves in bouquet-like rosette, somewhat fan-shaped, with toothed margins, glossy upper surface, and hairy undersides; leafstalks long, with swollen, air-filled bladders. Submersed leaves whorled, finely divided, and feather-like. Flowers white, small, with 4 petals, blooming July until fall frost. Fruit nut-like, with 4 barbs.

LOOK-ALIKES: None.

NOTES: Water chestnut is originally from Eurasia and Africa and is not yet known in Wisconsin. Where established in a few northeastern states, it grows in streams and lakes in quiet, often nutrient-rich water to 5 m deep on soft substrate. It is a nuisance species that can inhibit native plants and impede beach recreation and boats and can reduce oxygen levels. Once established, it spreads quickly.

fruit

SUBMERSED PLANTS

Submersed plants are those that grow with most of their leaves below the water surface. They can most easily be distinguished from each other by the shape and arrangement of their leaves. They are divided here into a few groups according to leaf arrangement: leaves may be (1) *opposite* (growing in pairs) or *whorled* (in groups of three or more along the stem), (2) *basal* (growing only from the base of the plant), or (3) *alternate* (growing singly and usually on alternate sides of the stem). An additional group in this section is (4) submersed plants with *finely divided* leaves (leaves that are distinctively thin and needle-like).

Submersed Plants with Opposite or Whorled Leaves

Plants in this section have mostly submersed leaves that grow either opposite each other in pairs or in *whorls* (groups of three or more) along the stem.

COMMON WATER STARWORT
Callitriche palustris
(formerly *C. verna*; Plantaginaceae)

DESCRIPTION: Submersed, with thin stems (10–20 mm long) and shallow roots. Floating leaves arranged in rosette; leaves rounded, 5 mm wide, and clustered near tip. Submersed leaves opposite, linear, and pale green, often with a two-pointed tip. Fruit tiny (1–1.4 mm long), growing in leaf axils, with wings, shallow grooves, and pits arranged vertically.

LOOK-ALIKES: Common waterweed. Autumnal water starwort (*C. hermaphroditica*)—special concern; very rare; no floating leaves; submersed leaves narrow, 5–15 mm long, and dark green; fruit 15–20 mm long, with deep groove. Large water starwort (*C. heterophylla*)—threatened; very rare; fruit round, small (only 1 mm wide), with shallow grooves, no wings, and pits not arranged in rows.

NOTES: Common water starwort is common in streams statewide, especially in N. Wisconsin. It is also sometimes found in lakes, preferring quiet, shallow, often cool, spring-fed water with muddy or sandy substrate. It provides habitat for invertebrates and fish, and its stems and fruits provide food for ducks.

floating leaves often in rosettes

fruit

MUSKGRASSES
Chara spp. (Characeae)

DESCRIPTION: Macroalgae resembling vascular plants. Stem-like structure 5 cm– 1 m tall, jointed, usually dark green. Leaf-like branchlets occurring in whorls of 6–16 at joints, usually not forked, with ridges that feel rough, and often brittle and coated with calcium carbonate. Flowers absent. Seed-like *oogonia* (female) and *atheridia* (male) very small, often yellow to orange, located at branchlet bases. Often emits strong skunk-like odor when crushed.

LOOK-ALIKES: Nitella and coontail; also naiads (*Najas* spp.)— leaves opposite and serrated.

NOTES: Muskgrasses are common statewide. They are found in mineral-rich waters up to 10 m deep on soft sediments. They provide habitat for invertebrates and young fish. Their fruits provide a very important food source for waterfowl, which may also feed on invertebrates and on other algae species growing on the surface of the muskgrass. Muskgrasses remove nutrients from the water and stabilize the substrate.

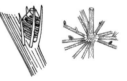

AUSTRALIAN SWAMP CROP
Crassula helmsii (Crassulaceae)

INVASIVE—PROHIBITED

DESCRIPTION: Submersed, with reddish stems occasionally branching. Leaves succulent, bright green, opposite, broadly lance-shaped, and short. Flowers white, small, with 4 petals.

LOOK-ALIKES: Brazilian waterweed, common waterweed, hydrilla, and oxygen-weed.

NOTES: Australian swamp crop is not yet known to be present in Wisconsin. It grows in ponds, in water up to 3 m deep. Originally from Tasmania, it forms dense mats that can outcompete native species, restrict flow, trap sediment, and reduce water quality.

BRAZILIAN WATERWEED
Egeria densa (Hydrocharitaceae)

INVASIVE—PROHIBITED

DESCRIPTION: Submersed, rooted or sometimes drifting. Stems occasionally branched. Leaves in whorls of 3–8 (usually 4–6), though lower leaves may be in whorls of 2–3. Leaves densely spaced, lance-shaped, 2–3 cm long, with finely serrated edges and smooth midveins. Flowers rare, small, white and greenish with 3 petals, extending roughly 2.5 cm above water.

LOOK-ALIKES: Australian swamp crop, common waterweed, hydrilla, and oxygen-weed.

NOTES: Brazilian waterweed has been found in an artificial pond in Portage County, though it is not yet known in natural waters of Wisconsin. It grows in lakes, ponds, pools, ditches, and streams, in quiet water up to 6 m deep, on sand, mud, or stone substrate. It can outcompete slow-growing native species, and it forms dense mats that restrict flow, trap sediment, and reduce water quality.

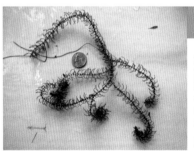

COMMON WATERWEED (elodea)
Elodea canadensis (Hydrocharitaceae)

DESCRIPTION: Submersed, with thin, branching stems up to 1 m long. Leaves bunched near stem tips, in whorls of 2–3, occasionally in whorls of 4. Leaves lance-shaped, pointed, stalkless, and small (average 2 mm wide, 5–15 mm long). Flowers small, white, with 3 petals, waxy, on long, thin stalk.

LOOK-ALIKES: Australian swamp crop, Brazilian waterweed, common water starwort, hydrilla, and oxygen-weed. Slender waterweed (*E. nuttallii*)—less common; leaves not bunched near stem tips; leaves and stems thinner; average leaf width 1.3 mm.

NOTES: Common waterweed is common statewide. It is found in water up to several meters deep, in fine substrate; it is tolerant of low light and resistant to disease. It provides habitat for invertebrates and fish, as well as food for waterfowl and muskrats.

HYDRILLA
Hydrilla verticillata (Hydrocharitaceae)

INVASIVE—PROHIBITED

DESCRIPTION: Submersed, often forming dense surface mats. Stems long, slender, with many branches. Leaves in whorls of 4–8, small (13–20 mm long, 1–5 mm wide) and pointed, with serrated edges and occasionally small barbs along midrib undersides. Leaf color usually green but may become yellow or brown. Flowers white, with 3 petals, small (4–8 mm wide), in leaf axils or floating. Blooming mid- to late summer. Reproduces with small tubers, turions, and fragmentation.

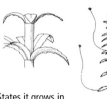
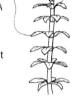

LOOK-ALIKES: Australian swamp crop, Brazilian waterweed, common waterweed, and oxygen-weed.

NOTES: Hydrilla has been found in an artificial pond in Marinette County; it is not yet known in natural waters of Wisconsin. Elsewhere in the United States it grows in lakes and medium to large rivers, in water up to 6 m deep, in varied conditions, and is tolerant of low light levels. A nuisance species from Asia, Africa, and Australia, hydrilla is fast-growing and forms dense mats. It outcompetes native species in other regions and is often considered the most problematic aquatic invasive plant in the country.

OXYGEN-WEED (African waterweed)
Lagarosiphon major (Hydrocharitaceae)

INVASIVE—PROHIBITED

DESCRIPTION: Submersed, forming dense mats. Stems long (to 6 m), narrow (3 mm), brittle, branching (especially at water surface). Leaves alternately spiraled around stem, small and lance-shaped (≤20 mm long, 2–3 mm wide), curving, stiff, densely crowded at stem tips, with visible midvein. Leaf edges with tiny teeth, though not rough to touch. Flowers tiny, white or pink, with 3 petals.

LOOK-ALIKES: Australian swamp crop, Brazilian waterweed, common waterweed, and hydrilla.

NOTES: Oxygen-weed grows in streams, rivers, ponds, and lakes, in open water to 7 m deep, preferring full sun. A nuisance species from Africa, it is not yet present in Wisconsin or anywhere in the United States. However, it is known to be fast-growing and to form dense mats, outcompeting native plants in other areas of the world.

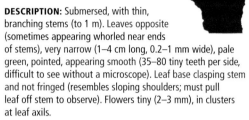

SLENDER NAIAD (bushy pondweed)
Najas flexilis (Hydrocharitaceae)

DESCRIPTION: Submersed, with thin, branching stems (to 1 m). Leaves opposite (sometimes appearing whorled near ends of stems), very narrow (1–4 cm long, 0.2–1 mm wide), pale green, pointed, appearing smooth (35–80 tiny teeth per side, difficult to see without a microscope). Leaf base clasping stem and not fringed (resembles sloping shoulders; must pull leaf off stem to observe). Flowers tiny (2–3 mm), in clusters at leaf axils.

LOOK-ALIKES: Brittle waternymph, muskgrasses, and sago and small pondweeds. Spiny naiad (*N. marina*)—leaves coarsely toothed and larger (0.5–4 cm long, 0.5–4.5 mm wide). Southern naiad (*N. guadalupensis*)—leaves wider (to 2 mm), less pointed, and less common in N. Wisconsin. Northern naiad (*N. gracillima*)—leaves fine with jagged base; usually in mineral-poor lakes.

NOTES: Slender naiad is common statewide. It is found in clear water up to several meters deep, in sandy or gravelly substrate, and is tolerant of disturbance. It provides habitat for invertebrates and fish and is an important food source for waterfowl, marsh birds, and muskrats.

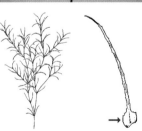

BRITTLE WATERNYMPH
Najas minor (Hydrocharitaceae)

INVASIVE—PROHIBITED

DESCRIPTION: Submersed, up to 2.5 m long, with many branches forming tufts near top. Leaves appearing opposite, subopposite, whorled, or in clumps; leaves slender, strongly curved, small (usually <3.5 cm long, 0.3–0.5 mm wide), pointed, and visibly serrated (with 7–15 tiny teeth per side). Leaf base broad and fringed (resembles sloping shoulders with fringe; must pull leaf off stem to observe). Leaves fall off easily when handled. Flowers small, 1–2 per plant, blooming from leaf axils. Seeds banana-shaped, purplish.

LOOK-ALIKES: Other naiads (*Najas* spp.)—leaves opposite, leaf base sometimes not fringed; also muskgrasses and sago pondweed.

NOTES: Brittle waternymph was recently discovered in a few south-central Wisconsin lakes. Originally from Eurasia and Africa, it is found in most states in the eastern United States. It can also grow in streams and ponds, preferring quiet water up to 5 m deep. Its fruits provide food for waterfowl, but it can outcompete native species, forming dense mats that restrict navigation.

NITELLA (sand grass, stonewort)
Nitella spp. (Characeae)

DESCRIPTION: Macroalgae resembling vascular plants. Stem-like structure up to 2 m tall (usually much shorter), hollow, branched, light to dark green, usually translucent. Leaf-like branchlets occurring in whorls of approximately 6–8, sometimes forking. Branches 1.5–3 mm wide; feel smooth, soft, and not ridged. Flowers absent. Small spore-producing, seed-like structures located at bases of branchlets. Odorless.

LOOK-ALIKES: Muskgrasses and coontail; also naiads (*Najas* spp.)—leaves opposite and serrated.

NOTES: Several species of nitella are common statewide and are difficult to tell apart from each other. They are found in deep water (to 12 m) or shallow water and may be found in acidic lakes or bogs. They tend to prefer soft sediments. Nitella species provide habitat for many invertebrates and other algae, which may be eaten by waterfowl and fish. Like muskgrasses, nitella species remove nutrients from the water and stabilize the stream substrate with their root-like structures.

stem   bud

Submersed Plants with Basal Leaves

Plants in this section have mostly submersed leaves that grow only from the base of the plant.

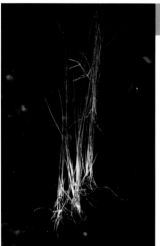

NEEDLE SPIKE-RUSH
Eleocharis acicularis (Cyperaceae)

DESCRIPTION: Submersed sedge (not a rush), occasionally emergent on shorelines. Stems delicate (to 0.5 mm thick), and short (3–15 cm long), in clumps carpeting the substrate and emerging from slender rhizomes. Leaves reduced to small sheaths at stem bases. Flowers rarely blooming in water, but if present, located atop each stem as a single oval spikelet 2.5–7 mm long and wider than stem.

LOOK-ALIKES: Creeping and bald spike-rushes—very common and similar to emergent form of needle spike-rush (page 42). Robbins' spike-rush (*E. robbinsii*)—special concern; rare; stems unsheathed; flowering stems bluntly 3-angled. Other spike-rushes such as matted spike-rush (*E. intermedia*), blunt spike-rush (*E. obtusa*), ovate spike-rush (*E. ovata*), and bright green spike-rush (*E. olivacea*)—stems thicker. Brown-fruited rush (*Juncus pelocarpus*)—outer leaves encompass inner leaves; horizontal lines visible in light.

NOTES: Needle spike-rush is common statewide, especially in N. Wisconsin. It is found in water to 2 m deep on sandy or firm substrate and is tolerant of some turbidity. It provides shelter for invertebrates, and food for waterfowl and muskrats. It is allelopathic, releasing chemicals that inhibit nearby plants.

WILD CELERY (eel-grass, tape-grass)
Vallisneria americana (Hydrocharitaceae)

DESCRIPTION: Mostly submersed, growing from rhizomes. Leaf arrangement basal. Leaves thin, tape-like, long (to 2 m long, 3–10 mm wide), slightly serrated, with a visible middle band when held to light. Leaves with irregular venation. Leaf tips sometimes trailing on water surface. Flowers tiny, on long spiraled stalks, not in spikes.

LOOK-ALIKES: Flowering-rush, ribbon-leaf pondweed, and the floating-leaf stage of bur-reeds and arrowheads.

NOTES: Wild celery is common statewide. It is found in water 0.3–3 m deep in firm substrate and is tolerant of turbid conditions. It provides good habitat for fish, and all of its parts provide an exceptional food source for waterfowl (especially canvasbacks) and muskrats.

Submersed Plants with Alternate, Thin Leaves

Plants in this section have mostly submersed leaves that grow singly along the stem in an alternate (not opposite) arrangement.

In Wisconsin streams, almost all submersed plants with alternate leaves are pondweeds (family Potamogetonaceae). Pondweeds are aquatic perennial plants that often have both submersed and floating leaves or only submersed leaves. Floating leaves, when present, are often rounded with a waxy upper surface. Submersed leaves are elongate and alternate with parallel veins and a prominent midvein. Flowers are usually small, arranged on an emergent spike, and greenish brown. Fruits are nutlets.

Pondweeds are abundant in Wisconsin streams; most of the pondweeds described below are common statewide. There are a variety of species found throughout the state. They are found in a variety of habitats, often in water 0.5–4 m deep, and they generally provide habitat for invertebrates and fish, as well as food for waterfowl and mammals.

Pondweed species can generally be distinguished by leaf shape, *stipules* (outgrowths at the leaf bases), and seeds. They can be difficult to tell apart in the field without a microscope and a close examination of their nutlets. The pondweeds in this guide are divided into two groups: (1) pondweeds with thin submersed leaves and (2) pondweeds with large submersed leaves. Note that some species could be placed in either group, so check both groups if you are having difficulty identifying a plant.

WATER STARGRASS
Heteranthera dubia (Zosterella dubia; Pontederiaceae)

DESCRIPTION: Submersed, with slender stems growing from rhizomes. No floating leaves. Submersed leaves alternate, thin (to 15 cm long, 2–6 mm wide), stalkless, without a major midvein. Flowers yellow, solitary, star-like, appearing to have 6 long petals.

LOOK-ALIKES: Flat-stem and small pondweeds.

NOTES: Water stargrass is common statewide. It is found in water up to 2 m deep, especially on mudflats. It is tolerant of turbid conditions. It provides habitat for fish as well as food for ducks and geese. Water stargrass is not a pondweed.

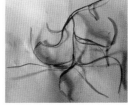

RIBBON-LEAF PONDWEED
Potamogeton epihydrus (Potamogetonaceae)

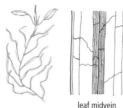

DESCRIPTION: Stems slightly flattened. Floating leaves (if present) elliptical (3–7 cm long, 8–20 mm wide), with long, thin stalk. Submersed leaves elongate (<20 cm long, 2–10 mm wide), ribbon-like, stalkless, with prominent pale band along midvein. Stipules 1–3 cm long and not fused to leaves.

leaf midvein

LOOK-ALIKES: Flat-stem pondweed and wild celery.

NOTES: Ribbon-leaf pondweed is common in N. Wisconsin. It is found in streams, ponds, and lakes, in soft water 1–2 m deep. It provides habitat for invertebrates and fish; its fruits provide food for waterfowl, particularly mallards; and its leaves and stems provide food for mammals such as muskrats and beavers.

FRIES' PONDWEED
Potamogeton friesii (Potamogetonaceae)

DESCRIPTION:
No floating leaves. Submersed leaves linear (3–7 cm long, 1.5–3 mm wide), stalkless with rounded tip, short beak, and 5–7 veins. Stipules white and string-like. Pair of glands on stem at leaf base. Winter buds with inner leaves in fan shape at 90° angle from outer leaves.

LOOK-ALIKES: Other narrow-leaved pondweeds, especially stiff pondweed (*P. strictifolius*)—stipules white, string-like; usually no glands; leaves stiff and pointed with 3–5 veins.

NOTES: Fries' pondweed is common in N. and E. Wisconsin. It is found in shallow water, providing habitat for invertebrates and fish as well as food for ducks and geese.

FLOATING-LEAF PONDWEED
Potamogeton natans (Potamogetonaceae)

DESCRIPTION: Floating leaves broad (5–10 cm long, 2–4.5 cm wide), with a heart-shaped base; leaf blade attaching to leafstalk at 90° angle, with stalk area adjacent to blade often pale-colored. Submersed leaves thin (10–40 cm long, 1–2 mm wide), stem-like, with 3–5 veins. Stipules not fused to leaves. Fruit wrinkled.

LOOK-ALIKES: Oakes' pondweed (*P. oakesianus*)—smaller leaves (2.5–6 cm long) and smooth fruit. Spotted pondweed (*P. pulcher*)—endangered; stems and leafstalks with prominent black spots; submersed leaves with wavy margin. In flowing water, long-leaf pondweed. Water smartweed.

NOTES: Floating-leaf pondweed is common statewide. It is found in water up to 1.5 m deep and is tolerant of various substrates and water conditions. It provides habitat for invertebrates and fish, as well as food for waterfowl, muskrats, deer, beavers, and moose.

BLUNT-LEAF PONDWEED
Potamogeton obtusifolius (Potamogetonaceae)

DESCRIPTION: No floating leaves. Submersed leaves linear (3–10 cm long, 1–3.5 mm wide; compare with small pondweed, page 72), with blunt tips and often red tint. Pair of glands on stem at leaf base. Stipules leaf-like (not stringy), 5–15 mm long, often wrapping around stem early in season and decomposing late in season.

LOOK-ALIKES: Other narrow-leaved pondweeds—leaves thinner.

NOTES: Blunt-leaf pondweed is uncommon and is found in N. Wisconsin. It grows in shallow water. It provides habitat for invertebrates and fish, and its seeds and tubers provide food for ducks, geese, and mammals.

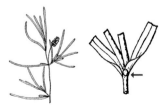

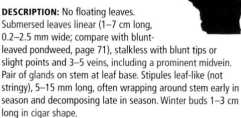

SMALL PONDWEED (slender pondweed)
Potamogeton pusillus (Potamogetonaceae)

DESCRIPTION: No floating leaves.
Submersed leaves linear (1–7 cm long,
0.2–2.5 mm wide; compare with blunt-
leaved pondweed, page 71), stalkless with blunt tips or
slight points and 3–5 veins, including a prominent midvein.
Pair of glands on stem at leaf base. Stipules leaf-like (not
stringy), 5–15 mm long, often wrapping around stem early in
season and decomposing late in season. Winter buds 1–3 cm
long in cigar shape.

LOOK-ALIKES: Leafy pondweed (*P. foliosus*)—very similar;
no glands at leaf nodes. Stiff pondweed (see Fries'
pondweed look-alikes, page 70). Blunt-leaf pondweed,
Fries' pondweed, and water stargrass.

NOTES: Small pondweed is common statewide. It is found
in water up to 3 m deep and is tolerant of turbid conditions.
It provides habitat for invertebrates and fish, as well as being an important food source for
waterfowl and mammals such as muskrats and moose.

FERN PONDWEED (Robbins' pondweed)
Potamogeton robbinsii (Potamogetonaceae)

DESCRIPTION: Stems round. No floating
leaves. Submersed leaves linear
(12 cm long, 6 mm wide), growing in
2 rows, stalkless, finely serrated, stiff, dark green-brown, and
resembling a fern. Leaf base clasping stem, with small lobes.

LOOK-ALIKES: Flat-stem pondweed.

NOTES: Fern pondweed is found mainly in
N. and E. Wisconsin. It grows in the deepest
water (4.5–6 m) of any pondweed. It provides
habitat for invertebrates and fish, especially
northern pike.

SPIRAL-FRUITED PONDWEED
Potamogeton spirillus (Potamogetonaceae)

DESCRIPTION: Stems slender, growing from rhizomes. Floating leaves (if present) elliptical (7–35 mm long, 2–13 mm wide). Submersed leaves often curved back, linear (1–8 cm long, 0.5–2 mm wide). Stipules fused to leaves for more than half the stipule length. Fruits clustered, with each fruit resembling a spiraling disk, which forms in midsummer.

LOOK-ALIKES: Water-thread pondweed (*P. diversifolius*)—special concern; leaves slightly narrower and not curved. Snail-seed pondweed (*P. bicupulatus*)—special concern; leaves narrow; floating leaves pointed near tip.

NOTES: Spiral-fruited pondweed is sporadically found in N. Wisconsin. It grows in shallow water, providing sediment stabilization, habitat for invertebrates and fish, and food for ducks and geese.

fruit

VASEY'S PONDWEED
Potamogeton vaseyi (Potamogetonaceae)

SPECIAL CONCERN

DESCRIPTION: Floating leaves (if present) elliptical (8–15 mm long) with 5–9 prominent veins. Submersed leaves hair-like (2–6 cm long, 0.2–1 mm wide). Stipules not fused to leaves.

LOOK-ALIKES: Water-thread pondweed (*P. diversifolius*)— leaves often slightly broader; stipules partially fused to leaf base.

NOTES: Vasey's pondweed is found in N. Wisconsin and is rare. It grows in shallow water, providing habitat for invertebrates and fish, as well as food for waterfowl.

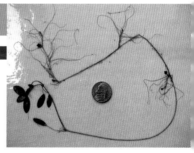

FLAT-STEM PONDWEED
Potamogeton zosteriformis (Potamogetonaceae)

DESCRIPTION: No floating leaves. Stems flattened, branching at an angle. Submersed leaves linear (5–20 cm long, 2–5 mm wide), stiff with pointed tip, many veins, and prominent midvein.

LOOK-ALIKES: Fern pondweed and water stargrass.

NOTES: Flat-stem pondweed is common statewide. It is found in water up to 3.5 m deep on soft substrate. It provides habitat for invertebrates and fish, as well as food for waterfowl and mammals such as beavers and deer.

SAGO PONDWEED
Stuckenia pectinata (formerly
Potamogeton pectinatus; Potamogetonaceae)

DESCRIPTION: No floating leaves. Often forming large mats. Submersed leaves very thin (3–10 cm long, 0.5–1.5 mm wide) with sharp tips and one vein, arranged in fan-like clusters. Stipules fused around leaf as sheath. Flower spike underwater.

LOOK-ALIKES: Brittle waternymph and naiads (*Najas* spp.)—leaves opposite and serrated. Thread-leaf pondweed (*S. filiformis*)—uncommon; leaves bluntly tipped; fruit smaller. Sheathed pondweed (*S. vaginata*)—threatened; leaves bluntly tipped; stipule sheaths inflated.

NOTES: Sago pondweed is common statewide. It is found in streams and lakes, usually in quiet water <2 m deep. It is tolerant of high turbidity. It provides habitat for young fish, and its fruit and tubers provide a critical food source for waterfowl.

Submersed Plants with Alternate, Broad Leaves

ALPINE PONDWEED (red pondweed)
Potamogeton alpinus (Potamogetonaceae)

DESCRIPTION:
Stems unbranched.
Floating leaves (if
present) oval (<6 cm long, 2.5 cm wide),
stalked, with leaf base tapering to the
leafstalk. Submersed leaves elongate
(4–20 cm long, 0.5–2 cm wide), stalkless,
with slightly rounded tip, prominent
midvein, and 7–9 reddish-brown veins.

LOOK-ALIKES: Variable, Illinois, and large-leaf pondweeds.

NOTES: Alpine pondweed is locally found in
N. Wisconsin, where it is uncommon. It grows
in lakes, ponds, and streams, usually in cold
water. It provides habitat for fish, and its
fruits provide food for waterfowl.

LARGE-LEAF PONDWEED (cabbage)
Potamogeton amplifolius (Potamogetonaceae)

DESCRIPTION: Stems thick (1–3.5 mm
wide). Floating leaves (if present) elliptical,
large, with long stalks and many veins.
Submersed leaves very broad (4–7 cm wide), broadly lance-shaped, arching, with sharp tips (but not needle-like), slightly
wavy and folded along midrib, and >25 veins. Stipules leaf-like
(not stringy), large (3.5–12 cm), pointed, not fused to leaves.

LOOK-ALIKES: Alpine, Illinois, and white-stem
pondweeds, and water smartweed.

NOTES: Large-leaf pondweed is common
statewide. It is found in clear water up to 3 m
deep, in soft substrate. It is sensitive to high
turbidity and top-cutting from motorboats. Its
broad leaves provide excellent habitat for
invertebrates and fish, and its large fruits
provide important food for waterfowl.

CURLY-LEAF PONDWEED
Potamogeton crispus (Potamogetonaceae)

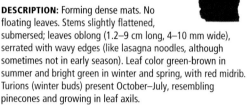

INVASIVE—RESTRICTED

DESCRIPTION: Forming dense mats. No floating leaves. Stems slightly flattened, submersed; leaves oblong (1.2–9 cm long, 4–10 mm wide), serrated with wavy edges (like lasagna noodles, although sometimes not in early season). Leaf color green-brown in summer and bright green in winter and spring, with red midrib. Turions (winter buds) present October–July, resembling pinecones and growing in leaf axils.

LOOK-ALIKES: Clasping-leaf pondweed.

NOTES: Curly-leaf pondweed is common statewide. It is found in medium to large rivers and in lakes, preferring water 1–4 m deep with soft substrate. It is tolerant of low light, high turbidity, and cold winter temperatures. It provides habitat for invertebrates and fish under ice in winter, but it is a nuisance species. It forms dense mats in spring that impede boats, and its July die-offs contribute to algal blooms and high turbidity. Curly-leaf pondweed is native to Eurasia, Africa, and Australia.

VARIABLE PONDWEED
Potamogeton gramineus (Potamogetonaceae)

DESCRIPTION: Stems short, thin. Floating leaves (if present) with long stalk and 11–19 veins. Submersed leaves linear to lance-shaped, <1 cm wide, with 3–7 veins; stalkless, but blade tapers slightly at stem. Stipules 1–3 cm long, not fused to leaf, with stipule tips blunt.

LOOK-ALIKES: Illinois pondweed and alpine pondweed.

NOTES: Variable pondweed is common statewide. It is found in shallow water. It provides habitat for invertebrates and fish; its fruits and tubers provide food for waterfowl; and its leaves, stems, and fruits provide food for mammals such as muskrats.

ILLINOIS PONDWEED
Potamogeton illinoensis (Potamogetonaceae)

DESCRIPTION: Stems thick (up to 5 mm wide). Floating leaves (if present) elliptical, with short stalk and >13 veins. Submersed leaves broad (2–5 cm wide), lance-shaped, arched, sharp, slightly wavy, and folded along midrib, with pointed tips and 9–19 prominent veins. Stipules leaf-like (not stringy), large (4–10 cm), and not fused to leaves.

LOOK-ALIKES: Variable, alpine, large-leaf, and long-leaf pondweeds.

NOTES: Illinois pondweed is common statewide. It is found in clear water up to 3 m deep; it is intolerant of high turbidity. Its broad leaves provide good habitat for invertebrates and fish, and it provides food for waterfowl and mammals such as beavers and deer.

LONG-LEAF PONDWEED
Potamogeton nodosus (Potamogetonaceae)

DESCRIPTION: Stems up to 3 m long. Leaves long, narrow, lance-shaped, with 7–15 veins, and on long stalks. Floating leaves 5–13 cm long (including stalk) and 1–4 cm wide. Submersed leaves up to 30 cm long and <2.5 cm wide. Stipules long (up to 10 cm), not fused to leaves, decomposing during the summer.

LOOK-ALIKES: Floating-leaf and Illinois pondweeds, and water smartweed.

NOTES: Long-leaf pondweed is sporadic statewide, especially in flowing water. It is found in streams and rivers and sometimes lakes, usually in flowing water, and it is tolerant of high turbidity and eutrophication. Long-leaf pondweed provides habitat for invertebrates and fish; its fruits provide food for waterfowl; and its leaves and stems provide food for mammals such as beavers and moose.

arrow points to stipules

floating leaves

77

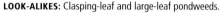

WHITE-STEM PONDWEED
Potamogeton praelongus (Potamogetonaceae)

DESCRIPTION: Stems zigzagging and thick. No floating leaves. Submersed leaves oblong to lance-shaped (up to 30 cm long, <4.5 cm wide), stalkless and wrapping up to halfway around the stem, with 3–5 prominent veins and 11–35 weaker veins. Leaf tip boat-shaped (margins folding toward each other), splitting when pressed. Stipules white, string-like (fibrous), and not fused to leaves.

LOOK-ALIKES: Clasping-leaf and large-leaf pondweeds.

NOTES: White-stem pondweed is common in N. and E. Wisconsin. It is found in clear water <4 m deep, in soft substrate; it is intolerant of high turbidity or degraded water quality. It provides valuable habitat for fish; its fruits provide food for ducks and geese; and its leaves and stems provide food for mammals such as muskrats and deer.

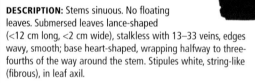

CLASPING-LEAF PONDWEED
(Richardson's pondweed)
Potamogeton richardsonii (Potamogetonaceae)

DESCRIPTION: Stems sinuous. No floating leaves. Submersed leaves lance-shaped (<12 cm long, <2 cm wide), stalkless with 13–33 veins, edges wavy, smooth; base heart-shaped, wrapping halfway to three-fourths of the way around the stem. Stipules white, string-like (fibrous), in leaf axil.

LOOK-ALIKES: Curly-leaf and white-stem pondweeds. Redhead pondweed (*P. perfoliatus*)—very rare; leaves smaller (1–5 cm long), and leaf base completely wrapping around stem.

NOTES: Clasping-leaf pondweed is common statewide. It is found in water up to 4 m deep on soft substrate, and it is tolerant of disturbance. It provides habitat for invertebrates and fish; its fruits provide food for waterfowl; and it is eaten by mammals such as muskrats.

stipule

Submersed Plants with Finely Divided Leaves

Plants in this section have mostly submersed leaves that are distinctly thin and needle-like. Some plants in this section, such as water marigold, also have other types of leaves. However, the thinly divided submersed leaves of these species are the most common form.

A few species in this section, namely, Eurasian water-milfoil and coontail, are among the most common invasive aquatic plants in Wisconsin. It is useful to be able to distinguish these common invasives from look-alike natives such as northern water-milfoil.

WATER MARIGOLD
Bidens beckii (*Megalodonta beckii*; Asteraceae)

DESCRIPTION: Usually submersed, though sometimes emergent. Emergent leaves opposite, lance-shaped, toothed, and stalkless. Submersed leaves opposite, with each leaf finely divided into 3 main sections. Leaf pair appearing like a whorl of 6 smaller branched leaves. Flowers very rare, yellow, showy, daisy-like, and 2–3 cm wide.

LOOK-ALIKES: Bladderworts, coontail, fanwort, water crowfoots, and water-milfoils.

NOTES: Water marigold is common in N. Wisconsin and found sporadically in the south. It grows in streams and lakes, in clear water up to 3.5 m deep. It provides cover for fish, and its fruits provide food for birds.

FANWORT (cabomba)
Cabomba caroliniana (Cabombaceae)

INVASIVE—PROHIBITED

DESCRIPTION: Submersed and often rooted. Stems long, appearing tubular underwater. Floating leaves (if present) alternate, and small (1 cm long). Submersed leaves opposite or whorled, finely divided, with long stalks. Flowers white and small (1 cm wide) with 6 petals.

LOOK-ALIKES: White water crowfoot, water marigold, common bladderwort, coontail, water-milfoils.

NOTES: Fanwort is not yet present in Wisconsin, but it has been observed in Michigan. It is found in lakes, ponds, ditches, and streams, in quiet water up to 2.5 m deep. Originally from South America, it reproduces quickly to form dense mats below the water surface, impeding native plants and boats.

COONTAIL
Ceratophyllum demersum (Ceratophyllaceae)

DESCRIPTION: Submersed, partially free-floating, in thick, evergreen stands that may be loosely attached to substrate (roots not present). Stems long (to 3–4 m), trailing, rigid, branching frequently. Most leaves in whorls of 5–12, 1.5–4 cm long, and crowded near tip of stem, creating "coon tails." Leaves flattened, toothed, and forking 1–2 times. Flowers inconspicuous in leaf axils, blooming June–September.

LOOK-ALIKES: Fanwort, muskgrasses, spiny hornwort, water crowfoots, water marigold, water-milfoils, and bladderworts.

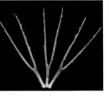

NOTES: Coontail is abundant statewide. It is found in lakes, marshes, ditches, streams, and river backwaters, in quiet water. It is tolerant of low light and cold water. It can be a nuisance species, but it also reduces water nutrient levels and provides habitat. Coontail's evergreen leaves provide important habitat during winter for invertebrates, especially scuds. It also provides habitat for fish, and its leaves, stems, and fruits provide food for waterfowl.

SPINY HORNWORT
Ceratophyllum echinatum (Ceratophyllaceae)

DESCRIPTION: Submersed, partially free-floating. Stems long, trailing, not rigid; may be loosely anchored to substrate. Leaves in whorls of 5–12, mostly evenly spaced on stem, but may be crowded at tip. Leaves round, usually untoothed, with small spines on leaf margins, branching 3–4 times. Flowers inconspicuous in leaf axils.

LOOK-ALIKES: Coontail.

NOTES: Spiny hornwort is found mostly in N. Wisconsin, where it is locally uncommon. It grows in lakes and ponds in quiet water up to 2 m deep.

PARROT FEATHER
Myriophyllum aquaticum (Haloragaceae)

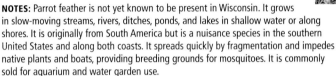

INVASIVE—PROHIBITED

DESCRIPTION: Submersed to emergent, often forming dense mats. Stems long (to 2 m), unbranched, greenish blue, emerging up to 30 cm above water. Leaves in whorls of 4–6, 2.5–5 cm long, and closely spaced. Leaves slender and divided into 10–18 pairs of leaflets, resembling feathers, with flattened midrib and short stalk. Emergent leaves stiff, bright green, with a waxy coating. Submersed leaves not stiff, brown, and deteriorating. Flowers white, tiny (0.5 mm wide), in emergent leaf axils.

LOOK-ALIKES: Eurasian and northern water-milfoils; also coontail, fanwort, and water marigold.

NOTES: Parrot feather is not yet known to be present in Wisconsin. It grows in slow-moving streams, rivers, ditches, ponds, and lakes in shallow water or along shores. It is originally from South America but is a nuisance species in the southern United States and along both coasts. It spreads quickly by fragmentation and impedes native plants and boats, providing breeding grounds for mosquitoes. It is commonly sold for aquarium and water garden use.

NORTHERN WATER-MILFOIL
(common water-milfoil)
Myriophyllum sibiricum
(formerly *M. exalbescens*; Haloragaceae)

DESCRIPTION: Submersed, not usually forming dense mats. Stem long (to 3 m), usually light-colored (whitish, pale green, or pale pink). No floating leaves. Submersed leaves rigid when out of water, in whorls of 4–5, up to 4 cm long. Leaves feathery, resembling a fish skeleton, and divided into 4–12 pairs of leaflets; leaflets at base longer than those at tip. When present, flower stalks emergent, to 15 cm long, with tiny emergent leaves (1–3 mm long) beneath flowers. Flowers with 4 petals. Winter buds conical, on side branches and at top of plant in autumn.

LOOK-ALIKES: Eurasian water-milfoil. Various-leaved water-milfoil (*M. heterophyllum*)—whorls of 4–6, closely spaced (≤10 mm apart), with occasional scattered alternate leaves. Whorled water-milfoil (*M. verticillatum*)—leaves stalkless; flower bracts lobed. Also coontail, fanwort, parrot feather, and water marigold.

NOTES: Northern water-milfoil is common statewide. It is found in lakes, in clear water up to 5 m deep, on soft substrate, and it is sensitive to turbid or eutrophic conditions. Northern water-milfoil provides habitat for invertebrates and fish, and its leaves and fruits provide food for waterfowl.

EURASIAN WATER-MILFOIL
Myriophyllum spicatum (Haloragaceae)

INVASIVE—RESTRICTED

DESCRIPTION: Submersed, forming dense surface mats. Stems long, often reddish pink, slender, and widely branched. No floating leaves. Submersed leaves 2–4 cm long in whorls of 4 (3–5), which are widely spaced along stem (2–3 cm). Leaves feathery, hanging limply when out of water, resembling fish skeleton when underwater, and divided into 12–20 V-shaped pairs of leaflets, which are mostly of equal lengths. Flowers not usually present. Flower stalks emergent and 2–4 cm long, with 1 tiny bract (1–3 mm long) beneath each flower. Flowers 4-petaled. No winter buds.

LOOK-ALIKES: Northern water-milfoil. Various-leaved water-milfoil (*M. heterophyllum*)—in whorls of 4–6, closely spaced (≤10 mm apart), with occasional scattered alternate leaves. Whorled water-milfoil (*M. verticillatum*)—leaves stalkless; flower bracts lobed. Also coontail, fanwort, parrot feather, and water marigold.

NOTES: Eurasian water-milfoil is found sporadically statewide but can be locally abundant. It grows in streams, rivers, and lakes, in water up to 4.5 m deep. It thrives in turbid, hot conditions, but is also tolerant of cool water in the early spring. These factors help it to form the dense canopies that shade out native species and restrict navigation. It provides habitat for a relatively low diversity and density of invertebrates. Its leaves, stems, and fruits provide limited food for waterfowl.

WHITE WATER CROWFOOT
Ranunculus aquatilis (Ranunculaceae)

DESCRIPTION: Submersed with long, weak, branching stem. No floating leaves. Submersed leaves alternate, small (1–2 cm long), stiff, and finely divided. Leafstalks wrapping around stem. Flowers white with yellow center, appearing 5-petaled, 1–1.5 cm wide, blooming June–August.

LOOK-ALIKES: Fanwort, common and flat-leaf bladderworts, coontail, water marigold, and yellow water crowfoot.

NOTES: White water crowfoot is common statewide. It is found in quiet, usually shallow water up to 2 m deep. It provides habitat for invertebrates and fish, including trout; its leaves, stems, and fruits provide food for waterfowl.

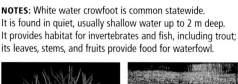

YELLOW WATER CROWFOOT
Ranunculus flabellaris (Ranunculaceae)

DESCRIPTION: Submersed with long, branching stem. Submersed leaves alternate, small, finely divided and stiff. Emergent leaves flat and divided into 3 main parts. Flowers yellow, appearing 5-petaled, 1.25–2.5 cm wide; each flower stalk long, thick, with 1 flower, blooming April–June.

LOOK-ALIKES: Coontail, water marigold, and white water crowfoot.

NOTES: Yellow water crowfoot is poisonous to eat and may cause a skin rash if touched. It is sporadically distributed, mostly in S. Wisconsin, growing in quiet, shallow water. It provides habitat for invertebrates and fish, and its leaves, stems, and fruits provide food for waterfowl.

CREEPING BLADDERWORT
Utricularia gibba (Lentibulariaceae)

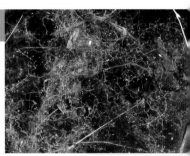

DESCRIPTION: Submersed, free-floating in tangled mats. Stems delicate, about 10 cm long. "Leaves" (leaf-like stems) alternate, forking 1–2 times. Bladders scattered, tiny, and few. Flowers yellow, 5-petaled, 2-lipped, small (0.5 cm long); 1–3 flowers per flower stalk, blooming June–August.

LOOK-ALIKES: Other bladderworts, coontail, and water marigold. Small bladderwort (*U. minor*)— "leaves" flattened; bladders scattered throughout.

NOTES: Creeping bladderwort is uncommon statewide. It grows in quiet water, from shorelines to deep water, often around floating-leaf plants, providing habitat for fish. Its bladders trap small zooplankton or invertebrates to supplement the plant's nutrient intake.

FLAT-LEAF BLADDERWORT
Utricularia intermedia (Lentibulariaceae)

DESCRIPTION: Submersed, free-floating but sometimes appearing rooted. Stems thin, commonly 15–30 cm long. "Leaves" (leaf-like stems) alternate, forking 3–7 times, flattened with midrib. Bladders only on separate, "leafless," colorless branches. Flowers yellow, 5-petaled, 2-lipped, with lower lip twice as long as upper lip, 1.3 cm long; 2–4 flowers per flower stalk, blooming July–August.

LOOK-ALIKES: Other bladderworts, coontail, water marigold, and water crowfoots.

NOTES: Flat-leaf bladderwort is common statewide. It is found in lakes, ponds, bogs, and ditches, floating in quiet, shallow water or loosely buried in mucky sediment. Its bladders trap small zooplankton or invertebrates to supplement the plant's nutrient intake.

COMMON BLADDERWORT
Utricularia vulgaris (Lentibulariaceae)

DESCRIPTION: Submersed, free-floating. Stem long (up to 3 m). "Leaves" (branches) alternate, forking 3–7 times, with small spines along edges. Bladders tiny, numerous, scattered, resembling translucent green to dark seeds. Flowers held above water, yellow, 5-petaled, large (up to 2.5 cm wide), 2-lipped; clusters of 4–20 flowers, blooming June–August.

LOOK-ALIKES: Twin-stemmed bladderwort (*U. geminiscapa*) and small bladderwort (*U. minor*)—smaller; spines only on tips of leaf divisions. Purple bladderwort (*U. purpurea*)—whorled leaves, bladders on tips of leaf divisions, and purple flowers. Coontail, fanwort, water marigold, and white water crowfoot.

NOTES: Common bladderwort is common statewide. It is found in lakes, ponds, streams, bogs, and ditches, in quiet water, floating or loosely attached to substrate. It provides habitat for invertebrates and fish and feeding opportunities for fish in areas that cannot support rooted plants. Its bladders trap small zooplankton or invertebrates to supplement the plant's nutrient intake.

ALGAE

The term *algae* encompasses a diverse array of organisms, some of which closely resemble plants. True algae are simpler and more primitive than plants—most species photosynthesize, but algae lack plants' complex root, stem, leaf, and reproductive structures. (Some organisms commonly called "algae," e.g., blue-green algae, are actually bacteria rather than algae.)

Two forms of plant-like green algae, muskgrasses and starry stonewort, are included previously under "Submersed Plants with Opposite or Whorled Leaves" (page 62) because they structurally resemble the plants in that section. The two additional forms included here, filamentous green algae and didymo, are more amorphous in appearance. Both may indicate poor water quality.

Note that freshwater sponges are also plant-like organisms that could be mistaken for algae. However, sponges are actually invertebrates, so we have placed them in that section of this guide (page 132).

FILAMENTOUS GREEN ALGAE
(pond scum, water silk)
class Chlorophyceae

DESCRIPTION: Algae in long, trailing strands, often forming hair-like growths on submerged objects (logs, rocks, other vegetation), or in dense floating mats with air bubbles. Varying shades of green. Texture varies by genera (4 common types): *Cladophora* branched to nearly unbranched, rough like wet strands of cotton (some species are large and horsehair-like); *Spirogyra* and relatives slippery (and bright green); *Oedogonium* unbranched and rough like strands of wet cotton; *Pithophora* branched and coarse like horsehair.

LOOK-ALIKES: Didymo, freshwater sponges (page 132). Mosses (phylum Bryophyta)—generally more structured in appearance and with tiny leaves.

NOTES: Filamentous green algae are common statewide. They are found in streams, rivers, lakes, and ponds, in shallow water attached to rocks, logs, and vegetation, or floating in dense mats. Populations typically peak in the spring and then decline. Because they require high nutrient levels, their recurring presence may indicate organic pollution. They are often a nuisance because they cover native plants and stream habitat, and they do not provide a food source for wildlife.

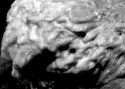
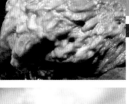

DIDYMO (rock snot)
Didymosphenia geminata

INVASIVE—PROHIBITED

DESCRIPTION: Freshwater diatom (alga). Initially appearing as small bubbly clumps on submerged rocks. Later blooming into thick yellowish brown mats up to 15 cm thick capable of covering large areas and can form long filamentous strands many centimeters long. Surfaces feel like wet cotton or thick wet felt and are not slimy or green.

LOOK-ALIKES: Other stalk-forming diatoms, filamentous algae, freshwater sponges (page 132). Mosses (phylum Bryophyta)—generally greener and more structured in appearance.

NOTES: Didymo is not yet present in Wisconsin except in Lake Superior, where it may be seen along the shore. It is native to Lake Superior and is not problematic there, but a more aggressive form has been found in scattered locations in the United States, particularly in the West. If encountered in rivers or other inland water bodies, didymo should be reported (see page 19). It prefers streams and rivers with cool, clear water and grows in full sun attached to rocks, logs, and vegetation. It covers and degrades stream habitat and lowers dissolved oxygen levels. It was originally from northern latitudes and appeared to prefer low-nutrient environments, but it now appears to also thrive in nutrient-rich waters.

Invertebrates

Alderflies and dobsonflies
order Megaloptera
(p. 90)

Large, elongate, and flattened body; head and thorax dark and hardened; large jaws; 7–8 pairs of lateral filaments; 1–2 end filaments.
Size: 10–90 mm

Beetles
order Coleoptera
(p. 92)

Larvae have a hardened head; adults have a hardened body and hardened, protective forewings form straight line down back.
Size: 1–70 mm

Caddisflies
order Trichoptera
(p. 95)

Larvae usually with cases or nets; elongate; head and thorax hardened and dark; 2 hooks on end (of abdomen); no wing pads; antennae not visible.
Size 3–35 mm

Damselflies and dragonflies
order Odonata
(p. 100)

Larvae have a wide head; large eyes; long, hinged lower lip.
Size: 13–62 mm

Mayflies
order Ephemeroptera
(p. 105)

Larvae usually have 3 tails; gills along abdomen; wing pads; single claw on each leg.
Size 2–32 mm

Stoneflies
order Plecoptera
(p. 111)

Larvae have an elongate, flattened body; long antennae; wing pads; 2 tails; 2 claws on each leg; no gills on middle of abdomen.
Size 3–70 mm

True bugs
order Hemiptera
(p. 115)

Elongate beak or cone, hidden when not feeding; no gills; larvae have wing pads; adults have 2 pairs of wings with ends overlapping when folded.
Size: 3–45 mm

True flies
order Diptera
(p. 118)

Larvae have an elongate, fleshy body with stubby "legs."
Size 2–60 mm

NONINSECTS

 Crustaceans subphylum Crustacea (p. 121) — Hard body armor; fused head and thorax; 5–8 appendages on thorax; smaller appendages on abdomen. Size: 4–150 mm

 Earthworms subclass Oligochaeta (p. 123) — Soft, elongate, round in cross section; short hairs; without suction disks. Size: 1–30 (max 150) mm

 Leeches subclass Hirudinea (p. 124) — Soft, elongate, flattened body with suction disk on end(s); segmented; no hairs. Size: 5–450 mm

 Mites and spiders class Arachnida (p. 125) — 4 pairs of legs. Size: 0.5–50 mm

 Mussels and clams class Bivalvia (p. 127) — 2 hinged hard shells enclosing soft body. Size: 1–190 mm

 Planarians class Turbellaria (p. 128) — Soft, elongate, unsegmented, flattened body, with 2 eyespots; head often arrow-shaped. Size: 1–10 (max 30) mm

 Snails class Gastropoda (p. 129) — Coiled hard shell enclosing soft body. Size: 2–70 mm

 Sponges phylum Porifera (p. 132) — Variously shaped, resembling moss; growing on submerged rocks, logs, and plants. Size: 1–300 mm

Invertebrates are animals without backbones. Thousands of different invertebrate species live in and along Wisconsin streams. Along with being a fascinating part of stream ecosystems, these animals are vital components of the community structure and functioning of aquatic and terrestrial ecosystems, and they are also important biological indicators of environmental conditions.

Key Traits

Over 80 percent of the earth's invertebrates are grouped in the phylum Arthropoda, which includes spiders, water mites, crustaceans, and insects. These animals have segmented bodies, a hard outer skeleton (*exoskeleton*), and jointed, flexible legs. The remaining invertebrates presented in this guide are in the following phyla: Annelida (worms and leeches), characterized by ring-like segmentation along the entire length of their bodies; Mollusca (snails, clams, and mussels), characterized by hardened shells protecting fleshy bodies; Platyhelminthes (flatworms, including planarians), characterized by soft, unsegmented bodies; and Porifera (sponges), which have encrusting or finger-like growth forms that attach to submerged rocks and tree limbs and are often mistaken for algae.

The invertebrates in this guide are often referred to as *macroinvertebrates* since they can be seen and usually identified without magnification. The animals presented are those most common to Wisconsin streams. For simplicity, they are separated into insects and noninsects, even though noninsects are extremely diverse taxonomically. These animals are primarily described at the family level, since more precise taxonomic identification usually requires a microscope, extensive knowledge of invertebrate anatomy, and the use of detailed taxonomic keys. (Note that in this guide, numbering is always front to back for invertebrates with many appendages or segments; e.g., the most anterior appendage is labeled "segment 1." Body lengths do not include tails and antennae.) All scientific names in this section (i.e., Dytiscidae) are family names unless otherwise noted.

Biology

Invertebrate life in streams is quite diverse, and so are the biological characteristics presented by these animals.

Many aquatic invertebrate species reproduce asexually or can switch between sexual and asexual reproduction depending upon environmental conditions. Most species have male and female sexes, produce eggs and sperm, and mate to fertilize the eggs.

Invertebrate life cycles range from quite simple to relatively complex. Planarians (a type of flat-worm) can simply fragment their bodies, and the pieces that break off grow into new individuals. In contrast, some mayfly species must shed their exoskeletons (*molt*) up to forty-five times to accommodate the growth and development necessary to emerge from the water as winged adults.

The longevity of stream invertebrates is also quite varied. Insects like mosquitoes may live between three and one hundred days as adults, while mussels live between ten and one hundred years. *Voltinism* refers to the number of generations or broods an animal has per year. Short-lived animals like mosquitoes may be *multivoltine*, having more than one generation per year; animals that have one generation per year are termed *univoltine*, while animals that require more than a year for each generation are referred to as *semivoltine*.

Food sources for stream invertebrates include terrestrial plant matter, aquatic plants, *periphyton* (a mixture of algae, fungi, diatoms, and bacteria), *detritus* (decaying plant and animal matter), and other animals. Some invertebrates are known as *shredders*, since they shred leaves that fall into the water. Much of what these animals shred drifts downstream as fine particulates and, along with algal cells and detritus, is eaten by *filterers*, animals that filter this material from the water. Filterers may do their filtering with silken nets (net-spinning caddisflies) or mucus-covered gills (mussels and clams), or they may collect material with fine hairs growing from their forelegs (brush-legged mayflies) or from the tops of their heads (black fly larvae). Many invertebrates are *grazers*, scraping periphyton off the streambed, aquatic plants, or submerged tree limbs and branches (mayflies, caddisflies, true flies, and others). Lastly, numerous invertebrates are *predators* (caddisflies, dragonflies, stoneflies, and others), eating other invertebrates. Species such as giant water bugs and fishing spiders will also prey on small fish, frogs, and tadpoles.

Ecological Notes

From the headwaters to the mouths of streams as they flow into larger rivers or lakes, there is a natural continuum of change in the physical and chemical makeup of streams that results in predictable changes in the streams' invertebrate populations. This predictability is called the *river continuum concept*. Shredders often dominate headwater streams due to the headwaters' high inputs of leaf litter and their low in-stream production of algae and aquatic macrophytes. (Algae and macrophytes are sparser in headwaters since small streams tend to be shaded by riparian trees, shrubs, and grasses.) Farther downstream, the quantity of shredded fine organic particles increases, resulting in greater numbers of species and of individual collectors and gatherers that take advantage of this particulate food source. As streams widen, more sunlight reaches the stream and allows greater in-stream photosynthetic production by microscopic plants, which are fed upon by grazing invertebrates. The relative proportion of invertebrate predators generally remains constant upstream and down.

The importance of energy inputs such as organic matter and sunlight to stream productivity has been recognized for decades. But only recently have studies revealed that energy flowing out of streams in the form of winged insects is critically important to the biological productivity of riparian ecosystems. A number of invertebrate, mammalian, and avian species rely on adult aquatic insects as a key food source. These animals often inhabit riparian areas and time their reproductive cycle to take advantage of the emerging insects to feed their young.

Macroinvertebrates identified to the family level provide useful information on the ecology, environmental conditions, and functioning of streams. For each entry in this section, *intolerant* or *tolerant of pollution* refers to the animal's ability (in its aquatic stage) to cope with human activities that degrade watershed or stream conditions. Human-induced effects on streams may include increased turbidity, excessive streamed siltation, increased nutrient levels, low dissolved oxygen, and stream flow or habitat alterations. Pollution tolerance is generalized for each invertebrate family in this guide, although tolerances can vary widely within a taxonomic family.

INSECTS (CLASS INSECTA)

Over a million insect species have been described worldwide, and the true number is undoubtedly much larger. Insects are thought to make up about 90 percent of all animal species on earth. The oldest definitive fossil of an insect is estimated to be 396 million years old.

Insects are characterized by three distinct body segments (head, thorax, and abdomen—note that the abdomen is the most posterior segment), three pairs of segmented legs, compound eyes, and two antennae. They usually have wings as adults and often display wing pads when immature. The word *insect* is from the Latin term *insectum*, which roughly translates into "cut into sections," referring to the characteristic three body segments and jointed legs.

All insects undergo *metamorphosis*, hatching from eggs as larvae and eventually developing into winged adults. There are two types of metamorphosis: complete and incomplete. *Complete metamorphosis* includes four life stages: egg, larva, pupa, and adult. The larva often looks worm-like and very different from the adult. After the larval stage, the insect develops into a *pupal* stage, during which the pupa (often enclosed in a cocoon) makes a dramatic transformation into a winged adult. *Incomplete metamorphosis* includes three life stages: egg, larva, and adult. The larva resembles a wingless version of the adult, gradually becoming an adult through a series of *molts*, sheddings of the exoskeleton that accommodate growth and development.

The term *nymph* has in the past been used to describe the immature (larval) stage of insects with incomplete metamorphosis. But entomologists now typically limit this term to describing the immature stage of true bugs (Hemipterans), which undergo incomplete metamorphosis and thus have three life stages. True bugs' nymphal stage is often nearly indistinguishable from the adult stage, and both nymphs and adults inhabit the same environment (either in the water or on the water's surface).

Stream insects are often described as being aquatic or semiaquatic. *Aquatic* insects have at least one life stage that lives underwater. *Semiaquatic* insects do not live underwater but have at least one life stage associated with the water's surface (e.g., water striders).

Insects are found within the phylum Arthropoda, which also includes arachnids such as spiders and water mites and crustaceans such as crayfishes and freshwater shrimps. Within the phylum, insects are further classified into the subphylum Hexapoda and the class Insecta.

ALDERFLIES AND DOBSONFLIES (ORDER MEGALOPTERA)

Megalopterans are a relatively small group of insects, with three hundred species identified worldwide. The fossil record is poor, and the evolutionary age of these animals is unclear. There are twelve species in two families of Megaloptera in Wisconsin.

Megaloptera larvae are aquatic, while all other life stages (egg, pupa, and adult) are terrestrial. Adults deposit eggs on structures overhanging the water such as vegetation, log jams, and boulders. After one to two weeks, eggs hatch, and larvae immediately drop into the water. Underwater for one to three years, larvae then crawl a few meters from the water to pupate in moist soil or under logs, often leaving en masse during spring thunderstorms. After undergoing complete metamorphosis, winged adults emerge from May to July to live and mate for three to ten days in the riparian area. Megalopterans produce one generation every one to four years.

Unless otherwise noted, general characteristics of larvae are bodies elongate and somewhat flattened; head large and dark-colored; jaws (mandibles) large and conspicuous; a long single filament or two pairs of hooks extending from the end of the abdomen; seven or eight pairs of lateral filaments sticking out from abdominal segments that aid in respiration (not locomotion); all legs ending with a pair of claws; head and thorax hardened (sclerotized); and abdomen soft. Terminal appendages and lateral filaments are important in distinguishing between the two families that occur in Wisconsin. Adults are large, 25–75 mm long, with large conspicuous jaws and wings, and dark-bodied. The wings are often dark-colored and held tent-like over the abdomen; wing venation is prominent.

The word *Megaloptera* is from the Greek *megal* (large or giant) and *ptera* (wings), referring to the large size of the adult's wings. Megalopteran larvae are commonly referred to as hellgrammites by anglers.

DOBSONFLIES (hellgrammites)
Corydalidae (3 genera, 4 species in Wisconsin)

DESCRIPTION (LARVA): Body elongate, 25–65 mm long; among Wisconsin's largest insects. Caterpillar-like; somewhat flattened top to bottom (dorsoventrally compressed). Head large, hardened (sclerotized), dark-colored; jaws large. All 3 segments of thorax hardened; abdomen soft. First 8 as well as 10th abdominal segments with lateral filaments. Two fleshy appendages (each with 2 hooks) extending from posterior end of abdomen; no long terminal filament.

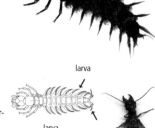

larva

larva

adult

DESCRIPTION (ADULT): 25–80 mm (including wings); striking in appearance due to large size of body, wings, and jaws. Head ant-like (rounded with long antennae and conspicuous mandibles); wings often twice the length of the body; wing venation prominent.

LOOK-ALIKES: Alderfly larvae and adults.

NOTES: Dobsonflies are uncommon statewide and very rare in areas with intensive agriculture or urban development. Larvae are found mainly in streams under rocks in riffles; some species are also found in weedy ponds and marshes and along lake margins. They are intolerant of pollution, especially species that inhabit flowing water. The numerous lateral filaments are often mistaken for legs but are actually used to facilitate oxygen uptake. Dobsonfly larvae (often referred to as hellgrammites) are voracious predators that have a strong influence on aquatic invertebrate populations and can inflict a painful bite to humans if carelessly handled. They take 2–4 years to reach maturity, pupating in underground chambers on land and typically emerging in June. Adults are weak fliers that are secretive and short-lived, often staying close to the water in the riparian vegetation.

ALDERFLIES
Sialidae (1 genus, 7 species in Wisconsin)

DESCRIPTION (LARVA): Body elongate, 10–28 mm long (including terminal filament). Head hardened (sclerotized), large and dark-colored. All 3 segments of thorax hardened; abdomen soft. First 7 abdominal segments with lateral filaments. Long single filament (with hairs) extending from end of abdomen.

larva

larva

adult

DESCRIPTION (ADULT): Up to 25 mm in length, including wings. Wings held tent-like over body; wings translucent black or dark brown, with conspicuous venation.

LOOK-ALIKES: Dobsonfly larvae and adults.

NOTES: Alderflies are common statewide. Larvae are found in streams, rivers, lakes, and marshes, often inhabiting silt and detritus that accumulate in pools and other areas of quiet water. The lateral filaments on the larvae are often mistaken for legs, but rather than being used for locomotion, these aid in oxygen uptake. Adults are weak fliers but good runners, staying close to the margins of the aquatic habitats from which the larvae have emerged. Larvae are moderately tolerant of pollution and are voracious predators that have a strong influence on aquatic invertebrate populations. They can inflict a painful bite to humans if carelessly handled.

BEETLES (ORDER COLEOPTERA)

The insect order Coleoptera evolved around 300 million years ago and has an estimated 400,000 species worldwide, which is more than any other animal order. Coleoptera are thought to represent over 25 percent of all known animal species on earth. While over 90 percent of beetle species are terrestrial, there are numerous *aquatic* or *semiaquatic* species, meaning that they have at least one life stage that occurs underwater or on water. There are 369 aquatic beetle species identified from Wisconsin; these are grouped into 14 families.

Beetles undergo complete metamorphosis, having an egg, larval, pupal, and winged adult stage. Of the aquatic beetle species, larvae are often aquatic, pupae are usually terrestrial, and adults are sometimes aquatic. Aquatic beetles are unique among insects in that some species have both a larval and an adult stage that are aquatic. Adults usually emerge from pupation in the fall, may be active or dormant in winter, and mate and lay eggs in the spring. The majority of aquatic beetles produce one generation per year.

Beetle larvae are characterized by a hardened (sclerotized) head, a thorax with 3 pairs of segmented legs, and no wing pads. Adults are characterized by a hardened body, hardened forewings (*elytra*) that meet in a straight line down the center of the back when folded, and membranous hind wings that are covered by the forewings when folded.

The word *Coleoptera* is from the Greek *koleon* (sheath) and *ptera* (wings), referring to the elytra.

adult

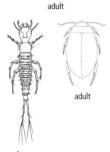

adult

larva

PREDACEOUS DIVING BEETLES
Dytiscidae (32 genera, 143 species in Wisconsin)

DESCRIPTION (LARVA): Body elongate, small to large, 2–70 mm long. Head dark-colored and hardened (sclerotized); 3 pairs of 5-segmented legs, each with 2 claws. Rarely encountered.

DESCRIPTION (ADULT): Body small to large, 2–25 mm long. Body shape highly variable, typically oval-shaped and streamlined; antennae thin; hind legs strong, developed for swimming. Most species black or brown.

LOOK-ALIKES: Whirligig beetle larvae and adults.

NOTES: Predaceous diving beetles are fairly common to abundant statewide, though larvae are rarely seen. Both larvae and adults are predators that inhabit aquatic vegetation in ponds, lakes, and slow-moving water in streams and rivers. Adults emerge in late spring or early summer, having overwintered as adults in water or in sheltered terrestrial habitats. They are strong swimmers. Adults rely on atmospheric oxygen stored under their wings that is replenished by breaking the water surface with the tip of the abdomen.

RIFFLE BEETLES
Elmidae (6 genera, 24 species in Wisconsin)

larva

DESCRIPTION (LARVA): Body elongate, sclerotized, worm-like, 1–8 mm long; ovoid or concave in cross section. Strongly segmented with 3 thoracic and 9 abdominal segments; last segment with hinged lid that protects the gills. Legs may be visible from above. Legs with 4 segments that end with a single claw. Color dark brown and tan.

larva

DESCRIPTION (ADULT): Body small, 2–5 mm; ovoid and hard. Antennae slender. Legs long compared with body length, visible from above, in 3 segments terminating in 2 claws. Color dark brown or black with light stripes or spots.

LOOK-ALIKES: Midge larvae and net-spinning caddisfly larvae.

NOTES: Riffle beetles are common statewide. They are found in cold or cool streams in fast-flowing, well-oxygenated water, in springs, and along some wave-swept lakeshores, crawling slowly on stones, hiding under rocks, and burrowing in or living on woody debris. They are scrapers, eating mainly algae and diatoms off of rocks. Both larvae and adults are aquatic, which is rare among insects. Most species take 1 or more years to complete their life cycle. Adult riffle beetles trap an air bubble on their abdomen to use as an underwater breathing apparatus; they are moderately tolerant of pollution.

adult   adult

WHIRLIGIG BEETLES
Gyrinidae (2 genera, 25 species in Wisconsin)

larva

DESCRIPTION (LARVA): Rarely seen; 6–30 mm long; elongate, somewhat flattened, centipede-like. Legs with 5 segments that each end in 2 claws. 10 abdominal segments with pairs of lateral filaments that aid in oxygen uptake, not locomotion (2 pairs of filaments on last segment). Abdomen ends in 4 small hooks. Color pale.

larva

DESCRIPTION (ADULT): 3–15 mm long; body hard, oval, flattened. Two pairs of eyes, 1 pair above and 1 below the waterline; can look above water and underwater simultaneously. Antennae club-shaped. Middle and back legs short and flattened. Color metallic black. Adults move quickly and erratically across the water surface, often in large groups.

adult

LOOK-ALIKES: Predaceous diving beetle larvae and adults.

NOTES: Whirligig beetles are common statewide, though larvae are rarely seen. They are found in ponds, lakes, rivers, and streams in quiet water. Larvae are found on submersed vegetation; adults, while good divers, are usually seen on the water's surface. They are predators as larvae and predators or scavengers as adults. Adults often create waves on the water surface to sense potential food items. Most species of whirligig beetle complete their life cycle in one year. While good fliers, adults must climb onto emergent structures to take flight. Adults breathe atmospheric oxygen and carry an air bubble held under the elytra (forewings), which they use as an underwater oxygen source. When handled or attacked they secrete a milky, defensive substance that smells like ripe apples in some species and strongly acrid or pungent in others. They are moderately tolerant of pollution.

adult

adults

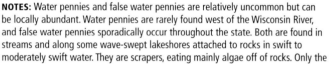

WATER PENNIES AND FALSE WATER PENNIES
Psephenidae (water penny—genus *Psephenus*,
1 species in Wisconsin; false water penny—
genus *Ectopria*, 2–3 species in Wisconsin)

larva (dorsal view)

DESCRIPTION (LARVA): Body disk-like, 5–8 mm long, very distinct, very flat, resembling a penny. Edges of "penny" smooth or saw-toothed. Legs and head obscured from view from above. 4 leg segments, with single claw at end of each leg. Water pennies usually bronze to dark yellowish; false water pennies typically various shades of brown and often match the color of the rocks they live on.

DESCRIPTION (ADULT): Body 4–6 mm long, somewhat flattened, and in various "beetle-shaped" body forms.

LOOK-ALIKES: Other adult beetles.

NOTES: Water pennies and false water pennies are relatively uncommon but can be locally abundant. Water pennies are rarely found west of the Wisconsin River, and false water pennies sporadically occur throughout the state. Both are found in streams and along some wave-swept lakeshores attached to rocks in swift to moderately swift water. They are scrapers, eating mainly algae off of rocks. Only the larvae are aquatic—adults are found clinging to rocks and logs *above* the water surface in riffles and along shorelines. Both water pennies and false water pennies are moderately sensitive to pollution.

larva (ventral view)

larva (ventral view)   larva (dorsal view)

CADDISFLIES (ORDER TRICHOPTERA)

Nearly 12,000 species of caddisflies have been described worldwide, but there are undoubtedly many more species. The earliest known fossil records of caddisflies are thought to be 185 million years old. The order Trichoptera includes 257 species in 19 families identified from Wisconsin.

Caddisfly larvae and pupae are both aquatic and a very important component of aquatic eco-systems because they have a widespread distribution and they make up a large proportion of the invertebrate biomass in most streams. Larvae also break down organic matter and are a key food source for other aquatic invertebrates, fish, birds, spiders, terrestrial insects, and bats.

Caddisflies are closely related to butterflies and moths (order Lepidoptera) and, like caterpillars, have silk glands. The silk is used to construct cases for shelter and camouflage, nets for filter feeding, cocoons for pupation, and silk strands to anchor to substrate.

Caddisflies undergo complete metamorphosis, having an egg, larval, pupal and adult life stage. Many caddisflies are "case builders": they use sand grains, small stones, or vegetation for the con-struction of shelters. All individuals within a family construct the same type of case, which can be used in taxonomic identification. Once mature, larvae build cocoons within the cases and pupate over the course of several weeks. Winged adults emerge from their case, swim to the water's surface, and immediately take flight. For most species, this emergence takes place early in the morning, and the newly emerged adults seek shelter in streamside vegetation as the day progresses.

During the adult stage, caddisflies return to the water toward dusk to mate and deposit eggs. The females of some species will deposit eggs on the water's surface, while other species will dive or crawl into the water and place eggs on submerged plants and rocks. Caddisflies produce one generation every six months to two years. Adult caddisflies can live for up to a month. Most species lack the highly synchronized mass emergences often associated with mayflies and other insect orders. At any time in spring, summer, or fall, at least some adults may be seen flying over the water or resting in streamside vegetation. Caddisflies can be identified at a distance by their erratic (moth-like) flight behavior low over the water at dawn or dusk.

Unless otherwise noted, general types and characteristics of caddisfly larvae include the following: They are case builders: they use sand grains, small stones, or vegetation for the construction of shelters. They are free-living: they build retreats out of detritus, algae, and mosses and use filter nets attached to rocks or vegetation to filter-feed. Their bodies are elongate; antennae are very small, not visible without magnification; thoracic segments are hardened, without wing pads; the abdomen is often with gills; and the abdomen ends in two hooked appendages.

Adult caddisflies are moth-like in appearance, folding their wings like tents over their backs; anten-nae are typically longer than the body; and most species have tan, brown, or black wings that are solid-colored or have a speckled coloration pattern.

The word *Trichoptera* is from the Greek *trichos* (hair) and *ptera* (wings), referring to the small hairs on the wings of adults. The word *caddisfly* is from the Middle English *cadaz* (cotton or silk), referring to the silk they produce.

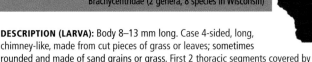

CHIMNEY CASE-MAKER CADDISFLIES (American sedges, grannoms, humpless case-maker caddisflies)
Brachycentridae (2 genera, 8 species in Wisconsin)

DESCRIPTION (LARVA): Body 8–13 mm long. Case 4-sided, long, chimney-like, made from cut pieces of grass or leaves; sometimes rounded and made of sand grains or grass. First 2 thoracic segments covered by hard, darkened plates; third thoracic segment with small, hard, darkened patches. First abdominal segment without dorsal and lateral humps. Thorax often bright green (photo is of a preserved specimen). Gills unbranched or absent. Forelegs with long hairs (setae) used to filter-feed.

larva (preserved specimen)

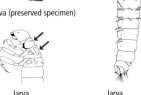

DESCRIPTION (ADULT): 12–15 mm long; antennae as long as body; body dark brown; wings light tan when emerging and tan to brownish tan when returning to the water to lay eggs.

LOOK-ALIKES: Little brown sedge larvae (family Lepidostomatidae)—cases composed of larger square pieces of vegetation.

larva   larva

NOTES: Chimney case-maker caddisflies are common in W., N., and central Wisconsin. They are found in small, spring-fed streams to large rivers, in fast water, attached to logs, rocks, and vegetation. They prefer cool or cold water and have a low pollution tolerance. Depending on species, they are collector/filterers or collector/gatherers. They produce 1 generation per year and sometimes every 2 years, emerging in spring to late summer depending on species.

case   adult

SADDLE CASE-MAKER CADDISFLIES
Glossosomatidae (3 genera, 6 species in Wisconsin)

DESCRIPTION (LARVA): Small, 3–7 mm long. Case resembles tortoise shell, composed of fine gravel and sand. Underside of case with a "strap" across the middle composed of smaller sand particles. Abandons case when distressed. Only first thoracic segment covered by hard plate. No humps on first abdominal segment. No gills on abdomen.

larva

DESCRIPTION (ADULT): Small, 5–8 mm; antennae as long as body; wings mottled brown and tan.

LOOK-ALIKES: None.

case

NOTES: Saddle case-maker caddisflies are common statewide. They are found in very clean streams and rivers and along lakeshores in cool, clear, swift water, usually atop clean rocks. They are highly intolerant of pollution. They are scrapers, eating mainly algae scraped off of rocks. They produce 1 generation per year, emerging in summer.

larva

case

adult

SNAIL CASE-MAKER CADDISFLIES
Helicopsychidae (1 genus, 1 species in Wisconsin)

DESCRIPTION (LARVA): Case snail-shaped, built out of small sand grains. Body small, curled inside of case; rarely collected outside of case.

larva

DESCRIPTION (ADULT): 5–7 mm; brownish or mottled wings.

larva

LOOK-ALIKES: None.

adult

NOTES: Snail case-maker caddisflies are sporadically distributed statewide. They are found in streams and occasionally along lakeshores, in moderately swift water attached to clean rocks and logs. They are intolerant of pollution. They are scrapers, eating mainly algae scraped off of hard substrates. They produce 1 generation per year, emerging during summer.

case

NET-SPINNING CADDISFLIES
(spotted sedges, speckled sedges)
Hydropsychidae (7 genera, 32 species in Wisconsin)

DESCRIPTION (LARVA): Body 14–18 mm. No case, but lives in a retreat composed of algae and detritus that is attached to aquatic vegetation or rocks. Often seen crawling, caterpillar-like, on rocks that have been removed from the water. All 3 thoracic segments covered by dark-colored hard plates (sclerotized). Underside of abdomen covered in rows of feathery gills. Tuft of hairs on pair of anal claws. Abdomen often green or grayish green.

larva

DESCRIPTION (ADULT): 12–18 mm; antennae longer than body. Body tan to brownish tan, wings tan to mottled tan and brown.

LOOK-ALIKES: Green rock worm larvae (family Rhyacophlidae)—very bright green. Also finger-net caddisfly larvae (family Philopotamidae), midge larvae, and riffle beetle larvae.

larva

NOTES: Net-spinning caddisflies are very abundant statewide. The most numerous and widely distributed caddisfly family in Wisconsin, they are found in nearly every stream in the state. Their fragile retreats (not cases) are built using silk webbing. These retreats are nondescript clumps of detritus, algae, and moss, attached to rocks or aquatic vegetation in flowing water. Net-spinning caddisflies are collector/filterers; a filter-feeding web-like apparatus 4–8 mm in diameter is often visible as part of the retreat. These caddisflies are intolerant to moderately tolerant of pollution. They produce 1–2 generations per year, emerging typically at dawn from April to September. As adults they fly to streamside vegetation during the day, then toward dusk they return to the stream to mate and lay eggs. As is typical of caddisflies, adults are moth-like, with erratic flight movements, flying low over the water surface at dawn and dusk.

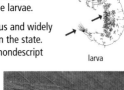

adult

larva

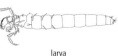

larva

LONG-HORNED CADDISFLIES
Leptoceridae (8 genera, 42 species in Wisconsin)

DESCRIPTION (LARVA): Body 7–15 mm long. Case is a long, cylindrical tube; construction design and materials quite varied among species—some made completely of silk; others of sand grains and twigs or conifer needles; still others spiraling and tubular, made of plant leaf material.

DESCRIPTION (ADULT): 10–17 mm; very slender body and wings; antennae nearly twice as long as body.

LOOK-ALIKES: None.

NOTES: Long-horned caddisflies are common statewide. They are found in streams, rivers, lakes, and marshes, on vegetation, sand, and rocky substrates. Most species are omnivorous. They are moderately tolerant of pollution. They produce 1 generation per year, emerging in late spring or summer. The white miller (*Nectopsyche* spp.) is a white-colored group familiar among fly fishers, emerging in midsummer.

adult

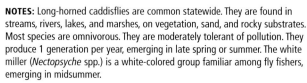

NORTHERN CASE-MAKER CADDISFLIES (orange sedges)
Limnephilidae (17 genera, 46 species in Wisconsin)

DESCRIPTION (LARVA): Body 8–35 mm long. Case tubular, built out of small stones and sand grains (often for species in cool, flowing water) or vegetation such as twigs, leaves, or pieces of bark (often for species in warmer, quieter water). Head round. First 2 thoracic segments covered by hard plates; third segment only covered by small hard patches. First abdominal segment with dorsal and lateral humps. Second-to-last abdominal segment covered by hardened plate. Abdomen with gills.

DESCRIPTION (ADULT): Antennae longer than body; thorax dark brown; legs, abdomen, and antennae lighter brown; wings tan to tannish brown or orange brown; venation prominent.

larva

LOOK-ALIKES: Strong case-maker caddisfly larvae (family Odontoceridae).

NOTES: Northern case-maker caddisflies are common statewide and can be locally abundant. They are found in small streams, large rivers, ponds, lakes, and marshes in varied habitats—attached to rocks or vegetation or crawling on the stream bottom. They are moderately tolerant of pollution, although the family has a wide range of tolerances, depending on the species. Species with vegetation cases are shredders, and species with stone cases are scrapers that graze on algae. Northern case-maker caddisflies produce 1 generation per year. They typically emerge at dawn from May to September, fly to streamside vegetation during the day, and over the course of several days to several weeks return to the water to mate and lay eggs toward dusk. Adults are moth-like, with erratic flight movements, and can be seen flying low over the water surface at dawn and dusk.

larva

larva

case   larva   adult

STRONG CASE-MAKER CADDISFLIES
Odontoceridae (1 genus, 1 species in Wisconsin)

larva

DESCRIPTION (LARVA): Body 10–20 mm long; first 2 thoracic segments covered with hardened plates, third plate partially hardened; body light green. Case is an elongated tube, slightly curved, constructed of uniformly sized sand grains that are strongly cemented together.

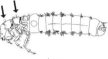

larva

DESCRIPTION (ADULT): Body 13–18 mm long, green to black; wings dark grayish brown; legs usually black; antennae as long as wings.

LOOK-ALIKES: Northern case-maker caddisfly larvae (family Limnephilidae).

adult

NOTES: Strong case-maker caddisflies are sporadically found throughout Wisconsin but are uncommon in the southeast. They primarily inhabit small, cool, sand- and gravel-bottomed streams. They are very intolerant of pollution. The cased larvae burrow in sand and fine gravel and feed on algae growing in the substrate. Larvae take 2 years to mature and pupate in early spring, when large numbers of the pupal cases can be found attached to the undersides of rocks. Adults primarily emerge in June.

FINGER-NET CADDISFLIES
Philopotamidae (3 genera, 6 species in Wisconsin)

DESCRIPTION (LARVA): Body 13–17 mm long. No case; builds fragile tubular retreats and nets of very fine silk threads. Head long, smooth. T-shaped structure (labrum) extending from mouth; structure is used to clean nets. Only first thoracic segment covered by hard plate (sclerotized). No gills on abdomen. Body often translucent orange; head darker orange or yellow.

larva   larva

DESCRIPTION (ADULT): Small, 5–9 mm; dark body and wings.

LOOK-ALIKES: Net-spinning caddisfly larvae (family Hydropsychidae); midge larvae.

adult

NOTES: Finger-net caddisflies are common statewide. They are found in small streams to large rivers, building retreats in fast water under rocks and logs. They are intolerant of organic pollution or excessive sedimentation and are collector/filterers. They produce 1–2 generations per year, emerging in late spring and early summer. Species in the genus *Chimarra* begin to emerge in late April (the earliest emergence of any Wisconsin caddisfly) and are referred to as small black caddis or tiny black sedges by fly fishers.

labrum

DAMSELFLIES & DRAGONFLIES (ORDER ODONATA)

The order Odonata is divided into two suborders: dragonflies (Anisoptera) and damselflies (Zygoptera). Over 6,500 species of odonates have been identified worldwide. They are a relatively old group of insects that have changed little in form over their 300 million years of existence on earth (although some fossil dragonflies have a wingspan of 45 cm!). There are 161 species in 9 families of odonates identified from Wisconsin. The word *Odonata* is from the Greek *odon* (tooth), referring to the "teeth" on the mandibles of the dragonfly larvae.

Odonate larvae are often referred to as nymphs and live in a variety of habitats. Approximately two-thirds of odonate species are associated with lake, pond, or wetland environments, and the remainder are found in or around flowing water environments. The families most common to streams are described in this guide.

Odonates are often migratory. Adults of some dragonfly species fly into Wisconsin from more southern states in the spring, and some species that emerge in Wisconsin may fly south in late summer or fall. Both of these groups follow flyways along the Mississippi River and Lake Michigan, similar to some migratory birds. Adult migrants from other states are typically seen in Wisconsin beginning in April.

Odonates are relatively long-lived insects, producing one generation every one to four years, depending upon species and local climate. The larval stage is aquatic and lasts much longer than the adult terrestrial stage. Adult males and females of many species fly in tandem while mating. Females deposit eggs by dipping their abdomens into the water while in flight or land on shoreline vegetation and insert eggs inside or on vegetation to avoid predators. Eggs usually hatch after several weeks but may take as long as two months, depending on species and water temperatures. Eggs can remain dormant for up to six months during harsh environmental conditions. Larvae undergo incomplete metamorphosis (they resemble adults) and crawl from the water to shed their larval exoskeletons and emerge as winged adults. The larval life stage usually lasts longer in Wisconsin than in warm climates and can range from ten months up to four years depending upon the species; adults survive for about one month.

Odonates are voracious predators throughout their lives, and larvae can be the top predator in ecosystems that lack fish. Larvae may stalk prey, or they may wait motionlessly for insects, tadpoles, or occasionally small fish to approach, then quickly extend and grasp the prey with their large, flexible lower lip (labium). The relatively large compound eyes (containing up to 30,000 individual lenses) of both the larvae and adults are evidence that they are visual predators.

Adults are strong, fast fliers (up to 35 mph) and are extremely adept aerial predators (hence the common names of pondhawk, meadowhawk, river cruiser, etc.). They catch prey while in flight, including insects and aerially drifting spiders. Adults can significantly reduce mosquito and biting fly populations, and in turn they are important food for birds, fish, frogs, spiders, and other dragonfly species. Adult males of some species are territorial, patrolling areas to ward off other males that may compete for food or mates, even guarding individual females with which they have mated. After mating, a male may also remain attached to the female while eggs are laid to ensure that other males don't remove his sperm from the female with a special scraping tool on the body and insert their own sperm.

Damselflies (suborder Zygoptera)

Damselfly larvae have the following characteristics: body elongate and slender; head wider than body; abdomen ending in three elongate tail-like, leaf-shaped gills (which break off easily when specimens are collected); and longest gills more than one-third the abdomen length. Gills are used both for breathing and in locomotion. Adult damselflies are often dark blue or green, with bright, iridescent, elongate bodies. They can be distinguished from dragonfly adults by having a more slender abdomen than most dragonfly species and by their ability to fold their wings, which are then held at a 45-degree angle above the abdomen when at rest. Damselflies usually produce 1 generation per year.

BROAD-WINGED DAMSELFLIES
Calopterygidae (2 genera, 4 species in Wisconsin)

larva

DESCRIPTION (LARVA): Body large, 30–40 mm long. First antennal segment much longer than the other segments combined. Legs relatively long, stilt-like. Front edge of lower lip (labium) with diamond-shaped notch; hairs absent. "Broad-winged" refers to wing pads on larva. Middle gill shorter than 2 lateral gills; gills without veins. Slow crawler.

DESCRIPTION (ADULT): Wings not strongly narrowed at base, usually dark-colored or grayish.

LOOK-ALIKES: Narrow-winged damselfly larvae.

NOTES: Broad-winged damselflies are common statewide. Larvae are found in streams, especially in woodlands, and inhabit slow-moving water on bank vegetation, snags, or undercut banks. They are moderately tolerant of organic pollution and are predators. They produce 1 generation every 1–2 years.

adult   larva   antennae

NARROW-WINGED DAMSELFLIES
Coenagrionidae (7 genera, 31 species in Wisconsin)

larva

DESCRIPTION (LARVA): Body relatively short, 13–35 mm long. Antennal segments of equal length; lower lip (labium) wide at base and only slightly larger toward tip. Gills leaf-shaped and of equal length; gills without veins. Slow crawler.

DESCRIPTION (ADULT): Wings strongly narrowed at base.

LOOK-ALIKES: Broad-winged damselfly larvae.

NOTES: Narrow-winged damselflies are common statewide and are the most numerous and diverse family of Wisconsin damselflies. Larvae are found in streams clinging to vegetation and rocks, often along lake margins. Narrow-winged damselflies are highly tolerant of pollution and are predators. They produce 1 generation every 1–2 years.

larva

adult

DAMSELFLIES & DRAGONFLIES (order Odonata)

Dragonflies (suborder Anisoptera)

Dragonfly larvae have the following characteristics: a hinged lower lip (labium); large, conspicuous compound eyes; a broad and stubby body; a head that is narrower than the body; and an abdomen ending in three to five short, stiff points. Adults are similar in body form to larvae, with a hinged lower lip and large, conspicuous compound eyes. Adults also have two pairs of large, clear wings held horizontally from a robust thorax; a long and narrow abdomen; and on some species the abdomen has a bulbous end (e.g., in club-tail dragonflies).

The coloration of the head, thorax, abdomen, wings, and wing venation can be used to identify adults and can often be seen using close-focusing binoculars when adults land nearby. Behavioral traits such as how dragonflies perch (horizontally or vertically), flying height above land or water, amount of time spent flying versus at rest, time of day when in flight, and so on can also aid in species identification.

DARNER DRAGONFLIES
Aeshnidae (7 genera, 16 species in Wisconsin)

DESCRIPTION (LARVA): Body large, 30–62 mm long, elongate. Antennae with 6–7 segments of approximately equal lengths, not club-shaped. Lower lip (labium) flattened when viewed from side.

DESCRIPTION (ADULT): Abdomen long and slender, lacking bulbous tip. Most colorful of Wisconsin dragonfly families; often with blue, green, or yellow abdominal spots.

LOOK-ALIKES: None.

NOTES: Darner dragonflies are common statewide; they are the most common of Wisconsin resident and migrant dragonflies. Larvae are found in lakes and ponds and along stream margins under stones, logs, and coarse woody debris. They have 1–3-year life cycles and are intolerant to moderately tolerant of organic pollution. Darner dragonflies are predators, actively stalking and seizing prey with their hinged labium.

larva

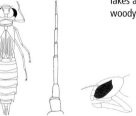

larva   antenna   labium

adult

102

SPIKE-TAIL DRAGONFLIES
Cordulegastridae (1 genus, 3 species in Wisconsin)

DESCRIPTION (LARVA): Body large, 30–45 mm long, often appearing hairy. Eyes small knobs at front of head. Antennae with 7 segments of approximately equal length. Front of lower lip (labium) enlarged, with irregular teeth; labium spoon-shaped, not flattened, when viewed from side.

DESCRIPTION (ADULT): Eyes green, meet at a point on top of head; 2 broad yellow stripes on sides of thorax.

LOOK-ALIKES: None.

NOTES: Spike-tail dragonflies are common statewide. Larvae are found in small, clear woodland streams, burrowing in sand and silt substrate. They are intolerant of organic pollution and are predators. They produce 1 generation every 3–4 years.

larva

adult

labium

larva

CLUB-TAIL DRAGONFLIES
Gomphidae (10 genera, 32 species in Wisconsin)

DESCRIPTION (LARVA): Body 25–45 mm long. Antennae with 4 segments, club-shaped: third segment longer and wider; fourth segment tiny, nearly invisible. Lower lip (labium) flattened when viewed from side; without thick hairs. Abdomen sometimes flattened top to bottom (dorsoventrally), tapering to a rounded or blunt point.

DESCRIPTION (ADULT): Eyes widely separated at top of head; bodies usually have greenish or yellowish markings on thorax. Abdomen usually with bulbous end.

LOOK-ALIKES: None.

NOTES: Club-tail dragonflies are common statewide. Larvae are found in streams, rivers, and lakes and often burrow in sand or silt substrate. They are intolerant to moderately tolerant of pollution and are predators. They typically produce 1 generation per year, with some species taking up to 4 years to reach maturity.

larva

adult

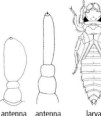

antenna   antenna   larva

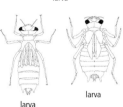

larva

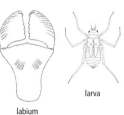

larva

labium

larva

larva

larva

DESCRIPTION (LARVA): Body 18–42 mm long, stout. Antennae with 6–7 segments of approximately equal length. Front of lower lip (labium) enlarged, with regular teeth; labium spoon-shaped, not flattened, when viewed from side. Often camouflaged by coloration or thick layer of silt on body.

DESCRIPTION (ADULT): Variable-colored bodies; wings usually have color patterns (wings not transparent).

LOOK-ALIKES: Green-eyed skimmer larvae (family Corduliidae)—uncommon in Wisconsin.

NOTES: Common skimmer dragonflies are very common statewide. Larvae are found in ponds, lakes, and marshes and sometimes along stream and river margins, in weeds or burrowing in substrate. They are tolerant of low dissolved oxygen and are predators. They produce 1 generation per year, though they sometimes take 2 years to reach maturity. Two large groups within this family are the king skimmers (*Libellula* spp.) and the meadowhawks (*Sympetrum* spp.).

adult

MAYFLIES (ORDER EPHEMEROPTERA)

The mayfly order, Ephemeroptera, is a relatively small group of insects with about 2,500 species identified worldwide. It is a very old group, thought to have evolved about 350 million years ago. There are at least 130 species in 21 families of mayflies identified from Wisconsin.

Mayflies undergo incomplete metamorphosis: larvae, often referred to as nymphs, resemble wingless adults, and as they grow, they gradually become adults through many molts (sheddings of exoskeleton). They have a greater number of molts—twelve to forty-five—than any other order of aquatic insect. Mayfly eggs are always laid in water, the larvae are always aquatic, and adults are terrestrial. When ready to emerge from the water, larvae either swim or float to the surface or crawl out of the water. Upon emerging, a larva immediately molts to become a *subimago*, or winged pre-adult, characterized by bluish, opaque wings; subimagos are referred to as *duns* by fly fishers. This life stage is unique to mayflies. Within a very brief time span (one minute to two days), the subimago molts a final time to become an adult with transparent wings; the adult then mates as part of a large breeding swarm. The female returns to the water to lay eggs and then dies, usually within a few hours or up to a day. The dead mayflies often drift downstream on the water surface with wings spread apart and are referred to as *spinners* by fly fishers.

The word *Ephemeroptera* is from the Greek *ephēmeros* (lasts a day) and *ptera* (wings), referring to the brevity of the adult life stage. The adult life stage is so brief that the adults of many mayfly species lack functional mouthparts or digestive tracts, instead focusing solely on reproduction.

Because the adult stage of life is so brief, mayfly adults emerge together and congregate in highly synchronized breeding swarms to ensure reproduction. These emergence patterns often occur in specific months and at certain times of day or night. During this time, adults are vulnerable to predation by spiders, dragonflies, birds, bats, and fish. Mayflies are also an important link in stream and terrestrial food chains, since the larvae primarily eat plants and detritus, and in turn both larvae and adults are fed upon by numerous aquatic and terrestrial animals.

Most mayflies have a low tolerance of organic pollution associated with low dissolved oxygen concentrations, so the presence of mayflies generally indicates good water quality.

Unless otherwise noted, mayfly larvae have the following characteristics: eyes positioned on the sides of the head; thorax with one pair of visible wing pads and three pairs of segmented legs; a single claw at the end of each leg; dorsal gills along the abdomen; and three (or sometimes two) manysegmented tails (caudal filaments). The larvae of mayfly families can be distinguished from one another using the shape and position of the gills and the shape of the claws. Adult mayflies have upright wings and appear as miniature "sailboats" when on the water's surface. Adults of most species are often distinguished by the presence or absence of posterior wings and by the patterns of the wing veins.

Since a few mayfly species have only two tails as larvae, and the tails often break when specimens are collected, they may appear similar to stoneflies (order Plecoptera). However, mayfly larvae can be distinguished from other insects by the presence of abdominal gills (i.e., gills on the most posterior body segment) and by the single claw at the end of each leg—stoneflies have two claws on the end of each leg and gills located on the thorax between the legs. In addition, mayfly larvae move their bodies up and down in an "M" motion, while stoneflies move side to side in an "S" motion.

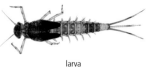 **MAYFLIES** (order Ephemeroptera)

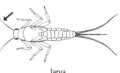

larva

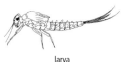

larva

larva

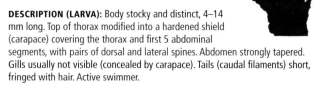

BLUE-WINGED OLIVES (small minnow mayflies)
Baetidae (12 genera, 26 species in Wisconsin)

DESCRIPTION (LARVA): Often very small, 3–12 mm; torpedo-shaped; antennae usually 2–3 times longer than width of head. Gills are plates of varying shape, not feathery. Two to three tails (caudal filaments); middle tail sometimes shorter than the other 2. Fast swimmer.

DESCRIPTION (ADULT): Among Wisconsin's smallest mayflies; rarely exceeds 10 mm in length (including tails); 2 tails present; male with unique large, upturned (turbinate) eyes; hind wings reduced in size, veinless, or absent; wings transparent. Adult characteristically wags abdomen and tails side to side when at rest. Immature winged stage (subimago): bluish-colored wings and often light green body.

LOOK-ALIKES: Other mayfly larvae and adults, especially prong-gilled mayflies (family Leptophlebiidae).

NOTES: Blue-winged olives are abundant statewide, inhabiting nearly every stream in Wisconsin. They are also common in ponds and along weedy lakeshores and are found in swift or quiet water on vegetation or pebbles and cobbles. They are intolerant to moderately tolerant of pollution and are scrapers, grazing algae off of substrate. Most species produce 1 generation per year (univoltine), while some produce 2 generations (bivoltine). Some species are the earliest of mayfly emergers in Wisconsin, taking flight in March through June from riffle areas; emergence is often triggered by snow squalls, light rain, or heavily overcast conditions. A second generation emerges in late summer and fall.

subimago

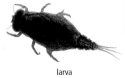

larva

larva

ARMORED MAYFLIES
Baetiscidae (1 genus, 3 species in Wisconsin)

DESCRIPTION (LARVA): Body stocky and distinct, 4–14 mm long. Top of thorax modified into a hardened shield (carapace) covering the thorax and first 5 abdominal segments, with pairs of dorsal and lateral spines. Abdomen strongly tapered. Gills usually not visible (concealed by carapace). Tails (caudal filaments) short, fringed with hair. Active swimmer.

DESCRIPTION (ADULT): Small size and shape, similar to larval body form, having a stout thorax and strongly tapered abdomen; 3 tails. Wings transparent. Immature winged stage (subimago): Wings with dark brown or black mottling.

LOOK-ALIKES: None.

NOTES: Armored mayflies are found statewide but are uncommon in S.E. Wisconsin. They inhabit streams and rivers, particularly pools and runs. They are often found along the margins of sandy streams that have a thin layer of silt (in which they partially burrow), at the bases of rooted vegetation, or in woody debris. They are intolerant of pollution. Armored mayflies are collector/gatherers and produce 1 generation per year, emerging in May and early June.

adult

SMALL SQUARE-GILL MAYFLIES
Caenidae (4 genera, 13 species in Wisconsin)

larva

DESCRIPTION (LARVA): Body small, 2–8 mm long. 1 pair of large, square, plate-like, and fringed gill protectors on second abdominal segment, touching or overlapping at midline and covering the other gills. Last several segments of abdomen without gills.

DESCRIPTION (ADULT): Small, 3–4 mm; yellowish thorax and strongly tapered abdomen; 3 tails; hind wings absent.

LOOK-ALIKES: Other mayfly larvae, especially little stout crawlers (family Leptohyphidae), prong-gilled mayflies (family Leptophlebiidae), and spiny crawler mayflies (family Ephemerellidae).

NOTES: Small square-gill mayflies are common statewide. They are found in streams, lakes, and wetlands in quiet water. They are tolerant of low oxygen levels and are collector/ gatherers or scrapers. They have an extremely brief adult stage—emerging subimagos molt quickly into imago stage, mate, and die within a few hours of emergence from the aquatic stage. Both larvae and adults are some of Wisconsin's smallest mayflies.

adult

gill protectors

larva

SPINY CRAWLER MAYFLIES
Ephemerellidae (8 genera, 21 species in Wisconsin)

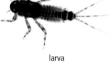

larva

DESCRIPTION (LARVA): Body flattened from top to bottom (dorsoventrally), 4–15 mm long. Gills are plates that overlap and are held over abdomen. Gills absent from anterior abdominal segments 1–3, present on segments 3–7 or 4–7, absent from last segments. Sharp to blunt spines often present on dorsal surfaces of head, thorax, or abdomen. When threatened, assumes a "scorpion" pose: curls tails and abdomen over body so that tails project forward in front of head. Slow swimmer.

larva

DESCRIPTION (ADULT): 8–12 mm, excluding tails. 3 tails. Body color varies, usually ranging from tan to reddish brown with lighter-colored banding along abdomen; wings clear with amber-colored veins.

LOOK-ALIKES: Other mayfly larvae, especially brush-legged mayflies (family Isonychiidae), little stout crawlers (family Leptohyphidae), prong-gilled mayflies (family Leptophlebiidae), and small square-gill mayflies (family Caenidae).

gills

NOTES: Spiny crawler mayflies are found statewide and are common in N. and W. Wisconsin. They inhabit streams and rivers and are found along wave-swept lakeshores; larvae are abundant in clean, fast-flowing streams in early spring and autumn. Most species are intolerant of pollution. They are collector/gatherers, eating mainly plant detritus. They mature in 1 year and emerge in the spring through the summer, depending on species. In general, given the number of different species' emergences (hatches), spiny crawler mayflies, particularly those in the genus *Ephemerella*, are of great importance to fly fishers. Several of these important species common in Wisconsin go by the common names of Hendricksons (*E. subvaria*), with peak emergences in late April and early May in midafternoon; sulphers (*E. dorothea*), emerging from May to July and peaking in June in mid- to late evening; and pale evening duns (*E. invaria*), emerging in May and peaking in mid-June in midafternoon and later in the day as summer progresses.

adult

107

MAYFLIES (order Ephemeroptera)

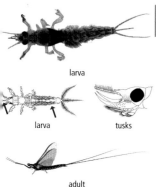

larva

larva   tusks

adult

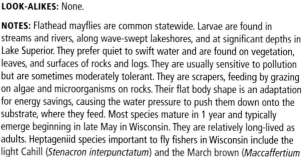

COMMON BURROWING MAYFLIES
Ephemeridae (3 genera, 6 species in Wisconsin)

DESCRIPTION (LARVA): Body large, elongate, 10–30 mm long—largest of Wisconsin mayflies. Pair of tusks projecting forward from head, with upturned ends (visible from dorsal view). Forelegs wide for burrowing. Abdominal gills feathery, held over abdomen dorsally; gills beat rhythmically. 3 tails. Swims with up-and-down, porpoise-like motion.

DESCRIPTION (ADULT): Largest of Wisconsin adult mayflies; 20–35 mm, excluding tails. Final winged adult stage often with brown and yellow banded coloration on dorsal side of each abdominal segment.

LOOK-ALIKES: Other mayfly larvae, especially hacklegills (family Potamanthidae—broader and shorter bodies; smaller, less feathery gills; lacking robust forelegs) and pale burrowing mayflies (family Polymitarcyidae—lacking feathery gills).

NOTES: Common burrowing mayflies are widespread in N. and W. Wisconsin. They are found in streams, rivers, and lakes, burrowing in soft sediments, creating a U-shaped tunnel, and beat their gills to create water flow through the burrow to obtain food and oxygen. The openings of these burrows look like "worm holes" in the soft sediment of shallow water along stream margins. These mayflies are moderately tolerant of pollution. They are collector/gatherers, eating small organic particles. Species in the genus *Hexagenia* have synchronized late evening (about 9:00 p.m. to midnight) emergences triggered by hot humid days in June and July where the winged adults can number in the billions, so numerous they are detected on weather radar. The adults gather on roads and bridges in such great numbers along the Mississippi and Wisconsin Rivers and the Great Lakes that snow removal equipment is occasionally used to clear roads. *Hexagenia* emergences are popular among fly fishers because the "hex hatch" causes large trout to go on feeding frenzies during their emergence and during the subsequent return of females to the water to lay eggs.

FLATHEAD MAYFLIES
Heptageniidae (11 genera, 26 species in Wisconsin)

larva

larva

larva

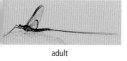

adult

DESCRIPTION (LARVA): Body 5–20 mm in length. Body, head, and legs flattened from top to bottom (dorsoventrally); legs appear muscular. Gills are single and plate-like. Eyes positioned on top of head, not sides. No mouth parts visible from dorsal view. 3 tails. Clings tightly to substrates and crawls quickly.

DESCRIPTION (ADULT): Body 4–20 mm long, excluding tails. Two long tails, often twice the length of the body. Wing venation distinct; leading edge of front wing often pigmented.

LOOK-ALIKES: None.

NOTES: Flathead mayflies are common statewide. Larvae are found in streams and rivers, along wave-swept lakeshores, and at significant depths in Lake Superior. They prefer quiet to swift water and are found on vegetation, leaves, and surfaces of rocks and logs. They are usually sensitive to pollution but are sometimes moderately tolerant. They are scrapers, feeding by grazing on algae and microorganisms on rocks. Their flat body shape is an adaptation for energy savings, causing the water pressure to push them down onto the substrate, where they feed. Most species mature in 1 year and typically emerge beginning in late May in Wisconsin. They are relatively long-lived as adults. Heptageniid species important to fly fishers in Wisconsin include the light Cahill (*Stenacron interpunctatum*) and the March brown (*Maccaffertium vicarium*), with both species emerging as winged adults in June and July from early afternoon until midevening.

108

BRUSH-LEGGED MAYFLIES
Isonychiidae (1 genus, 2 species in Wisconsin)

DESCRIPTION (LARVA): Body elongate, 8–17 mm long. Forelegs with fringe of long hairs (setae) on inner margins. Gills are small oval plates with tufts of filaments under plates on abdominal segments 1–7. Center tail (caudal filament) and inner margins of outer tails densely fringed with hairs. Distinctive dark stripe with light center line running down dorsal side of head, thorax, and abdomen.

larva

larva

DESCRIPTION (ADULT): 10–12 mm, excluding tails. Male with large upturned (turbinate) eyes and often a mahogany-colored body. First (anterior) pair of legs dark brown, and 2 posterior pairs of legs light tan-colored. Wings without coloration or mottling.

adult

LOOK-ALIKES: Cleft-footed minnow mayfly larvae (family Metretopodidae), primitive minnow mayfly larvae (family Siphlonuridae), prong-gilled mayfly larvae (family Leptophlebiidae), and spiny crawler mayfly larvae (family Ephemerellidae)— all 4 with more robust thorax and more tapered abdomen and lacking long hairs (setae) on inner margins of front legs.

NOTES: Brush-legged mayflies are found statewide and can be locally abundant. They are found in streams and rivers in moderate to swift water, clinging to vegetation or root masses. They are intolerant of pollution and are primarily collector/filterers, eating algae and diatoms filtered from water using the long hairs (setae) on the inner margins of their forelegs, though they are occasionally carnivorous. Most species require 1–2 years to mature. Larvae climb up on rocks and logs to emerge from the water. 1 brush-legged mayfly important to fly fishers is commonly referred to as the slate drake (*Isonychia bicolor*); it emerges from dawn to dusk from early May to mid-July.

LITTLE STOUT CRAWLERS (tricos)
Leptohyphidae (formerly Tricorythidae; 1 genus, 3 species in Wisconsin)

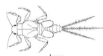

DESCRIPTION (LARVA): Very small, 3–10 mm long. Thorax appears stout relative to abdomen. Gills absent from abdominal segment 1, present on segments 2–6. Gills on segment 2 are plate-like, oval to triangular in shape. 3 tails, middle tail longer than lateral tails; tails often covered with fungal growth.

larva

larva

DESCRIPTION (ADULT): Very small, 5–6 mm. Thorax stout relative to abdomen. Hind wings absent. 3 tails. Thorax dark brown to black, abdomen grayish black, wings clear.

LOOK-ALIKES: Small square-gill mayfly larvae (family Caenidae) and spiny crawler mayfly larvae (family Ephemerellidae).

NOTES: Little stout crawlers are common statewide and can be locally abundant. They most commonly occur in slow-flowing streams and rivers, inhabiting vegetation, gravel, detritus, sand, and silt. They are poor swimmers, clinging or crawling on substrate. They are collector/gatherers and are moderately tolerant of pollution. Despite being small, they often emerge in great numbers, and the breeding swarms can be seen over 100 m from streams. Emergence ranges from late July into September, occurring in the early to midmorning. They are an important but often challenging hatch for fly fishers, since they are very small and emerge in such great numbers that the trout have many flies to choose from.

adult

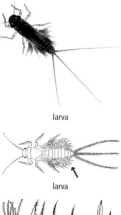

larva

larva

gills

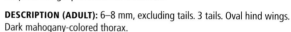

PRONG-GILLED MAYFLIES
Leptophlebiidae (4 genera, 7 species in Wisconsin)

DESCRIPTION (LARVA): Body 4–15 mm long. Most gills forked or variable in shape, usually slender or with slender filaments (finger-like projections) that are easily broken off when specimens are collected. Gills held at sides of abdomen. No plate-like gill protectors on abdomen.

DESCRIPTION (ADULT): 6–8 mm, excluding tails. 3 tails. Oval hind wings. Dark mahogany-colored thorax.

LOOK-ALIKES: Larvae of blue-winged olives (family Baetidae), brush-legged mayflies (family Isonychiidae), small square-gill mayflies (family Caenidae), spiny crawler mayflies (family Ephemerellidae); and small stoneflies.

NOTES: Prong-gilled mayflies are common statewide. They are found in clean streams, ponds, and lakes, in protected areas under rocks, in leaf packs, in woody debris, and among tree roots. They are intolerant of pollution and are omnivorous collector/gatherers. They require 1 year to mature and, depending upon species, primarily emerge in late May to early June. Species in the genus *Paraleptophlebia* are commonly called blue quills and small mahogany duns by fly fishers and emerge in May to early June in the late morning to midafternoon.

adult

STONEFLIES (ORDER PLECOPTERA)

The order Plecoptera is a relatively small group of insects, with approximately two thousand species described worldwide. Fossilized stoneflies have been found dating as far back as 54 million years ago, but their fossil record is fragmented, and there is some evidence that these animals may have evolved as long as 280 million years ago. There are fifty-eight species of stoneflies in eight families identified from Wisconsin.

All stonefly larvae are aquatic and are generally found in fast, cold, well-oxygenated streams on hard substrate or in leaf packs. Most stoneflies have primitive respiratory organs and in general are more sensitive to organic pollution than most other aquatic insects. As a result, they are often the first insects to be extirpated from streams due to polluted runoff from human activities.

Stoneflies undergo incomplete metamorphosis. Adult females deposit eggs on the water surface, on underwater substrate, or along streambanks. The eggs hatch, producing larvae that look like wingless adults. Mature larvae crawl out of the water onto streambanks, rocks, or logs to shed their exoskeletons and emerge as winged adults. Adults live one to four weeks, eating leaves, algae, lichen, or flowers; some do not feed at all, depending on the species. Adult males attract females by "drumming," or beating the abdomen against a hard surface, until the female responds and eventually arrives to mate. Plecoptera generally produce one generation per year, though some species take two or three years for the larvae to mature into winged adults.

The Euholognatha suborder includes families that emerge in winter and rely on glycogen (a sugar compound that acts like antifreeze) in their bodies to survive, while members of the Systellognatha suborder generally emerge in summer or fall.

Adult stoneflies are weak fliers and are secretive, hiding in streamside vegetation while looking for mates. Their four wings are visible and distinctive during flight, making it possible to identify them as stoneflies at some distance.

Unless otherwise noted, general characteristics of stonefly larvae are an elongate and flattened body; long antennae; two pairs of distinct wing pads present on thorax of mature larvae; head possessing moderately developed and widely separated eyes; two claws on the end of each leg; no gills on abdominal segments (some gills may be visible on thorax behind leg bases); and two long tails (caudal filaments) at the end of the abdomen. Stonefly larvae crawl on stream bottoms or swim side to side, snake-like, in an "S" motion. Gills and wing pads are used to distinguish between different families. Adult stonefly characteristics include an elongate and soft body, with elongate wings held flat over the body and extending beyond the tip of the abdomen; prominent wing venation; and two tails at the end of the abdomen.

Stonefly larvae are occasionally misidentified as mayflies, but mayfly larvae can be distinguished by the gills seen on their abdomens, and most mayflies (but not all species) have three tails (caudal filaments). In addition, mayflies swim up and down in an "M" motion that differs from stoneflies' side-to-side swimming.

The word *Plecoptera* is from the Greek *plekein* (to braid) and *ptera* (wings), thought either to refer to the distinctive venation of the wings or to how the large hind wings of the adult are folded under its front wings when the insect is not in flight.

larva

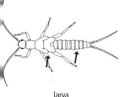

larva

SMALL WINTER STONEFLIES (little black stoneflies)
Capniidae (2 genera, 11 species in Wisconsin)

DESCRIPTION (LARVA): Body small, 3–6 mm long, elongate, cylindrical. Hind wing pads nearly parallel to each other, with little divergence from thorax (not pointing outward). Body color often dark.

DESCRIPTION (ADULT): Small, 5–7 mm; dark-colored; 2 tails.

LOOK-ALIKES: Rolled-winged stonefly larvae (family Leuctridae)—wing pads longer and more slender.

NOTES: Small winter stoneflies are found statewide but are less common in S. Wisconsin. They are found in small streams and occasionally medium-sized rivers, in moderate to swift water, in gravel or detritus. They are intolerant of pollution. Shredders, they eat mainly algae and detritus. They produce 1 generation per year. Small winter stoneflies are among Wisconsin's earliest emerging insects of the year. They are often seen crawling on ice and snow along streambanks in late winter, and they crawl into tiny snow caverns to seek shelter from severe cold. Some adult forms have very small, flightless wings to avoid being blown away from streams by winter winds.

adult

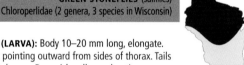

GREEN STONEFLIES (sallflies)
Chloroperlidae (2 genera, 3 species in Wisconsin)

DESCRIPTION (LARVA): Body 10–20 mm long, elongate. Wing pads not pointing outward from sides of thorax. Tails shorter than abdomen. Brownish-yellow coloration.

DESCRIPTION (ADULT): Body 6–15 mm long; often greenish or yellowish.

LOOK-ALIKES: Patterned stonefly larvae (family Perlodidae).

NOTES: Green stoneflies are common in N. Wisconsin. They are found in streams, in cool, flowing water on stone and gravel substrate, and sometimes in leaf packs or woody debris. They are intolerant of pollution. They are predators, eating mainly midge larvae. They produce 1 generation per year, emerging from May to July.

larva

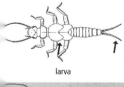

larva

adult

STONEFLIES (order Plecoptera)

BROWN STONEFLIES
Nemouridae (5 genera, 8 species in Wisconsin)

DESCRIPTION (LARVA): Body 5–20 mm, often hairy in appearance. Wing pads diverge greatly from midline of thorax. Hind legs, when pulled back, extend past tip of abdomen. Body color brown.

DESCRIPTION (ADULT): Tail inconspicuous and reduced to 1 segment.

LOOK-ALIKES: None.

NOTES: Brown stoneflies are found statewide but are less common in S.E. Wisconsin. Most species are found in small, spring-fed streams, although several species are found in large rivers and along the margins of lakes. They prefer cold water; some species prefer soft sediment, while others are associated with leaf packs and woody debris. They are shredders, eating mainly diatoms and detritus,

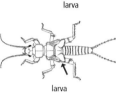

larva

adult

larva

and are intolerant of pollution. They produce 1 generation per year. Most species emerge in spring and early summer, with a few smaller-sized species emerging in the fall.

COMMON STONEFLIES (golden stoneflies)
Perlidae (7 genera, 10 species in Wisconsin)

DESCRIPTION (LARVA): Body 20–50 mm long. Feathery gills on thorax behind base of each leg. Striking, highly contrasting pattern of yellow and brown or black. Fast crawler; very active.

larva

DESCRIPTION (ADULT): Body 9–40 mm in length, yellowish or brownish but not green. Remnants of gills visible on ventral areas between legs.

LOOK-ALIKES: Patterned stonefly larvae (family Perlodidae).

larva

NOTES: Common stoneflies are found statewide, widespread especially in N. Wisconsin. They are found in streams and rivers, usually in riffles, under stones, and in snags and leaf packs where invertebrate prey are abundant. They are intolerant of pollution. Some species exhibit aggressive territorial behavior toward other individuals of the same species. They produce 1 generation every 1–3 years and emerge from May to July, typically at night, crawling up onto rocks and logs.

adult

STONEFLIES (order Plecoptera)

larva

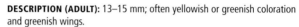

PATTERNED STONEFLIES
(little yellow stoneflies, yellow sallies)
Perlodidae (3 genera, 14 species in Wisconsin)

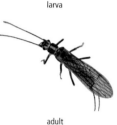

larva

larva

DESCRIPTION (LARVA): Body 10–50 mm long, elongate, slender. Hind wing pads pointing outward from sides of thorax; front wing pads do not point outward. No feathery gills on thorax. Tails as long as or longer than length of abdomen. Highly patterned; color pattern similar to common stoneflies (family Perlidae, page 113) but less striking. Fast crawler.

DESCRIPTION (ADULT): 13–15 mm; often yellowish or greenish coloration and greenish wings.

LOOK-ALIKES: Common stonefly larvae (family Perlidae) and green stonefly larvae (family Chloroperlidae).

NOTES: Patterned stoneflies are common statewide but less common in south-central Wisconsin. They are found in clean streams and along the shorelines of cold lakes, usually in flowing water under stones, woody debris, and leaf packs. They are intolerant of pollution. Though all patterned stoneflies are predators as larvae, adults of some species feed on pollen. They produce 1 generation per year, emerging from April to July.

adult

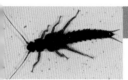

larva

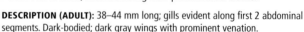

GIANT BLACK STONEFLIES (salmonflies)
Pteronarcyidae (1 genus, 2 species in Wisconsin)

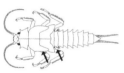

larva

DESCRIPTION (LARVA): Body large, 15–70 mm long (largest of Wisconsin stoneflies); stocky. Wing pads point outward from sides of thorax. Feathery gills behind leg bases on thorax and on first 2 abdominal segments. Dark brown or black, without striking color patterns. Slow crawler.

DESCRIPTION (ADULT): 38–44 mm long; gills evident along first 2 abdominal segments. Dark-bodied; dark gray wings with prominent venation.

LOOK-ALIKES: None.

NOTES: Giant black stoneflies are sporadically found in N. and S.W. Wisconsin and are uncommon to common, depending on locale. They inhabit streams and rivers, preferring cold, fast water in leaf packs and woody debris. They are intolerant of pollution, though they are occasionally found in waters that are slightly warmer than typical stonefly habitat. They are shredders, eating mainly detritus. In rivers of the western United States, they are an important food item for trout, although they are less important for trout in Wisconsin streams. They require 3 years to mature in Wisconsin, emerging from late April to July.

adult

TRUE BUGS (ORDER HEMIPTERA)

There are over 50,000 species of true bugs on earth. These animals are a relatively recent group of insects, having evolved only about 300,000 years ago. There are at least sixty-seven aquatic and twenty-six semiaquatic species in eleven families identified from Wisconsin. All aquatic and semiaquatic true bugs are in the suborder Heteroptera.

True bugs undergo incomplete metamorphosis, meaning that the larvae (often called nymphs) resemble adults. Eggs are laid underwater and hatch in late spring or early summer. After four or five molts (sheddings of the exoskeleton), nymphs become mature adults by fall. Adults hibernate during the winter in mud or plant debris, in shallow water or on shore. They mate in the spring, usually in the water. Members of this order usually produce one to two generations per year.

True bugs usually obtain oxygen from the atmosphere rather than the water, so they can tolerate environments with low dissolved oxygen levels. They tend to prefer quiet water.

Both nymphs and adults are characterized by an elongate beak or short cone (folded under the head when not feeding), three pairs of segmented legs, two claws at the end of at least some legs, and no gills. There are a few differences between nymphs and adults. Nymphs have less hardened bodies and lack wings but often have wing pads on the thorax. Adults usually have two pairs of wings: forewings with the basal half hardened and the outer half membranous; and shorter, membranous hind wings. When folded, the forewings rest on top, with the membranous ends overlapping. Families of Hemiptera can often be distinguished from each other by shape and length of antennae, legs, and beak.

The word *Hemiptera* is from the Greek *hemi* (half) and *ptera* (wings), referring to the basal half of the wings, which tends to be leathery, and the outer portion, which is membranous.

GIANT WATER BUGS
Belostomatidae (2 genera, 3 species in Wisconsin)

DESCRIPTION (NYMPH AND ADULT): Body large, 25–45 mm long, oval and flattened. Forelegs similar in shape to those of a praying mantis. Head triangular with large eyes. Rostrum (beak) tucked under head.

LOOK-ALIKES: None.

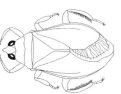

NOTES: Giant water bugs are common statewide. They are found in lakes, ponds, and marshes and occasionally in slower-moving waters of streams and rivers. They are voracious piercer predators of small fish, tadpoles, frogs, snails, and insects, grasping prey with their forelimbs, using their rostrum to inject a protein-dissolving enzyme into the body of the prey, and then sucking out the liquefied contents. They can inflict painful wounds on humans if carelessly handled. They breathe atmospheric oxygen and are tolerant of organic pollution and low dissolved oxygen environments. They usually produce 1–2 generations per year. Females of some species lay clusters of eggs on the backs of the adult males. Adults fly to deep rivers or lakes to overwinter along the shoreline.

adult feeding on a fish

WATER BOATMEN
Corixidae (9 genera, 49 species in Wisconsin)

DESCRIPTION (NYMPH AND ADULT): Body oval, flattened on top, 3–11 mm long. Antennae concealed below eyes and shorter than head. Eyes large. Beak short, broad, cone-shaped, resembling continuation of head. Foot (tarsus) of foreleg scoop-like, with fringe of hairs (setae). Usually dark gray, brown, or black with yellow striated markings on dorsal side. Eyes usually reddish. Very fast swimmer.

LOOK-ALIKES: Backswimmers (family Notonectidae)—no "scoops" on forelegs; hind legs much longer than others; often swim upside down.

NOTES: Water boatmen are common statewide. They are found in streams, rivers, lakes, ponds, and marshes in quiet, shallow, often vegetated water. Adults fly frequently. Depending on species, they are herbivores, detritivores, or piercers of plants and algae. They are tolerant to highly tolerant of organic pollution. They breathe underwater using an air bubble held under their wings. Water boatmen are an important food source for fish. They generally produce 1–2 generations per year. Adults fly to deep rivers or lakes to overwinter along the shoreline.

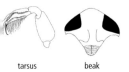

tarsus   beak

WATER STRIDERS
Gerridae (7 genera, 12 species in Wisconsin)

DESCRIPTION (NYMPH AND ADULT): Body elongate and slender, 3–18 mm long. Antennae longer than head. Beak cylindrical. Legs long, thin. First segment (femur) of posterior legs reaching well beyond tip of abdomen when extended straight back. Wings vary among species; some species wingless. Both larva and adult skate on water surface. Since their legs do not break through the surface film, dark oval shadows are visible where legs touch the water surface.

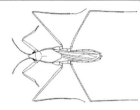

LOOK-ALIKES: Broad-shouldered water striders (family Veliidae)—femur much smaller, not reaching far beyond tip of abdomen.

NOTES: Water striders are very common statewide. They are found in ponds, lakes, and marshes, along the margins of streams, and in rivers, preferring quiet water. Both nymphs and adults inhabit the water surface. They are predators, eating mainly insects trapped in the surface film, using vibrations on the water surface to sense struggling prey.

WATER SCORPIONS
Nepidae (2 genera, 4 species in Wisconsin)

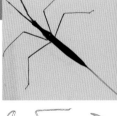

DESCRIPTION (NYMPH AND ADULT): Body very elongate, 15–45 mm, excluding respiratory tube. Legs long and narrow, with front legs "praying mantis–like." Antennae hidden below eyes. Respiratory tube extends "backward" (posteriorly) from abdomen; tube thin and nearly the length of combined thorax and abdomen. Body dark brown or black, leathery in appearance.

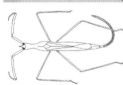

LOOK-ALIKES: Marsh treaders (family Hydrometridae)—antennae long; lack respiratory tube.

NOTES: Water scorpions are common statewide. They are found in lakes, ponds, and marshes and in undercut banks along streams and rivers, preferring quiet water. They are ambush predators, using their front legs to grasp prey, and are often seen clinging to vegetation, oriented head down, with the tip of the breathing tube extending above the water surface to breathe air.

TRUE FLIES (ORDER DIPTERA)

Over 150,000 species have been identified worldwide in the true fly insect order, which is thought to have existed for at least 250 million years. The oldest definitive true fly fossil is of a crane fly estimated to be 225 million years old. The true flies have the greatest ecological and biological diversity of any insect order and include such animals as deer flies and mosquitoes. Over one-third of true fly species are in the family Chironomidae (midges). True flies have a tremendous influence, both beneficial and detrimental to humans, such as midges that pollinate plants and mosquitoes that transmit diseases. There are at least 660 species of true flies in 19 families identified from Wisconsin.

True flies undergo complete metamorphosis, having an egg, larval, pupal, and winged adult stage. Among aquatic true flies, larvae and pupae are always aquatic, and adults are always terrestrial. True fly species produce a varying number of generations per year.

True fly larvae have the following characteristics: an elongate, fleshy body that is often divided into many segments; no wing pads or segmented legs; and *prolegs* (short, fleshy appendages) extending laterally from the thorax and/or abdomen. Adult true flies (like all adult insects) have the following characteristics: three pairs of legs, three body segments (head, thorax, and abdomen), two antennae, and *compound eyes* (made up of hundreds or thousands of lenses). Families can be distinguished from each other at the larval stage by head shape, the number and location of prolegs, and the shape of terminal appendages.

The word *Diptera* is from the Greek *di* (two) and *ptera* (wings). This refers to true fly adults having two wings, unlike most other winged insects, which typically have four wings.

WATER SNIPE FLIES
Athericidae (1 genus, 1 species in Wisconsin)

DESCRIPTION (LARVA): Body elongate, 10–18 mm long. Head pointy, reduced, withdrawn into thorax. Paired prolegs (fleshy, short legs) bearing hooks on underside of abdominal segments 1–7. A single proleg on the underside of abdominal segment 8; 2 tails (caudal appendages) fringed with hairs.

larva

larva

DESCRIPTION (ADULT): 8–12 mm long; abdomen stout with dark bands of color and pointed end; wings transparent with dark, mottled coloration.

LOOK-ALIKES: Crane fly larvae; deer and horse fly larvae (family Tabanidae)—both anterior and posterior ends are pointed. Also deer and horse fly adults (family Tabanidae)—much larger (15 and 25 mm in length, respectively); tip of abdomen rounded on both.

adult

NOTES: Water snipe flies are common statewide. They are found in stream riffles, often under rocks. Adult females have the interesting habit of laying egg masses on the undersides of tree limbs overhanging streams or on the undersides of bridges. The female remains with the eggs until she dies, attracting other females to the site to lay their eggs and die. The dead flies and the egg masses accumulate in grayish-colored clumps. When the eggs hatch, the larvae drop into the water. As predators, water snipe flies eat mainly other aquatic insects such as midge larvae or mayfly larvae. They are intolerant of pollution.

MIDGES
Chironomidae (103 genera in Wisconsin; species number unknown)

DESCRIPTION (LARVA): Body elongate, worm-like, 2–20 mm long. Head hardened (sclerotized), rounded, and distinct from thorax. Two pairs of ventral prolegs (fleshy, short legs): 1 pair at first segment of thorax (near head), the other on last segment of abdomen. Prolegs ending with series of small hooks. Body color green, tan, or pink to blood red.

larva

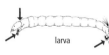

larva

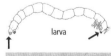

larva

DESCRIPTION (ADULT): Size varies greatly; 2–25 mm long. Delicate-looking, wings clear; abdomen extends past wing tips and is often upturned at posterior end. Male with fuzzy antennae.

LOOK-ALIKES: Net-spinning caddisfly larvae (family Hydropsychidae) and riffle beetle larvae. Mosquito adults (family Culicidae)—lack "fuzzy" antennae; have needle-shaped mouth (proboscis); and vary greatly in size, rarely larger than 15 mm in length.

adult

NOTES: Midges are very common statewide, often locally very abundant—thousands of larvae per square meter of stream or lake bed. They are found in virtually all water body types in widely varying habitats: in soft sediment and detritus, on rocks, and on vegetation. Larvae of many species are highly tolerant of organic pollution and low dissolved oxygen levels, especially species with high hemoglobin concentrations, which result in a red body color. Called "blood midges" or "bloodworms," their presence can indicate organic enrichment. Midges eat mainly fine organic matter and are either collector/gatherers, scrapers, collector/filterers, or predators, depending on species. They are often an important food source for other invertebrates, fish, and waterfowl. They produce varying numbers of generations per year. Adults can be seen "dancing" in large swarms above lawns, shrubs, or water, or swarming around lights near water. Midges are some of the earliest emergers in Wisconsin, seen flying above streams and riparian vegetation as early as February.

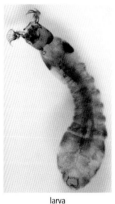

BLACK FLIES
Simuliidae (5 genera, 30 species in Wisconsin)

DESCRIPTION (LARVA): Small, 3–15 mm long; body bowling pin–shaped, with posterior third of body enlarged. Head hardened (sclerotized) and separate from thorax. Mouth usually with pair of "mouth brushes." Single proleg (fleshy, short leg) present on ventral side of anterior end of thorax. Abdomen terminating in ring of hooks resembling a suction disk, used to attach to substrate.

DESCRIPTION (ADULT): Similar to a housefly but much smaller (2–4 mm long), with slightly reduced head size relative to thorax or abdomen and wings strongly overlapped when not in flight.

LOOK-ALIKES: House fly adults (family Muscidae)—much larger, 8–12 mm; wings more widely spread (divergent) when not in flight.

larva

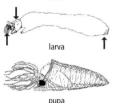

larva

pupa

NOTES: Black flies are common to very abundant statewide. They are found in streams and rivers in moderate to swift current attached to rocks, logs, and vegetation, often in large patches of thousands of animals in uniform rows. They attach to substrate and vegetation with their abdominal hooks and will drift downstream on silken threads up to 1 m long. They are intolerant to tolerant of pollution, depending upon the species; when abundant, they often indicate moderate organic pollution or very good water quality. They are collector/filterers, extending mouth brushes like a parasol to collect detritus, algae, and bacteria, and they often produce several generations per year. Adult females feed on the blood of birds or mammals and produce painful bites and welts. Black flies swarm in large numbers and are often a nuisance to humans, livestock, and wildlife.

larvae clinging to substrate

adult

larva

CRANE FLIES
Tipulidae (14 genera, 52 species in Wisconsin)

DESCRIPTION (LARVA): Body 3–60 mm long, cylindrical, stout, caterpillar-like, thick-skinned (some species called "leatherjackets"). Head reduced, withdrawn into thorax; anterior end of head pointy. Abdomen often with fleshy lumps or short hairs. Posterior segment of abdomen usually with 2 holes (spiracles), located on flattened area, surrounded by up to 7 pairs of irregularly shaped, finger-like projections. Body color white, tan, gray, or dark brown, often translucent.

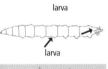

larva

DESCRIPTION (ADULT): Similar to a mosquito but much larger (25–75 mm in length). Abdomen slender; legs extremely long; lacking piercing mouth (proboscis).

LOOK-ALIKES: Water snipe fly larvae (family Athericidae). Also deer and horse fly larvae (family Tabanidae)—one-third the size of crane fly larvae; lacking finger-like projections on posterior segment. Mosquito adults (family Culicidae)—piercing mouth (proboscis) present; body 5–20 times smaller than crane fly adults.

adult

NOTES: Crane flies are common statewide. Larvae are found in streams, ponds, marshes, and lakes, in leaf packs, on algal mats, sand, and snags, and under rocks. Larvae are shredders, predators, or collector/gatherers, depending on species, eating leaves that fall into the water from streamside vegetation, other invertebrates, or detritus. They are intolerant to moderately tolerant of pollution and usually produce 1 generation per year. Larvae of shredder species break down leaves, making fine particulate organic matter available to other invertebrates. Adult crane flies are weak fliers and are active at night or in shady areas during daylight. They feed on nectar or not at all and live only for a few days.

NONINSECTS

For simplicity, we have grouped macroinvertebrates that are not insects together, even though they are actually quite a diverse collection of animals and are not closely related. One thing that these organisms do have in common is that they all lack physical features that define insects. In particular, they lack three pairs of segmented legs, three body segments, compound eyes, and wings or wing pads. Additionally, unlike insects, these animals do not go through metamorphosis—juveniles closely resemble adults.

Many of the following animals are difficult to identify to species, family, or even order level without a microscope and taxonomic keys. Thus, with the exception of snails and crustaceans, they are grouped at the higher taxonomic level of class. In contrast, mussels, clams, and crayfishes are often possible to identify to species. They are only mentioned briefly in this section but are described in detail in their own separate sections of this guide.

CRUSTACEANS (SUBPHYLUM CRUSTACEA)

The subphylum Crustacea includes three orders commonly found in Wisconsin streams: Amphipoda (scuds), Isopoda (aquatic sow bugs), and Decapoda (crayfishes and shrimps). Aquatic sow bugs and scuds are described here, while crayfishes are described in a separate section of this guide (page 133).

Crustaceans often have the following characteristics: an exoskeleton composed of calcium carbonate and chitin; a body divided into a *cephalothorax* (fused head and thorax) and abdomen (sometimes fused to the cephalothorax); two pairs of antennae; mouth parts that move laterally; five to eight segmented appendages on the cephalothorax or thorax, often with two branches or forks; and smaller, less conspicuous appendages on the abdomen.

The word *crustacean* is from the Latin *crusta* (hard covering).

SCUDS (sideswimmers, freshwater shrimps)
order Amphipoda, families Gammaridae and Hyalellidae

DESCRIPTION: Body 5–20 mm; flattened from side to side (laterally compressed). Back arched; body segments visible; tan or light pink. Two pairs of antennae of nearly equal length. 7 pairs of walking legs on thorax: first 2 pairs with large claw; remaining pairs with simpler, pointed claw. 6 pairs of small appendages on underside of abdomen, used for swimming. Swims rapidly on its side; very active.

LOOK-ALIKES: Aquatic sow bugs.

NOTES: Scuds are common to very abundant statewide, except in north-central Wisconsin waters that are low in calcium carbonate—calcium is needed for their exoskeleton development. They are found in springs, streams, ponds, and lakes, in cold, shallow waters, among aquatic plants or in silt and detritus. Species in the family Gammaridae are moderately intolerant of pollution; members of the Hyalellidae family are tolerant of pollution. Scuds are collector/gatherers, eating mainly detritus, and they are an important food source for other invertebrates and fish. They generally produce 1 generation per year. The word *Amphipoda* is from the Greek *amphi* (both kinds) and *pod* (foot), referring to amphipods' 2 different kinds of legs for walking and swimming.

CRAYFISHES (crawfishes, crawdads)
order Decapoda

DESCRIPTION: Body large: up to 15 cm, not including claws or antennae. Body cylindrical, divided into *cephalothorax* (fused head and thorax) and abdomen. Hardened shell protects head and thorax, with tip projecting between eyes. Two pairs of antennae, 1 much longer than the other. 5 pairs of segmented legs on thorax, first pair with large claws. Small appendages on underside of tail; tail with broad flipper at end.

LOOK-ALIKES: None in wadeable streams.

NOTES: Crayfishes are common statewide. There are 8 species of crayfishes in Wisconsin, 2 of which are invasive. For more information on crayfishes, see "Crayfishes," page 133.

AQUATIC SOW BUGS
order Isopoda, family Asellidae

DESCRIPTION: Body 4–18 mm long, flattened from top to bottom (dorsoventrally). Abdomen with segmented plates, shield-like at rear. Two pairs of antennae, 1 pair much longer than the other. 7 pairs of long walking legs, first pair with enlarged hinged claws. Each thorax segment with shelf-like projection from body on each side. 6 pairs of short appendages under abdomen, with last pair appearing like flat tails.

LOOK-ALIKES: Scuds.

NOTES: Aquatic sow bugs are common statewide. They are found in ditches, streams, ponds, wetlands, and lakes, in shallow water, among aquatic plants or in detritus or silt. They are tolerant to very tolerant of pollution and are indicators of nutrient enrichment and/or organic wastes. They are collector/gatherers, eating detritus. Although aquatic sow bugs are found throughout North America, there is relatively little published information on them in Wisconsin and elsewhere. To date, 4 species have been identified from this state. The word *Isopoda* is from the Greek *iso* (equal) and *pod* (foot), referring to the similarity of all appendages on the body; this is in contrast to scuds (Amphipoda), which have 2 types of legs.

EARTHWORMS (CLASS CLITELLATA, SUBCLASS OLIGOCHAETA)

AQUATIC EARTHWORMS
subclass Oligochaeta

DESCRIPTION: Body usually 1–30 mm long, sometimes to 100 mm; elongate, round in cross section. Ring-like segments (usually 40–200), most with short hairs. No suckers, head, or appendages present.

LOOK-ALIKES: Leeches.

NOTES: Aquatic earthworms are common statewide. They are found in streams, ponds, lakes, and marshes in soft substrates. They are collector/gatherers. They are tolerant of pollution and able to absorb dissolved oxygen through their skin. Abundant populations of aquatic earthworms may indicate severe organic pollution and/or low dissolved oxygen levels. The word *Oligochaeta* is from the Greek *olig* (long) and *chaitē* (hair), referring to earthworms' elongate bodies with small tufts of hair. The tufts of hair are retractable and used to gain traction when moving.

LEECHES (CLASS CLITELLATA, SUBCLASS HIRUDINEA)

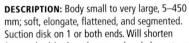

LEECHES
subclass Hirudinea

DESCRIPTION: Body small to very large, 5–450 mm; soft, elongate, flattened, and segmented. Suction disk on 1 or both ends. Will shorten (retract body) when threatened and elongate when swimming. No hairs present. Usually dark gray, brown, or black, often with colorful patterns of stripes, spots, and/or pigmented rings on top of body.

LOOK-ALIKES: Aquatic earthworms and planarians.

NOTES: Leeches are common statewide. They are found in marshes, lakes, and streams, usually in slow-flowing or stagnant water, attached to vegetation or other solid substrates. They are highly tolerant of pollution. The taxonomy, geographic distributions, and ecology of leeches are very poorly understood in Wisconsin, the United States, and worldwide. While commonly thought of as "bloodsuckers" feeding on the blood of fishes, turtles, salamanders, birds, and mammals, many leeches are not parasitic but rather are scavengers of carrion or are predators of aquatic worms, other leeches, insect larvae, and mollusks.

MITES AND SPIDERS (CLASS ARACHNIDA)

Within the phylum Arthropoda and subphylum Chelicerata is the class Arachnida, which contains horseshoe crabs, scorpions, spiders, ticks, and mites. Four pairs of walking legs distinguish arachnids from all other arthropods. Worldwide, about 100,000 terrestrial arachnids have been identified, and the true number is undoubtedly much greater. Freshwater arachnids (nearly all are mites) are a relatively small group of about 5,000 species, although the taxonomy of these animals is poorly understood, and thousands of additional species likely exist. The ancestors of spiders and mites first appeared in the fossil record about 445 million years ago.

While a variety of spider taxa live near water, the fishing spider (family Pisauridae) is described in this guide since it is often a conspicuous member of aquatic communities. Though not a truly aquatic animal, it dives underwater to hunt prey and avoid predators and can stay submerged for extended periods by relying on oxygen from air bubbles clinging to its body that function as an underwater breathing apparatus.

MITES AND SPIDERS (class Arachnida)

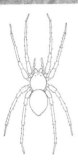

FISHING SPIDERS
order Araneae, family Pisauridae (1 genus, 3 species in Wisconsin)

DESCRIPTION: Body up to 50 mm across, including legs. Two body segments: cephalothorax (head and thorax fused together) and abdomen. 4 pairs of legs, 2 "fangs" (chelicerae), and 8 eyes. Typically brown or gray with patterned spots of white and black.

LOOK-ALIKES: Wolf spiders (family Lycosidae)—usually with hairier, more robust bodies.

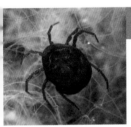

NOTES: Fishing spiders are fairly common to abundant statewide. They are found along the margins of streams, rivers, and lakes, as well as in marshes and wetlands. Many spiders in the Pisauridae family are active hunters that search for insects, worms, and other spiders; others are "ambush predators" that wait for prey to come to them. Fishing spiders are very common around ponds and streams, often hunting for prey on the water's surface, usually by holding on to vegetation at the water's edge. Like all spiders, they hatch from eggs, and their young look like miniature adults. They shed their exoskeletons as they grow. After laying eggs, a female fishing spider will wrap them in a silk egg sack. She will then carry the egg sack in her *chelicerae* (mouthparts) until the eggs are nearly ready to hatch. When hatching time arrives, the female will build a "nursery" in which the eggs can hatch. The nursery consists of a few leaves woven together with silk, forming a protective pocket into which the egg sack is placed.

WATER MITES
order Trombidiformes

DESCRIPTION: Body small, 0.5–3 mm in diameter, including legs; spherical, without obvious segmentation. Antennae absent. One pair of finger-like projections (pedipalps) in front of body. 4 pairs of segmented legs (3 pair on larvae, but adults usually collected). Often bright red, orange, black, or green. Fast swimmer.

LOOK-ALIKES: None.

pedipalps in front of body

NOTES: Water mites are abundant statewide. They are found in lakes, marshes, streams, and rivers, usually in vegetated areas. They are moderately tolerant of pollution. Water mites are parasites as larvae and predators as adults. They can occur in high densities (thousands per square meter of streambed) and are extremely diverse, inhabiting many different ecological niches and parasitizing a large number of aquatic hosts: insects, crayfish, mussels, and fish. Their influence on aquatic communities is poorly understood and vastly underestimated.

MUSSELS AND CLAMS (CLASS BIVALVIA)

Wisconsin has fifty-one species of native freshwater mussels; over forty species of native fingernail clams; and three exotic species of bivalves: the zebra mussel, the quagga mussel, and the Asian clam. Over half of Wisconsin's native species are listed as endangered, threatened, or of special concern. Mussels can often be identified to species; mussels and clams are covered in a separate section of this guide (page 141).

MUSSELS AND CLAMS
class Bivalvia

DESCRIPTION: Two shells, connected along 1 side by a hinge. Asymmetrical (mussels) or symmetrical (clams) when held flat in the palm. Fleshy foot and siphons protrude from the shell when undisturbed in the water.

LOOK-ALIKES: None in wadeable streams.

NOTES: As a group, mussels and clams are abundant statewide, found in lakes, temporary ponds, rivers, and streams. Native mussels have a complex and fascinating life cycle; for detailed information about mussels and clams, see "Mussels and Clams," page 141.

spike (*Elliptio dilatata*)

PLANARIANS (CLASS TURBELLARIA)

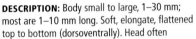

PLANARIANS
class Turbellaria

DESCRIPTION: Body small to large, 1–30 mm; most are 1–10 mm long. Soft, elongate, flattened top to bottom (dorsoventrally). Head often triangle-shaped. Two eyespots usually present. No segments. No appendages. Mouth and anus combined as 1 opening on underside at midbody. Top usually dark-colored or mottled; underside usually light gray without markings. Glide slowly along on benthic substrate or in sample containers.

LOOK-ALIKES: Leeches.

NOTES: Planarians are common statewide. They are found crawling on top of or under rocks in streams, rivers, lakes, ponds, and wetlands, usually in shallow, slow-moving water. A total of thirty-one species have been identified from Wisconsin, but both the ecology and taxonomy of these animals are poorly understood, and the true number of species that inhabit Wisconsin is likely much higher. Planarians are moderately tolerant of pollution and may indicate organic pollution when found in large numbers. They are predators, eating other invertebrates. Planarians have the interesting physiological ability to regenerate damaged body parts. Lab experiments have shown that if a planarian's head is cut in 2, the animal will grow 2 heads, and if the animal is cut in half down the middle, the 2 parts will grow into 2 separate animals. A planarian can reproduce asexually by fragmenting its body—each piece that breaks off eventually develops into a new animal. The word *Turbellaria* is from the Latin *turba* (stir), referring to the minute turbulence created when a planarian glides across substrate.

SNAILS (CLASS GASTROPODA)

The class Gastropoda contains snails, limpets, and slugs; snails and limpets are found in Wisconsin streams. There are an estimated seventy-four species of snails in ten families in Wisconsin.

Limpets have a single, somewhat flattened, conical shell that is 3–5 mm wide, and they attach to submerged rocks and plants with a fleshy foot. There is little published information on their ecology and distribution in Wisconsin, and they are not described in this guide. Snails and limpets are closely related to mussels and clams (class Bivalvia)—both are in the phylum Mollusca. Mussels and clams are described in detail in a separate section of this guide.

Snails hatch from a gelatinous mass of eggs laid in the water. Hatchlings resemble adult snails with fewer coils (adults generally have four or more coils). They do not undergo metamorphosis or shed their shells as they grow. Snails usually produce one generation per year.

Snails are important to stream ecosystems: they provide food for predators such as other invertebrates and scrape (and eat) algae off of plants, increasing plants' ability to photosynthesize. Some snail species are intermediate hosts of many parasites, including black spot (a trematode), which infects a number of Wisconsin fish species.

Snails can generally be divided into two groups: gill-breathing snails and lung-breathing snails. Gill-breathing snails use gills to obtain dissolved oxygen; lung-breathing snails use a sack-like structure to obtain atmospheric oxygen, usually visiting the water surface periodically to refill the "lung." Because gill-breathers rely on dissolved oxygen, their presence can indicate normal concentrations of dissolved oxygen in a water body. Lung-breathers are more tolerant of low dissolved oxygen levels, so it is helpful to discern gill-breathers from lung-breathers. Since gill-breathing snails are very difficult to tell apart, this guide groups together the families of gill-breathers that are found in Wisconsin.

Snail families can be distinguished from each other by the size and shape of the shell and the presence or absence of an operculum. The *operculum* is a hard plate that, for most families of gill-breathing snails, closes over the shell opening when the snail's body is withdrawn inside. (The exception is Pleuroceridae, a gill-breathing family without opercula.) Lung-breathing snails do not have opercula; when these snails are withdrawn into their shells, the shell opening remains uncovered. Additionally, since the operculum is attached to the snail's body, when a snail dies, its empty shell is left without an operculum.

To summarize: if a snail has an operculum, it is a gill-breather and may indicate normal concentrations of dissolved oxygen. However, if a shell does not have an operculum, it may be *either* a lung-breather, a gill-breathing member of Pleuroceridae, or the empty shell of a dead snail.

For gill-breathers, the operculum is carried on the top of the foot when the snail's body is partly extended outside of the shell; at such times, the operculum may be hard to see. To determine whether a live snail has an operculum, it may be easiest to pick the snail up out of the water, inducing it to completely withdraw into its shell.

Left- or right-handedness is another key to telling many snail families apart. A snail is said to be *left-handed* if, when the pointed end is oriented upward and the opening is facing the observer, the shell's opening is on the left side of the shell; *right-handed* snails have the opening on the right side when positioned this way. All individuals of the same species have the same "handedness," and all snails in Wisconsin's gill-breathing families are right-handed. However, one lung-breathing family (Lymnaeidae) is also right-handed, so this trait must be used along with other traits to determine whether a snail is gill-breathing or lung-breathing.

The word *Gastropoda* is from the Greek *gaster* (stomach) and *pod* (foot), referring to the fact that part of a snail's digestive system lies in the fleshy foot that projects from the shell.

SNAILS (class Gastropoda)

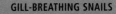

DESCRIPTION: Body small to large, protected by calcareous shell. "Right-handed"—shell opening is on the right when narrow end is pointed up and opening faces observer. When live snail withdraws into shell, shell opening may be sealed off by operculum (hard or slightly flexible lid-like structure) rather than being open. Sides of the shell often bulge out, making the shell appear swollen.

LOOK-ALIKES: Lymnaeid snails (family Lymnaeidae); also see New Zealand mudsnail below.

NOTES: Gill-breathing snails are common to abundant statewide. They are found in streams, rivers, lakes, and marshes, on rocks, vegetation, detritus, or sediment. They are intolerant to moderately tolerant of pollution. Live specimens of gill-breathing snails usually use opercula to close off their openings when removed from water. (The exception is family Pleuroceridae, which does not have opercula. Dead specimens also lose their opercula.) Gill-breathing snails are scrapers, eating mainly algae scraped from hard substrate. The invasive New Zealand mudsnail, one gill-breathing species in the family Hydrobiidae, is described in detail below.

INVASIVE—PROHIBITED

DESCRIPTION: Body very small (maximum shell length 5 mm), protected by a calcareous shell. "Right-handed"—shell opening is on the right when narrow end is pointed up and opening faces observer. Coiling with 5 or 6 whorls (a higher number than most native North American snail species). When live snail withdraws into shell, shell opening sealed off by operculum (hard or slightly flexible, lid-like structure) rather than being open. Shell relatively elongate compared to most other Wisconsin aquatic snail species. Shell color varies from dark or light brown to gray.

LOOK-ALIKES: Other gill-breathing snails, especially other species in the family Hydrobiidae.

NOTES: The New Zealand mudsnail is native to freshwater lakes and streams and estuaries in New Zealand and is well established in Australia and parts of Europe. Mudsnail populations consist mostly of asexually reproducing females, which bear live young that are genetic clones of the female. This snail was first discovered in the United States in the Snake River in Idaho in 1987 and in Lake Ontario in 1991, and has since spread widely in western rivers and streams and in the Great Lakes. The western clone's shell is elongate while the Great Lakes clone is broader, suggesting that these two populations arrived in the United States through different pathways. Inland populations of New Zealand mudsnails in Wisconsin were first documented in 2013 from invertebrate samples collected from Black Earth Creek in Dane County in 2012. The specimens were elongate, suggesting an introduction from western U.S. waters. Mudsnail densities can fluctuate widely and reach over 500,000 individuals per square meter of stream bottom. Mudsnails feed on plant matter, algae, and bacteria, and may compete with native aquatic insects, snails, and crustaceans for food and space. While eaten by fish, they can pass through the digestive tract of many species unharmed, providing no nutritional value to the fish. The mudsnail cannot withstand temperatures above 30° C (86° F) for extended periods of time, dry conditions, or freezing, although in cool, moist conditions it can withstand long periods out of water and can be spread by boaters, anglers, and others in contact with infested waters.

LYMNAEID SNAILS
family Lymnaeidae

DESCRIPTION: Body small to medium, protected by calcareous shell. "Right-handed"—shell opening is on the right when narrow end is pointed up and opening faces observer. Shell opening *never* sealed off by operculum (hard or slightly flexible lid-like structure); fleshy body visible. Shell surface appears smooth, with no visible grooves/striations. If present, striations only longitudinal (parallel to shell axis from tip to base, as in photo); striations never spiral (parallel to spiral of shell).

LOOK-ALIKES: Gill-breathing snails, especially family Pleuroceridae.

NOTES: Lymnaeid snails are common statewide. They are most often found in quiet water on firm substrate. They use an air sac to obtain atmospheric oxygen and are moderately to highly tolerant of pollution. They are scrapers, eating mainly algae scraped from hard substrate.

PHYSID SNAILS
family Physidae

DESCRIPTION: Body small, protected by calcareous shell. "Left-handed"—shell opening is on the left when narrow end is pointed up and opening faces observer. Shell opening *never* sealed off by operculum (hard or slightly flexible lid-like structure); fleshy body visible. Sides of the shell bulge out; shell appears swollen.

LOOK-ALIKES: None.

NOTES: Physid snails are common to abundant statewide. They are found in quiet or flowing water, most often on firm substrate. They use an air sac to obtain atmospheric oxygen and are moderately to highly tolerant of pollution. They are scrapers, eating mainly algae scraped from hard substrate.

PLANORBID SNAILS
family Planorbidae

DESCRIPTION: Body small, protected by calcareous shell. Shell coiled flat, not extended into a rising spiral. Shell opening *never* sealed off by operculum (hard or slightly flexible lid-like structure).

LOOK-ALIKES: None.

NOTES: Planorbid snails are common statewide. They are found in quiet or flowing water, most often on soft substrate. They are moderately to highly tolerant of pollution, and they are scrapers, eating mainly algae scraped from hard substrate.

SPONGES (PHYLUM PORIFERA)

FRESHWATER SPONGES
family Spongillidae

DESCRIPTION: Small masses; smooth, textured, or wavy, sometimes with finger-like projections. Delicate to very firm or gritty texture (never slimy or filmy). Structure composed of tiny needle-like structures (spicules), which can be used to distinguish species but can only be seen with a microscope. Reproductive internal buds (gemmules) resemble tan poppy seeds, appearing in late summer or fall. Color usually green or yellowish tan; may also be beige or brown.

LOOK ALIKES: Aquatic mosses (phylum Bryophyta)—with distinctive branching; filamentous algae (phylum Chlorophyta)—grows long, hair-like strands.

NOTES: Freshwater sponges are found sporadically statewide, and relatively little is known about them. They often resemble plants, mosses, or algae but are actually multicellular animals. They are found in lakes, rivers, streams, and bogs, in shallow water, attached to rocks, logs, and vegetation. Some species are sensitive to pollution and may indicate good water quality, but as a group this trait is not consistent. If encountered, they should not be removed from the water.

Crayfishes

Crayfishes are among the most visible creatures in many Wisconsin streams and can be delightful to catch and identify. They are usually the largest invertebrates in streams.

Crayfishes are found in the subphylum Crustacea and the order Decapoda, which also includes shrimps. Wisconsin's only freshwater shrimp, the Mississippi grass shrimp (*Palaemonetes kadiakensis*; special concern), is very rarely encountered and only in deep, lake-like stretches of streams. For that reason, only crayfishes are described in this book.

There are eight species of crayfishes found in Wisconsin, all of which belong to the family Cambaridae. Two species are invasive: rusty crayfish (*Orconectes rusticus*) and red swamp crayfish (*Procambarus clarkii*). The rusty crayfish is widespread and established in Wisconsin, while the red swamp crayfish had only been found in three artificial stormwater ponds as of 2012 and should be reported if found (see page 19). All of the other six crayfish species are native.

Crayfish are sometimes referred to as crawfish or crawdads. The word *crayfish* is from the Old High German *krebiz* (crab) and *fish*. The word *Decapoda* is from the Greek *deka* (ten) and *pod* (foot), referring to the number of walking legs on members of this order.

Basic Identification

Crayfish identification can be very difficult in the field. Identification is often only possible using mature breeding male specimens (see below); very young or nonbreeding specimens may not exhibit distinct markings. Hybridization of the four *Orconectes* species may also occur and further complicate identification. Certain traits such as body color also vary within species.

Although identification is difficult, it is important to note that there are only three crayfish species commonly found throughout the state: the northern clearwater, virile, and rusty crayfishes. These three species often constitute more than 90 percent of specimen collections, while all other species are either uncommon or only found in localized areas.

We have made an effort to keep terminology simple, but there are still a few terms that are helpful when describing crayfish anatomy. Like many other invertebrates, crayfish are divided into three main body segments: the head, thorax ("middle"), and abdomen ("tail"). However, the head and thorax of a crayfish are fused into a *cephalothorax*, which is protected on the top (dorsal) side by a hardened shell called a *carapace*. The *rostrum* is the front tip of the carapace between the eyes. The *areola* is the space between the pair of seams on the carapace that curve like an hourglass. (In some species this space is nonexistent because the lines touch.) See the diagram on page 134 for an illustration of crayfish terms.

Crayfish generally have the following characteristics: two pairs of antennae, one much longer than the other; a cylindrical body divided into a cephalothorax and tail (abdomen); a carapace with a rostrum; five pairs of segmented legs on the thorax, first pair with large claws; small appendages (pleopods) on the underside of the tail; and a broad flipper (telson and uropods) at the end of the tail.

Key features used to tell crayfishes apart are body marking *pattern* (not color, which varies), rostrum, areola, claws, and first pleopods. One distinguishing trait is the presence or absence of a central ridge running front to back on the rostrum. Note that this ridge is small and can often best be detected by running a fine point (e.g., a pencil tip or a knife) gently along the center of the rostrum. Likewise, the presence or absence of *marginal spines* on the sides of the rostrum can also be distinct from species to species.

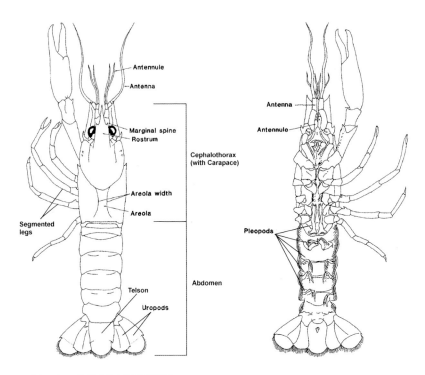

crayfish anatomy: dorsal (*left*) and ventral (*right*)

Feeding and Burrowing

Crayfish are omnivorous collector/gatherers, often eating mainly detritus, as well as vegetation, invertebrates, fish eggs, and fish.

In Wisconsin all crayfishes at least occasionally burrow in streambanks or in nearby marshes and fields. Burrowing has many important purposes for crayfish, including egg laying, protection from predation, moving below the frost line during freezing, and moving to the water table during dry periods. Crayfish burrows also provide refuge for other invertebrates and amphibians.

One additional purpose of burrows is to help crayfish tolerate low dissolved oxygen levels. All crayfishes use gills, located on the sides of the cephalothorax, to "breathe" oxygen dissolved in water. (Crayfish can live outside of water for long periods as long as they keep their gills covered in a film of moisture.) Burrows help maximize air flow to the water/air interface, which increases the dissolved oxygen concentration of the water inside the burrow.

Different crayfishes have different burrowing habits. The devil and prairie crayfishes are *primary burrowers*, spending almost their entire lives underground and not in surface water. They usually only leave to feed at night, on rainy days, or after a spring egg hatch. The calico crayfish is a *secondary burrower*, living mainly in the surface water but also spending significant amounts of time in burrows. The other Wisconsin species are *tertiary burrowers*, only retreating to burrows during events such as winter freezing or drought or to lay eggs.

It generally is not possible to distinguish crayfish species solely on burrow appearance. Burrow appearance can vary by substrate type, and different species of crayfishes have been observed sharing a single burrow. However, primary burrowers (the devil and prairie crayfishes) tend to construct the most complex burrows. A burrow that has multiple entrances and structures such as "chimneys" and/or that is located some distance from surface water likely indicates the presence of one of these two primary burrowers.

Life Cycle and Reproduction

Wisconsin crayfishes often mate in late summer to winter. After mating, the female lays eggs in late fall to spring, attaching the eggs to her abdomen with a sticky substance. For most species, the eggs hatch in spring between March and June. Young crayfish continue to cling to their mother's abdomen until they molt (shed their skin) two or three times. Only a small percentage survive long enough to breed; for instance, only 3 percent of newly hatched rusty crayfish reach sexual maturity.

For species that spend most of their time in burrows, mating takes place within the burrow. After juveniles detach and move independently, adult females leave the burrows. Juveniles leave the burrows by early summer.

Surviving males molt into a special breeding form known as the Form I male. Form I males have distinct features useful for species identification (see below). After the mating season, males molt back to a juvenile body form while continuing to increase in size (as with all moltings). A male with this postmating juvenile form is known as a Form II male. It may be adult-sized, but its features are less distinct and not as useful for species identification.

Some crayfishes have been documented to live at least two breeding seasons before dying, although documentation of the longevity of crayfishes is scarce.

How to Tell if a Crayfish is a Form I (Breeding) Male

The first pleopods of Form I males are the most reliable trait for distinguishing crayfish species from each other. Recall that the *pleopods* are the small appendages on the underside of the abdomen (*not* the larger, more conspicuous legs on the anterior half of the body). The *first* pleopods are the pair closest to the front of the body.

Unfortunately, the pleopods are small, and to be used for identification they must be observed with a hand lens and often detached from the body. For this reason, the species descriptions in the crayfish section focus on other traits such as color patterns, areola, and rostrum. However, in case it is possible for you to examine the first pleopods to help with species identification, we include the following description of how to tell whether your crayfish is a Form I male (page 136), and in each species description we include an illustration of the Form I male first pleopods.

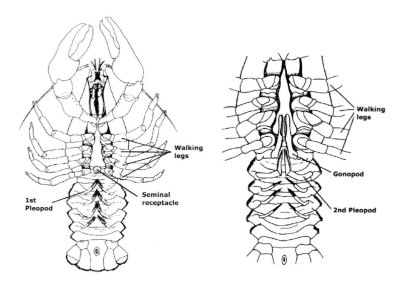

female (*left*) vs. Form I male (*right*)

On females, the first pleopods are translucent and inconspicuous compared with the other pleopods, and a reproductive depression called a *seminal receptacle* is visible between the final pair of walking legs (see diagram on page 135). If a specimen fits this description, it is a female. On males, the first pleopods are more conspicuous and are called *gonopods*. The gonopods are oriented differently from the other pleopods: they point forward and are located on the underside of the cephalothorax.

In males of the Form I life stage, the gonopods are used for reproduction and tend to be long with ends that are yellow to brown, hardened (sclerotized), and pointed. On juvenile or Form II males, the gonopods tend to be shorter and rigid, though still conspicuous compared to the first pleopods of females. The ends of Form II gonopods are never pointed. The hardness and color of the gonopod ends are hard to see on some crayfishes, though, particularly the prairie and white river crayfishes, which both have hairs (setae) covering the ends of their gonopods.

DEVIL CRAYFISH
Cambarus diogenes

DESCRIPTION: Rostrum (tip between eyes) with no central ridge or marginal spines. Hourglass seams on back joined (areola not present). Claws toothed; hinged "finger" of large claw with wide notch near base. Tail flattened.

LOOK-ALIKES: Prairie and white river crayfishes.

NOTES: The devil crayfish is found statewide and is fairly common except in N.E. Wisconsin. It inhabits streams, ditches, marshes, and ponds, preferring quiet water flowing over fine substrate. It is tolerant of varied conditions, including low dissolved oxygen levels. A primary burrower, it is usually found in its burrows, not in surface water. Burrows may be complex and covered with "chimneys."

Form I
male
gonopod

CALICO CRAYFISH
Orconectes immunis

DESCRIPTION: Rostrum (tip between eyes) broad, with no central ridge or marginal spines. Hourglass seams on back narrowly spaced at center, widely spaced ahead and behind. Hinged "finger" of large claw with notch and tuft of fibers near base. Mottling on body. Claws with orange tips.

LOOK-ALIKES: Northern clearwater, rusty, and virile crayfishes.

NOTES: In Wisconsin the calico crayfish is found sporadically, mainly in the southeast, and is uncommon. It inhabits streams, rivers, ponds, and lakes, preferring quiet, vegetated water flowing over muddy substrate. It is tolerant of high water temperatures and low dissolved oxygen levels. It is outcompeted by the virile crayfish when the two are found in the same water body. The calico crayfish is a secondary burrower, living mainly in surface water but also spending a significant amount of time in burrows, especially during drought.

fibers at claw hinge

Form I
male
gonopod

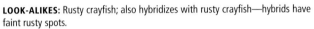

NORTHERN CLEARWATER CRAYFISH
Orconectes propinquus

SPECIAL CONCERN

DESCRIPTION: Body small. Rostrum (tip between eyes) narrow, with straight edges and raised ridge in center (running front to back; variable) and with distinct marginal spines. Hourglass seams on back widely spaced. Body color brown or gray (gray in clear water). Broad, dark band along top of tail; tail with light sides. Claw tips orange with black bands (bands sometimes faint).

LOOK-ALIKES: Rusty crayfish; also hybridizes with rusty crayfish—hybrids have faint rusty spots.

NOTES: The northern clearwater crayfish is found statewide and is abundant in S. and N.E. Wisconsin. It inhabits lakes and streams in clear to turbid or stained water. It prefers gravelly or rocky substrate and/or abundant vegetation, hiding under rocks or in vegetation mats. This species is moderately tolerant of high temperatures and is an opportunistic scavenger. It lives almost entirely in the surface water and does not usually burrow. Its population appears to be declining in recent years, possibly due to competition with the invasive rusty crayfish, although data is scarce.

Form I
male
gonopod

RUSTY CRAYFISH
Orconectes rusticus

INVASIVE—RESTRICTED

DESCRIPTION: Rostrum (tip between eyes) with edges curving inward (concave) or sometimes straight; with no central ridge and with distinct marginal spines. Hourglass seams on back narrowly spaced. Dark spots on body. Often, but not always, with rusty spot on each side, sometimes absent or faint. Front dorsal edges of abdominal (tail) segments with rusty bands. Claws large, tips orange with black band.

LOOK-ALIKES: Northern clearwater and virile crayfishes; hybridizes with both, but rusty spots much fainter in hybrids.

NOTES: The rusty crayfish is very common statewide. It inhabits streams and lakes and is found in varied habitats, often with rocks, logs, or vegetation. The rusty crayfish is tolerant of pollution and large temperature changes and is a voracious herbivore. It can spread quickly and remove vegetation. It sometimes burrows along banks, but it lives mainly in the surface water. Although it is listed as a restricted species by the Wisconsin DNR, there are some exceptions for this species. For example, as of 2012 it may be used as live bait on the Mississippi River (or as dead bait on other waters); and it may be possessed, transported, or transferred without a permit as long as it is not released. These exceptions may be subject to change in subsequent years.

Form I
male
gonopod

CRAYFISHES

VIRILE CRAYFISH
Orconectes virilis

DESCRIPTION: Body large. Rostrum (tip between eyes) with straight edges, with no central ridge, and with distinct marginal spines. Hourglass seams on back narrowly spaced but never touching. Abdomen with pairs of brown (darkened) spots. Claws often bluish, with white, wart-like bumps and thin gap when closed. Claw tips orange without black band (sometimes orange tips very small). Tail with 4 rows of angular spots running front to back.

LOOK-ALIKES: Northern clearwater, prairie, rusty, and white river crayfishes; also hybridizes with rusty crayfish—hybrids have faint rusty spots.

NOTES: The virile crayfish is very common statewide. It inhabits lakes, rivers, and streams and is found in varied habitats, often under rocks or in vegetation. It is tolerant of pollution and high water temperatures and is an aggressive scavenger. It is outcompeted by the nonnative rusty crayfish when the 2 are found in the same water body. It lives mainly in the surface water but sometimes burrows along banks.

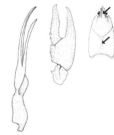

Form I
male
gonopod

WHITE RIVER CRAYFISH
Procambarus acutus

SPECIAL CONCERN

DESCRIPTION: Rostrum (tip between eyes) wedge-shaped, with long, narrow taper and only small indents at tip, and no marginal spines. Hourglass seams on back narrowly spaced. Very dark bumps on claws; many small bumps on body. Black band along top of tail.

LOOK-ALIKES: Red swamp crayfish.

NOTES: In Wisconsin the white river crayfish is sporadically distributed, mainly in the southeast, and is uncommon. It inhabits streams, rivers, ditches, ponds, and lakes. It prefers quiet, moderately turbid, vegetated water flowing over soft substrate but is tolerant of varied conditions. This species lives mainly in the surface water but enters burrows over winter or during drought.

Form I
male
gonopod

139

CRAYFISHES

RED SWAMP CRAYFISH
Procambarus clarkii

INVASIVE—PROHIBITED

DESCRIPTION: Rostrum (tip between eyes) wedge-shaped, with only small indents near tip. Hourglass seams on back touching in center. Bright red bumps on claws; many small bumps on body. Body color red (rarely blue). Tail with black stripe.

Form I
male
gonopod

LOOK-ALIKES: White river crayfish.

NOTES: As of 2012 the red swamp crayfish has been found in 3 artificial ponds in S.E. Wisconsin; it is rare and was likely eradicated from 2 of the 3 ponds. It inhabits streams, rivers, ponds, lakes, and marshes, preferring quiet water; it is tolerant of water level fluctuations. It lives mainly in the surface water but sometimes burrows along banks and may move over land between water bodies. The red swamp crayfish is a voracious omnivore: it removes vegetation, consumes fish and amphibian eggs, creates turbid water, and outcompetes native crayfishes. It is the most widely consumed and introduced crayfish in the world and is commonly sold for food or aquariums.

PRAIRIE CRAYFISH
Procambarus gracilis

SPECIAL CONCERN

DESCRIPTION: Rostrum (tip between eyes) blunt and broad, without marginal spines. Hourglass seams on back narrowly spaced or joined. Body color often reddish brown.

LOOK-ALIKES: Devil and virile crayfishes.

NOTES: The prairie crayfish is rare and in Wisconsin is found only in the southeastern part of the state. It inhabits streams, ditches, marshes, fields, and ponds, preferring quiet water. A primary burrower, this crayfish only enters surface water during fall copulation; after spring egg hatch; or at night to forage during warm, moist conditions. Burrows may be complex and covered with "chimneys."

Form I
male
gonopod

140

Mussels and Clams

Mussels and clams are mollusks (phylum Mollusca), related to snails and slugs. They are in the class Bivalvia, a name indicating that they have two shells (or *valves*) that fit together. Wisconsin has fifty species of native freshwater mussels that inhabit many of our lakes, rivers, and streams; over forty species of native fingernail clams; and three exotic species of bivalves: the zebra mussel, the quagga mussel, and the Asian clam. The invasive Asian clam was brought over from Southeast Asia and released for food. The invasive quagga and zebra mussels came to North America in the ballast water of ships and are spread primarily by anglers and recreational boaters.

The words *mussel* and *clam* are often used interchangeably. In general, clams can be distinguished from mussels by their symmetry: clam shells are symmetrical, and mussels are asymmetrical when viewing them broadside (i.e., holding them flat in the palm of the hand).

Different mussel and clam species can be hard to tell apart, and it helps to know several terms to describe their shells; see page 144 for a diagram of mussel shell anatomy. The outside of the shell is covered in a thin layer called the *periostracum*, which can vary in color and may have patterns. The inside of the shell is called the *nacre*, which is the typical "mother of pearl" color but which can also be purple, lavender, orange, blue, or green in addition to being white or "pearly." The two shells are connected by a hinge near the *umbo*, the raised part of the shell where the shell first formed (sometimes called the *beak*).

Though mussels and clams may look simple, they have complex internal anatomy. Terms like *dorsal*, *ventral*, *anterior*, and *posterior* apply to mussels and clams just as they apply to other animals. The *dorsal* part of the shell is the hinged side, and the *ventral* side is the side where the shell opens. In mussels, anterior and posterior can be determined by holding the mussel in the palm of the hand. The *anterior* part is the shorter end as measured from the beak; the *posterior* part is the longer end. Clams similarly have an anterior and posterior, but because of their symmetry and small size these can be difficult to determine.

FRESHWATER MUSSELS

Key Traits

Important shell features for identification of mussels include color, size, and overall shape, as well as features such as bumps, ridges, wings, and rays or patterns on the shell. Typical shapes include elongate, triangular, round, and square; the shell shape diagram (page 142) illustrates these and other mussel shapes. When viewed from the side, mussels may be *compressed* or *inflated*, as in the shell width diagram. Some species also have different shell shapes according to their gender.

Because mussels can look alike to the untrained eye, we have divided this section into three subsections based mainly on overall appearance. The three categories are *bumpy or ridged (not smooth)*, *smooth*, and *invasive*. Wisconsin's invasive mussels are distinctively small and prolific and are easy to tell apart from native mussels. Smooth mussels have been further divided into *elongate or oval* and *triangular, round, or winged*. None of these are taxonomic differences, but mussels are arranged alphabetically by scientific name within each category.

Internal anatomy is not useful for identification of live mussels because they do not open willingly, and we don't want to kill them to identify them. We identify live mussels by external characteristics,

SHELL SHAPE

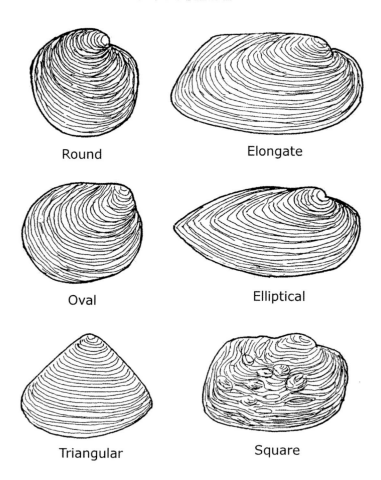

Round

Elongate

Oval

Elliptical

Triangular

Square

but when dead shells are available, we can use both internal and external characteristics. Internally, some mussel species can be distinguished by differences in their "teeth," which are not true teeth but are internal structures designed to help the two shells hinge together (not to help with eating). Mussels have two sets of teeth, both located inside the shell near the dorsal edge. *Lateral teeth* are elongated ridges located along the hinge; *pseudocardinal teeth* are triangular, serrated, and located anterior to the hinge. The *beak cavity* is another useful internal feature. It is the depression on the inside of the umbo, and different species' beak cavities vary from shallow to deep. Some mussels have highly reduced teeth, and some have no teeth at all, depending on the species. The mussel shell anatomy diagram on page 144 illustrates external and internal shell features that may be referenced in this guide.

Descriptions in this guide are based solely on external features for live mussels and on internal and external shell features for the empty shells of dead mussels.

Life Cycle and Biology

Freshwater mussels can be incredibly long-lived, often living for many decades. For most of their lives, they lead solitary lives on the bottoms of rivers and streams, taking in oxygen and filtering algae and

SHELL WIDTH

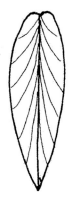 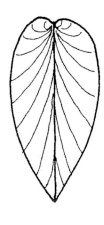 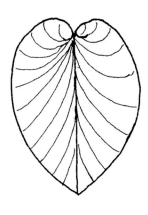

COMPRESSED   NORMAL   INFLATED

other organic material from the water for food through their *incurrent siphon* and releasing their waste through their *excurrent siphon*. They are generally sedentary but can move when necessary using their large muscular "foot," similar to that of a snail.

Freshwater mussels have an amazingly complex and fascinating life history (see diagram on page 145). The male releases sperm into the water, where it is siphoned in by the female (1); the eggs are fertilized within the gills of the female, and fertilized eggs are called *glochidia*. Glochidia have two shells but contain only one muscle for snapping shut and only rudimentary internal organs. Glochidia need to attach to a host species to develop fully and disperse. The host is usually a fish, though one species of mussel uses the mudpuppy, and some hosts are not known. Many mussels use a group of closely related fish species as hosts, while other mussels are specific to one host fish species.

Mussel species have developed extraordinary measures to ensure they complete this critical link to attract and attach to their host (2). Species with a predatory fish host have developed lures that look remarkably like minnows, crayfish, or other prey items. When the fish comes to investigate, the female mussel expels her glochidia onto the fish, where they attach to the gills. Other species release their glochidia in an egg mass called a *conglutinate*. Conglutinates vary in size and shape and look like worms or other food items preferred by nonpredatory species. Some conglutinates are so intricate that they look like the larvae of insects, complete with eyespots and the ability to attach to rocks. One mussel species in Wisconsin, the snuffbox, actually grabs the head of its host fish. No matter what strategy mussels use, it ensures that they get their young on the right host.

The glochidia obtain nutrients from the host as well as a free ride, but they are generally harmless. During the infestation on the host (3), which usually lasts only a few weeks but can take up to a few months, the immature mussels grow very little but develop all their internal organs. When the young mussel is ready, it drops off the fish as a juvenile and settles in the sediment, where it may stay for the next half of a century (4).

Ecological Notes

Freshwater mussels are one of the most endangered groups of animals in North America and globally; in North America over 70 percent are either rare or extirpated. In Wisconsin over half of our mussel species are listed as either endangered, threatened, or of special concern. Common culprits for mussel declines include habitat alteration, water quality degradation, and invasive species. Mussel die-offs occur because of disease, nutrient loading, pesticides, heavy metals, and siltation. Dams create

Mussel Shell Anatomy

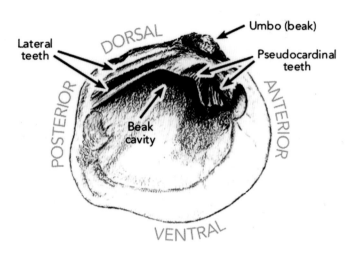

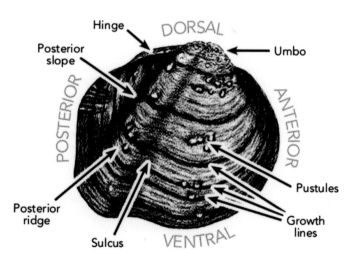

interior (*top*) and exterior (*bottom*) anatomy of mussel shells

silt-laden impoundments, which suffocate mussels and cause habitat alteration from lack of flow, cold temperatures, and loss of host species that are essential for mussel reproduction.

Invasive species are increasingly becoming a problem for native mussels. Zebra and quagga mussels not only outcompete native mussels but also often grow on top of them, smothering them and causing starvation. Invasive black carp (*Mylopharyngodon piceus*; prohibited and not yet present in Wisconsin as of 2012) could also prove to be devastating to native mussel populations because they are voracious *molluscavores* (mollusk eaters).

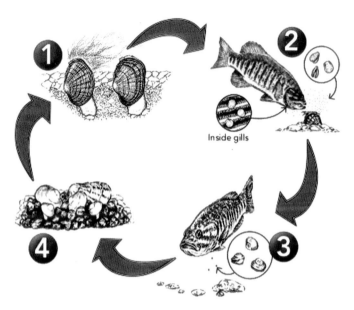

Inside gills

life cycle of a mussel

Although live mussels were historically harvested commercially, it is currently illegal to take them from Wisconsin waters. However, empty mussel shells may be collected, except for shells of threatened or endangered species. Also, no shell material may be collected from the Saint Croix and Namekagon Rivers, according to National Park Service regulations. Live mussels can be examined but should be returned to the water.

BUMPY OR RIDGED MUSSELS (Not Smooth)

BUMPY OR RIDGED (NOT SMOOTH) MUSSELS

The following mussels have some sort of external sculpture such as bumps or ridges—they are not smooth.

THREERIDGE
Amblema plicata

DESCRIPTION: Shell round to elongate, thick; shell thickness and size vary widely by habitat. Anterior end rounded; posterior end rounded or bluntly pointed. Dorsal margin straight; ventral margin straight or curved. 3 or more roughly parallel ridges on posterior half; anterior smooth. Outer shell (periostracum) dark green, brown, or black and lighter when younger. Lateral and pseudocardinal teeth heavy. Inner shell white. Length up to 18 cm.

LOOK-ALIKES: Rock pocketbook and washboard.

NOTES: The threeridge is found statewide in small to large rivers or impoundments and is often found in mud, sand, or gravel. Its host fishes include basses, catfishes, gars, perches, sauger (*Sander canadensis*), and sunfishes.

ROCK POCKETBOOK
Arcidens confragosus

THREATENED

DESCRIPTION: Oval to square, moderately inflated, heavily sculpted. Two rows of knobs extend from umbo and become ridges and irregular folds closer to shell margin. Outer shell (periostracum) green to dark brown. Lateral teeth poorly developed; pseudocardinal teeth present. Beak cavity moderately deep. Inner shell white. Length up to 15 cm.

LOOK-ALIKES: Threeridge and washboard.

NOTES: The rock pocketbook is found in the Mississippi, Saint Croix, and Wisconsin Rivers in mud or sand substrate. Its host fishes are American eel (*Anguilla rostrata*), crappies, freshwater drum, gizzard shad (*Dorosoma cepedianum*), and rock bass.

PURPLE WARTYBACK
Cyclonaias tuberculata

ENDANGERED

DESCRIPTION: Shell round, thick, covered with tubercles except anterior quarter. Tubercles present on wing extending out from umbo. Outer shell (periostracum) brown. Pseudocardinal and lateral teeth heavy. Beak cavity very deep. Inner shell purple or white with purple edge. Length up to 13 cm.

LOOK-ALIKES: Mapleleaf, pimpleback, and winged mapleleaf.

NOTES: The purple wartyback is found in the Chippewa, Flambeau, Mississippi, Pine, Rock, and Saint Croix Rivers and their tributaries. It prefers large rivers with swift currents and rocky substrate. Its host fishes are bullheads, channel catfish, and flathead catfish (*Pylodictis olivaris*).

FLUTED-SHELL
Lasmigona costata

DESCRIPTION: Elongate, moderately thick, compressed. Anterior end rounded; posterior slope with numerous small ridges or ruffles extending along slope to edge of shell. Outer shell (periostracum) yellow to green, with green rays when young and brown when older. Lateral teeth poorly developed, and pseudocardinal teeth present. Beak cavity shallow. Inner shell white, and can be salmon-colored in the beak cavity. Length up to 13 cm.

LOOK-ALIKES: Creek heelsplitter.

NOTES: The fluted-shell is found statewide in small streams to large rivers with soft or coarse substrate. It has many species of host fishes, including common carp.

WASHBOARD
Megalonaias nervosa

SPECIAL CONCERN

DESCRIPTION: Large, heavy, elongate or squarish. Anterior end rounded; posterior somewhat truncate (shortened). Heavily sculpted with ridges and folds that extend onto the posterior wing. Outer shell (periostracum) dark brown or black, lighter in juveniles. Pseudocardinal and lateral teeth well developed. Inner shell white. Length up to 25 cm.

LOOK-ALIKES: Rock pocketbook and threeridge.

NOTES: The washboard is found in the Mississippi and Saint Croix Rivers. It prefers large rivers with moderate current and mud substrate. Its host fishes are American eel (*Anguilla rostrata*), basses, bowfin, catfishes, gizzard shad (*Dorosoma cepedianum*), and sunfishes.

147

THREEHORN WARTYBACK
Obliquaria reflexa

DESCRIPTION: Somewhat triangular, thick, with a single row of large knobs that radiate down the center of the shell from the umbo to the margin. Knobs offset when viewed from the side. Outer shell (periostracum) yellow, green, or brown, sometimes with faint rays. Teeth well developed. Inner shell white or pearly. Length up to 8 cm.

LOOK-ALIKES: Pimpleback, sheepnose, and wartyback.

NOTES: The threehorn wartyback is found in the Chippewa, Embarrass, Mississippi, Saint Croix, Wisconsin, and Wolf Rivers and their tributaries. It prefers large rivers and may be found in soft or coarse substrate. Its host fishes are common shiner and longnose dace.

SHEEPNOSE (bullhead)
Plethobasus cyphyus

STATE AND FEDERALLY ENDANGERED

DESCRIPTION: Oblong to somewhat triangular, thick, slightly inflated. Anterior end rounded; posterior end bluntly pointed. A row of small broad knobs extends intermittently from umbo to shell margin along center of shell; knobs can be subtle. Outer shell (periostracum) yellow to dark brown, lighter when younger. Teeth well developed. Beak cavity shallow. Inner shell white. Length up to 10 cm.

LOOK-ALIKES: Hickorynut, round pigtoe, threehorn wartyback, and Wabash pigtoe.

NOTES: The sheepnose is found in the Chippewa, Flambeau, Mississippi, and Wisconsin Rivers in stable sand or gravel substrate. Its host fish is the sauger (*Sander canadensis*).

WINGED MAPLELEAF
Quadrula fragosa

STATE AND FEDERALLY ENDANGERED

DESCRIPTION: Squarish, thick, and somewhat inflated. Anterior end rounded; posterior end square or truncate (shortened). Two rows of bumps (pustules) separated by a shallow groove (sulcus) extend from umbo to shell margin, with pustules extending along ridges to prominent posterior wing. Teeth well developed. Beak cavity very deep. Inner shell white. Length up to 10 cm.

LOOK-ALIKES: Mapleleaf, monkeyface, and purple wartyback.

NOTES: The winged mapleleaf is found in the Saint Croix River and was historically also found in the Wisconsin River. It prefers a substrate of stable sand or mixed sand and gravel. Its host fishes are blue catfish (*Ictalurus furcatus*) and channel catfish.

MONKEYFACE
Quadrula metanevra

THREATENED

DESCRIPTION: Rounded or squarish; thick shell, with large pustulous knobs along posterior ridge; bumps (pustules) and small ridges radiating out from knobs. Posterior margin of shell indented. Outer shell (periostracum) yellow to brown or black with green chevron markings (may not be visible in older shells). Teeth heavy. Inner shell white. Length up to 13 cm.

LOOK-ALIKES: Mapleleaf, pimpleback, purple wartyback, and winged mapleleaf.

NOTES: The monkeyface is found in the Chippewa, Manitowoc, Mississippi, Rock, Saint Croix, and Wisconsin Rivers. It prefers swift, large rivers and may be found in gravel or sand and gravel substrate. Its host fishes are basses, bluegill, green sunfish, and sauger (*Sander canadensis*).

WARTYBACK
Quadrula nodulata

THREATENED

DESCRIPTION: Rounded, thick. Anterior rounded; posterior moderately truncate (shortened). Two prominent rows of paired knobs or pustules extend from umbo to shell margin; shallow groove (sulcus) between rows. Small posterior wing with no bumps or ridges extends from posterior ridge. Outer shell (periostracum) yellow to brown. Teeth well developed. Beak cavity deep. Inner shell white. Length up to 10 cm.

LOOK-ALIKES: Mapleleaf, pimpleback, and threehorn wartyback.

NOTES: The wartyback is found in the Chippewa, Manitowoc, Mississippi, Rock, Saint Croix, and Wisconsin Rivers in soft or coarse substrate. Its host fishes are basses, bluegill, catfishes, and crappies.

PIMPLEBACK
Quadrula pustulosa

DESCRIPTION: Rounded and thick. Anterior and posterior ends rounded; posterior half or more covered with bumps (pustules). Outer shell (periostracum) yellow to dark brown; a broad green ray often extends short distance from umbo but does not reach margin. Teeth well developed. Beak cavity deep. Inner shell white. Length up to 10 cm.

LOOK-ALIKES: Mapleleaf, monkeyface, purple wartyback, threehorn wartyback, wartyback, and winged mapleleaf.

NOTES: The pimpleback is found statewide. It exploits impoundments and is also found in medium to large rivers in either soft or coarse substrate and flowing water. Its host fishes are brown and black bullheads, channel catfish, and flathead catfish (*Pylodictis olivaris*).

MAPLELEAF
Quadrula quadrula

SPECIAL CONCERN

DESCRIPTION: Squarish, thick; anterior end rounded. Two rows of bumps (pustules) separated by a shallow groove (sulcus), with prominent ridge extending out to smooth posterior wing. Outer shell (periostracum) green to dark brown and lighter when younger. Pseudocardinal teeth well developed. Beak cavity deep. Inner shell white. Length up to 13 cm.

LOOK-ALIKES: Monkeyface, pimpleback, purple wartyback, wartyback, and winged mapleleaf.

NOTES: The mapleleaf is found in the Fox, Mississippi, Saint Croix, Wisconsin, and Wolf Rivers. It prefers medium to large rivers and impoundments and may be found in mud, sand, or gravel substrate. Its host fishes are brown and black bullheads, channel catfish, and flathead catfish (*Pylodictis olivaris*).

PISTOLGRIP (buckhorn)
Tritogonia verrucosa

THREATENED

DESCRIPTION: Elongate, thick, and compressed. Anterior end rounded; posterior end square or truncate (shortened) in males and more elongate and rounded in females. Shell covered with irregular bumps (pustules), including prominent posterior ridge. Teeth well developed. Beak cavity deep. Outer shell (periostracum) dark green, brown, or black. Length up to 20 cm.

LOOK-ALIKES: Rock pocketbook.

NOTES: The pistolgrip is found in the Black, Chippewa, Eau Claire, Mississippi, Sugar, Wisconsin, and Wolf Rivers and their tributaries. It inhabits medium to large rivers, preferring swift current and firm substrate. Its host fishes are brown and yellow bullheads and flathead catfish (*Pylodictis olivaris*).

SMOOTH MUSSELS

Elongate or Oval (Smooth) Mussels

All of the mussels below are smooth, not bumpy or ridged. Rather than being triangular or having wings extending out to the side, they tend to be elongate (more oval-shaped than circular).

MUCKET
Actinonaias ligamentina

DESCRIPTION: Oblong, robust, large, moderately compressed to slightly inflated. Anterior end rounded; posterior end bluntly pointed. Outer shell (periostracum) smooth, yellowish brown with green rays that disappear as shell gets darker brown with age. Teeth well developed. Inner shell white, rarely pink or salmon. Length up to 15 cm.

LOOK-ALIKES: Ellipse, fatmucket, Higgins eye, and plain pocketbook.

NOTES: The mucket is found statewide in medium to large rivers with mixed gravel and sand substrate. Its host fishes are banded killifish, basses, crappies, perches, and sunfishes.

CYLINDRICAL PAPERSHELL (cylinder)
Anodontoides ferussacianus

DESCRIPTION: Elongate, thin shell; anterior end rounded; posterior bluntly rounded, cylindrical. Outer shell (periostracum) smooth, shiny, yellow to green to brown, may have fine green rays. Teeth absent. Inner shell white or silvery. Length up to 10 cm.

LOOK-ALIKES: Creeper, giant floater, paper pondshell, and salamander mussel.

NOTES: The cylindrical papershell is found statewide in small streams. It prefers mud and sand substrate. Its host fishes are darters, minnows (cyprinids), sticklebacks, and white sucker.

SPECTACLECASE
Cumberlandia monodonta

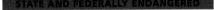
STATE AND FEDERALLY ENDANGERED

DESCRIPTION: Very elongate and compressed; thin when young to moderately thick when older. Ventral margin often concave in the middle. Outer shell (periostracum) black to brown. Pseudocardinal teeth poorly developed; lateral teeth absent. Inner shell white. Length up to 20 cm.

LOOK-ALIKES: Black sandshell, salamander mussel, and spike.

NOTES: The spectaclecase is found in the Chippewa, Flambeau, and Saint Croix Rivers and their tributaries. It prefers large rivers with large rocks. Its host fishes are unknown.

EASTERN ELLIPTIO
Elliptio complanata

SPECIAL CONCERN

DESCRIPTION: Elongate or oblong, usually compressed. Pronounced posterior ridge; anterior rounded. Outer shell (periostracum) brown or black and cloth-like in appearance. Lateral and pseudocardinal teeth well developed. Inner shell whitish to purplish. Length up to 15 cm.

LOOK-ALIKES: Black sandshell, creek heelsplitter, and spike.

NOTES: The eastern elliptio is found in rivers and streams in the Lake Superior and Lake Michigan basins, namely the Bad, Menominee, and White Rivers and their tributaries. Its host fishes are banded killifish, basses, crappies, perches, and sunfishes.

SPIKE
Elliptio dilatata

DESCRIPTION: Elongate, solid shell moderately inflated. Anterior end rounded; posterior end pointed. Outer shell (periostracum) brown to black but greenish when young. Teeth well developed with short lateral teeth. Beak cavity very shallow. Inner shell usually purple, sometimes white. Length up to 13 cm.

LOOK-ALIKES: Black sandshell, eastern elliptio, elephant ear, ellipse, and spectaclecase.

NOTES: The spike is found statewide in small to large streams in mud, sand, or gravel. Its host fishes are basses, catfishes, crappies, gizzard shad (*Dorosoma cepedianum*), perches, sauger (*Sander canadensis*), and sculpins.

PLAIN POCKETBOOK
Lampsilis cardium

DESCRIPTION: Large, round to oblong, inflated. Anterior end rounded; posterior end bluntly pointed in males and truncate (shortened) in females. Outer shell (periostracum) yellow to green or brown (may be pink or blue when young), often with dark green rays. Teeth well developed. Inner shell white, sometimes pink. Length up to 15 cm.

LOOK-ALIKES: Fatmucket, fat pocketbook, Higgins eye, and mucket.

NOTES: The plain pocketbook is found statewide in small creeks to large rivers in mud, sand, or gravel substrate. Its host fishes are basses, perches, and sunfishes.

male (*top*), female (*bottom*)

FATMUCKET
Lampsilis siliquoidea

DESCRIPTION: Elongate; may be thick or thin, compressed when young and more inflated with age. Anterior end rounded; shell dimorphic with posterior end bluntly pointed in males and truncate (shortened) and inflated in females. Outer shell (periostracum) yellow to dark green, tan, or brown, with green rays of various widths. Length up to 13 cm.

LOOK-ALIKES: Mucket, plain pocketbook, and yellow sandshell.

NOTES: The fatmucket is found statewide in small streams to large rivers, lakes, and impoundments. Its host fishes are basses, minnows, perches, and sunfishes.

male (*top*), female (*bottom*)

YELLOW AND SLOUGH SANDSHELLS
Lampsilis teres

ENDANGERED

DESCRIPTION: Elongate, relatively thick, smooth. Anterior end rounded; shell dimorphic, with posterior end pointed in males and truncate (shortened) in females. Outer shell (periostracum) light to dark yellow, sometimes with light green rays, especially when young. Teeth well developed. Beak cavity moderately deep. Inner shell white, sometimes with cream or salmon near the beak cavity. Length up to 15 cm.

LOOK-ALIKES: Black sandshell and fatmucket.

NOTES: The yellow and slough sandshells are 2 varieties (subspecies) of the same species: *Lampsilis teres anodointoides* (yellow sandshell) and *L. teres teres* (slough sandshell). They are found in the Mississippi, Wisconsin, and Wolf Rivers. They prefer large, swift rivers with sandy substrate. Their host fishes are basses, gars, sturgeon, and sunfishes.

slough sandshell (*top*),
yellow sandshell (*bottom*)

CREEK HEELSPLITTER
Lasmigona compressa

DESCRIPTION: Elongate or oblong, thin, slightly compressed. Anterior end rounded; posterior end truncate (shortened), with slight posterior ridge. Outer shell (periostracum) green to brown, may have green rays. Pseudocardinal teeth reduced; lateral teeth not well developed. Beak cavity very shallow. Inner shell white, may be cream or salmon-colored in beak cavity. Length up to 15 cm.

LOOK-ALIKES: Eastern elliptio, fluted-shell, and white heelsplitter.

NOTES: The creek heelsplitter is found statewide in streams to medium-sized rivers with soft or coarse substrate. Its host fishes are black crappie, slimy sculpin, spotfin shiner, and yellow perch.

FRAGILE PAPERSHELL
Leptodea fragilis

DESCRIPTION: Shell oblong or elliptical; thin and fragile when young, may be thicker with age; somewhat compressed. Anterior end rounded; posterior end rounded in males and broadened in females, with a posterior wing that extends along the dorsal edge, which is less prevalent with age. Outer shell (periostracum) yellow to brown, often with numerous light green rays. Teeth thin. Inner shell iridescent white and pink. Length up to 15 cm.

LOOK-ALIKES: Pink papershell.

NOTES: The fragile papershell is found statewide. It may be found in streams of all sizes with mud, sand, or gravel substrate. Its host fish is the freshwater drum.

BLACK SANDSHELL
Ligumia recta

DESCRIPTION: Elongate, moderately thick. Outer shell (periostracum) smooth and shiny, dark green or black, sometimes rayed. Sexually dimorphic, with the anterior end rounded and females more truncate (shortened) and inflated posteriorly, males more pointed posteriorly. Teeth well developed. Inner shell white, purple, or combination. Length up to 20 cm.

LOOK-ALIKES: Spectaclecase, spike, and yellow sandshell.

NOTES: The black sandshell is found statewide. Its host fishes are bluegill, largemouth bass, crappies, and sauger (*Sander canadensis*).

female (*top*), male (*bottom*)

GIANT FLOATER
Pyganodon grandis

DESCRIPTION: Large, thin (very thin in young), elongate, with inflated umbos elevated above hinge line. Anterior end rounded; posterior end bluntly pointed. Shell size and shape highly variable depending on type of habitat. Teeth absent. Inner shell white or iridescent. Length up to 18 cm.

LOOK-ALIKES: Creeper, cylindrical papershell, flat floater, and paper pondshell.

NOTES: The giant floater is found statewide in a variety of habitats, including lakes and slow river sections with mud substrate. Its host fishes are bullheads, darters, freshwater drum, gars, gizzard shad (*Dorosoma cepedianum*), and skipjack herring (*Alosa chrysochloris*).

SMOOTH MUSSELS (Elongate or Oval)

SALAMANDER MUSSEL
Simpsonaias ambigua

THREATENED

DESCRIPTION: Small, very thin, elongate or oblong, and moderately compressed. Anterior and posterior ends rounded. Posterior ridge rounded and not prominent. Outer shell (periostracum) smooth, dull, yellowish tan to copper brown to dark brown. 1 thin pseudocardinal tooth in each valve, almost negligible; lateral teeth absent. Beak cavity shallow. Inner shell white or iridescent, may have salmon color near beak. Length up to 5 cm.

LOOK-ALIKES: Cylindrical papershell, lilliput, and spectaclecase.

NOTES: The salamander mussel is found in the Black, Chippewa, Eau Claire, Flambeau, Saint Croix, Wisconsin, and Wolf Rivers and their tributaries. It prefers large rivers and is found under large rocks in mud, silt, or sand. Its host is the common mudpuppy, a species of salamander.

CREEPER (bankclimber, strange floater)
Strophitus undulatus

DESCRIPTION: Oblong or elliptical, thin to moderately thick shell, inflated. Anterior end rounded; posterior end bluntly pointed, sometimes truncated. Shell smooth and shiny, dark green, brown, or black. Teeth greatly reduced; lateral and pseudocardinal teeth only as slightly thickened ridges. Beak cavity moderately shallow. Inner shell cream, salmon, or white. Length up to 12 cm.

LOOK-ALIKES: Cylindrical papershell, giant floater, and paper pondshell.

NOTES: The creeper is found statewide in small streams to medium rivers and sometimes in large rivers. Its host fishes are banded killifish, basses, chubs, and sunfishes.

LILLIPUT
Toxolasma parvus

DESCRIPTION: Very small, oblong, inflated. Anterior and posterior ends rounded. Outer shell (periostracum) with cloth-like texture, green or brown color. Teeth well developed. Beak cavity moderately deep. Inner shell iridescent, silver, purple, lavender, and sometimes pink. Length up to 2.5 cm, usually less.

LOOK-ALIKES: Salamander mussel.

NOTES: The lilliput is found statewide but is never common, and, due to its small size, it is often overlooked. It inhabits both rivers and small streams and is found in soft substrate. Its host fishes are sunfishes.

PAPER PONDSHELL
Utterbackia imbecillis

DESCRIPTION: Shell small, thin, oblong, very compressed when young, and more inflated when older. Anterior end rounded; posterior end pointed; dorsal margin straight; ventral margin rounded. Hinge line straight, umbos below hinge line. Teeth absent. Beak cavity shallow or absent. Inner shell white or iridescent. Length up to 10 cm.

LOOK-ALIKES: Creeper, cylindrical papershell, giant floater, and salamander mussel.

NOTES: The paper pondshell is found statewide but is uncommon and is limited to areas with soft substrate. It inhabits streams, rivers, ponds, and lakes. Its host fishes are banded killifish, basses, perches, and sunfishes.

ELLIPSE
Venustaconcha ellipsiformis

THREATENED

DESCRIPTION: Small, elongate, thick for its size. Anterior end rounded; posterior end bluntly pointed. Ventral margin slightly curved to straight. Shell smooth, sometimes with a few folds on posterior half when older. Outer shell (periostracum) dark green to brown, with wavy green rays at the posterior end. Teeth well developed and heavy. Beak cavity shallow. Inner shell white. Length up to 10 cm.

LOOK-ALIKES: Mucket, spike, and rainbow shell.

NOTES: The ellipse is found primarily in S.E. and S. Wisconsin but also in the Yellow River and its tributaries. It prefers shallow, flowing streams with stable substrate. Its host fishes are brook stickleback, darters, and sculpins.

male (*top*), female (*bottom*)

RAINBOW SHELL
Villosa iris

ENDANGERED

DESCRIPTION: Small, elongate; shells sexually dimorphic: compressed in males and inflated in females. Anterior end rounded; posterior end rounded in females and bluntly pointed in males. Outer shell (periostracum) yellow to green to brown with dark green rays, which appear to be broken or not continuous. Teeth well developed. Beak cavity shallow. Inner shell white and highly iridescent. Length up to 5 cm.

LOOK-ALIKES: Ellipse, fatmucket, and mucket.

NOTES: The rainbow shell is found mainly in E. Wisconsin in the Ashippun, Mukwonago, Pigeon, Rock, and Yellow Rivers and their tributaries. It prefers shallow, flowing streams with sand and gravel substrate. Its host fishes are largemouth and smallmouth basses.

Triangular, Round, or Winged (Smooth) Mussels

All of the mussels below are smooth, not bumpy or ridged. Rather than being elongate, they are more triangular or round in overall shape and/or have an edge that is pointed or extends out like a wing.

ELKTOE
Alasmidonta marginata

SPECIAL CONCERN

DESCRIPTION: Elongate, triangular, inflated. Anterior end rounded; posterior ridge sharply angled, ending in blunt point. Outer shell (periostracum) green to brown, with numerous dark green rays and speckling. Poorly developed teeth, with laterals absent and pseudocardinals thin. Beak cavity moderately deep. Inner shell white. Length up to 12 cm.

LOOK-ALIKES: Deertoe and snuffbox.

NOTES: The elktoe is found statewide in small streams to large rivers. It prefers sand, rock, and gravel substrate. Its host fishes are redhorses, rock bass, suckers, and warmouth.

SLIPPERSHELL
Alasmidonta viridis

THREATENED

DESCRIPTION: Very small, oblong, somewhat inflated. Anterior end rounded; posterior ridge high and round and posterior slope flattened. Shell green to gray with numerous rays. Lateral teeth poorly developed. Beak cavity moderately deep. Inner shell white and iridescent. Length usually <2.5 cm.

LOOK-ALIKES: Elktoe.

NOTES: The slippershell is found in E. Wisconsin in streams draining to Lake Michigan. It inhabits small to medium streams with hard (mineral-rich) water and sand or gravel substrate. Its host fishes are banded and Johnny darters and mottled sculpin.

FLAT FLOATER
Anodonta suborbiculata

SPECIAL CONCERN

DESCRIPTION: Rounded, compressed, and thin-shelled. Anterior end rounded; posterior end very slightly pointed; ventral margin very rounded. Slight posterior ridge with wing extension. Outer shell (periostracum) yellow or brown, with possible light green rays and glossy texture. Teeth absent. Inner shell pink, orange, silvery iridescent. Length up to 18 cm.

LOOK-ALIKES: Giant floater and pink papershell.

NOTES: The flat floater is found in the Chippewa, Saint Croix, and Wisconsin Rivers, preferring backwater areas. Its host fishes are unknown.

BUTTERFLY
Ellipsaria lineolata

ENDANGERED

DESCRIPTION: Triangular, thick. Anterior end rounded; posterior end bluntly pointed. Males compressed; females only slightly more inflated. Posterior ridge sharply angled. Outer shell (periostracum) yellow to brown, with a pattern of broken rays. Teeth well developed. Beak cavity shallow to moderately deep. Inner shell white. Length up to 12 cm.

LOOK-ALIKES: Deertoe.

NOTES: The butterfly is found in the Mississippi, Saint Croix, and Wisconsin Rivers in sand, rock, or gravel substrate. Its host fishes are freshwater drum, green sunfish, and sauger (*Sander canadensis*).

ELEPHANT EAR
Elliptio crassidens

ENDANGERED

DESCRIPTION: Triangular, heavy. Anterior end rounded; posterior end pointed. Posterior ridge prominent and angled. Outer shell (periostracum) brown to black. Lateral and pseudocardinal teeth well developed. Beak cavity shallow. Inner shell usually light purple, sometimes pink or white. Length up to 12 cm.

LOOK-ALIKES: Mucket and spike.

NOTES: The elephant ear is found in the Mississippi and Saint Croix Rivers. Its host fish is unknown but is suspected to be the skipjack herring (*Alosa chrysochloris*). It is rarely found and may soon be extirpated.

SNUFFBOX
Epioblasma triquetra

STATE AND FEDERALLY ENDANGERED

DESCRIPTION: Small, triangular, thick for its size. Anterior end rounded; posterior ridge sharply angled, with finely grooved posterior slope. Shells dimorphic: males more elongate, with a rounded ventral margin; females very inflated, with a straight ventral margin and serrated edges or hooks on the posterior margin of the shell. Outer shell (periostracum) yellow to green, with disjunct rays or chevrons. Teeth well developed. Beak cavity fairly deep. Inner shell white. Length up to 5 cm.

LOOK-ALIKES: Deertoe, elktoe (female snuffbox), and fawnsfoot (male snuffbox).

NOTES: The snuffbox is found in the Embarrass, Saint Croix, and Wolf Rivers and their tributaries. It prefers riffle areas of medium to large streams. Its host fishes are banded sculpin and logperch. Female snuffbox grab the head of the host fish and hold on until all their glochidia have been deposited on the gills of the fish.

male (*top*), female (*bottom*)

EBONYSHELL
Fusconaia ebena

ENDANGERED

DESCRIPTION: Solid, round, heavy, inflated. Anterior and posterior ends rounded. Shell smooth, with slightly elevated ridges. Outer shell (periostracum) dark brown to black but light when younger. Pseudocardinal teeth well developed. Beak cavity very deep. Inner shell pearly white. Length up to 10 cm.

LOOK-ALIKES: Higgins eye, hickorynut, round pigtoe, and Wabash pigtoe.

NOTES: The ebonyshell is found in the Mississippi, Saint Croix, and Wisconsin Rivers in gravel, sand, or mud substrate. Its host fish is the skipjack herring (*Alosa chrysochloris*). It is rarely found and may soon be extirpated.

WABASH PIGTOE
Fusconaia flava

DESCRIPTION: Triangular. Anterior end rounded; posterior end bluntly pointed. Wide, shallow groove (sulcus) present near slight dorsal ridge. Cloth-like texture. Reddish brown to dark brown in adults; can be yellowish when younger. Teeth well developed. Beak cavity deep. Inner shell white, sometimes pink. Length up to 12 cm.

LOOK-ALIKES: Deertoe, ebonyshell, round pigtoe, and sheepnose.

NOTES: The Wabash pigtoe is found statewide in creeks to large rivers in mud, sand, or gravel substrate. Its host fishes are bluegill, crappies, creek chub, and silver shiner.

male (*top*), female (*bottom*)

HIGGINS EYE
Lampsilis higginsii

STATE AND FEDERALLY ENDANGERED

DESCRIPTION: Round to oblong, thick and inflated. Anterior end rounded; posterior end bluntly pointed in males or truncated in females. Outer shell (periostracum) smooth, yellowish, dark green, or brown with green rays. Pseudocardinal teeth well developed. Beak cavity deep. Inner shell white, sometimes pink by beak cavity. Length up to 10 cm for females, 15 cm for males.

LOOK-ALIKES: Fat pocketbook, hickorynut, mucket, and plain pocketbook.

NOTES: The Higgins eye is found in the Mississippi, Saint Croix, and Wisconsin Rivers. It prefers large rivers with flowing water and sand substrate. Its host fishes are basses, freshwater drum, walleye, and sauger (*Sander canadensis*).

WHITE HEELSPLITTER
Lasmigona complanata

DESCRIPTION: Large, round, and compressed. Thin when young and thick when older. Anterior end rounded; posterior end bluntly pointed. Pronounced dorsal wing extends posteriorly. Outer shell (periostracum) dark green or brown to black. Pseudocardinal teeth well developed; lateral teeth poorly developed. Beak cavity shallow to moderately deep. Inner shell white. Length up to 20 cm.

LOOK-ALIKES: Creek heelsplitter and pink heelsplitter.

NOTES: The white heelsplitter is found statewide in streams and rivers with mud, sand, or gravel substrate. Its host fishes are common carp, crappies, green sunfish, and largemouth bass.

HICKORYNUT
Obovaria olivaria

DESCRIPTION: Oval or egg-shaped; thick, solid, inflated. Anterior and posterior ends rounded. Shell smooth, lustrous, olive green to brown, with faint rays. Teeth well developed. Beak cavity shallow. Inner shell white or iridescent. Length up to 10 cm.

LOOK-ALIKES: Ebonyshell, Higgins eye, round pigtoe, and Wabash pigtoe.

NOTES: The hickorynut is found in the Chippewa, Eau Claire, Embarrass, Flambeau, Menominee, Mississippi, Saint Croix, Wisconsin, and Wolf Rivers and their tributaries. It prefers large rivers with sand or mixed sand and gravel substrate. Its host fish is the shovelnose sturgeon (*Scaphirhynchus platorhynchus*).

ROUND PIGTOE
Pleurobema sintoxia

DESCRIPTION: Shell variable: round and compressed in small streams, round to triangular and inflated in large rivers. Anterior end rounded; posterior end bluntly pointed, ventral margin rounded. Outer shell (periostracum) reddish brown or dark brown. Teeth well developed. Beak cavity moderately shallow. Inner shell white, sometimes pink. Length up to 12 cm.

LOOK-ALIKES: Ebonyshell, sheepnose, and Wabash pigtoe.

NOTES: The round pigtoe is found statewide in small streams to large rivers in sand or mixed substrate. Its host fishes are bluegill and minnows (cyprinids).

PINK HEELSPLITTER
Potamilus alatus

DESCRIPTION: Large, squarish oval, thick, and compressed. Prominent posterior wing extending beyond hinge. Shell smooth, dark green to brown to black, with dark green rays when young. Teeth well developed; beak cavity shallow. Inner shell usually purple, lavender. Length up to 18 cm.

LOOK-ALIKES: Fragile papershell, pink papershell, and white heelsplitter.

NOTES: The pink heelsplitter is found statewide in medium to large rivers with mud or mixed mud, sand, and gravel substrate. Its host fish is the freshwater drum.

PINK PAPERSHELL
Potamilus ohiensis

SPECIAL CONCERN

DESCRIPTION: Oval, thin, fragile, and compressed. Anterior and posterior ends rounded. Well-developed posterior dorsal wing and less developed anterior dorsal wing, creating a V shape over the umbo when not worn off. Outer shell (periostracum) tan to brown, with faint green rays. Teeth thin. Beak cavity shallow. Inner shell pink or lavender. Length up to 12 cm.

LOOK-ALIKES: Flat floater, fragile papershell, and pink heelsplitter.

NOTES: The pink papershell is found in the Chippewa, Mississippi, Saint Croix, and Wisconsin Rivers and their tributaries. It prefers medium to large rivers with silt, mud, or sand substrate. Its host fishes are crappies and freshwater drum.

FAWNSFOOT
Truncilla donaciformis

THREATENED

DESCRIPTION: Small, elongate, moderately inflated. Anterior end rounded; posterior end pointed; ventral edge rounded. Outer shell (periostracum) yellow to green, with chevrons or zigzag markings along rays. Teeth well developed. Beak cavity moderately shallow. Inner shell white. Length up to 5 cm.

LOOK-ALIKES: Deertoe, snuffbox.

NOTES: The fawnsfoot is found in the Chippewa, Eau Claire, Mississippi, Saint Croix, Wisconsin, and Wolf Rivers. It prefers large rivers or the lower reaches of medium streams and can be found in sand and gravel substrate. Its host fishes are freshwater drum and sauger (*Sander canadensis*). Its numbers are declining in Wisconsin—once widespread and abundant, it is now rarely found.

DEERTOE
Truncilla truncata

DESCRIPTION: Triangular, thick, somewhat inflated. Anterior end rounded; posterior end pointed, with a sharply angled posterior ridge. Outer shell (periostracum) green, yellow, blue, brown. Rays highly variable. Teeth well developed. Inner shell white, sometimes pink. Length up to 8 cm.

LOOK-ALIKES: Fawnsfoot and Wabash pigtoe.

NOTES: The deertoe is found in the Chippewa, Embarrass, Fox, Mississippi, Saint Croix, White, Wisconsin, and Wolf Rivers and their tributaries. It prefers medium to large rivers with mud, sand, and gravel substrate. Its host fishes are freshwater drum and sauger (*Sander canadensis*).

INVASIVE MUSSELS

There are two invasive mussels known to occur in Wisconsin: the closely related zebra and quagga mussels. They were originally native to eastern Europe and were brought over to the Great Lakes in the ballast of boats, where they spread to our inland rivers and lakes, disrupting the native ecosystems. Unlike the complex life history of our native mussels that require a host species, these two invasive species simply release massive quantities of their free-swimming young (*veligers*) to the water column. An adult female zebra mussel can produce up to one million free-swimming veligers each year. After drifting in the water for several weeks, the veligers settle onto and attach to most substrates, including sand, silt, rock, pilings, piers, and any other available surfaces, where they grow into adult mussels.

In some areas, invasive mussels completely cover the substrate, including native mussels, preventing them from getting food and suffocating them. They are responsible for the near extinction of native mussel populations in portions of the Great Lakes and adjacent water bodies. They are a nuisance to swimmers and boaters, as their empty shells are sharp and accumulate on beaches and in boating channels and have proven very expensive for industrial and municipal water users to prevent or eliminate if the mussels get in water pipes. Zebra mussels can tolerate a wide range of environmental conditions; adults can survive out of water for seven days, and young are easily transported by recreational boaters and anglers. The spread of invasive mussels can be prevented by thoroughly drying boats and associated equipment and not transporting water between water bodies.

2012 distribution

QUAGGA MUSSEL
Dreissena bugensis

INVASIVE—PROHIBITED

ZEBRA MUSSEL
Dreissena polymorpha

INVASIVE—RESTRICTED

quagga mussel (*top*), zebra mussel (*bottom*)

DESCRIPTION: Small, triangular, elongate shells with alternating light and dark bands and highly variable patterns. No pseudocardinal or lateral teeth (as in native mussels). May have *byssus*: black, thread-like hairs used for attachment of shell to other surfaces. Often found in clusters attached to each other, rocks, piers/pilings, or native mussels. Length up to 4 cm.

LOOK-ALIKES: Quagga and zebra mussels look very similar but differ slightly in shell shape, the quagga having 1 side more flattened and being less "striped" in appearance.

NOTES: Zebra and quagga mussels are separate species but overlap in appearance, habitat, and behavior; it is most practical to group them together. They are found in Lake Michigan and Lake Superior as well as Lake Winnebago and other inland lakes and rivers. They do not require a fish host to complete their life cycle and can become extremely abundant. Both species compete with native mussels for food and oxygen. They cover the native mussels' shells, suffocating and starving them and preventing movement. They are easily transported by boaters and anglers, and care should be taken to inspect and remove them.

FINGERNAIL CLAMS

CLAMS

The word *clam* is from the Greek *klamma* (constriction), referring to the two tightly closed shells. Like mussels, clams are filterers, eating mainly plankton, detritus, and bacteria. Our native clams are referred to as pea clams or fingernail clams due to their small size. There are over forty species of fingernail clams in Wisconsin.

Clams are hermaphrodites, having both sexes in each individual, with internal fertilization. Developing young are incubated within their mother, and newborn clams look like miniature copies of the adults. They do not require a fish host like our native mussels but release their young directly into the water column. They live one to two years and are an important food for many fishes and birds.

FINGERNAIL CLAMS

FINGERNAIL CLAMS (pea clams)
family Pisidiidae (formerly Sphaeriidae)

DESCRIPTION: Small, rounded to oval, and inflated (round like a pea). White or cream to light brown. May have very fine concentric rings; smooth on the surface. Symmetrical: hinge centered or only slightly off center. Length up to 1.3 cm.

LOOK-ALIKES: Asian clam. Also small juvenile mussels, but juvenile mussels are elongate, and the hinge is skewed off center.

NOTES: Fingernail clams are abundant statewide. They are found in lakes, wetlands, seasonal ponds, large rivers, and small streams; most species are found in slow-flowing water in sandy or silty substrate. They burrow partly or entirely into the substrate. Most species are intolerant of pollution and low oxygen levels, but a few are extremely tolerant.

ASIAN CLAMS

ASIAN CLAM
Corbicula fluminea

INVASIVE—PROHIBITED

DESCRIPTION: Small; yellowish brown to black, with numerous evenly spaced raised concentric rings on the shell surface. Shell slightly triangular and symmetrical: umbo centered. Young shells may have purple stripe on umbo; inside is white or purple. Length up to 4 cm.

LOOK-ALIKES: Fingernail clams.

NOTES: The invasive Asian clam has the potential to become very abundant, and it competes with native clams and mussels for food and space. It is found in Lakes Michigan and Superior, the Saint Croix and Mississippi Rivers, and recently Lake Winnebago and a few inland streams. It prefers warm water and is most frequently found at warm-water discharge sites, such as in the thermal plume of power plants, where it can overwinter. It also appears to be able to overwinter in warm water bodies if the winter is not severe. If it spreads beyond its current distribution, it will likely spread to similarly warm sites. It does not require a fish host to complete its life cycle and prefers sandy or muddy substrate. This clam was brought over from Asia for food and can be extremely abundant in temperate parts of this country. In Wisconsin it is at the northern extent of its range and is not currently widespread.

Fishes

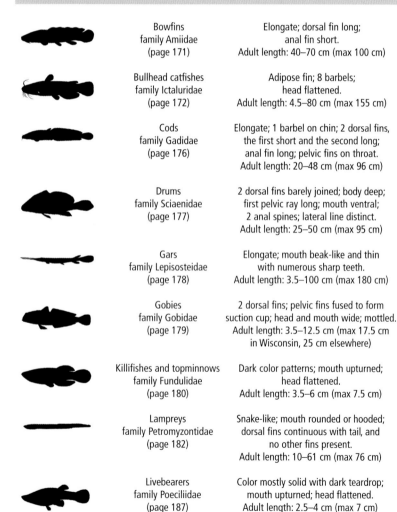

Bowfins family Amiidae (page 171)		Elongate; dorsal fin long; anal fin short. Adult length: 40–70 cm (max 100 cm)
Bullhead catfishes family Ictaluridae (page 172)		Adipose fin; 8 barbels; head flattened. Adult length: 4.5–80 cm (max 155 cm)
Cods family Gadidae (page 176)		Elongate; 1 barbel on chin; 2 dorsal fins, the first short and the second long; anal fin long; pelvic fins on throat. Adult length: 20–48 cm (max 96 cm)
Drums family Sciaenidae (page 177)		2 dorsal fins barely joined; body deep; first pelvic ray long; mouth ventral; 2 anal spines; lateral line distinct. Adult length: 25–50 cm (max 95 cm)
Gars family Lepisosteidae (page 178)		Elongate; mouth beak-like and thin with numerous sharp teeth. Adult length: 3.5–100 cm (max 180 cm)
Gobies family Gobidae (page 179)		2 dorsal fins; pelvic fins fused to form suction cup; head and mouth wide; mottled. Adult length: 3.5–12.5 cm (max 17.5 cm in Wisconsin, 25 cm elsewhere)
Killifishes and topminnows family Fundulidae (page 180)		Dark color patterns; mouth upturned; head flattened. Adult length: 3.5–6 cm (max 7.5 cm)
Lampreys family Petromyzontidae (page 182)		Snake-like; mouth rounded or hooded; dorsal fins continuous with tail, and no other fins present. Adult length: 10–61 cm (max 76 cm)
Livebearers family Poeciliidae (page 187)		Color mostly solid with dark teardrop; mouth upturned; head flattened. Adult length: 2.5–4 cm (max 7 cm)

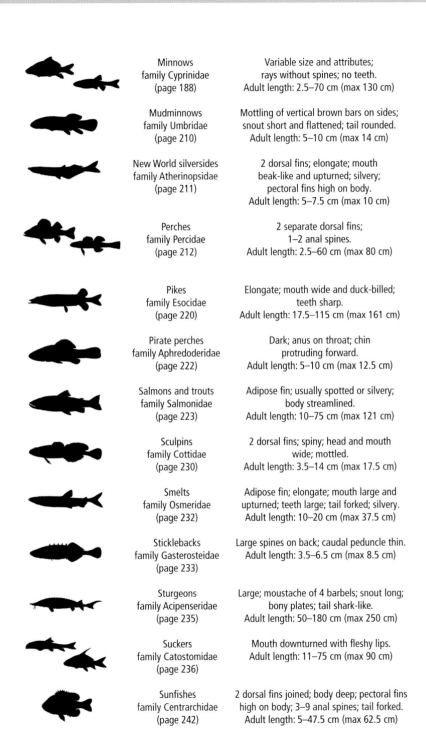

Minnows
family Cyprinidae
(page 188)

Variable size and attributes;
rays without spines; no teeth.
Adult length: 2.5–70 cm (max 130 cm)

Mudminnows
family Umbridae
(page 210)

Mottling of vertical brown bars on sides;
snout short and flattened; tail rounded.
Adult length: 5–10 cm (max 14 cm)

New World silversides
family Atherinopsidae
(page 211)

2 dorsal fins; elongate; mouth
beak-like and upturned; silvery;
pectoral fins high on body.
Adult length: 5–7.5 cm (max 10 cm)

Perches
family Percidae
(page 212)

2 separate dorsal fins;
1–2 anal spines.
Adult length: 2.5–60 cm (max 80 cm)

Pikes
family Esocidae
(page 220)

Elongate; mouth wide and duck-billed;
teeth sharp.
Adult length: 17.5–115 cm (max 161 cm)

Pirate perches
family Aphredoderidae
(page 222)

Dark; anus on throat; chin
protruding forward.
Adult length: 5–10 cm (max 12.5 cm)

Salmons and trouts
family Salmonidae
(page 223)

Adipose fin; usually spotted or silvery;
body streamlined.
Adult length: 10–75 cm (max 121 cm)

Sculpins
family Cottidae
(page 230)

2 dorsal fins; spiny; head and mouth
wide; mottled.
Adult length: 3.5–14 cm (max 17.5 cm)

Smelts
family Osmeridae
(page 232)

Adipose fin; elongate; mouth large and
upturned; teeth large; tail forked; silvery.
Adult length: 10–20 cm (max 37.5 cm)

Sticklebacks
family Gasterosteidae
(page 233)

Large spines on back; caudal peduncle thin.
Adult length: 3.5–6.5 cm (max 8.5 cm)

Sturgeons
family Acipenseridae
(page 235)

Large; moustache of 4 barbels; snout long;
bony plates; tail shark-like.
Adult length: 50–180 cm (max 250 cm)

Suckers
family Catostomidae
(page 236)

Mouth downturned with fleshy lips.
Adult length: 11–75 cm (max 90 cm)

Sunfishes
family Centrarchidae
(page 242)

2 dorsal fins joined; body deep; pectoral fins
high on body; 3–9 anal spines; tail forked.
Adult length: 5–47.5 cm (max 62.5 cm)

| | Temperate basses
family Moronidae
(page 248) | 2 dorsal fins barely joined; body deep;
3–9 anal spines; tail forked.
Adult length: 12.5–80 cm (max 103 cm) |
| | Trout-perches
family Percopsidae
(page 249) | Adipose fin; dusky spots; head large.
Adult length: 5–10 cm (max 15 cm) |

Over 30,000 fish species have been identified worldwide. Wisconsin currently has 159 known species, which is more than most states and many countries. Over 100 of these species inhabit Wisconsin streams for at least a part of their life.

The oldest fish fossils in the world are estimated to be approximately 500 million years old. Lampreys are the oldest group of living Wisconsin fishes; the earliest lamprey fossils appeared 360 million years ago. Other primitive fishes that live in Wisconsin today include sturgeons, which evolved over 200 million years ago; and garfish and bowfins, whose fossil records are over 100 million years old. Bony fishes (superclass Osteichthyes), from which the majority of Wisconsin's fishes have evolved, first appeared in the fossil record about 395 million years ago, but those generally looked very different from the bony fishes living today. (Note that the word *fish* can be pluralized to either *fish* or *fishes*. In general, *fish* refers to multiple individuals of the same species; *fishes* is used when indicating or distinguishing among multiple species.)

Key Traits

Most Wisconsin fish species have scales (except lampreys, sculpins, catfishes, paddlefish, and sturgeons) and skeletons composed of bone (except lampreys). For other fishes, such as eels and burbot, the scales are so small and smooth that the average person might think these fishes are scaleless. Body shape varies among fish species, and different shapes allow fishes to specialize in different types of movement and occupy different habitats. For example, the elongate bodies of muskellunge and other pikes allow bursts of speed to capture prey, whereas deep-bodied bluegills and other panfishes are more maneuverable and adept at capturing prey in weedy environments. Trouts' and suckers' long and tapered shape allows for efficient swimming in fast-flowing environments.

In distinguishing fish species from each other, it is helpful to know some terminology of fish body structures; the diagram below illustrates a few key terms. Along with body size and shape, fin location and shape are helpful for identification. For example, some species' dorsal fins are separated into two fins, one spiny and one soft. Other species, such as trouts and salmons, have an adipose fin located behind the dorsal fin (not pictured below). Some species can be distinguished from each other by differences in the number of fin rays, especially in the dorsal and anal fins; rays are counted from anterior to posterior, as indicated in the diagram. Scale appearance (large or small, smooth or rough, subtle or distinctly outlined) can also help with species identification, as can lateral line appearance and eye and jaw position. Color may vary widely among individuals within a species depending largely on age,

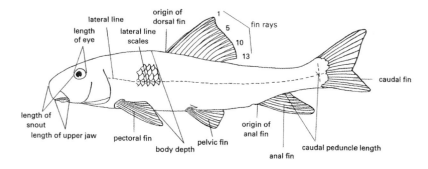

sex, breeding status, and water chemistry, but colors and pigmentation patterns can nevertheless be useful for identification.

Fish have certain organs that are specially designed for life underwater. All fishes use gills to extract oxygen from the water, although a few species such as central mudminnows, bowfins, and gars can also breathe by gulping air. A majority of fishes have a gas bladder to control buoyancy (burbot, lampreys, and sculpins do not).

Fish sense their environment through a variety of means. Some fishes use their gas bladder to detect pressure waves caused by predator or prey movement or to sense changes in water depth or currents. Minnows, suckers, and catfish have a small series of bones, termed the *Weberian apparatus*, in contact with the bladder that make them particularly sensitive to pressure waves. Many fish species have a *lateral line* on each side of their body comprised of a series of hundreds of sensory cells to aid in finding prey and avoiding predators and to help some species with synchronized schooling behavior. Fish lack external ears but have an internal ear that detects sound and helps orient the fish in a weightless environment. Fish also do not have eyelids, though they do sleep by ignoring certain visual stimuli. They have paired nostrils (a single nostril in lampreys) for smelling, with sensitivities thought to be similar to those of humans in some fish species and hundreds of times more sensitive in others. They have taste buds on their jaws, lips, and tongue. Burbot, some members of the minnow family, and sturgeons, as well as catfishes, bullheads, and madtoms have taste buds on their barbels. Catfishes, bullheads, and madtoms also have taste buds scattered over their entire body and tail that aid in finding food in murky water and at night.

Life Cycle and Reproduction

Stream fishes have varying strategies and ecological requirements for reproduction. Most minnow species are relatively short-lived and become sexually mature at a young age. For example, on average fathead minnows may live for two to three years and become sexually mature at four to five months. Brook trout live a bit longer: in the wild, they live an average of three to four years, and males can be sexually mature within their first year of life and females typically in their second year. Some species, such as lake sturgeon, may live over one hundred years in the wild and may not reach sexual maturity until twenty-five years of age.

Except for the nonnative western mosquitofish, all Wisconsin fishes lay eggs that are externally fertilized, meaning that the male fertilizes the eggs after they have been laid by the female. Some species build nests in which to lay the eggs, while others do not. Redhorse species, for example, do not build nests but release tens of thousands of small (2–3 mm diameter) eggs in fast-flowing riffles and rapids in April and May. Their eggs are heavier than water and adhesive: they stick to rocks or settle into crevices among the rocks. Depending upon water temperature, the eggs hatch within approximately a week. No parental care is given to the eggs or fry. Similarly, common carp do not build nests or care for the eggs or fry; each female simply broadcasts as many as a million 1–2 mm diameter adhesive eggs over aquatic plants and soft sediment in May and early June; the eggs hatch in about a week.

Female brook and brown trout dig shallow depressions (*redds*) with their body and tail in gravel streambeds in October through December. The females release between 200 and 2,000 eggs that are 3–5 mm in diameter. The eggs are fertilized by the male and then covered with gravel by the female. The eggs remain buried for four to five months until spring. Trout eggs hatch while buried in the streambed, and the emerging "sac fry" get nourishment from a yolk sac until their bodies are fully developed; the fry then emerge from the gravel.

Hornyhead chubs pile small stones into mounds that may be over a meter in diameter and 15–30 cm high on the streambed. The mounds are used as a communal nest by other species such as common shiner, rosyface shiner, and southern redbelly dace. Some fishes, such as members of the sunfish family and some minnow species, provide parental care to their eggs by fanning their nests to keep the eggs clear of silt that would suffocate them and by guarding against predators such as crayfish or other fish. Male smallmouth bass may guard their fry for up to a month after they hatch.

Brook stickleback males build nests out of aquatic vegetation they glue together with body secretions. Each male defends his territory and entices a female into the nest with an elaborate courtship dance. Once the female lays her eggs, the male drives her off, fertilizes the eggs, and guards the eggs until they hatch a week later, herding any escaping fry back into the nest for a few days after hatching.

Most Wisconsin fishes spawn in spring or summer, although most salmons and trouts spawn in fall and early winter. Burbot are Wisconsin's earliest-spawning fish of the calendar year, laying eggs under the ice in lakes, streams, and the waters of the Great Lakes in January and February.

Ecological Notes

Water temperature strongly influences what fish species are likely to be found in a stream. Trouts and salmons, sculpins, and longnose sucker are restricted to living in coldwater streams—they tolerate a relatively narrow temperature range that can only rarely exceed 21°C (70°F) for more than a week (such as during late summer low-flow conditions). The vast majority of other Wisconsin stream fish species can tolerate a wider range of water temperatures.

Coldwater or "trout streams" are dominated by groundwater seeping into the streambed or flowing into streams via springs. Wisconsin groundwater has a stable, cool temperature, flowing out of the earth at about 12°C (53°F) year-round. Wisconsin's geology, land formations, soil types, and land use determine whether a stream's water source is primarily this cold groundwater or surface runoff, which can be warm or cold depending on the time of year. Good quality coldwater streams tend to have few fish species (often only two or three), whereas a similar-sized warmwater stream can contain more than twenty species. In parts of the state where groundwater dominates, such as the Driftless Area of the southwest and along glacial moraines, the presence of coldwater species such as brook trout and sculpins indicates healthy environmental conditions.

Stream size can affect the presence or absence of fish species. In general, as streams increase in size and water temperature, there is a corresponding increase in the number of species found. Headwater streams usually support only a few fish species. If these streams are dominated by surface runoff, there may be only a few hardy minnow species; if these streams are fed by groundwater, they may support more environmentally sensitive species such as brook or brown trout and sculpins. As streams get larger and warmer, the fish assemblage shifts to include more darter, minnow, and sucker species. In larger streams, the top predators are often basses, pikes, or catfishes.

Stream fishes feed on a variety of food types. The majority of Wisconsin's stream fishes rely on small crustaceans, aquatic insect larvae, and zooplankton as food for at least a part of their lives. Trouts and many sucker and minnow species feed on aquatic and terrestrial insects and small crustaceans throughout their lives. A smaller number of species, such as adult brown trout, basses, bowfin, gar, and pikes, feed on crayfish, frogs, and fish. Also present may be herbivores, detritivores, omnivores, or planktivores, including carp and some other minnow species, some suckers, and immature lampreys, which feed on a wide variety of invertebrates, plants, and detritus that are sucked or scraped from the stream bottom or filtered from the water column. Filtering is achieved using tiny finger-like projections on the gills called *gill rakers*.

Fish species vary in their tolerance of various types of environmental degradation, and the fish assemblages found in a stream are good indicators of ecosystem condition. By volume, soil flowing off of croplands and urban construction sites is the greatest pollutant affecting streams both nationally and in Wisconsin. This sediment smothers important streambed habitat and makes water turbid, which affects fishes' ability to find food. Sediment also warms the water via increased solar heating. Phosphorus flowing off of crop fields and urban areas promotes algae growth, which causes a shift toward poorer food sources for stream invertebrates, which are the base of the food chain. Excess nutrients in streams, such as phosphorus and nitrogen, increase not only algae but also other aquatic plant growth, which increases the fluctuation in dissolved oxygen concentrations in the water. Wide fluctuations are stressful to both invertebrates and fish. Habitat alterations due to sedimentation, streambank erosion, riparian corridor development, or straightening of stream channels also have strong negative effects on stream fish assemblages. Lastly, groundwater withdrawal can reduce the amount and thermal stability of water flowing into a stream, which is the living space for fish and other aquatic animals.

BOWFINS (AMIIDAE)

Amiidae was once a large family of primitive fishes that were most abundant during the Mesozoic period (250 to 65 million years ago). Today, only one species remains, and it is found only in North America.

Bowfins have the ability to gulp air and can tolerate low dissolved oxygen concentrations in water. They can also swim both forward and backward. They are advanced among primitive fishes in terms of caring for young: the bowfin male builds and guards the nest, then protects the young for six to eight weeks after they hatch. There are reports of protective male bowfins even propelling themselves out of the water toward perceived threats.

The word *Amiidae* is from the Greek *amia* (a kind of shark).

BOWFIN
Amia calva   40–70 (max 100) cm

juvenile

DESCRIPTION: Body moderately long, stout. Mouth large, with numerous canine-like teeth. Nostrils prominent. 2 barbel-like structures present on snout. Dorsal fin base long, rays short; anal fin base short. Back and sides olive; belly whitish; pectoral, pelvic, and anal fins often green. Often dark mottling on body. Juveniles with black spot near top of tail base.

LOOK-ALIKES: Burbot.

NOTES: The bowfin is uncommon to common in large rivers and lakes in the Mississippi and Lake Michigan basins and in their low-gradient tributaries (especially during spawning). It prefers clear, vegetated water. The bowfin is only moderately tolerant of overall environmental degradation, but it can gulp air for breathing to survive in habitats with very low dissolved oxygen levels. It is omnivorous but eats mainly fish and invertebrates. The bowfin sometimes enters tributaries to spawn or feed. Spawning occurs from April to June over nests made by clearing vegetation.

BULLHEAD CATFISHES (ICTALURIDAE)

Ictaluridae is an exclusively North American family, one of thirty families of catfishes worldwide. Seven species of catfishes are found in Wisconsin streams. An eighth species, the flathead catfish (*Pylodictis olivaris*), is found in large rivers. Members of the bullhead catfish family have large heads that are flattened top to bottom (dorsoventrally); minute, sharp teeth arrayed in broad pads; 8 prominent whisker-like barbels; exclusively soft fin rays, except for 1 spinous fin ray at the anterior end of the dorsal fin and in each pectoral fin; and an elongated adipose fin. Species in this family lack scales and have thousands of taste buds covering their bodies and tails to help them sense food in turbid water or at night. These fishes tend to be nocturnal and swim along the bottom, with their barbels skimming along the stream or lake bed, searching for food. Bullhead catfishes are hosts for glochidia of a number of mussel species.

The bullhead catfishes found in Wisconsin streams can be divided into three groups: bullheads, madtoms, and the channel catfish. Bullheads and channel catfish are larger, popular game fishes and have an adipose fin that is not connected to the back and tail at the posterior end. Madtoms are smaller, are seldom seen, and have an adipose fin that is connected to the back and tail at the posterior end of the fin. Bullheads do well in enriched silt-bottomed waters and are often the only species to survive low-oxygen conditions.

The word *Ictaluridae* is from the Greek *ichthys* (fish) and *ailouros* (cat).

Catfishes with Forked Tails

CHANNEL CATFISH
Ictalurus punctatus

40–60 (max 85) cm

juvenile

large adult

DESCRIPTION: Head flattened top to bottom (dorsoventrally). 8 barbles; longest barbel longer than head. Spine on pectoral fins with teeth on posterior edge. Adipose fin not connected to tail. Anal fin rounded, with long base: 24–27 rays, including small rays. Tail deeply forked. In juveniles (10–30 cm long), body with dark spots on silvery bluish or olive background. Smaller juveniles (<10 cm) with black-tipped fins, no spots on body. Larger adults (>30 cm) also with few or no spots on body.

LOOK-ALIKES: None in wadeable streams.

NOTES: The channel catfish is common in the southern part of the state and is uncommon in the north. It inhabits large streams, rivers, and lakes, prefers warm water, and is moderately tolerant of environmental degradation. Juveniles are found largely in riffles, adults largely in pools. The channel catfish feeds most actively from sundown until midnight and has a broad diet, eating fish, crayfish, insects, and carrion. Spawning occurs from May to July in shelters under rocks or among tree roots. The channel catfish is highly valued as a game fish, especially along the Mississippi River. This fish is a host of the glochidia (parasitic young) of a large number of large river mussel species.

Bullheads (*Ameiurus* spp.)

BLACK BULLHEAD
Ameiurus melas (formerly *Ictalurus*)   15–25 (max 54.6) cm

DESCRIPTION: Head flattened top to bottom (dorsoventrally). Spine on each pectoral fin with slightly rough posterior edge but without saw-like teeth. Adipose fin not connected to tail. Anal fin base short: 17–21 rays, including smallest rays. Body a solid dark color; belly white to yellow. 8 barbles; chin barbels dark. Often a light vertical bar at tail base.

LOOK-ALIKES: Other bullheads; may hybridize with brown bullhead.

pectoral fin spine

NOTES: The black bullhead is common statewide. It inhabits lakes, ponds, and low-gradient streams and is tolerant of environmental degradation such as high turbidity; it is often the only survivor of low dissolved oxygen conditions. It prefers warm water. An opportunistic, nocturnal feeder, it eats mainly snails, leeches, aquatic insect larvae, fish, and carrion. Spawning occurs from April to June over mud or sand substrate under shelter such as matted vegetation, undercut banks, and logs or in muskrat tunnels. Large swirling masses of swimming young can be seen in spring. As these fish mature they become more solitary and secretive.

YELLOW BULLHEAD
Ameiurus natalis (formerly *Ictalurus*)   16.5–27.5 (max 39.4) cm

DESCRIPTION: Head flattened top to bottom (dorsoventrally). Spine on each pectoral fin with saw-like teeth on posterior edge (see brown bullhead for illustration, page 174). Adipose fin not connected to tail. Anal fin base long: 24–27 rays, including smallest rays. Body solid black to yellowish brown. 8 barbels; chin barbels white or yellow. No light bar at base of tail.

LOOK-ALIKES: Other bullheads.

pectoral fin spine

NOTES: The yellow bullhead is common statewide, though only sporadically found in S.W. Wisconsin. It inhabits lakes and midsized, low-gradient streams and prefers clear, warm water, although it is tolerant of environmental degradation such as high turbidity and low dissolved oxygen levels. It mainly eats insect larvae, snails, crayfish, fish, and carrion. Spawning occurs from May to July under shelter such as streambanks, logs, or tree roots.

BULLHEAD CATFISHES (Ictaluridae)

BROWN BULLHEAD
15–30 (max 44.5) cm
Ameiurus nebulosus (formerly *Ictalurus*)

DESCRIPTION: Head flattened top to bottom (dorsoventrally). Spine on each pectoral fin with saw-like teeth on posterior edge. Adipose fin not connected to tail. Anal fin base medium length: 21–24 rays, including smallest rays. Body yellowish brown or dark gray, often with dark mottling. 8 barbels; chin barbels dark. No light bar at base of tail.

pectoral fin spine

LOOK-ALIKES: Other bullheads; hybridizes with black bullhead.

NOTES: The brown bullhead is found statewide, although there are few occurrences in the Wisconsin River drainage. This species is found mainly in lakes and ponds, only rarely in streams in low-gradient reaches near lakes. It prefers warm water and can survive high turbidity and low dissolved oxygen concentrations but is moderately tolerant of overall environmental degradation. The brown bullhead eats insect larvae, snails, crayfish, fish, and carrion. Spawning occurs from May to July over mud, sand, or gravel substrate under shelter such as rocks, logs, or vegetation. In late autumn brown bullheads become sluggish and will burrow in bottom sediments for up to 24 hours, with only their mouths protruding above the stream or lake bottom.

Madtoms (*Noturus* spp.)

SLENDER MADTOM
7.5–11.5 (max 12.5) cm
Noturus exilis

ENDANGERED

DESCRIPTION: Head flattened top to bottom (dorsoventrally). Tooth pad on roof of mouth oval or rectangular, without tips that point to rear. Lower jaw only slightly shorter than upper jaw. 8 barbels. Spine on each pectoral fin with saw-like teeth on posterior edge. Adipose fin connected to tail. Tail rounded, relatively short (see tadpole madtom, page 175). Sometimes large light yellow spots in front of and behind dorsal fin; no dark lateral streaks. Tail, dorsal, and anal fins uniformly pigmented or with distinctive black edges. Light blotch on upper edge of tail.

short tail (A > B)

pectoral fin spine

LOOK-ALIKES: Stonecat and tadpole madtom; also burbot.

NOTES: The slender madtom was historically found from S. Wisconsin throughout the Rock River drainage, but in this state is currently found only in the southeast in the Bark and Oconomowoc Rivers and possibly in the Richland Creek watershed south of Monroe, where it is uncommon to rare. It inhabits streams and rivers, preferring swift, shallow, clear water with rocky substrate. It is intolerant of environmental degradation, including siltation and high turbidity, and it mostly eats insect larvae. Spawning occurs from May to June under rocks.

tooth pad

tooth pad

STONECAT
Noturus flavus

10–17.5 (max 30) cm

DESCRIPTION: Body long. Head flattened top to bottom (dorsoventrally). Overbite mouth: lower jaw noticeably shorter than upper. Tooth pad on roof of mouth crescent-shaped, with tips pointing to the rear. 8 barbels. Spine on each pectoral fin smooth, without teeth. Adipose fin connected to tail. Tail mostly square, relatively short (see tadpole madtom, below). Light spots in front of and behind dorsal fin; no dark lateral streaks. Pelvic fins completely light-colored; other fins uniformly dark or dark with light edges.

short tail (A > B)

LOOK-ALIKES: Other madtoms; also burbot.

tooth pad

tooth pad

NOTES: The stonecat is common statewide, though only sporadically in N. Wisconsin. It inhabits streams and small rivers, preferring the clear water of rocky riffles and pools. The stonecat is moderately tolerant of environmental degradation and short periods of low oxygen but is much less tolerant than most bullheads. It eats mainly insect larvae, though large individuals will occasionally consume fish. Spawning occurs from May to June under rocks.

TADPOLE MADTOM
Noturus gyrinus

4.5–8.9 (max 11.7) cm

DESCRIPTION: Body chubby anteriorly. Head flattened top to bottom (dorsoventrally). Tooth pad on roof of mouth oval or rectangular, without tips that point to the rear. 8 barbels. Spine on each pectoral fin smooth on posterior edge. Adipose fin connected to tail. Tail rounded or slightly pointed, relatively long (see other madtoms). Body a solid light brown color, with 3 dark lateral streaks on each side; dark vertical lines outline muscles. Fins usually dark with light edges.

long tail (A ≤ B)

LOOK-ALIKES: Slender madtom and stonecat; also burbot.

pectoral fin spine

tooth pad

NOTES: The tadpole madtom is common statewide except near Lake Superior, where it is rare. It inhabits medium to large low-gradient rivers, mainly in sloughs, backwaters, and tributary mouths, as well as lakes with extensive aquatic vegetation. It prefers quiet water with dense cover; eats insect larvae, crustaceans, and aquatic worms; and is moderately tolerant of environmental degradation. Spawning occurs from June to July under shelters such as logs or roots or in artificial cavities such as soda and beer cans.

CODS (GADIDAE)

The cod family has twenty-five species worldwide, all of which are found in the Northern Hemisphere, mostly in the Atlantic and Pacific Oceans. Cod (*Gadus* spp.) and haddock (*Melanogrammus aeglefinus*) are two well-known members of this family, important for human consumption. Gadidae is represented by only one species in Wisconsin, the burbot. Species in this family tend to have a large head with wide gill openings, bands of small teeth, and a single small barbel at the tip of the chin. The word *Gadidae* is from the Greek *gados* (fish).

Some more recent taxonomic classifications place burbot in its own family, Lotidae. *Lotidae* is from the French *la lotte* (monkfish, angler fish, or burbot).

BURBOT
Lota lota

20–48.3 (max 96) cm

DESCRIPTION: Body elongated, very slippery. Head large and flattened top to bottom (dorsoventrally); eyes small. 1 barbel at tip of chin. 2 dorsal fins; second dorsal fin very long. Anal fin also very long. Pelvic fins in front of pectoral fins. Body brown to yellow with mottling.

LOOK-ALIKES: Madtoms, bowfin.

NOTES: The burbot is sporadically distributed in Wisconsin and may be locally common, particularly in N. Wisconsin. It inhabits large rivers, lakes, and occasionally smaller tributaries, preferring cool, deep water, and is moderately tolerant of environmental degradation. It eats aquatic insects and crustaceans when small and mainly fish as an adult. Spawning occurs from January to March. While similar in taste to other species in the cod family, burbot is underutilized as a food fish in the United States.

DRUMS (SCIAENIDAE)

The drum family is composed of 160 species worldwide, 33 of which are found in the United States and Canada. Drums are mainly saltwater fishes that dominate in tropical and subtropical waters, but some species venture into freshwater habitats at times. Wisconsin is home to only one species.

Drums generally have a large head with heavy skull bones; bands of small, sharp teeth; prominent scales on the head and body; a distinct lateral line; two barely connected dorsal fins (one spiny, one soft); and an anal fin with two spines. The name "drum" comes from the fact that breeding males of most species can produce a drumming sound by vibrating muscles and tendons against the swim bladder. This drumming is associated with mating.

Many members of the drum family are valuable for sport and for human consumption. Wisconsin's only drum, the freshwater drum, is common in the southern half of the state. It is considered a nongame fish and thus is not regulated, although it experiences moderate sport-fishing harvest.

FRESHWATER DRUM
Aplodinotus grunniens   **25.4–50 (max 95.3) cm**

DESCRIPTION: Body deep. Back strongly arched. Scales highly visible on head, body, and bases of dorsal and anal fins. Lateral line extending through tail base. Mouth ventral; upper jaw extending to middle of eye. Teeth small, in broad bands on both jaws. 2 dorsal fins, barely connected. Pelvic fins each with first ray elongated (located adjacent to the single pelvic spine). 2 anal fin spines, second longer and stouter than first, and 7 rays. Tail rounded, square, or triangular (not forked). Color olive to silver, with whitish head, belly, and pectoral fins.

pelvic fin

LOOK-ALIKES: White perch.

NOTES: The freshwater drum occurs in several lakes and large rivers in the Mississippi and Lake Michigan basins, such as the Mississippi, Saint Croix, and Wisconsin Rivers and Lake Winnebago. It may move into the large pools of tributaries of these systems. It prefers turbid, deep water and is moderately tolerant of overall environmental degradation. It eats mainly invertebrates, including mollusks, and fish. Spawning occurs from April to July in deep, open water. It is the only freshwater fish in North America for which the eggs and larvae float on the water surface (eggs hatch 24–48 hours after spawning). It is an important host for the glochidia (parasitic young) of many mussel species. The freshwater drum is one of the few fish species in Wisconsin that will eat zebra mussels. This species is relatively long-lived, and fish collected from Lake Winnebago have been estimated to be over 40 years old.

GARS (LEPISOSTEIDAE)

The gar family has seven species worldwide, all of which are found in North America and two of which are found in Wisconsin. The longnose gar is the only gar found in Wisconsin streams. The shortnose gar (*Lepisosteus platostomus*) is restricted to larger rivers and associated lakes and impoundments.

Gars are primitive fish that have the ability to breathe air. They surface briefly to breathe every few minutes, except during winter. This ability to breathe air gives them a tolerance for very low concentrations of dissolved oxygen in water.

Historically, gars were seen as nuisance fish because they prey on other fishes, but they are becoming more appreciated for their ability to curb populations of invasives such as carp or overabundant panfish. Gars are the only hosts to the glochidia (parasitic young) of yellow sandshell mussels, which are endangered in Wisconsin.

The word *Lepisosteidae* is from the Greek *lepis* and *idos* (scale) and *osteon* (bone), referring to their bony scales, which are characteristic of many primitive fishes. The word *gar* is an Old English word meaning "spear," probably referring to the long, spear-like mouth with sharp teeth.

LONGNOSE GAR
Lepisosteus osseus

50–100 (max 180) cm

DESCRIPTION: Body long and cylindrical, with prominent, beak-like mouth and snout, which are flattened from top to bottom. Teeth needle-like. Scales rhomboid, visible along entire body. Dorsal fin (single) and anal fin set far back on body. Body gray to green above, whitish below, with diffuse black spots on posterior portion and on some fins. Juveniles often with broad, dark lateral stripe, with white stripe immediately below.

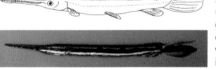

juvenile

LOOK-ALIKES: None in wadeable streams.

NOTES: In Wisconsin the longnose gar is found mainly in the southern half of the state. It is common in the Wolf, Fox, Mississippi, and lower Wisconsin River systems and also in some northwestern rivers. It is uncommon in N.E. Wisconsin. It prefers quiet water, mainly inhabiting lakes, reservoirs, and backwaters of large rivers, as well as the lower reaches of wadeable streams that drain into these bodies of water. The longnose gar is only moderately tolerant of overall environmental degradation, but it can breathe air to survive in habitats with low dissolved oxygen levels. Juvenile longnose gar eat zooplankton and larval fish; adults are ambush predators. Longnose gar often feed at the water's surface at night, lying motionless, waiting for prey to swim nearby; with a quick sideways slashing motion they capture fish in their toothy jaws. The longnose gar is typically found in streams during spawning, which occurs from May to early July.

GOBIES (GOBIDAE)

Gobiidae is a large family (at least 1,875 species) that is mostly tropical or subtropical and marine in distribution. *Gobiidae* is from the Latin *gobius* (goby). Gobies tend to be small, with the pelvic fins fused into a suction disk that anchors the fish to substrate.

The two species of Gobiidae found in Wisconsin, the round goby and the tubenose goby, are both native to the Black and Caspian Seas and invasive here. Both species were most likely transported to the Great Lakes in the 1990s in the ballast water of transoceanic ships. The tubenose goby (*Proterorhinus marmoratus*) is uncommon and has not yet been found in streams. It is too early to know whether it poses a threat to native ecosystems. The round goby, however, is of great concern due to its rapid and continuing spread, high abundance, and aggressive nature.

The round goby's introduction has already had serious consequences for parts of the Great Lakes ecosystem. It has caused declines of native species that use similar habitats, such as Johnny darter, logperch, and mottled and slimy sculpins. The round goby has been observed to eat the eggs and fry of game fishes such as smallmouth bass and lake sturgeon and may limit the populations of these species. Round goby feeding has also decreased the abundance of a variety of native invertebrate species that are consumed by a wide range of native fishes. Round gobies prey heavily on invasive dreissenid mussels (zebra and quagga mussels, page 163) and may reduce their abundance locally, but this predation is not believed to be sufficient to control populations of these two mussel species.

ROUND GOBY
Neogobius melanostomus
(formerly *Apollonia melanostomus*)

7.5–12.5 (max 17.5 in Wisconsin, max 25 elsewhere) cm

INVASIVE—RESTRICTED

DESCRIPTION: Head and mouth wide: when viewed from above, body tapering from wide head to narrow caudal peduncle. 2 dorsal fins. Pectoral fins large. Pelvic fins fused. Scales present (compare with sculpins, page 230). Mottled; first dorsal fin may have green tinge and distinct black spot. Juveniles are solid slate gray.

LOOK-ALIKES: Sculpins.

NOTES: The round goby is found along Great Lakes shorelines and nearshore reefs and in tributaries. It lives on the bottom and prefers rocky or gravel substrate. It can use its fused pelvic fins as a suction disk to anchor itself to vertical surfaces. It is moderately tolerant of environmental degradation such as high turbidity. It eats mainly invertebrates, especially isopods, insect larvae, and invasive zebra and quagga mussels, but it also consumes small fish and fish eggs. Spawning occurs from April to September.

pelvic fins

first dorsal fin

KILLIFISHES AND TOPMINNOWS (Fundulidae)

KILLIFISHES AND TOPMINNOWS (FUNDULIDAE)

The killifish and topminnow family is native to North America. Its Wisconsin species live mostly near the water surface, although the word *Fundulidae* is from the Latin *fundus* (bottom)—many non-Wisconsin species are less surface-oriented. There are three species in Wisconsin, all of which are found in streams. They tend to be small, with a dorsal, upturned mouth adapted for surface feeding, a flattened head and back, large eyes, and a dorsal fin that is located posterior (all or almost entirely behind) to pelvic fins.

BANDED KILLIFISH
Fundulus diaphanus

3.5–6.4 (max 7.5) cm

SPECIAL CONCERN

DESCRIPTION: Body long, slender. Mouth upturned. Dorsal fin origin slightly in front of anal fin origin. Scales relatively small (see starhead topminnow, page 181). 10–20 thick green vertical bars on silver background (no mottling, no teardrop, no lateral stripe). Breeding males with prominent vertical bars, often green-gold iridescence on dorsal fin.

LOOK-ALIKES: Starhead and blackstripe topminnows; western mosquitofish.

NOTES: The banded killifish is found in E. and N.W. Wisconsin and is generally uncommon. It inhabits streams and lakes with aquatic vegetation, preferring quiet, shallow, clear, open water with sandy substrate. The banded killifish is moderately tolerant of environmental degradation. It is a schooling species that is less surface-oriented than the topminnows. It eats mainly aquatic insects and zooplankton. Spawning occurs from June to August.

180

STARHEAD TOPMINNOW
Fundulus dispar

3.5–5.5 (max 6.2) cm

ENDANGERED

DESCRIPTION: Body deep, compressed side to side (laterally). Mouth upturned. Dorsal fin origin behind anal fin origin. Scales large (see banded killifish, page 180). Silver-white spot on top of head (most visible when swimming). Dark teardrop under eye. 7–8 thin, dotted horizontal stripes on olive or silver background (no mottling, no thick vertical bars, no broad dark lateral stripe). Males with thin vertical bars; bars absent or diffuse in females.

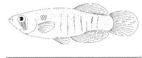

breeding male

LOOK-ALIKES: Banded killifish, blackstripe topminnow, and western mosquitofish.

NOTES: The starhead topminnow is rare and in Wisconsin is found only in the southern part of the state. It inhabits medium to large rivers and a few shallow vegetated lakes, preferring quiet, shallow, slightly turbid, vegetated backwaters and sloughs. The starhead topminnow is moderately tolerant of environmental degradation, and it eats mainly terrestrial insects that fall or are blown into the water and zooplankton. Spawning occurs from June to July.

BLACKSTRIPE TOPMINNOW
Fundulus notatus

3.5–6 (max 7.5) cm

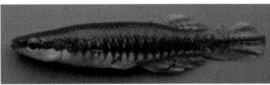

DESCRIPTION: Body slender (males deeper-bodied). Mouth upturned. Dorsal fin origin behind anal fin origin. Silver-white spot on top of head (most visible when swimming). Wide blue-black stripe from snout to tail. No teardrop below eye. Dorsal, anal, and tail (caudal) fins tannish or yellowish in males and spotted in both sexes. Males with vertical crossbars on stripe; females with straight margin on stripe.

LOOK-ALIKES: Banded killifish, starhead topminnow, and western mosquitofish.

female

NOTES: In Wisconsin the blackstripe topminnow is found mainly in the southeast and is common. It inhabits low-gradient streams, rivers, ditches, and occasionally lakes, preferring quiet water near the surface. The blackstripe topminnow is moderately tolerant of environmental degradation, and it eats mainly terrestrial insects that fall or are blown into the water and algae. Spawning occurs from June to July.

LAMPREYS (Petromyzontidae)

LAMPREYS (PETROMYZONTIDAE)

Lampreys are primitive, eel-like fishes that lack jaws, scales, and bone and have only dorsal and caudal (tail) fins. They are found throughout the world, mainly in temperate regions. Their populations are declining in many states in the Upper Midwest. There are five native lamprey species in Wisconsin and one invasive species, the sea lamprey. These six species are grouped into three genera: *Ichthyomyzon* (four species), *Lampetra* (referred to as *Lethenteron* by some biologists), and *Petromyzon*.

Lampreys have distinct larval, intermediate, and adult life stages. Larvae, called *ammocoetes*, are more commonly encountered in wadeable streams than adults. They are blind. They live as filter feeders for three to seven years prior to metamorphosis, burrowing into the sandy or silty substrate of pools or runs. Metamorphosis typically occurs in winter and lasts approximately six months, during which time the lampreys are called *transformers*. Finally, the adult life stage lasts only one to two months. Adults may be found in streams in spring during spawning, in riffles. All lampreys die soon after spawning.

Adult lampreys do not feed, but three Wisconsin species are parasitic in an additional intermediate life stage between transformer and adult. For these species—the chestnut, silver, and sea lampreys—winter metamorphosis leads to a parasitic life stage in which they spend one year feeding on the blood of other fish before becoming fully mature adults. (As with nonparasitic species, the adult life stage lasts only one to two months.) During the parasitic stage, they resemble adults.

Both larval and adult lampreys have elongated, scaleless bodies, suction disk mouths, a single median nostril in front of the eyes, seven pore-like gill openings, one or two dorsal fins continuous with the tail, and no other fins. The family name *Petromyzontidae* is from the Latin *petra* (stone) and the Greek *myzo* (to suckle) and *odontos* (teeth), referring to their habit of clinging to rocks with their distinctive tooth-filled suction disk mouths.

Identifying lampreys to the species level is difficult and sometimes impossible. Ammocoetes can seldom be identified to species, and *Ichthyomyzon* ammocoetes cannot be distinguished from each other in the field. Head and mouth structure is key to identification of adults and requires knowledge of several terms unique to lampreys—see the diagrams below and the glossary for definitions of unfamiliar terms.

Lamprey ammocoetes can be distinguished from adults. An ammocoete has a hood-like mouth (without a *papillary fringe*), a *sieve apparatus* that fills the mouth opening, a lack of teeth, and rudimentary eyes. In contrast, an adult has a round or oval mouth with a papillary fringe, no sieve apparatus within the mouth opening, teeth present, and functional eyes. As adults, the four *Ichthyomyzon* species can be distinguished from other Wisconsin lampreys by a single, continuous dorsal fin. The two remaining species (American brook and sea lampreys) have two distinct dorsal fins. Adults can most easily be identified to species by the size of their suction disk and by whether their *circumoral teeth* are *unicuspid* (one-pointed) or *bicuspid* (two-pointed).

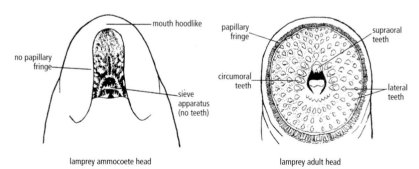

lamprey ammocoete head

lamprey adult head

Because they depend on filter feeding as ammocoetes, lampreys are sensitive to pollutants, and their presence may indicate good water quality. Several lamprey species—the brook lampreys and the sea lamprey—tend to be found in cool and cold, moderate- to high-gradient streams, so they are often associated with trout, sculpins, burbot, and certain minnows and darters.

CHESTNUT LAMPREY
Ichthyomyzon castaneus   12.5–23.5 (max 27.1) cm

ammocoete

adult

ammocoete

DESCRIPTION: Body elongate, with round sucking mouth. Single dorsal fin, connected to tail, with shallow notch.

DESCRIPTION (AMMOCOETE): Hood-like mouth without teeth; eyes rudimentary; indistinguishable from other *Ichthyomyzon* ammocoetes.

DESCRIPTION (ADULT): Oral disk that, when expanded, is as wide as or wider than maximum body diameter. 2 supraoral teeth narrowly separated; 4 pairs of bicuspid (2-pointed) circumoral teeth; 7–8 lateral teeth per radiating row. Lateral pores dark.

adult

adult

LOOK-ALIKES: Southern brook lamprey; also northern brook and silver lampreys.

NOTES: The chestnut lamprey is found in the western two-thirds of the state (not in the Lake Superior basin) and is uncommon to common. It inhabits midsized streams to large rivers and is intolerant of environmental degradation. Ammocoetes prefer unvegetated water with silty sand substrate; adults prefer flowing, shallow water with gravel or larger rocks. Postlarval chestnut lampreys are parasitic on the blood of fish species such as suckers, catfishes, paddlefish, and northern pike for nearly a year before reaching full maturity. Spawning occurs from April to June, with a peak in May in rocky riffles and runs. Chestnut lampreys sometimes spawn together with southern brook lampreys.

NORTHERN BROOK LAMPREY
Ichthyomyzon fossor   10–13.5 (max 17.1) cm

ammocoete

adult

ammocoete

DESCRIPTION: Body elongate, with round sucking mouth. Single dorsal fin, connected to tail, sometimes with shallow notch.

DESCRIPTION (AMMOCOETE): Hood-like mouth without teeth; eyes rudimentary; indistinguishable from other *Ichthyomyzon* ammocoetes.

DESCRIPTION (ADULT): Oral disk that, when expanded, is narrower than maximum body diameter. 2 supraoral teeth narrowly separated; other teeth unicuspid (1-pointed), small, blunt. Lateral pores light-colored.

adult

adult

LOOK-ALIKES: Silver lamprey; also chestnut and southern brook lampreys.

NOTES: The northern brook lamprey is found sporadically statewide; it is common in the Red Cedar and Wolf River drainages. It inhabits midsized streams and rivers, preferring moderately warm, clear water, and it is intolerant of environmental degradation. Ammocoetes prefer quiet water, often burrowing into soft substrate and filter-feeding on algae; adults prefer riffles and runs. This species is nonparasitic; spawning occurs from April to June.

SOUTHERN BROOK LAMPREY
Ichthyomyzon gagei

20–23.5 (max 27.1) cm

ammocoete

ammocoete

adult

DESCRIPTION: Body elongate, with round sucking mouth. Single dorsal fin, connected to tail.

DESCRIPTION (AMMOCOETE): Hood-like mouth without teeth; eyes rudimentary; indistinguishable from other *Ichthyomyzon* ammocoetes.

adult

DESCRIPTION (ADULT): Oral disk that, when expanded, is narrower than maximum body diameter. 2–3 supraoral teeth narrowly separated; 3–4 pairs of bicuspid (2-pointed) inner circumoral teeth (see chestnut lamprey for additional illustration, page 183). Lateral pores dark.

LOOK-ALIKES: Chestnut lamprey; also northern brook and silver lampreys.

NOTES: Despite its name, the southern brook lamprey is found in sporadic locations in N. Wisconsin, where it is uncommon to common. (It is called "southern" because, outside of Wisconsin, it is found mostly in the southern United States.) It inhabits small streams and rivers, preferring shallow, cool, clear water, and it is intolerant of environmental degradation. Ammocoetes often burrow in silty sand in runs and pools, while adults prefer riffles and runs. This species is nonparasitic. Spawning occurs from May to June in gravelly riffles or under rocks.

SILVER LAMPREY
Ichthyomyzon unicuspis

10.3–32.6 (max 38.5) cm

ammocoete

ammocoete

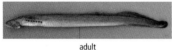

adult

DESCRIPTION: Body elongate, with round sucking mouth. Single dorsal fin slightly notched.

DESCRIPTION (AMMOCOETE): Hood-like mouth without teeth; eyes rudimentary; indistinguishable from other *Ichthyomyzon* ammocoetes.

adult

adult

DESCRIPTION (ADULT): Oral disk that, when expanded, is as wide as or wider than maximum body diameter. 2 supraoral teeth narrowly separated; 4 pairs of unicuspid (1-pointed) circumoral teeth (rarely 1 bicuspid tooth); 6–7 lateral teeth per radiating row; 3 teeth in anterior row. Lateral pores slightly darkened, dark in larger specimens. Young adult light yellow tan; older adult blue or blue gray.

LOOK-ALIKES: Northern brook lamprey; also chestnut and southern brook lampreys.

NOTES: The silver lamprey is sporadically distributed in Wisconsin and is uncommon to common. It inhabits lakes and large rivers, preferring fairly clear water over gravel or sand substrate, and it is intolerant of environmental degradation. Postlarval silver lampreys are parasitic, feeding on the blood of fish species such as catfishes, sturgeons, suckers, and paddlefish for nearly a year before reaching full maturity. Spawning occurs from April to June in riffles of medium or large rivers or the lower reaches of their tributaries.

AMERICAN BROOK LAMPREY
Lampetra appendix (also known as *Lethenteron*)　　　**13–19.4 (max 20.2) cm**

ammocoete

DESCRIPTION: Body elongate, with round sucking mouth. 2 distinct dorsal fins.

DESCRIPTION (AMMOCOETE): Hood-like mouth without teeth; eyes rudimentary. Tail bluntly pointed, light near edges. Lower half of upper lip and area under eye light; wide light band above gill openings; lower edge of caudal peduncle light.

DESCRIPTION (ADULT): Oral disk that, when expanded, is wider than maximum body diameter. 2 supraoral teeth widely separated; 3 pairs of bicuspid circumoral teeth; no lateral teeth beyond those mentioned. Body brown; darker above, pale below; no mottling.

LOOK-ALIKES: Sea lamprey.

NOTES: The American brook lamprey is widespread in W. Wisconsin and found sporadically elsewhere; it is found especially in the Red Cedar, Black, Wisconsin, and Rock River drainages but not in the Lake Superior basin. It inhabits small streams to midsized rivers and is intolerant of environmental degradation. Ammocoetes often burrow in the silty sand of pools; adults prefer cool, clear water with sandy, gravelly riffles and runs. This species is nonparasitic. Spawning occurs from April to May over gravel substrate.

ammocoete

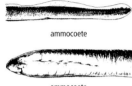

ammocoete

ammocoete

ammocoete

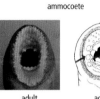

adult　　　adult

adult

 # LAMPREYS (Petromyzontidae)

SEA LAMPREY
Petromyzon marinus

35–61 (max 76) cm

INVASIVE—RESTRICTED

ammocoete

ammocoete

ammocoete

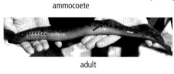
ammocoete

adult

adult

adult

DESCRIPTION: Body elongate, with round sucking mouth. 2 distinct dorsal fins.

DESCRIPTION (AMMOCOETE): Hood-like mouth without teeth; eyes rudimentary. Tail rounded, dark almost to edges. Body solid dark brown or gray. Lower half of upper lip and area under eye dark; narrow light band above gill openings; lower edge of caudal peduncle dark.

DESCRIPTION (ADULT): Large size. Oral disk, when expanded, as wide as or wider than maximum body diameter. 2 supraoral teeth narrowly separated; 4 pairs of bicuspid (2-pointed) circumoral teeth, 5–7 lateral teeth per radiating row. Body light brown with mottling.

LOOK-ALIKES: American brook lamprey.

NOTES: The sea lamprey is uncommon. Ammocoetes inhabit quiet pools of streams that are tributaries to the Great Lakes, burrowing in soft sediments with their heads exposed to filter-feed on algae and detritus. Adults inhabit the open waters of the Great Lakes. Postlarval sea lampreys feed on the blood of commercially important species such as lake trout (*Salvelinus namaycush*), salmons, lake whitefish (*Coregonus clupeaformis*), and other fish species for nearly a year before reaching sexual maturity. Adult lampreys then migrate from the Great Lakes into tributary streams to spawn. Spawning occurs from April to July, over gravel or sand substrate, in cool or coldwater streams. The sea lamprey is a nuisance species, contributing to the mortality of Great Lakes fishes. Millions of dollars are spent each year by Canada and the United States to apply chemical lampricides in tributary streams to kill lamprey ammocoetes or to maintain physical or electrical barriers to upstream movement of the spawning adults.

186

LIVEBEARERS (POECILIIDAE)

The livebearer family has about 150 species, most of which are found in the tropics. Many of the tropical species are important in the aquarium trade, including the guppy (*Poecilia reticulata*), green swordtail (*Xiphophorus hellerii*), and platy (*X. maculatus*). As its common name implies, the family is characterized by fish that use internal fertilization and give live birth to live young rather than laying eggs. The word *Poeciliidae* is from the Greek *poikilos* (with different colors), referring to the bright colors of some of the tropical species, most notably the guppy.

The western mosquitofish is the only livebearer species found in Wisconsin streams. Native to the southeast United States, it has been introduced throughout the world for mosquito control. Its effectiveness in controlling mosquitoes is debatable, but its negative impacts on indigenous organisms in many areas are not. It is an aggressive species that has reduced or eliminated native fishes, amphibians, and invertebrates, especially in the southwest United States, Australia, and southern Europe. It may also precipitate algae blooms by reducing populations of zooplankton and other invertebrates that feed on algae.

WESTERN MOSQUITOFISH
Gambusia affinis   2.5–4 (max [females] 7.1) cm

INVASIVE—PROHIBITED

DESCRIPTION: Body very small, usually <25 mm, only rarely >35 mm. Head flattened on top. Mouth upturned. 1 dorsal fin; dorsal fin origin behind anal fin origin. Lateral line absent. Tail rounded. Body color solid tan or olive, sometimes with a few dark spots, especially on back; sometimes a short, dark, and iridescent horizontal band behind gills. Dark teardrop under eye. Breeding males may be black.

LOOK-ALIKES: Banded killifish and topminnows; juvenile cyprinids (minnows, etc.).

eastern mosquitofish (*G. holbrooki*); image is also representative of the western mosquitofish

NOTES: The western mosquitofish was stocked in Wisconsin in the 1940s but did not persist. In 2009 established populations were discovered in Pool 11 of the Mississippi River (Grant County) and in the Sugar River at Brodhead (Green County) in S.W. Wisconsin. These were probably introduced accidentally with bait shipments of fathead minnows from fish farms in the southern United States. Elsewhere in the United States, this species inhabits rivers, lakes, streams, and ponds, preferring the shallow margins of quiet, vegetated water. It is tolerant of environmental degradation, including low oxygen levels, high turbidity, and siltation. An aggressive predator, it eats mainly insect larvae at the water's surface, but it may also eat eggs, larvae, and juveniles of other fish species. It gives birth to live young, probably from May to September; it matures in 4–6 weeks and can produce several generations per year.

MINNOWS (CYPRINIDAE)

The family Cyprinidae is the largest family of freshwater fishes in the world, with at least 2,400 species; its members are found in North America, Africa, and Eurasia. The family is also the most diverse in Wisconsin, with 47 species found in the state. Of those, 35 are found in wadeable streams, all of which are native except for common carp and goldfish. Cyprinids vary greatly in size and attributes, but they generally have soft-ray fins and toothless jaws. The word *Cyprinidae* is from the Greek *kyprinos* (goldfish).

We have separated the Cyprinidae into three broad groups based on general appearance and morphology: (1) carp and goldfish; (2) chubs, dace, minnows, and stonerollers; and (3) shiners. Not all of these are taxonomic categories and this grouping is not meant to imply that species within a group are necessarily more closely related to each other than they are to members of another group. We have, however, separated the shiners because all of Wisconsin's shiners belong to five genera: *Cyprinella*, *Luxilus*, *Lythrurus*, *Notemigonus*, and *Notropis*. The Ozark minnow (*Notropis nubilus*) is taxonomically a shiner, so we have included it in the shiner section.

All of these groupings may be confusing. But the most important thing to keep in mind is that chubs, dace, minnows, shiners, and stonerollers often resemble each other, so be sure to peruse the entire Cyprinidae section for look-alikes.

Common Carp and Goldfish

Carp are among the largest species in the minnow family. Five species of carp have been observed in Wisconsin, all of which were introduced from Eurasia. Common carp is the only species that is widespread in the state. Goldfish, a type of carp, are also occasionally seen in streams. The others are not included here because they are not found in wadeable streams. These are bighead, grass, and silver carp—*Hypophthalmichthys nobilis*, *Ctenopharyngodon idella*, and *H. molitrix*, respectively (all prohibited). Collectively known as Asian carp, they are established farther south in the Mississippi River and have only been observed in Wisconsin a few times, although there is great concern that they may become established here.

Common carp and goldfish both have a large, deep body, large scales, and a forked tail. Both species also appear to have spines in their dorsal and anal fins, although these are not true spines but rather hardened bundles of soft-ray elements.

GOLDFISH
Carassius auratus

15–30 (max 45) cm

INVASIVE—RESTRICTED

DESCRIPTION: Body deep, thick. Mouth terminal. No barbels. Scales large; <32 lateral line scales. Dorsal fin base long, with 1 saw-toothed "spine," 15–21 rays; origin slightly ahead of or above pelvic fin origin. Tail large. Color variable: bright orange to olive to brown or black; sometimes orange with black mottles. No black spot at anterior base of scales.

LOOK-ALIKES: Common carp; also bigmouth buffalo and quillback; hybridizes with common carp.

NOTES: The goldfish is found in S. Wisconsin but is generally rare in wild settings. It prefers warm, shallow, vegetated water of sluggish streams, lakes, and reservoirs. It is omnivorous, feeding on aquatic worms, insect larvae, snails, clams, algae, and other aquatic plants. The goldfish is tolerant of environmental degradation. It was introduced from Asia historically, and new introductions continue due to the aquarium trade; viable populations now exist in some water bodies. Although it is listed as restricted by the Wisconsin DNR, it may be possessed, transported, or transferred without a permit as part of the aquarium trade as long as it is not released. Like other restricted species, it may not be used or possessed in any way on streams, rivers, lakes, or other water bodies. Spawning occurs from April to August over aquatic vegetation or willow roots. While on average the goldfish lives six or seven years, it may live up to thirty years.

COMMON CARP
Cyprinus carpio

40–70 (max 120) cm

INVASIVE—RESTRICTED

DESCRIPTION: Body thick, strongly arched back, and flattened below. Mouth subterminal. 2 barbels on each side of upper jaw; rear barbel much larger. Dorsal fin base long, with 1 doubly serrated "spine" and 17–21 rays; dorsal fin origin slightly anterior to or above pelvic fin origin. Anal fin with 1 serrated "spine" and 4–6 rays. Scales large; >32 lateral line scales. Body brassy olive above, light below. On back and sides, black spot at anterior base of scales. Anal fin and tail red orange on large adults.

LOOK-ALIKES: Bigmouth buffalo, goldfish, quillback, and other suckers; hybridizes with goldfish.

NOTES: The common carp is common to abundant statewide, especially in S. Wisconsin, although rare in the Lake Superior basin. It inhabits the shallows of lakes and small to large rivers, preferring warm, shallow, turbid, vegetated pools with silty substrate. It is tolerant of environmental degradation such as low dissolved oxygen and turbidity. The common carp is omnivorous and uses teeth in the back of its mouth to grind plant matter, snails, small mollusks, and insect larvae. In the late 1880s the common carp was stocked by the thousands throughout the state. To date no other fish species has caused as great and widespread damage to aquatic ecosystems in Wisconsin and across the United States as the common carp. By "rooting up" aquatic plants and resuspending bottom sediments and nutrients that reduce habitat and water quality, this fish has profound negative environmental impacts. Attempts to eradicate the common carp have been expensive and mostly unsuccessful. Spawning occurs from April to August in shallow, weedy areas. Large females can produce over a million eggs each year.

Chubs, Dace, Minnows, and Stonerollers

Chubs, dace, minnows, and stonerollers are common names for a variety of species found in the family Cyprinidae. Multiple species sharing a similar common name (e.g., chubs) may have some distinct group traits, but these are not necessarily consistent.

Fishes in these groups are generally small (usually <175 mm), with a single dorsal fin and a forked tail. They sometimes have small barbels at the corners of their mouths, usually have relatively high numbers of lateral line scales, usually have seven or eight anal fin rays, and often have diffuse mottling on their sides.

CENTRAL STONEROLLER
Campostoma anomalum   7.5–15 (max 22.5) cm

DESCRIPTION: Body nearly round in cross section. Mouth subterminal; lower jaw not fleshy, with hard edge ("chisel"; depress lower lip with pencil to observe). No barbels. 49–55 lateral line scales; 39–46 circumferential scales (see diagram; compare with largescale stoneroller, page 192). Mottled, sometimes with lateral stripe. Dorsal fin with dark crescent (not consistent in juveniles). Breeding males have tubercles on head (more tubercles near nostrils than largescale stoneroller), orange-yellow hue, and dark stripe on anal fin.

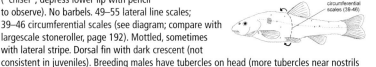

circumferential scales (39-46)

LOOK-ALIKES: Largescale stoneroller; also longnose and western blacknose dace, suckermouth minnow, and white sucker; juveniles may be confused with creek and gravel chubs. Hybridizes with longnose and southern redbelly dace.

NOTES: The central stoneroller is abundant in S. Wisconsin and found sporadically in central and N.W. Wisconsin. It inhabits small to midsized streams and occasionally rivers, preferring warm, usually swift water with coarse substrate. The central stoneroller is moderately tolerant to overall environmental degradation, though it is sensitive to high turbidity. It eats mainly algae. Spawning occurs from May to June and possibly July. Central stoneroller schools migrate upstream seeking quiet, shallow water, where the males dig small, round nests in gravel.

MINNOWS (Cyprinidae)

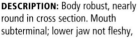

LARGESCALE STONEROLLER
Campostoma oligolepis

7.5–15 (max 20) cm

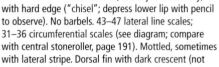

circumferential scales (31-36)

DESCRIPTION: Body robust, nearly round in cross section. Mouth subterminal; lower jaw not fleshy, with hard edge ("chisel"; depress lower lip with pencil to observe). No barbels. 43–47 lateral line scales; 31–36 circumferential scales (see diagram; compare with central stoneroller, page 191). Mottled, sometimes with lateral stripe. Dorsal fin with dark crescent (not consistent in juveniles). Dark spot on base of tail. Breeding males have tubercles on head (fewer tubercles near nostrils than central stoneroller), red-orange hue.

LOOK-ALIKES: Central stoneroller, longnose and western blacknose dace, suckermouth minnow, and white sucker; juveniles may be confused with creek and gravel chubs. Hybridizes with longnose dace.

NOTES: The largescale stoneroller is abundant in N. and central Wisconsin (though absent from the Lake Superior basin) and is found sporadically in the south. It inhabits medium to large streams, preferring pools near swift riffles. It is sensitive to siltation, but it is moderately tolerant of overall environmental degradation. It eats mainly algae. Spawning occurs in June, in swift, deep water, over large, round gravel nests.

REDSIDE DACE
Clinostomus elongatus

6.5–10 (max 11.5) cm

SPECIAL CONCERN

breeding male

DESCRIPTION: Body elongated. Snout long, pointed. Mouth very large, upturned, extending to back of eye. No barbels. Lower lip slightly forward of upper lip. Body color green blue above, with stripes on sides: thin gold stripe above darker, thicker orange-red stripe. Colors brighter in breeding males.

LOOK-ALIKES: Creek chub, and northern and southern redbelly dace; hybridizes with all of these and with common shiner.

NOTES: The redside dace is distributed sporadically through the southern three-fourths of Wisconsin, although it has been extirpated from S.E. Wisconsin. It inhabits small streams and rivers, preferring cool, quiet, or moderately swift water. It is intolerant of environmental degradation, including high temperatures and turbidity. It eats mainly terrestrial insects and aquatic insect larvae and spawns from May to June in gravelly riffles.

192

LAKE CHUB
Couesius plumbeus   10–17.5 (max 22.5) cm

DESCRIPTION: Body elongated. Snout slightly overhanging mouth. Mouth slightly subterminal, extending almost to eye. Small barbel in corner of mouth. Scales small. Back and upper sides lead gray and silver to silvery white beneath. Often faintly mottled with diffuse lateral stripe. No spot at dorsal fin base. In breeding males, rosy spot at base of pectoral fins and pinkish or reddish belly.

LOOK-ALIKES: Creek chub and its look-alikes; pearl dace.

NOTES: The lake chub is found along the shores of the Great Lakes, as well as in their tributaries during spawning around April to May. It is rarely encountered except during spawning, when it is uncommon (Lake Michigan tributaries) to common (Lake Superior tributaries). Spawning habitat varies. It generally prefers cool, shallow water with boulders. The lake chub is only moderately tolerant of overall environmental degradation but can survive in highly turbid waters. Adults eat insects; juveniles eat small crustaceans.

GRAVEL CHUB
Erimystax x-punctatus (formerly *Hybopsis*)   5–8.5 (max 10) cm

ENDANGERED

DESCRIPTION: Body slender, almost round in cross section. Snout long, overhanging mouth. Mouth small, subterminal. Small barbel in corner of mouth. Sides olive gray, silvery, or tan, with dark X-, Y-, and W-shaped markings. Belly white; fins transparent.

LOOK-ALIKES: Small shiners; also longnose and western blacknose dace, suckermouth minnow, juvenile stonerollers, and juvenile white sucker.

NOTES: The gravel chub is rare and in Wisconsin is found only in the south in the Rock River basin. It inhabits large streams to large rivers and strongly prefers swift, deep, clear, unvegetated water with gravel substrate. It is intolerant of environmental degradation, particularly turbidity and siltation. The gravel chub's diet consists of algae and detritus. Spawning occurs from May to June.

	BRASSY MINNOW
3.5–7.5 (max 9.5) cm	*Hybognathus hankinsoni*

DESCRIPTION: Snout long, blunt, rounded, slightly overhanging mouth. Dorsal fin rounded. No dark pigmentation on sides. Sometimes with a brassy color (especially breeding males).

breeding male

LOOK-ALIKES: Bluntnose and fathead minnows.

NOTES: The brassy minnow is a schooling species that is uncommon to common statewide. It inhabits small to midsized streams and northern bogs, preferring mostly quiet, clear water. The brassy minnow is moderately tolerant of environmental degradation. Omnivorous, it eats largely plankton and algae. Spawning occurs from May to June in vegetated areas.

	PEARL DACE
7.5–12.5 (max 15) cm	*Margariscus margarita* (formerly *Semotilus*)

DESCRIPTION: Body elongated. Mouth small, terminal, extending almost to eye. Barbels inconspicuous or absent, anterior to corners of mouth. Scales small. Often mottled, with diffuse dark lateral stripe. Adult males often with reddish or pinkish belly below dark lateral stripe. Females often yellow to red.

LOOK-ALIKES: Creek and lake chubs; hybridizes with northern redbelly dace.

NOTES: The pearl dace is uncommon to common statewide, though it is rare in S.W. Wisconsin. It inhabits low-gradient headwater streams, preferring cool, clear water often associated with wetland drainage, and it is moderately tolerant of environmental degradation. It eats mainly insect larvae and algae. Spawning occurs from March to April over gravel substrate.

HORNYHEAD CHUB
Nocomis biguttatus   8.9–15 (max 22.5) cm

DESCRIPTION: Body robust, almost round in cross section. Mouth small, slightly subterminal, extending almost to front of eye. Small barbel present at corner of mouth. Anterior dorsal scales relatively large, not much smaller than lateral line scales nor crowded anteriorly. Tail usually brown. Juveniles with yellow-orange fins, reddish tail. Often dark, diffuse lateral stripe and spot at tail base, especially in juveniles. Breeding males have orange spot behind eye and tubercles on head.

breeding male

LOOK-ALIKES: Creek chub and its look-alikes, and suckermouth minnow; hybridizes with common shiner.

NOTES: The hornyhead chub is common statewide. It inhabits midsized streams to small rivers, preferring the shallow, clear water of riffles and pools. It is moderately tolerant of environmental degradation and eats mainly snails, insect larvae, and zooplankton. Spawning occurs from May to July over large mound nests of gravel, which are guarded by the males.

SUCKERMOUTH MINNOW
Phenacobius mirabilis   6.5–10 (max 12.5) cm

DESCRIPTION: Body slender, round in cross section. Snout extending beyond mouth. Mouth inferior. Lips thick, fleshy, plicate (folded), and papillose (with bumps); lateral lobes thickened. 7 (sometimes 6) anal fin rays. Body olive brown above, silver white below, with thin, dark lateral stripe; not mottled. Dark spot at base of tail. Pelvic and anal fins whitish.

LOOK-ALIKES: Gravel and hornyhead chubs, and stonerollers; also juvenile redhorses, juvenile spottail shiner, and juvenile white sucker.

NOTES: The suckermouth minnow is found in S. and especially S.W. Wisconsin; it is uncommon to common. It inhabits streams and small rivers, preferring warm, swift, turbid, unvegetated water of riffles with coarse, silt-free substrate. It is moderately tolerant of environmental degradation and eats mainly insect larvae by rooting around in streambed gravel. Spawning occurs from July to August.

MINNOWS (Cyprinidae)

NORTHERN REDBELLY DACE
3.5–6 (max 8) cm
Phoxinus eos

breeding male

DESCRIPTION: Body elongated. Snout blunt, short. Mouth small, strongly upturned. Lower lip just ahead of upper lip (compare with southern redbelly dace, below). No barbels. Scales tiny. 2 black lateral stripes. Breeding males with golden-red (rarely green) belly, yellow fins.

LOOK-ALIKES: Finescale, redside, and southern redbelly dace. Hybridizes with common shiner and finescale, pearl, and redside dace.

NOTES: The northern redbelly dace is abundant in N. Wisconsin, found sporadically in S. Wisconsin, and rare in the Driftless Area of the southwest. It inhabits sluggish streams, beaver ponds, and boggy lakes, preferring vegetated water. The northern redbelly dace is moderately tolerant of environmental degradation. Mainly herbivorous, it eats mostly filamentous algae and diatoms (phytoplankton). Spawning occurs from May to August in mats of filamentous algae.

SOUTHERN REDBELLY DACE
5–7.5 (max 8.9) cm
Phoxinus erythrogaster

breeding male

DESCRIPTION: Body elongated. Snout triangular, with tip rounded. Mouth small, somewhat upturned. Upper lip just ahead of lower lip (compare with northern redbelly dace, above). No barbels. Scales tiny. 2 black lateral stripes. Breeding males with striking red belly; yellow fins.

LOOK-ALIKES: Finescale, northern redbelly, and redside dace; hybridizes with central stoneroller, common shiner, creek chub, and redside dace.

NOTES: The southern redbelly dace is common in S. Wisconsin. It inhabits small to midsized streams with swift currents and gravel or cobble substrate, preferring the clear water of pools or riffles. It strongly prefers to be in schools. The southern redbelly dace is moderately tolerant of environmental degradation. Mainly herbivorous, it eats mostly phytoplankton. Spawning occurs from May to July in riffles, often over other minnows' nests.

FINESCALE DACE
Phoxinus neogaeus   6.1–10 (max 12.5) cm

DESCRIPTION: Body stout. Snout blunt. Mouth medium-sized, oblique (at ~45° angle). No barbels. Scales tiny. Dark "cape" on back above single dark lateral stripe. Breeding males with upcurved pectoral fins, reddish-yellow lateral stripe.

breeding male

LOOK-ALIKES: Creek chub and northern and southern redbelly dace; hybridizes with northern redbelly dace.

NOTES: The finescale dace is uncommon to common in N. Wisconsin and rare in central Wisconsin. It inhabits sluggish streams, beaver ponds, and boggy lakes, preferring cool water. It is moderately tolerant of environmental degradation and eats mainly insect larvae and zooplankton. Spawning occurs from April to June in sheltered depressions.

BLUNTNOSE MINNOW
Pimephales notatus   4–7.5 (max 11) cm

DESCRIPTION: Body elongated, round in cross section. Snout rounded, blunt. Mouth small, horizontal, subterminal, extending almost to front of eye. Dorsal fin origin slightly behind pelvic fin origin. First dorsal fin ray short, spaced widely from other rays in larger individuals. 7 anal fin rays. Small, crowded scales in front of dorsal fin. Faint to dark stripe from eye to black spot at tail base. Breeding males darker, with barbel-like structures at corners of mouth, tubercles on snout.

breeding male

LOOK-ALIKES: Blackchin, blacknose, and weed shiners; creek chub; and other minnows.

NOTES: The bluntnose minnow is abundant statewide. It inhabits streams, small rivers, lakes, and occasionally large rivers, preferring clear water, though it is tolerant of turbid water and overall environmental degradation. An omnivorous bottom feeder, it often eats zooplankton, aquatic insect larvae, and terrestrial insects. Spawning occurs from May to August. Males excavate nests underneath logs and rocks, and they guard the nests and fan the eggs to keep them free of sediment.

breeding male
snout

MINNOWS (Cyprinidae)

FATHEAD MINNOW
Pimephales promelas

2.5–6.5 (max 9) cm

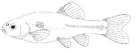

breeding male

DESCRIPTION: Body stout, ovoid in cross section, often with fat belly. Mouth small, upturned, not reaching front of eye. Dorsal fin rounded. 7 anal fin rays. Scales in front of dorsal fin small, crowded. Breeding males with black head, dark body, 2 light vertical bands, and tubercles on snout.

LOOK-ALIKES: Brassy and bluntnose minnows; creek chub.

NOTES: The fathead minnow is uncommon to common statewide. It prefers small, quiet streams and small, shallow, vegetated lakes. The fathead minnow is tolerant of environmental degradation, including high turbidity and low oxygen. It feeds on algae, insect larvae, and zooplankton. Spawning occurs from May to August underneath logs or rocks in nests prepared and guarded by the males. This species is commonly used by anglers for bait, so fathead minnows that have escaped from bait buckets may be found almost anywhere.

LONGNOSE DACE
Rhinichthys cataractae

7.5–10 (max 14) cm

DESCRIPTION: Body elongated. Head flattened top to bottom (dorsoventrally). Snout projects well over mouth (1–3 mm). Mouth inferior; lips fleshy. Upper lip connected to snout by fleshy bridge (frenum). Small barbels at corners of mouth. Dark mottling on back and sides with a small cream- or white-colored spot at the anterior origin of the dorsal fin and another small cream- or white-colored spot at the dorsal origin of the caudal fin.

LOOK-ALIKES: Gravel chub, western blacknose dace, and stonerollers; hybridizes with stonerollers, common shiner, and creek chub.

NOTES: The longnose dace is found in the northern, central, and western portions of the state but is absent from south-central Wisconsin and rare in the southeast. It inhabits streams and small rivers, preferring the cool, very swift water of rocky riffles, and it also occurs along exposed, wave-washed rocky shores of the Great Lakes. The longnose dace is moderately tolerant of environmental degradation. It eats aquatic insect larvae. Spawning occurs from April to June over gravel substrate.

WESTERN BLACKNOSE DACE (blacknose dace)
Rhinichthys obtusus   6.4–10 (max 12.5) cm

DESCRIPTION: Body chunky (stout). Head flattened top to bottom (dorsoventrally). Snout barely projects over mouth (<1 mm). Mouth subterminal, slightly oblique (at ~45° angle). Upper lip connected to snout by fleshy bridge (frenum). Small barbels at corners of mouth. Mottling on sides, sometimes forming irregular stripe posteriorly. Juveniles with prominent black lateral stripe. Breeding males with distinct orange or red lateral stripe.

LOOK-ALIKES: Gravel chub, longnose dace, and stonerollers.

breeding male

juvenile

NOTES: The western blacknose dace is common to abundant statewide. It inhabits headwater streams and small rivers, preferring cool, swift water of riffles and runs. The western blacknose dace is tolerant of environmental degradation. It eats mainly aquatic insect larvae and, to a lesser extent, algae. Spawning occurs from May to early July over gravel substrate.

WESTERN BLACKNOSE DACE *vs.* LONGNOSE DACE

Longnose dace: snout longer, overhangs mouth 1–3 mm.
Western blacknose dace: snout shorter, overhangs mouth <1 mm. Body more stout (chunky).

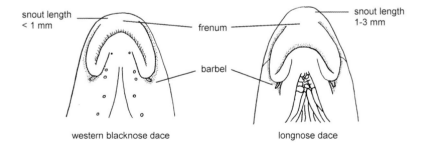

snout length < 1 mm

frenum

snout length 1-3 mm

barbel

western blacknose dace

longnose dace

MINNOWS (Cyprinidae)

CREEK CHUB
7.5–17.5 (max 30) cm | *Semotilus atromaculatus*

DESCRIPTION: Mouth terminal and large, extending almost to middle of eye. Barbel absent or very small, anterior to corner of mouth. Scales near head small and crowded. Lateral line complete. Often dark spot at anterior base of dorsal fin. Back dark olive, becoming silvery white on sides and belly. Often dark lateral stripe.

LOOK-ALIKES: Bluntnose and fathead minnows; finescale, pearl, and redside dace; hornyhead and lake chubs; lake chubsucker; and stonerollers. Hybridizes with common shiner and longnose, redside, and southern redbelly dace.

NOTES: The creek chub is abundant statewide. It inhabits streams and small rivers, preferring mostly clear water, but is tolerant of environmental degradation such as turbidity, siltation, and eutrophication. An opportunistic feeder, it eats mainly aquatic insect larvae, although large adults eat fish. Spawning occurs from May to July in gravel runs in nests dug by the males. Creek chubs are hosts for mussel glochidia (parasitic young).

Shiners

Shiners are a subgroup of the minnow family that includes the genera *Cyprinella*, *Luxilus*, *Lythrurus*, *Notemigonus* and *Notropis*. Shiners are usually small (adults 35–175 mm; most <85 mm), with no barbels, silvery scales, eight anal fin rays (several exceptions), a dorsal fin origin above the pelvic fin origin, and an absence of bright colors outside of the breeding season. Since there are many similar shiner species, be sure to compare specimens encountered in the field with all shiner species in this section, not only with those listed as look-alikes.

Shiners with Deep Bodies, Tall Lateral Line Scales

STRIPED SHINER
Luxilus chrysocephalus (formerly *Notropis*)   5.8–15 (max 23) cm

ENDANGERED

DESCRIPTION: Body deep. 9 anal fin rays. Anterior lateral line scales diamond-shaped, tall and narrow, with anterior black spots. Up to 17 predorsal scales (on back, between head and dorsal fin origin; compare with common shiner, page 202, which has 19–28 predorsal scales). Breeding males with lead-blue head and back, pink sides, tubercles on head.

breeding male

LOOK-ALIKES: Common shiner; hybridizes with common shiner (common × striped shiner hybrid has ~18 predorsal scales).

NOTES: The striped shiner is very rare and has possibly been extirpated in Wisconsin. If it is still present, it is found only in the lower Milwaukee River drainage of S.E. Wisconsin. Outside of Wisconsin, it inhabits small streams to midsized rivers, preferring mostly the clear water of runs or shallow pools. The striped shiner is moderately tolerant of environmental degradation. It eats mainly aquatic insect larvae. Spawning occurs from May to June in gravelly riffles.

MINNOWS (Cyprinidae)

COMMON SHINER
6.4–15 (max 20) cm   *Luxilus cornutus* (formerly *Notropis*)

breeding male

DESCRIPTION: Body deep. 9–10 anal fin rays. Anterior lateral line scales diamond-shaped, tall and narrow, with anterior black spots in larger specimens. 19–28 predorsal scales (on back, between head and dorsal fin origin; compare with striped shiner, page 201, which has up to 17 predorsal scales).

Breeding males with lead-colored back and head, pink to rose body color, and reddish ventral fins, with tubercles on head.

LOOK-ALIKES: Striped shiner; also redfin and spotfin shiners. Hybridizes with creek and hornyhead chubs; longnose, northern redbelly, redside, and southern redbelly dace; and carmine, rosyface, redfin, and striped shiners.

NOTES: The common shiner is common statewide. It is found in small streams to small rivers and lakes in various habitats. It is moderately tolerant of environmental degradation and eats mainly aquatic insect larvae and plant matter. Spawning occurs from May to July, mainly over gravelly riffles and often over the nests of hornyhead chubs.

Shiners with "Mouse Tracks" along Lateral Line but No Lateral Stripe

BIGMOUTH SHINER
3.5–5.5 (max 8) cm   *Notropis dorsalis*

A>B

DESCRIPTION: Body arched. Head flattened on top. Snout long. Mouth horizontal, subterminal. Upper jaw length greater than eye diameter (A>B in diagram); jaw extending to below pupil. Eyes upwardly directed.

LOOK-ALIKES: Mimic and sand shiners.

NOTES: The bigmouth shiner is locally common statewide, especially in W. Wisconsin; it is absent from the Lake Superior basin. It inhabits streams and rivers, preferring open, unvegetated water with sand flats. The bigmouth shiner is only moderately tolerant of overall environmental degradation but can survive high turbidity and siltation. Insect larvae, crustaceans, and algae are its main food. Spawning occurs from May to August.

202

SAND SHINER
Notropis stramineus

3.5–6.5 (max 8) cm

DESCRIPTION: Mouth terminal, slightly oblique (at ~45° angle). Jaw extending only to front margin of eye. 6–8 (usually 7) anal fin rays. Anterior lateral line scales not tall (compare with mimic shiner, below). Dusky stripe often present along back but interrupted at anterior edge of dorsal fin and expanding into dark wedge at dorsal fin origin.

LOOK-ALIKES: Bigmouth and mimic shiners.

NOTES: The sand shiner is common in most of the state and found sporadically in the north. It inhabits mainly medium to large streams and rivers, preferring clear, unvegetated water; it is moderately tolerant of overall environmental degradation. It eats mainly zooplankton, aquatic insect larvae, and crustaceans. Spawning occurs from May to August.

MIMIC SHINER
Notropis volucellus

3.5–6.5 (max 7.5) cm

DESCRIPTION: Snout blunt, slightly overhanging. Mouth subterminal, slightly oblique (at ~45° angle). Upper jaw length less than eye diameter (A<B in diagram). Anterior lateral line scales >3 times as tall as wide. Dorsal stripe usually complete from nape to tail.

LOOK-ALIKES: Bigmouth and sand shiners; also channel shiner (*Notropis wickliffi*; only found in large rivers).

A<B

NOTES: The mimic shiner is absent in S.W. Wisconsin and found sporadically in the west-central part of the state. It inhabits lakes and medium to large rivers, preferring the clear, open water of pools and runs with firm bottoms. It is moderately tolerant of environmental degradation and eats aquatic insect larvae, crustaceans, and algae. Spawning occurs from May to July. It closely resembles the channel shiner (*Notropis wickliffi*), which is found in large rivers. In Wisconsin the channel shiner inhabits the lower Chippewa, Mississippi, Saint Croix, Wisconsin, and Wolf Rivers; the mimic shiner is also found in these rivers, but the channel shiner predominates.

MINNOWS (Cyprinidae)

Shiners with a Black Lateral Stripe

	PUGNOSE SHINER
3.5–5 (max 6) cm	*Notropis anogenus*

THREATENED

DESCRIPTION: Mouth very small and strongly upturned, nearly vertical. 8 anal fin rays. Dorsal scales outlined in pigment. Dark lateral stripe extending around snout, lower lip, and chin. Black wedge-shaped spot on base of tail.

LOOK-ALIKES: Blackchin, blacknose, and weed shiners.

NOTES: In Wisconsin the pugnose shiner is found mainly in the southeast and northwest and is rare. It inhabits lakes and streams, preferring quiet, shallow, clear, vegetated water. The pugnose shiner is intolerant of overall environmental degradation, including high turbidity. It eats mainly algae and aquatic insect larvae. Spawning occurs from June to July.

	BLACKCHIN SHINER
3.5–5.6 (max 7) cm	*Notropis heterodon*

DESCRIPTION: Body robust. Snout triangular with tip rounded. Mouth terminal, oblique (at ~45° angle), small, not extending to below front of eye. 8 anal fin rays (compare with weed shiner, page 206). Dorsal scales strongly outlined. Black lateral stripe that often forms a zigzag pattern; stripe extending around snout; chin with black pigment. Small black spot at tail base.

LOOK-ALIKES: Blacknose, pugnose, and weed shiners; Ozark and bluntnose minnows.

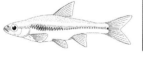

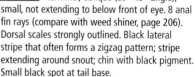

NOTES: The blackchin shiner is found sporadically statewide; it is absent from the southwest. It inhabits lakes, bogs, and streams, preferring quiet, clear, vegetated water. The blackchin shiner is intolerant of environmental degradation, such as high turbidity and siltation, and eats mainly aquatic insect larvae and zooplankton. Spawning occurs from June to August.

204

BLACKNOSE SHINER
Notropis heterolepis   3.5–6.5 (max 8.5) cm

DESCRIPTION: Body slender. Snout triangular with tip rounded, projecting slightly beyond lower jaw. Mouth inferior, nearly horizontal. Dorsal fin origin slightly behind pelvic fin origin. 7–8 anal fin rays. Black lateral stripe extending around snout but NO black pigment on chin. Within stripe, black crescents, the tips of which point obliquely toward the rear. Spot at tail base absent or not pronounced.

LOOK-ALIKES: Blackchin, pugnose, and weed shiners; bluntnose minnow.

NOTES: The blacknose shiner is found statewide; it is common in N. and rare in S.W. Wisconsin. It inhabits lakes and streams, preferring quiet, clear, vegetated water. The blacknose shiner is intolerant of environmental degradation such as siltation and persistently high turbidity, but it can survive winter oxygen depletion. It eats mainly crustaceans and aquatic insect larvae and spawns from June to August.

OZARK MINNOW
Notropis nubilus   3.5–7.5 (max 8.5) cm

THREATENED

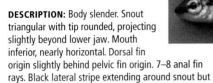

DESCRIPTION: Mouth small, upturned. Lateral line scales round. Black lateral stripe extending to upper lip and snout, often absent from lower lip and chin. Dark olive or brown above, silver white below. Tail with small black spot at base. Breeding adults with yellow hue.

LOOK-ALIKES: Shiners.

breeding male

NOTES: The Ozark minnow is found in the Red Cedar River drainage basin and S.W. Wisconsin. It inhabits small to midsized streams, preferring quiet, clear water with cobble substrate; it is intolerant of environmental degradation, particularly siltation. It eats mainly algae. Spawning occurs from May to August over gravel, often over the nests of the hornyhead chub.

MINNOWS (Cyprinidae)

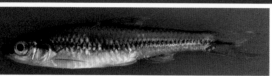

WEED SHINER
Notropis texanus

3.5–5.1 (max 6.5) cm

SPECIAL CONCERN

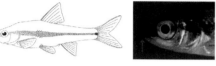

DESCRIPTION: Body moderately robust. Snout blunt. Mouth terminal, oblique (at ~45° angle), extending to just below front of eye. Dorsal fin origin slightly in front of pelvic fin origin. 7 anal fin rays (compare with blackchin and pugnose shiners, page 204). Dorsal and lateral line scales diamond-shaped. Black lateral stripe extending around snout on both lips. Stripe often appears wider in front of dorsal fin. Light streak just above lateral line. Black spot on tail base, sometimes streaking to end of fin; slightly separated from lateral stripe.

LOOK-ALIKES: Blackchin, blacknose, and pugnose shiners; bluntnose minnow.

NOTES: The weed shiner is found in the Fox/Wolf River drainage and the Mississippi River basin and is generally uncommon. It inhabits large rivers and the lower reaches of their tributaries, preferring sloughs, backwaters, and other areas of quiet water. The weed shiner is intolerant of environmental degradation. It eats aquatic insect larvae and detritus. Spawning occurs from June to July.

Other Shiners

SPOTFIN SHINER
Cyprinella spiloptera (formerly *Notropis*)

5–8.8 (max 21.5) cm

breeding male

DESCRIPTION: Body moderately deep (adults). Snout pointed. Mouth strongly oblique (at 45° angle). Lateral line scales diamond-shaped. Dorsal fin origin slightly behind pelvic fin origin. 8 anal fin rays. Body silvery with bluish cast. Dark blotch on posterior part of dorsal fin (only a few speckles of pigment on small specimens). Breeding males with steel-blue upper sides grading to cream-colored below and yellow lower fins; scales darkly outlined.

LOOK-ALIKES: Common, golden, and redfin shiners.

NOTES: The spotfin shiner is common statewide, except it is found only sporadically in N. Wisconsin and absent from the Lake Superior basin. It inhabits small to large rivers and is moderately tolerant of turbidity and siltation. It eats mainly terrestrial insects and aquatic insect larvae, crustaceans, and plant matter. Spawning occurs from May to September, usually under the bark of submerged logs or in rock crevices.

REDFIN SHINER
Lythrurus umbratilis (formerly *Notropis*)

3.5–6.5 (max 8.5) cm

THREATENED

DESCRIPTION: Dorsal fin origin slightly behind pelvic fin origin. 10–12 (usually 11) anal fin rays. Lateral line decurved. Dorsal fin origin with diffuse dark spot. Dark, diffuse blotch on posterior part of dorsal fin (adults). Breeding males steel blue, especially on back, with pinkish-red fins.

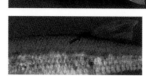

LOOK-ALIKES: Common, golden, and spotfin shiners.

NOTES: In Wisconsin the redfin shiner is found mostly in the south and is rare. It inhabits streams, small rivers, and impoundments, preferring warm, quiet, turbid water, which is often found in pools and protected inlets. The redfin shiner is moderately tolerant of environmental degradation. It eats mainly terrestrial insects, aquatic insect larvae, and algae. Spawning occurs from June to August over sunfish nests.

breeding male

GOLDEN SHINER
Notemigonus crysoleucas

7.5–17.5 (max 30.5) cm

DESCRIPTION: Body deep (adults). Mouth small, upturned. Dorsal fin origin behind pelvic fin origin. 11–14 anal fin rays. Lateral line strongly decurved. Fleshy, scaleless keel in front of anal fin (only clearly visible in larger individuals). Golden color. Juveniles often with dusky silvery lateral band.

juvenile

LOOK-ALIKES: Other shiners.

NOTES: The golden shiner is common statewide. Self-sustaining populations inhabit streams and small shallow lakes, preferring quiet, vegetated water. However, the golden shiner is a common bait minnow, so escapees from bait buckets may be encountered anywhere. This species is tolerant of environmental degradation, including winter oxygen depletion. A surface feeder, it eats largely zooplankton, aquatic insect larvae, and algae. Spawning occurs from late May to August over vegetation beds and in active largemouth bass nests.

fleshy keel

207

MINNOWS (Cyprinidae)

3.5–8.5 (max 12.5) cm

 EMERALD SHINER
Notropis atherinoides

DESCRIPTION: Snout short and rounded. Mouth terminal, oblique (at ~45° angle), extending to front of eye. Dorsal fin origin somewhat behind pelvic fin origin. 10–12 (usually 11) anal fin rays.

LOOK-ALIKES: Brook silverside and carmine and rosyface shiners.

NOTES: The emerald shiner is common statewide, though found only sporadically in N. Wisconsin. It is found in large lakes (including the Great Lakes), large rivers, and the lower reaches of their tributaries, preferring the clear water of pools. While once common, it has largely disappeared from Lake Michigan, likely due to competition from alewife (*Alosa pseudoharengus*). The emerald shiner is moderately tolerant of environmental degradation. It eats mainly zooplankton and aquatic insect larvae. Spawning occurs from May to August in gravelly shallows.

5–10 (max 13.7) cm

 SPOTTAIL SHINER
Notropis hudsonius

DESCRIPTION: Snout projecting slightly beyond upper lip. Mouth slightly subterminal, nearly horizontal, extending to below front of eye. Black spot at base of tail (most visible on smaller fish).

LOOK-ALIKES: Other shiners; juvenile may be confused with suckermouth and bluntnose minnow.

NOTES: The spottail shiner is found statewide in large rivers but is uncommon in streams. It inhabits large rivers and lakes (including the Great Lakes) and sometimes their tributaries; it prefers the quiet water of pools or the moderate current of runs. The spottail shiner is intolerant of environmental degradation. It eats mainly aquatic insect larvae and zooplankton. Inland populations spawn from May to June in gravelly riffles or sandy shallows and in the river mouths of the Great Lakes.

carmine shiner

rosyface shiner

CARMINE SHINER
Notropis percobromus   3.5–7.6 (max 9) cm

ROSYFACE SHINER
Notropis rubellus   3.5–7.6 (max 9) cm

SPECIAL CONCERN (ROSYFACE SHINER)

breeding male

DESCRIPTION: These 2 species are identical in appearance and cannot be distinguished in the field except by distribution. Snout pointed (compare with emerald shiner, page 208). Mouth terminal, oblique (at ~45° angle), extending to beneath pupil. Dorsal fin origin strongly behind pelvic fin origin, around midpelvic fin. 9–13 (usually 10) anal fin rays. Breeders with red around operculum (gill cover), sometimes red covering lower half of body and blue-black back; color most intense in males.

LOOK-ALIKES: Brook silverside and emerald shiner; hybridize with common shiner.

NOTES: These 2 species have complementary distributions that do not overlap. In Wisconsin the carmine shiner is found throughout the Mississippi River basin (except in the Illinois-Fox River drainage in S.E. Wisconsin) and in the Lake Michigan basin in those river systems that drain to Green Bay (Fox, Wolf, Suamico, Oconto, Peshtigo, and Menominee). The rosyface shiner occurs in the Mississippi basin in the Illinois-Fox River drainage and in the Lake Michigan basin in systems that drain directly to Lake Michigan (Kewaunee, Twin, Manitowoc, Sheboygan, and Milwaukee). Neither species occurs in the Lake Superior basin. The carmine shiner is common in its preferred habitat, but the rosyface shiner is uncommon. Both species inhabit large streams to midsized rivers, preferring swift, clear water. They are intolerant of environmental degradation, including high turbidity and siltation. They eat mainly aquatic insect larvae and algae. Spawning occurs from May to June over gravel, often on hornyhead chub nests.

MUDMINNOWS (UMBRIDAE)

Umbridae is a small family of fishes found only in the Northern Hemisphere. There are only five species found worldwide, and the central mudminnow is the only species found in Wisconsin. Mudminnows have heads that are somewhat flattened top to bottom (dorsoventrally), short snouts, and rounded tails. In general, species in this family tend to inhabit small bog lakes and muddy ponds and sluggish, vegetated streams. They are capable of breathing atmospheric oxygen, which makes them tolerant of low dissolved oxygen levels in water. The word *Umbridae* is from the Latin *umbra* (shadow), referring to their rapid movements, which resemble those of shadows.

CENTRAL MUDMINNOW
Umbra limi

5–10 (max 14) cm

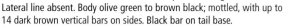

DESCRIPTION: Body robust, almost round in cross section. Lower jaw slightly protruding. Dorsal fin origin behind pelvic fin origin. Tail rounded. Lateral line absent. Body olive green to brown black; mottled, with up to 14 dark brown vertical bars on sides. Black bar on tail base.

LOOK-ALIKES: Darters, minnows, and topminnows.

NOTES: The central mudminnow is common statewide. It inhabits marshes, streams (particularly wetland-dominated streams), and ditches, preferring quiet, shallow, clear, vegetated water. The central mudminnow is tolerant of environmental degradation, particularly high water temperatures and low oxygen concentrations, due to its ability to gulp air. A bottom feeder, it eats mainly zooplankton, snails, fingernail clams, and fish. Spawning occurs in April, often in ponds created by spring flooding; it lays its eggs individually on vegetation.

NEW WORLD SILVERSIDES (ATHERINOPSIDAE)

New World silversides are a tropical and temperate family of approximately one hundred species. Twelve species are identified from Canada and the United States, ten of which are coastal saltwater or estuarine species. The brook silverside is the only species that is found in Wisconsin. Species in this family are generally small, with scaled heads, two dorsal fins, pectoral fins placed high on the body, and pelvic and anal fins with one spine each. Silversides are closely related to topminnows and killifishes.

BROOK SILVERSIDE
Labidesthes sicculus   5–7.5 (max 10) cm

DESCRIPTION: Body slender, elongated. Beak-like mouth located high on snout with a curved profile, the anterior part of the mouth horizontal and the posterior part sloping downward; lower jaw protruding forward. Pelvic fins far back with anterior

base below or behind end of pectoral fins. 2 dorsal fins on posterior half of back; first fin small, with 4 spines and origin above anal fin origin. Pectoral fins high on body. Anal fin elongated, sickle-shaped, with 1 spine and ≥20 rays. Translucent, solid silver, or pale green color; silvery lateral stripe.

LOOK-ALIKES: Elongated minnows (especially emerald, carmine, and rosyface shiners) and rainbow smelt.

NOTES: The brook silverside is common in lakes in the St. Croix River Basin and the lower three-fourths of the state (rare and possibly introduced in the Lake Superior basin), but it is uncommon in wadeable streams. It inhabits lakes, reservoirs, sloughs, and pools of medium to large rivers, preferring quiet, clear water. The brook silverside is moderately tolerant of environmental degradation. It is usually found near the water surface, eats mainly zooplankton, and may leap from the water for flying insects or in the moonlight. The brook silverside spawns only once, at age 1, and dies soon after. Spawning occurs from May to August.

PERCHES (PERCIDAE)

Percidae is comprised of a diverse array of approximately two hundred fishes distributed across the Northern Hemisphere. Their distribution is limited by water temperature, since they are adapted to living in temperate climates. The family includes both large fishes that are popular among anglers (e.g., walleye) and smaller, often colorful darters. There are nineteen species known from Wisconsin, one of which is introduced (the ruffe) and five of which are found only in large rivers and river impoundments. (These are the bluntnose darter [*Etheostoma chlorosomum*; endangered], crystal darter [*Crystallaria asprella*; endangered], river darter [*Percina shumardi*], sauger [*Sander canadensis*], and western sand darter [*Ammocrypta clara*; special concern].)

In general, perches have two separate dorsal fins (the second with only soft rays), pelvic fins placed well forward and almost below the pectoral fins, and a small anal fin with one or two spines.

Percidae is from the Greek *perkē* (perch).

Darters

Darters are freshwater fishes in the perch family that are found only in North America. They are small (most <85 mm), with a mouth that is terminal to subterminal and slightly oblique (at ~45° angle) to horizontal; two separate dorsal fins, the first wilh six or more spines; a square to slightly forked tail; and a light (white, cream, or yellow) belly. Certain species are brilliantly colored, especially during spawning. Many species have a *teardrop*, a dark bar or blotch below the eye.

One key trait for distinguishing some darters from each other is whether the gill membranes are broadly or narrowly joined. *Gill membranes* are the skin tissue connecting the bones (*branchiostegal rays*) located just posterior to the gills on the ventral side (underside) of the fish. *Broadly joined* gill membranes meet at an obtuse angle (>120°) at the midline; *narrowly joined* gill membranes form an acute angle (≤90°). The banded and fantail darters' gill membranes are broadly joined (figure A), while other darters' membranes are narrowly joined (figure B).

Darters are "bottom" fish that spend most of their time resting on the streambed propped up on their pectoral fins. They forage in the gravel for crustaceans and insect larvae, and most species also require clean substrate for spawning. Since they are often sensitive to turbidity and siltation, the presence of some species of darter indicates streams without excessive sedimentation.

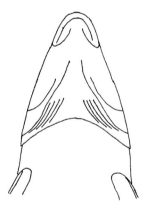

Figure A
broadly joined gill membranes (banded and fantail darters)

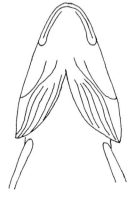

Figure B
narrowly joined gill membranes (other darters)

MUD DARTER
Etheostoma asprigene   3.5–5.1 (max 6.5) cm

SPECIAL CONCERN

DESCRIPTION: Body robust. Snout slightly rounded, blunt. Cheek fully scaled. Teardrop sometimes large. 2 separate dorsal fins, both with dark base, orange band, dark margin. 3 dark spots at base of tail, vertically arranged and often fused. 9–12 dark blotches on each side, often fused along lateral line as a stripe. Breeding males with green-blue vertical bars surrounded by orange pigment; belly orange red.

breeding male

LOOK-ALIKES: Banded, Iowa, least, and rainbow darters.

NOTES: The mud darter is uncommon and is found only in the Mississippi River basin. It prefers large, low-gradient rivers and their tributaries and overflow areas and is usually found in water <1.5 m deep. The mud darter is moderately tolerant of environmental degradation. It eats aquatic insect larvae and spawns in the spring.

RAINBOW DARTER
Etheostoma caeruleum   3.5–6.5 (max 7.5) cm

DESCRIPTION: Body robust. Snout somewhat pointed. Cheek unscaled. 2 separate dorsal fins. Teardrop faint or absent. Both dorsal fins with dark bands; first dorsal fin with orange base. Sides mottled, with 8–13 blue-green vertical bars, some extending over the back, forming 3 distinct "saddles." Breeding males brightly colored: blue bars on red-orange background; orange throat.

breeding male

LOOK-ALIKES: Banded, Iowa, and mud darters.

NOTES: The rainbow darter is common in the southwestern three-fourths of Wisconsin. It inhabits streams to large rivers, preferring rocky riffles or shallow runs with clear water. It is intolerant of overall environmental degradation, including siltation, high turbidity, and habitat degradation. It eats aquatic insect larvae, crustaceans, and zooplankton. Spawning occurs from April to June in gravelly riffles, where the male guards territories.

PERCHES (Percidae)

IOWA DARTER
Etheostoma exile

3.5–5.1 (max 7.5) cm

breeding male

DESCRIPTION: Body elongated; caudal peduncle long, narrow. Snout rounded. 2 separate dorsal fins. Lateral line incomplete, curved upward. Tan above; sides with dark brown mottling, 9–12 irregular blotches. Teardrop prominent, long. Tail and second dorsal fin with rows of brown speckles. Anal, pelvic, and pectoral fins transparent to dark, not red-orange as in least darter breeding males (page 215). No distinct "saddles" on back (compare with rainbow darter, page 213). Breeding males very colorful: first dorsal fin with blue edge and base, middle red band.

LOOK-ALIKES: Banded, Johnny, least, mud, and rainbow darters.

NOTES: The Iowa darter is uncommon to common statewide and found sporadically in S.W. Wisconsin. It inhabits bog ponds, lakes, and low-gradient streams and rivers, preferring shallow, mostly clear, vegetated water. The Iowa darter is intolerant of environmental degradation. It eats aquatic insect larvae, crustaceans, and zooplankton. Spawning occurs from April to June in shallow water, usually on fibrous roots or filamentous algae.

FANTAIL DARTER
Etheostoma flabellare

3.5–6.5 (max 7.5) cm

breeding male

DESCRIPTION: Body robust, with deep caudal peduncle. Snout straight, not rounded. Cheek unscaled. Gill membranes broadly joined (see figures A and B, page 212). 2 separate dorsal fins. Teardrop thin or absent. 8–9 thin horizontal stripes on each side of body. 9–13 irregular vertical bars on each side, often faint. Distinct black bands on tail and second dorsal fin. Breeding males with swollen golden tips of dorsal spines; body golden; head black.

LOOK-ALIKES: None in wadeable streams.

NOTES: The fantail darter is common statewide except in the Lake Superior basin, where it is absent. It inhabits small streams and sometimes midsized rivers, preferring warm water with rocky substrate. It is moderately tolerant of environmental degradation and eats aquatic insect larvae, crustaceans, and snails. Spawning occurs from April to June underneath rocks on the edges of riffles and in rocky runs.

214

LEAST DARTER
Etheostoma microperca   2.5–3.5 (max 4.5) cm

SPECIAL CONCERN

DESCRIPTION: Body length small.
Mouth strongly oblique (at 45° angle).
2 separate dorsal fins; 6 dorsal fin
spines (all in first fin). Pelvic fins longer
than pectoral fins. Lateral line absent or
short; few (0–7) lateral line pores.
Teardrop large, slanted back. Mottled
with 7–12 dark blotches on midline of
each side; markings not as clear as in
Johnny darter. First dorsal fin mottled.
Breeding males with red-orange pelvic
and anal fins and red spots on first dorsal fin.

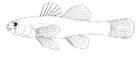

breeding male

LOOK-ALIKES: Iowa, Johnny, and mud darters.

NOTES: The least darter is widely distributed but generally uncommon, found sporadically in
N. and S.E. Wisconsin and only rarely in S.W. Wisconsin. It inhabits small lakes and low-gradient,
weedy streams, preferring clear water. It is intolerant of environmental degradation such as siltation,
and it eats mainly insect larvae and zooplankton. Spawning occurs from April to July in shallow
water, directly on vegetation.

JOHNNY DARTER
Etheostoma nigrum   3.5–6.5 (max 7.5) cm

DESCRIPTION: 2 separate dorsal fins.
Pelvic fins at least as long as pectoral
fins. Body never colorful. Teardrop short
or absent. Dark X-, Y-, and W-shaped
markings along lateral line. Breeding
males with black head, black anal and
pelvic fins, sometimes dark vertical bars.

LOOK-ALIKES: Banded, Iowa, and least
darters.

breeding male

NOTES: The Johnny darter is very common statewide and is the most widely distributed of the
perch species in Wisconsin streams. It inhabits small streams to large rivers and lakes, preferring
sand or gravel substrate, and is moderately tolerant of environmental degradation such as siltation.
It eats mainly midge and blackfly larvae and crustaceans. Spawning occurs from April to June under
large rocks or other objects.

PERCHES (Percidae)

BANDED DARTER
Etheostoma zonale

3.5–5 (max 6.5) cm

breeding male

DESCRIPTION: Body robust. Snout blunt. Mouth slightly subterminal. Cheek fully scaled. Gill membranes broadly joined (see figures A and B, page 212). 2 separate dorsal fins. Pectoral fins long, at least as long as head. Coloring mainly green: 9–13 green to gray bars on each side that join those of other side under belly. Bars often appear as mottles. Teardrop narrow, often broken into 2 spots. Dorsal fins and tail mottled. No distinct "saddles" on back (compare with rainbow darter, page 213). Breeding males with bright green vertical bands on sides and colorful fins with white tips; first dorsal fin with green edge, red base.

LOOK-ALIKES: Iowa, Johnny, mud, and rainbow darters.

NOTES: The banded darter is found in the southern two-thirds of Wisconsin and is uncommon to common. It inhabits medium to large streams and rivers with moderate to high gradients, preferring the clear water of riffles and runs. It is intolerant of environmental degradation, including high turbidity and siltation, and it eats mainly insect larvae. Spawning occurs from April to June.

LOGPERCH
Percina caprodes

9.4–12.5 (max 17.5) cm

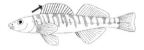

DESCRIPTION: Body elongated. Snout pointed, elongated, often with conical protuberance at tip and extending beyond lower lip. 2 separate dorsal fins. Teardrop distinct or inconspicuous. 15–25 thin bars along each side—some short, some long—that extend over the back and join bars on the other side. Dorsal fin and tail barred; other fins without much pigment. First dorsal fin lacking orange band. Black spot at tail base.

LOOK-ALIKES: Slenderhead darter; hybridizes rarely with blackside darter.

NOTES: The logperch is common statewide. It inhabits large streams, rivers, and lakes, preferring clear water with sand or rock substrate; it is moderately tolerant of environmental degradation. It eats mainly zooplankton as a juvenile and aquatic insect larvae and crustaceans as an adult. Spawning occurs from April to June over sand and gravel near shore.

PERCHES (Percidae)

GILT DARTER
Percina evides   5–6.6 (max 8.6) cm

THREATENED

DESCRIPTION: Snout short, curved downward. Cheek often unscaled. 2 separate dorsal fins. Teardrop distinct. No wavy black dorsal lines (as in blackside darter, page 217). Wide dusky greenish-black bars on sides, continuing on to back; yellow between bars. First dorsal fin often orange or amber at margin; orange band below edge. 2 large white or yellow areas on tail base. Breeding males with blue-green bars on back, bright orange underside.

breeding male

LOOK-ALIKES: Blackside darter; hybridizes rarely with blackside darter.

NOTES: The gilt darter is rare in Wisconsin, found only in the northwest in the St. Croix, Chippewa, and Black River drainages. It inhabits medium to large rivers, preferring the swift, clear water of riffles and runs with rocky substrate. It is intolerant of environmental degradation, including siltation and high turbidity, and it eats insect larvae. Spawning occurs in June, in riffles.

BLACKSIDE DARTER
Percina maculata   6–8.5 (max 11.1) cm

DESCRIPTION: Snout pointed. Mouth large, subterminal, horizontal. Cheek often unscaled. 2 separate dorsal fins. Teardrop very dark, prominent. Wavy black dorsal lines or mottling. First dorsal fin dusky, black at front along base. 6–9 black, ovoid blotches on each side that do not continue across back; blotches sometimes fused. Discrete black spot on tail (not always present).

LOOK-ALIKES: Gilt and slenderhead darters and logperch; hybridizes rarely with gilt darter and logperch.

NOTES: The blackside darter is common statewide except in the Lake Superior basin and far north-central Wisconsin, where it is absent. It inhabits medium to large streams and rivers, preferring runs with sand or rock substrate. The blackside darter is moderately tolerant of environmental degradation. It eats mainly insect larvae and zooplankton. Spawning occurs from April to June in moderately swift water over sand and gravel.

217

SLENDERHEAD DARTER
6–7.5 (max 8.5) cm	*Percina phoxocephala*

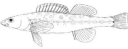

DESCRIPTION: Body elongated. Snout pointed, elongated; no conical protuberance. Cheek unscaled. 2 separate dorsal fins. Teardrop inconspicuous. Dark stripe from snout tip through eye to back of gills. First dorsal fin: bottom half dark, then distinct orange band, dark band, and light edge. Each side with 10–16 dark irregular vertical bars or blotches. Black spot at tail base.

LOOK-ALIKES: Blackside darter and logperch.

NOTES: The slenderhead darter is found sporadically statewide except in the Lake Superior basin, where it is absent. Where present, the slenderhead darter is uncommon to common. It inhabits large streams to large rivers, occupying swift, slightly turbid to turbid water. It is intolerant of environmental degradation such as siltation, and it eats mainly insect larvae. Spawning occurs in June in gravelly riffles.

Other Members of the Perch Family

	RUFFE
10–15 (max 22.5) cm	*Gymnocephalus cernuus*

INVASIVE—RESTRICTED

DESCRIPTION: Body short (<15 cm). Head scaleless. Mouth small, in "frown." 2 dorsal fins, long and tall, broadly joined together; spine tips sharp and not joined. Scales large. Adipose fin absent (compare with trout-perch, page 250). Tail forked. Many small dark blotches on sides, dorsal fin, and tail. Pectoral fins clear to pink.

LOOK-ALIKES: Trout-perch, walleye, and yellow perch.

NOTES: In Wisconsin the ruffe is found only in the Lake Superior basin, commonly in tributary mouths, but uncommonly farther upstream in the tributaries themselves. It inhabits nearshore areas of lakes and their tributaries, preferring quiet, turbid, unvegetated water. The ruffe is moderately tolerant of environmental degradation. It eats mainly aquatic insect larvae and crustaceans. Spawning occurs in May and June. The ruffe is believed to compete with native fishes for food and to prey on their eggs and larvae.

YELLOW PERCH
Perca flavescens

12.7–30 (max 42.5) cm

DESCRIPTION: Mouth large, extending to middle of eye. Canine-like teeth absent. Cheek scaled. 2 separate dorsal fins. Tail forked. Sides yellow; 6–9 green-brown "saddles" extending down each side as triangular bars. Eyes yellow to green. Black blotch at rear of first dorsal fin. Pectoral and pelvic fins yellow to red.

LOOK-ALIKES: Ruffe, trout-perch, and walleye.

NOTES: The yellow perch is common statewide in lakes but is less common in streams and rivers. It inhabits lakes and small to large rivers, preferring vegetated pools. The yellow perch is moderately tolerant of environmental degradation, including low oxygen. Juveniles eat mainly zooplankton and aquatic insect larvae, and adults eat mainly fish. Spawning occurs from April to May in quiet, vegetated, or brushy water. The yellow perch is a popular game fish and was the mainstay of the "Friday night fish fry" until the near collapse in the 1980s of commercially harvested stocks in Lake Michigan and significantly reduced harvests in other areas in the Great Lakes.

WALLEYE
Sander vitreus (formerly *Stizostedion vitreum*)

36–60 (max 80) cm

DESCRIPTION: Body large, elongated, almost cylindrical. Snout long, pointed. Mouth large, extending beyond middle of eye. Canine-like teeth large. Cheek scaleless or nearly scaleless. 2 separate dorsal fins. Tail forked. Body brassy yellow with dark greenish-black blotches on back; 5–12 dusky "saddles" extending partway down each side, faint on adults. Eyes silver or cloudy. Fins yellow with dark bands. Black spots at rear of first dorsal fin, base of pectoral fins. Anal fin and lower lobe of tail with white tips. Juveniles with less robust body.

juvenile

LOOK-ALIKES: In wadeable streams, ruffe and yellow perch.

NOTES: The walleye is common statewide but uncommon in wadeable streams. It inhabits large rivers and lakes and occasionally tributaries, preferring quiet, clear water. The walleye is moderately tolerant of environmental degradation. It eats mainly fish. Spawning occurs from April to May in rocky lake shallows, floodplain marshes, or gravelly streams. The walleye is a popular game fish and is widely stocked.

PIKES (ESOCIDAE)

Pikes are highly predacious fish with a distinctive, torpedo-like shape. The pike family contains just five species distributed in the Northern Hemisphere, with three species found in Wisconsin. These are grass pickerel, muskellunge, and northern pike; the latter two are among the largest, most sought after game fish in the state. Members of this family have an elongated, cylindrical body, a duck-billed snout that is compressed top to bottom (dorsoventrally), a large mouth armed with sharp teeth, sensory pores on the underside of the jaw, and a single soft-rayed dorsal fin positioned far back on the body. The three Wisconsin species can be distinguished from each other by size, scaling of the cheek and *opercle* (gill-covering bone), and markings. The word *Esocidae* is from the Latin *esox* (pike).

	GRASS PICKEREL
17.5–27.5 (max 37.5) cm	*Esox americanus vermiculatus*

juvenile

DESCRIPTION: Body elongate, small (<20 cm). Mouth duck-billed. Both cheek and opercle fully scaled. Sensory pores on undersurface of jaw: 4 on each side (see northern pike for picture, page 221). Tail tips rounded. Backward-slanting teardrop under eye. Dark green to brown wavy bars along sides; thin yellow lines between. In juveniles, light lateral stripe from snout to tail; wavy bars not present.

LOOK-ALIKES: Muskellunge and northern pike; hybridizes with northern pike.

NOTES: The grass pickerel is found sporadically in the southern half of the state and in the Vilas County area where introduced; it is uncommon to common. It inhabits lakes, sloughs, and streams, preferring quiet, shallow, vegetated water. The grass pickerel is moderately tolerant of environmental degradation. It eats fish; spawning occurs in April.

PIKES (Esocidae)

NORTHERN PIKE
Esox lucius   50–90 (max 125) cm

DESCRIPTION: Body elongate, large.
Mouth duck-billed. Cheek fully scaled;
opercle scaled only on upper portion.
Sensory pores on undersurface of jaw: 4–6
(usually 5) on each side. Tail tips rounded.
Teardrop absent or faint. Dark green background
with rows of light, bean-shaped spots. Juveniles
have dark vertical bars (or spots) alternating with
thin, light bars; dark olive background abruptly
changes to white belly.

LOOK-ALIKES: Grass pickerel and muskellunge;
hybridizes with both.

juvenile

NOTES: The northern pike is common statewide except in S.W. Wisconsin and is a popular
game fish. It inhabits lakes, ponds, and low-gradient rivers and streams, preferring cool,
mostly clear, vegetated water. The northern pike is moderately tolerant of environmental
degradation. It eats mainly fish. Spawning occurs from March to April soon after the ice
thaws in flooded riparian vegetation and marshes.

sensory
pores on
undersurface
of jaw

MUSKELLUNGE
Esox masquinongy   75–115 (max 161.3) cm

DESCRIPTION: Body elongate, large
(adults). Mouth duck-billed. Both cheek
and opercle scaled only on upper portion.
Sensory pores on undersurface of jaw: 6–9 on each
side (see northern pike for picture, above). Tail tips
pointed. Teardrop absent or faint. Light olive color,
usually with dark narrow vertical bars (often faint)
or spots. Small juveniles have light lateral stripe on
dark mottled background. Larger juveniles have
broken dark vertical bars on light background,
middorsal yellow stripe.

juvenile

LOOK-ALIKES: Grass pickerel and northern pike; hybridizes with
northern pike.

tiger muskie: northern pike ×
muskellunge hybrid

NOTES: The muskellunge, or "muskie," is common in N. Wisconsin and rare
to common in S. and central Wisconsin. A popular game fish, its native range
was historically north-central Wisconsin, but it is widely stocked elsewhere. It inhabits lakes
and medium to large rivers, preferring quiet water. The muskellunge is intolerant of overall
environmental degradation, including siltation. It eats mainly fish. Spawning occurs from
April to May in shallow, vegetated bays with mucky substrate.

221

PIRATE PERCHES (APHREDODERIDAE)

The family Aphredoderidae has only one living species, the pirate perch, which lives only in Norh America and is found in Wisconsin streams. This family is distantly related to trout-perch (page 250) and to cavefishes (family Amblyopsidae). The pirate perch's most distinctive trait is the location of the anus in the throat region of the adult fish. A juvenile fish's anus is located just anterior to the anal fin (as in most fishes), and as the fish matures the anus migrates forward. The word *Aphredoderidae* is from the Greek *aphod* (excrement) and *dere* (throat).

PIRATE PERCH
Aphredoderus sayanus

5–10 (max 12.5) cm

SPECIAL CONCERN

DESCRIPTION: Body short, deep. Head large. Mouth large; lower jaw protruding. Tail square. Lateral line incomplete or absent. Anus on throat between gill membranes (adults). Gray to black above with specks of iridescent blue; belly yellow white. 1–2 black bars at base of tail. Fins dusky to black.

LOOK-ALIKES: None in wadeable streams.

NOTES: The pirate perch is found sporadically statewide but mostly near the lower reaches or floodplains of the Des Plaines, Mississippi, and Wisconsin Rivers, where it is uncommon. It inhabits ponds, sloughs, marshes, and pools of midsized streams to large rivers, preferring quiet, densely vegetated or brushy water with soft substrate. The pirate perch is moderately tolerant of environmental degradation. It eats aquatic insect larvae and crustaceans. Spawning occurs in May.

SALMONS AND TROUTS (SALMONIDAE)

Salmons and trouts are coldwater fishes that are extremely popular as game fish. The family Salmonidae is native to the Northern Hemisphere, but many of its sixty-six species have been introduced outside of their natural ranges for sportfishing.

All salmonids spawn in freshwater. Species that spend their adult lives in the ocean are *anadromous*, living partly at sea but migrating inland to spawn. Species introduced to Wisconsin from the western United States (such as the Chinook and coho salmons and rainbow trout) display a comparable behavior by spending most of their lives in the Great Lakes, then migrating into tributaries to spawn.

Salmons and trouts generally have a streamlined, somewhat elongated body; a large mouth; spineless fins; 1 dorsal fin; and an adipose fin. The adipose fin, located behind the dorsal fin, is found only in this family and a few others, such as smelts and bullhead catfishes. Trouts have 8–13 anal fin rays; salmons generally have 12–19. Breeding male salmon may have hooked jaws and humped backs. Salmonids are usually most easily told apart by color. Adults are easily discernible, but juveniles can be more difficult.

The brook trout is the only member of this family that is native to Wisconsin streams, but several other species have been introduced in the state, mostly intentionally. Although these species are listed as invasive and restricted by the Wisconsin DNR, they are propagated by the DNR for stocking in streams, lakes, and the Great Lakes. Several species (such as rainbow trout and brown trout) are part of the aquaculture industry and are produced primarily for food or for the stocking of private sportfishing ponds. According to state regulations, if used for aquaculture at a registered fish farm, they are allowed to be transported, possessed, and/or transferred (unlike most other restricted species).

The word *Salmonidae* is from the Latin *salmo* (salmon).

Trouts

RAINBOW TROUT (steelhead)
Oncorhynchus mykiss

inland 30–40 (max 74.9) cm

INVASIVE—RESTRICTED

DESCRIPTION (ADULT): Body streamlined, with large mouth and adipose fin. Light olive to bronze background with many small black spots; no dorsal vermiculations (worm-like markings). Spots cover most of sides, dorsal fin, and tail and are much smaller than pupil of eye; red or light-colored spots absent. Broad pink stripe often present on each side. Adipose fin with a few spots and edged in black. Steelhead (adult rainbow trout that have matured in the Great Lakes) with gray-blue to silver background and faint dark spots; pink stripe faint or absent.

juvenile

juvenile

DESCRIPTION (JUVENILE): Body color lighter. Each side with 5–10 parr marks (vertical bars or blotches), often thinner than space between marks. Adipose fin with dark margin.

LOOK-ALIKES: Brook and brown trout.

NOTES: The rainbow trout is native to the western slope of the Rocky Mountains. It is common statewide in streams, ponds, lakes, and the Great Lakes because of extensive stocking. Only a few Wisconsin lakes, streams, or rivers have self-sustaining populations. Although it is listed as restricted by the Wisconsin DNR, it is stocked as a part of the state's fisheries management program and is part of the aquaculture industry (see page 223). Wisconsin is the second-greatest producer of farm-raised rainbow trout in the United States, second only to Idaho. In streams, it prefers the cold, swift water of riffles and rapids. The rainbow trout is moderately tolerant of environmental degradation and eats terrestrial insects, aquatic insect larvae, crustaceans, zooplankton, and fish. Spawning occurs from March to May in riffles and gravel runs.

BROOK TROUT
Salvelinus fontinalis

10–30 (max 51) cm

DESCRIPTION (ADULT): Body streamlined, with large mouth and adipose fin. Dark olive to gray background with light-colored vermiculations (worm-like markings) on back, light spots and small red spots on sides. Red spots surrounded by bluish halos and much smaller than pupil of eye. Lower body fins orange red with black and white stripes along front edges. Adipose fin *not* edged in orange red, tail *not* deeply forked.

juvenile

DESCRIPTION (JUVENILE): Dark line along tip of chin. Each side with 7–9 parr marks (vertical bars), widest mark about equal to eye diameter. Spots and vermiculations less conspicuous; very young may be almost black, with dark speckling on belly. Adipose fin with dark margin.

juvenile

tiger trout: brook trout ×
brown trout hybrid

LOOK-ALIKES: Brown and rainbow trouts; hybridizes with brown trout. Hybrid (tiger trout) has zebra- or giraffe-like markings.

NOTES: The brook trout is common in N. and W. Wisconsin and uncommon in S.E. Wisconsin. Brook trout are propagated and stocked by the Wisconsin DNR as part of the state's fisheries management program. The Wisconsin DNR has also developed a wild trout program. Eggs and sperm are taken from naturally reproducing populations of brook trout captured from streams. The adult trout are returned to the stream and the offspring are raised in hatcheries and then stocked. "Wild" brook trout young have greater survivorship than offspring from hatchery broodstock. The wild trout are stocked in the same drainage basin from which the eggs were obtained to help maintain the genetic integrity of these trout populations. While commonly called a trout, technically a brook trout is a char (genus *Salvelinus*), a close relative to lake trout (*S. namaycush*) and several other species. It is Wisconsin's only native inland trout species. It inhabits spring-fed headwater streams and ponds, preferring cold, clear, well-oxygenated water, and is intolerant of siltation, turbidity, elevated water temperatures, and eutrophication. It eats mainly terrestrial insects, aquatic insect larvae, crustaceans, and fish. Spawning usually occurs from October to November in redds dug in gravelly riffles or spring-fed areas, with the fry emerging from the streambed in March and April.

SALMONS AND TROUTS (Salmonidae)

BROWN TROUT
Salmo trutta

25–40 (max 87.1) cm

INVASIVE—RESTRICTED

juvenile

juvenile

DESCRIPTION (ADULT): Body streamlined, with large mouth and adipose fin. Light olive brown above; yellow brown on sides; creamy on belly. No dorsal vermiculations (worm-like markings). Light background with dark spots: black spots on back, dorsal fin, and upper sides; red spots on sides; all types of spots often surrounded by pale halos. Spots often nearly as large as pupil of eye. White stripe at front edge of lower body fins not as pronounced as in brook trout. Adipose fin usually edged in orange red.

DESCRIPTION (JUVENILE): Tip of chin pale. Each side with 9–14 (usually 11) parr marks (vertical bars), all equal to or narrower than eye diameter. Belly with dark speckling; other spots less conspicuous. Adipose fin orange red, without dark margin.

LOOK-ALIKES: Brook and rainbow trouts; hybridizes with brook trout (see tiger trout photo under brook trout, page 225).

NOTES: The brown trout is native to Iceland, Europe, North Africa, and Asia. It was introduced to the United States in the late 1800s from eggs shipped from Germany and soon after with eggs from the British Isles—hence the common names "German" and "Loch Leven" (Scotland) brown trout. It is common statewide through stocking and subsequent natural reproduction. It inhabits streams and lakes with cold, mostly clear water but is slightly more tolerant of environmental degradation than the native brook trout and has replaced or outcompeted the brook trout in much of the brook trout's native range. Although the brown trout is listed as restricted by the Wisconsin DNR, it is propagated and stocked as a part of the state's fisheries management program and is part of the aquaculture industry (see page 223). It eats aquatic and terrestrial insects, snails, crustaceans (including crayfish), and fish. Spawning occurs from October to December in redds dug by the females in riffles and groundwater-fed areas, with the fry emerging in March and April.

226

Salmons

PINK SALMON
Oncorhynchus gorbuscha   30–50 (max 61) cm

INVASIVE—RESTRICTED

DESCRIPTION: Body streamlined, with large mouth and adipose fin. Back blue green; sides silvery; belly white. Back and both lobes of tail with oval-shaped black spots, sometimes as large as eye diameter. Breeders with white gums. Breeding males with distinctively humped back, dark head and back, and pink to brown stripe on each side. Juveniles are not found in streams.

breeding male

LOOK-ALIKES: Other salmons and trouts; hybridizes with Chinook salmon.

NOTES: The pink salmon is found in Lake Superior and rarely in Lake Michigan; adults may be found in tributary streams during spawning. It prefers cold, clear water and is moderately tolerant of overall environmental degradation. The pink salmon was accidentally introduced into the Great Lakes in 1955 when fish from a hatchery in Ontario, Canada were disposed of in a tributary to Lake Superior, and the fish subsequently dispersed throughout Lakes Superior, Michigan, and Huron. It eats zooplankton, insect larvae, crustaceans, and fish. Spawning occurs from September to October in runs or deep riffles over gravel substrate. Larvae immediately drift to lakes after hatching, so juveniles are not found in streams.

breeder

227

SALMONS AND TROUTS (Salmonidae)

INVASIVE—RESTRICTED

juvenile

juvenile

DESCRIPTION (ADULT): Body very large, streamlined, with large mouth and adipose fin. Back steel blue to green with black spots; sides silver; belly white. Tail with a few black spots, mainly on upper lobe; spots smaller than pupil of eye and sometimes faint. Breeders are dark, with more pronounced spots; lower gums pale to gray at tooth base; breeding males with dark blue-green back and head and reddish flanks.

breeder

breeding male

DESCRIPTION (JUVENILE): Anal fin sickle-shaped (first ray elongated) (compare with Chinook salmon, page 229); front of anal fin with white stripe, dark stripe behind. Back blue green; sides silvery. 8–12 narrow parr marks (vertical bars) on each side. Spots inconspicuous. Tail reddish.

LOOK-ALIKES: Other salmons and trouts. Fish newly arrived in spawning streams may closely resemble Chinook salmon, which have a relatively less sickle-shaped anal fin with a relatively longer fin base.

NOTES: The coho salmon is native to the Pacific Ocean along the Pacific Northwest of the United States, Canada, and Alaska and through stocking is found in the Great Lakes and their tributaries. Although it is listed as restricted by the Wisconsin DNR, it is propagated and stocked by the DNR as a part of the state's fisheries management program (see page 223). Nearly all Lake Michigan populations are sustained by stocking, but Lake Superior populations are self-sustaining, with good reproduction in the Bois Brule River system, Douglas County, and streams draining the Bayfield Peninsula. The coho salmon prefers cold, clear water but is moderately tolerant of overall environmental degradation. Juvenile coho salmon eat zooplankton and crustaceans, and adult fish eat primarily alewife (*Alosa pseudoharengus*) and rainbow smelt. Spawning occurs from October to December in redds dug in clean gravel substrate of riffles, with the fry emerging from the gravel in March and April.

CHINOOK SALMON (king salmon)
Oncorhynchus tshawytscha

45–70 (max 120.7) cm

INVASIVE—RESTRICTED

DESCRIPTION (ADULT): Body very large, streamlined, with large mouth and adipose fin. Silvery to light olive, with numerous small black spots on upper sides and both tail lobes; spots much smaller than pupil of eye. Breeders darker with more pronounced spots; lower gums black.

juvenile

juvenile

DESCRIPTION (JUVENILE): First ray of anal fin only slightly elongated (compare with coho salmon, page 228). Front of anal fin with white stripe, no dark stripe. Back blue green; sides silvery. 6–12 thick parr marks (vertical bars) as wide as or wider than spaces between.

breeding male

LOOK-ALIKES: Other salmons and trouts; hybridizes with pink salmon.

NOTES: The Chinook salmon is found in the Great Lakes and their tributaries. Although it is listed as restricted by the Wisconsin DNR, it is propagated and stocked as a part of the state's fisheries management program (see page 223). A few small naturalized populations of juvenile fish occur in Wisconsin's Lake Superior tributaries, and large naturalized populations occur in some Lake Michigan tributaries in the state of Michigan, but populations in Wisconsin's Lake Michigan tributaries are largely sustained by stocking. The Chinook salmon prefers cold, clear water but is moderately tolerant of environmental degradation. Juveniles eat aquatic insects and crustaceans, and adults eat alewife (*Alosa pseudoharengus*) and rainbow smelt. Spawning occurs from October to November over clean gravel substrate, with the fry emerging in March and April.

breeder

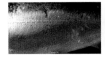

SCULPINS (COTTIDAE)

The sculpin family contains over three hundred species found in the Northern Hemisphere, including the Arctic. Most are marine, but species in the genus *Cottus* are found primarily in freshwater. Four species are found in Wisconsin, two of which are found in streams: the mottled sculpin and the slimy sculpin. Both of these inhabit cold water and are often associated with trout.

Wisconsin's two stream-dwelling sculpins are small, with a body shape that tapers from a wide head to a narrow caudal peduncle, a mouth that is very wide and terminal, an upper lip that protrudes beyond the lower lip, no scales, small prickles on the body below the lateral line near the first dorsal fin, an incomplete lateral line that begins near the gill covers and ends below the second dorsal fin, large pectoral fins, and mottling with dark irregular blotches. They are hard to tell apart from each other and should also be compared with the round goby, an invasive species.

The word *Cottidae* is from the Greek *kottos* (sculpin).

MOTTLED SCULPIN
Cottus bairdi

3.5–10.2 (max 13.7) cm

DESCRIPTION: Head flattened and mouth wide; when viewed from above, body tapering from wide head to narrow caudal peduncle. Pectoral fins large. Pelvic fins not fused, with no scales and 4 rays (compare with round goby, page 179). Caudal peduncle usually shorter than postorbital distance (B<A in diagram). Mottled.

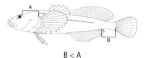

B < A

LOOK-ALIKES: Slimy sculpin, round goby.

NOTES: The mottled sculpin is common statewide except portions of west-central Wisconsin. It inhabits headwater streams to medium-sized streams and large lakes, preferring cold, clear water in sheltered areas of pools and riffles. It is intolerant of high turbidity and siltation. It eats crustaceans and aquatic insect larvae and is important in the diet of trout. Spawning occurs from April to May in cavities beneath rocks or logs. The spawning fish are oriented upside-down, and adhesive eggs are laid on the "roof" of the nest cavity.

SLIMY SCULPIN
Cottus cognatus   3.5–9 (max 11.1) cm

DESCRIPTION: Head flattened and
mouth wide; when viewed from above,
body tapering from wide head to
narrow caudal peduncle. 2 dorsal fins.
Pectoral fins large. Pelvic fins not fused,
with no scales and usually 3 rays (compare with round goby, page 179).
Caudal peduncle usually longer than postorbital distance (B>A in diagram).
Mottled; often 2 dark "saddles" under second dorsal fin.

B > A

LOOK-ALIKES: Mottled sculpin, round goby.

NOTES: The slimy sculpin is sporadically distributed in Wisconsin; it is found mostly in the southwest
and in the Lake Superior basin, where it can be locally common. It inhabits deep, clear lakes and
headwater streams, preferring the cold, moving water of rocky pools and riffles. It is intolerant of
high turbidity and siltation, and it eats mainly crustaceans and aquatic insect larvae. Spawning
occurs from April to May in cavities beneath rocks and logs. The spawning fish are oriented
upside-down, and the adhesive eggs are laid on the "roof" of the nest cavity.

SMELTS (Osmeridae)

SMELTS (OSMERIDAE)

Smelts are mainly marine fishes of the Northern Hemisphere. They generally are small and elongate, with large mouths, an adipose fin, and a silvery color. The word *Osmeridae* is from the Greek *osmē* (bad smelling).

There are thirteen species of smelt, only one of which lives in Wisconsin waters. This is the invasive rainbow smelt, originally from both the east and west coasts of North America. Rainbow smelt were first brought to the Great Lakes region in the early 1900s as food for salmon that were being stocked in Michigan, and it is generally believed that rainbow smelt were first established in the Great Lakes from fish stocked in Crystal Lake, Michigan (which has a tributary that flows into Lake Michigan), in 1912. Although the rainbow smelt was not originally intended as a sport fish itself, it has since become an important part of Wisconsin's fishery, for decades being netted by anglers along the shore of Lake Michigan and at the mouths of tributary streams and rivers and being an important forage fish for Lake Michigan salmon and trout. However, it is detrimental to the inland populations of some other game fish such as walleye and cisco (*Coregonus artedi*) because it preys on or competes with their young. In Lake Michigan its numbers fell sharply in the 1980s, likely due to competition with the exotic alewife (*Alosa pseudoharengus*), and today it is less common there. However, it is expanding its distribution in inland lakes.

RAINBOW SMELT
Osmerus mordax

10–20 (max 37.5) cm

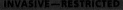
INVASIVE—RESTRICTED

DESCRIPTION: Body slender. Mouth large, reaching at least middle of eye. Large teeth on jaws, roof of mouth, and tongue. Adipose fin present. Tail deeply forked. Body silvery, with back pale green to blue; sides iridescent, sometimes with silver stripe along sides; belly white. Tail darkly pigmented. Smells like cucumbers.

LOOK-ALIKES: Brook silverside.

NOTES: In Wisconsin the rainbow smelt is found mainly in deep offshore water of the Great Lakes and the mouths of tributary rivers and some N. Wisconsin lakes. It is moderately tolerant of environmental degradation. Carnivorous, it eats mainly crustaceans and small fish. Spawning occurs from March to May in streams and rivers and the shallows of lakes.

STICKLEBACKS (GASTEROSTEIDAE)

Gasterosteidae is a small family of at least sixteen fishes found in the Northern Hemisphere. There are three species of stickleback in Wisconsin: two are native (brook and ninespine), and one is introduced (threespine). Sticklebacks are generally small (35–65 mm), with no scales, independent dorsal fin spines not connected to each other by membranes, fan-like pectoral fins set high on the sides, and a narrow caudal peduncle. The word *Gasterosteidae* is from the Greek *gaster* (stomach) and *osteon* (bone).

BROOK STICKLEBACK
Culaea inconstans   3.5–6.5 (max 8.5) cm

DESCRIPTION: Mouth dorsal, small, upturned. 4–6 short dorsal fin spines. Caudal peduncle slender, short, with no bony lateral keel. Breeding males jet black, sometimes copper-tinged.

LOOK-ALIKES: Other sticklebacks.

NOTES: The brook stickleback is common statewide. It inhabits small streams and small shallow lakes,

breeding male

preferring cool, slow-moving, mostly clear, vegetated water. It is tolerant of environmental degradation, including high turbidity, low dissolved oxygen, and habitat degradation. It is mainly carnivorous, feeding on zooplankton and aquatic insect larvae. Spawning occurs from April to May in shallow vegetation. Males build 1 or more nests out of aquatic vegetation, exhibit elaborate courtship behaviors, and guard the nest(s) until the eggs hatch.

STICKLEBACKS (Gasterosteidae)

THREESPINE STICKLEBACK
Gasterosteus aculeatus

3.5–6.5 (max 7.5) cm

INVASIVE—RESTRICTED

DESCRIPTION: Mouth terminal, slightly oblique (at ~45° angle). 2–4 (usually 3) short dorsal fin spines; last spine very short. Caudal peduncle slender, with bony lateral keel on each side. Often dark mottling on light background. Large males black, often with red on fins. Breeding males with blue sides; red or pink belly; bright blue eyes. Breeding females with pinkish posterior belly.

LOOK-ALIKES: Other sticklebacks.

NOTES: The threespine stickleback is found in shallow to deep water of Lakes Michigan and Superior, and, during spawning, it may be found in the lower reaches of tributaries. It is moderately tolerant of environmental degradation. It is carnivorous. Spawning occurs from May to June.

NINESPINE STICKLEBACK
Pungitius pungitius

3.5–6.5 (max 8.5) cm

DESCRIPTION: Mouth small, upturned. 8–11 (usually 9) short dorsal spines, angled alternately left and right. Caudal peduncle long, thin (wider than deep), with bony lateral keel on each side. Dark bars or mottles on light background. Breeding males with jet black belly and whitish pelvic fins.

LOOK-ALIKES: Other sticklebacks.

NOTES: The ninespine stickleback is common in offshore areas of Lakes Michigan and Superior and a few deep N. Wisconsin lakes. During spawning it may be found in nearshore areas and the lower reaches of tributaries. It prefers cold, quiet water and is moderately tolerant of environmental degradation, including short-term low concentrations of dissolved oxygen. It eats mainly zooplankton and aquatic insect larvae. Spawning occurs from May to June in vegetation in shallow water.

STURGEONS (ACIPENSERIDAE)

Sturgeons are large, primitive fishes valued for their meat and *caviar* (eggs). There are at least twenty-three species worldwide, of which many are threatened or endangered because of dams, pollution, and overharvest. They tend to be found in temperate to cold areas of the Northern Hemisphere. There are two species of sturgeons in Wisconsin: the lake sturgeon and the shovelnose sturgeon (*Scaphirhynchus platorynchus*). The lake sturgeon is sometimes found in wadeable streams, but the shovelnose sturgeon is an exclusively large-river species.

Sturgeons have large, elongated bodies, shovel-shaped snouts, ventral mouths, four barbels, bony *scutes* (plates) in five rows along their back and sides, and shark-like tails with large dorsal lobes.

The word *Acipenser* is Latin for *sturgeon*.

LAKE STURGEON
Acipenser fulvescens   115–180 (max 250) cm

SPECIAL CONCERN

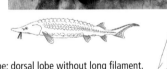

DESCRIPTION: Snout shovel-shaped, rounded. Mouth ventral. Lower lip with 2 papillose (bumpy) lobes. 4 smooth barbels. 5 rows of bony scutes (plates) along back and sides. Caudal peduncle partly naked, relatively short: shorter than distance from pelvic fin origin to anal fin origin. Tail with large dorsal lobe; dorsal lobe without long filament. Back and sides olive gray; belly white; fins brown or dark gray. Scutes on back and sides same color as skin.

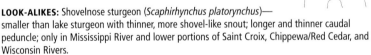

LOOK-ALIKES: Shovelnose sturgeon (*Scaphirhynchus platorynchus*)—smaller than lake sturgeon with thinner, more shovel-like snout; longer and thinner caudal peduncle; only in Mississippi River and lower portions of Saint Croix, Chippewa/Red Cedar, and Wisconsin Rivers.

NOTES: The lake sturgeon is found sporadically statewide; it is rare to common locally. It inhabits large rivers and lakes, including Great Lakes shoals and sometimes their tributaries. Strongholds for the lake sturgeon are the Chippewa/Flambeau, Menominee and lower Peshtigo, Saint Croix/Namekagon, Wisconsin, and Wolf/Fox/Lake Winnebago River systems. It prefers the deep water of pools and deep runs. The lake sturgeon is moderately tolerant of environmental degradation. It eats mainly invertebrates, especially crustaceans when young, and aquatic insects, fish, and fish carrion as an adult. The lake sturgeon becomes sexually mature when about 25 years old and may live up to 80 years. Spawning occurs from April to June in rocky areas along riverbanks and lake shoals.

SUCKERS (CATOSTOMIDAE)

Suckers are a large family (at least sixty-eight species) of generally bottom-dwelling fish found in the Northern Hemisphere. Many suckers that live in streams have sucker-like mouths that are *inferior*, or located ventrally on the head. The ventral orientation of their fleshy lips allows suckers to effectively forage for crustaceans, mussels, and aquatic insect larvae hidden under and among rocks and gravel on streambeds. The word *Catostomidae* is from the Greek *kata* (down) and *stoma* (mouth). Suckers' fleshy lips are an important trait for distinguishing species from each other. Some species have *plicate* (folded) lips, others have *papillose* (bumpy) lips, and others have combinations of both.

Redhorses (*Moxostoma* spp.)

Redhorses are a genus of the sucker family (*Moxostoma*). There are six species of redhorse in Wisconsin, four of which are found in wadeable streams. They are common in medium to large rivers and are somewhat to very sensitive to siltation and to organic and chemical pollution. Many species have red fins and/or tails.

Redhorses tend to be large and round in cross section, with the top of the head convex, generally *plicate lips* (arranged into long folds with grooves), and a solid body color. Juvenile redhorses can be confused with white sucker juveniles. Note that suckers that are not redhorses often have more *papillose* (bumpy) lips and more irregular body color patterns (e.g., mottling, blotches, etc.), and they usually lack red fins.

Redhorses with Red Tails (Individuals >10 cm)

SHORTHEAD REDHORSE
Moxostoma macrolepidotum

28–50 (max 55) cm

DESCRIPTION: Body slightly elongated, moderately compressed side to side (laterally). Head small: about 20 percent of length from snout to tail base. Snout pointed or slightly blunted, not overhanging mouth. Mouth small, ventral. Lips deeply plicate (folded), with folds of the lower lip divided into large bumps (papillae). Lower lip's rear margin nearly straight. Dorsal fin pointed, concave (slightly sickle-shaped). 12–13 scale rows around caudal peduncle (see greater redhorse diagram, page 237). Tail and ventral fins red or orange in life. Body color silver, bronze, gold, or copper; back dark olive.

LOOK-ALIKES: Other redhorses and suckers; juveniles may be confused with suckermouth minnow.

NOTES: The shorthead redhorse is common statewide, the most common of the redhorses in Wisconsin. It is found in medium to large rivers and occasionally lakes, preferring swift water. The shorthead redhorse is moderately tolerant of environmental degradation. It eats mainly crustaceans, aquatic insect larvae, and zooplankton. Spawning occurs from April to May in shallow gravelly areas in and around riffles.

GREATER REDHORSE
Moxostoma valenciennesi

40–60 (max 68) cm

SPECIAL CONCERN

DESCRIPTION: Body elongated. Head large: about 25 percent of length from snout to tail base. Snout slightly rounded but not overhanging mouth. Mouth large, ventral. Lips folded (plicate); with a few bumps (papillae) at corners. Lower lip often appearing swollen, with an obtuse, shallow, V-shaped rear margin. Dorsal fin slightly convex (slightly concave in juveniles). 16 scale rows around caudal peduncle (see diagram). Tail and ventral fins red. Body color silvery, bronze, golden, or copper.

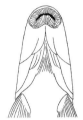

LOOK-ALIKES: Other redhorses and suckers; juveniles may be confused with suckermouth minnow.

NOTES: The greater redhorse is found sporadically statewide except in the Lake Superior basin and S.W. Wisconsin; it is uncommon. It inhabits medium to large rivers and lakes, preferring clear water with sand, gravel, or boulder substrate, and is intolerant of turbidity and siltation. It eats mainly crustaceans, mollusks, and aquatic insect larvae. Spawning occurs from May to June in moderate current in and near riffles.

Redhorses with Slate-Colored Tails (Individuals >10 cm)

SILVER REDHORSE
Moxostoma anisurum

30–50 (max 74.3) cm

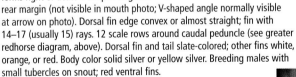

DESCRIPTION: Body large, stout; back slightly arched. Snout blunt, square or rounded, not overhanging mouth. Mouth ventral. Lower lip folds divided into small bumps (papillae). Lower lip forms right or acute V-shaped angle at rear margin (not visible in mouth photo; V-shaped angle normally visible at arrow on photo). Dorsal fin edge convex or almost straight; fin with 14–17 (usually 15) rays. 12 scale rows around caudal peduncle (see greater redhorse diagram, above). Dorsal fin and tail slate-colored; other fins white, orange, or red. Body color solid silver or yellow silver. Breeding males with small tubercles on snout; red ventral fins.

LOOK-ALIKES: Other redhorses and suckers; juveniles may be confused with suckermouth minnow.

NOTES: The silver redhorse is found statewide, especially in W. Wisconsin; it is uncommon to common. It inhabits medium to large rivers, preferring the deep, clear water of pools and runs. The silver redhorse is moderately tolerant of environmental degradation and eats mainly crustaceans, aquatic insect larvae, and algae. Spawning occurs from April to May.

breeding male

DESCRIPTION: Body robust; caudal peduncle thick top to bottom (dorsoventrally). Snout blunt or rounded but not overhanging mouth. Mouth ventral. Lips smoothly folded (plicate), without bumps. Lower lip arched or at a shallow angle at rear margin. Dorsal fin slightly sickle-shaped, with 10–15 (usually 13) rays. 11–14 (usually 12) scale rows around caudal peduncle (see greater redhorse diagram, page 237). Dorsal fin and tail slate-colored (tail may be reddish in small specimens); other fins white, orange, or red. Body color solid silvery, dark brassy, or bright gold. Breeding males with large tubercles on snout.

LOOK-ALIKES: Other redhorses and suckers; juveniles may be confused with suckermouth minnow.

NOTES: The golden redhorse is common statewide except in the Lake Superior basin and extreme N.E. Wisconsin. It inhabits streams and rivers, preferring the clear, unvegetated water of pools. It is moderately tolerant of environmental degradation and eats crustaceans, aquatic insect larvae, mussels, and algae. Spawning occurs from April to May in riffles.

Other Suckers

DESCRIPTION: Body large: 1–2 kg (2.2–4.4 lb) fish common. Mouth ventral. Lower lip forms a V, with halves meeting at ~90° angle. Dorsal fin sickle-shaped with long base; first ray very long, almost as long as fin base (normally a little shorter than in main photo).

LOOK-ALIKES: Bigmouth buffalo, common carp, and goldfish.

NOTES: The quillback is found statewide except in northeast and north-central Wisconsin and is probably introduced in the Lake Superior basin, where it is rare. It is common in large rivers and uncommon in wadeable streams, though more common in some streams during spawning. It inhabits large rivers with low gradients, preferring warm, quiet water, but it occupies riffles and runs during spawning. The quillback is moderately tolerant of environmental degradation. It is omnivorous, eating algae, mussels, and aquatic insect larvae. Spawning occurs from May to June over mud, sand, or gravel substrate.

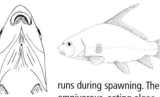

238

LONGNOSE SUCKER
Catostomus catostomus   30–45 (max 60) cm

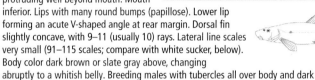

DESCRIPTION: Body elongated, round in cross section. Snout elongated, protruding well beyond mouth. Mouth inferior. Lips with many round bumps (papillose). Lower lip forming an acute V-shaped angle at rear margin. Dorsal fin slightly concave, with 9–11 (usually 10) rays. Lateral line scales very small (91–115 scales; compare with white sucker, below). Body color dark brown or slate gray above, changing abruptly to a whitish belly. Breeding males with tubercles all over body and dark or crimson lateral stripe. Juveniles often with 3 large, diffuse dark blotches on sides.

LOOK-ALIKES: Northern hog, spotted, and white suckers; redhorses.

NOTES: The longnose sucker is found in the nearshore waters of the Great Lakes, especially Lake Superior. It enters Great Lakes tributaries during spawning, often in large numbers, but is otherwise absent in Lake Michigan tributaries and rare in Lake Superior tributaries. A small inland population occurs in the Brule River on the Michigan border in N.E. Wisconsin. The longnose sucker prefers cold water and is intolerant of environmental degradation. It eats mussels, crustaceans, and aquatic insect larvae. Spawning occurs from April to May over gravel substrate with current.

WHITE SUCKER
Catostomus commersonii   24.1–45 (max 60) cm

DESCRIPTION: Body elongated, round in cross section. Snout short, rounded or square, barely overhanging mouth. Mouth ventral. Lips with many round bumps (papillose). Lower lip broad, fleshy (not cartilaginous as in stonerollers), forming an acute V-shaped angle at rear margin. Dorsal fin slightly concave to slightly convex, with 10–13 rays. Lateral line scales small (55–85 scales; compare with longnose sucker, above). Light background body color, often with dark irregular mottling, especially in juveniles. Dorsal fin and tail light slate-colored; other fins white or orange-tinged; no red fins; no dark crescent on dorsal fin. Breeding males with broad dark or reddish lateral stripe. Juveniles often with 3 diffuse dark blotches on each side.

juvenile

breeding male

LOOK-ALIKES: Lake chubsucker; longnose, spotted, and northern hog suckers; and redhorses. Juvenile white suckers may also be confused with lake chubsucker and with many minnows, including stonerollers, gravel chub, and suckermouth minnow.

NOTES: The white sucker is abundant statewide and is likely found in more Wisconsin streams than any other fish. It inhabits streams, rivers, and lakes and is found in various environmental conditions; it is very tolerant of environmental degradation, including high turbidity and siltation, but it also inhabits relatively clean "trout streams." It is omnivorous, feeding on algae, mussels, aquatic insect larvae, and crustaceans. Spawning occurs from April to May in fast-flowing water over gravel substrate.

239

LAKE CHUBSUCKER
Erimyzon sucetta

15–25 (max 30) cm

SPECIAL CONCERN

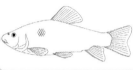

juvenile

DESCRIPTION: Body deep (especially adults). Snout blunt. Mouth subterminal; lips smoothly folded (plicate), without bumps (papillae). Barbels absent. Lateral line absent (compare with creek chub, page 200). Dorsal fin convex, with short base. Scales more diamond-shaped than those of white sucker (page 239). Back olive brown; sides yellowish; belly olive yellow. Sometimes with series of diffuse dark blotches on each side (adults). Juveniles with black stripe from tip of snout to base of tail; tail reddish.

LOOK-ALIKES: Creek chub and white sucker.

NOTES: In Wisconsin the lake chubsucker is found mainly in the upper Illinois and Rock River, lower Wisconsin River, and Wolf River drainages, where it is uncommon. It inhabits streams to large rivers and lakes, preferring quiet, clear water with dense vegetation. It is only moderately tolerant of overall environmental degradation, though it can tolerate low oxygen. It eats mainly crustaceans, aquatic insect larvae, mussels, and algae. Spawning occurs from March to July.

NORTHERN HOG SUCKER
Hypentelium nigricans

20–35 (max 50) cm

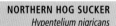

head cross
section

DESCRIPTION: Body elongated, heavier at front end; caudal peduncle long, narrow. Top of head strongly concave between eyes, which are oriented upward. Snout long, decurved; mouth protruding forward. Mouth inferior. Lips with many round bumps (papillae). Lower lip forming an acute V-shaped angle at rear margin. Lateral line scales large. Dorsal fin sickle-shaped. Sides mottled, with 5 black "saddles" on tan or olive background. Lips orange. All fins yellowish or tan.

LOOK-ALIKES: Longnose, spotted, and white suckers; redhorses.

NOTES: The northern hog sucker is found statewide except in the Lake Superior basin; it is common in streams and rivers in its preferred habitat of clear riffles and runs with silt-free bottoms. It is intolerant of environmental degradation, including high turbidity and siltation. A bottom feeder, it eats mainly crustaceans and aquatic insect larvae. Spawning occurs from April to May in gravelly riffles.

BIGMOUTH BUFFALO
Ictiobus cyprinellus   40–50 (max 124.5) cm

DESCRIPTION: Body robust. Mouth terminal, sharply oblique (at 45° angle). Often with a slight depression on the snout near the eyes. Dorsal fin sickle-shaped with long base; length of rays much shorter than length of fin base. Body brownish or greenish bronze; fins dark. Juveniles less deep-bodied.

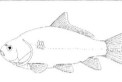

LOOK-ALIKES: Common carp, goldfish, and quillback.

NOTES: The bigmouth buffalo is found in the southern half of Wisconsin. It is uncommon to common in medium to large rivers and lakes and uncommon in wadeable streams near their juncture with larger waters. The bigmouth buffalo prefers deep, quiet water; it is only moderately tolerant of overall environmental degradation, though it can tolerate high temperatures and low oxygen. A midwater feeder, it eats mainly zooplankton and other invertebrates. Spawning occurs from April to May.

SPOTTED SUCKER
Minytrema melanops   27.9–45 (max 50) cm

DESCRIPTION: Body elongated, round in cross section. Snout blunt. Mouth ventral. Lips thin, smoothly folded (plicate; faint on upper lip). Lower lip forming an acute V-shaped angle at rear margin. Dorsal fin short, slightly sickle-shaped (adults) or straight (young), with 11–12 rays. Lateral line absent. Body olive to tan; fins dusky to white. Outer edge of dorsal fin dusky. Anterior edge of scales with square-shaped spots in regular

  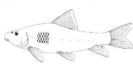

horizontal rows. Breeding males with tubercles on head and anal fin and sometimes with 2 black lateral stripes with pinkish stripe in between.

LOOK-ALIKES: Longnose, northern hog, and white suckers; redhorses.

NOTES: The spotted sucker is rarely encountered in streams and primarily inhabits large rivers such as the Mississippi, Saint Croix, Chippewa, Black, Des Plaines, and Wolf and their tributaries. It prefers off-channel areas of quiet, slightly turbid water with heavy vegetation. The spotted sucker is intolerant of environmental degradation. Spawning occurs in May in flowing water.

241

SUNFISHES (CENTRARCHIDAE)

Sunfishes are deep-bodied, often colorful fish that belong to a small family of twenty-seven species found only in North America. There are eleven species of sunfishes found in Wisconsin streams, though most sunfishes are more often found in lakes or large rivers. They are Wisconsin's most popular game fish.

Sunfishes tend to have bodies that are deep and strongly compressed from side to side (laterally); no teeth on the tongue; two dorsal fins that are broadly joined and appear to be one fin; the first dorsal fin with six to thirteen spines, the second with only soft rays; pectoral fins placed moderately high on the body, with pelvic fins almost directly below; and an anal fin with three to seven spines near the front. All sunfishes build nests to spawn, with the males guarding the eggs and the newly hatched fry.

Many sunfishes hybridize, especially in the genus *Lepomis*. Hybrids tend to resemble a mix of the two parent species.

The word *Centrarchidae* is from the Greek *kentron* (thorn) and *archos* (anus), probably referring to the spines in the anal fin.

Crappies

WHITE CRAPPIE
Pomoxis annularis

16.5–30 (max 42) cm

DESCRIPTION: Body deep, compressed side to side (laterally). Mouth large, upper jaw extending to middle of eye. Predorsal region (from snout to base of dorsal fin) very long, arched, with a shallow dip over eye. Dorsal and anal fin base lengths shorter than distance between eye and dorsal fin origin. 5–6 (usually 6) dorsal spines, first shorter than last. Body white, often with mottling organized into 6–9 dusky bars on each side; bars widest at top (less pronounced in juveniles). Tail, dorsal, and anal fins with wavy black bands, spots.

LOOK-ALIKES: Black crappie; also hybridizes with black crappie.

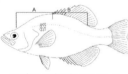

very long predorsal region (A > B)

NOTES: In Wisconsin the white crappie is found mostly in the southern part of the state, where it is uncommon to common, but it also occurs in scattered areas of N. Wisconsin. It inhabits mainly lakes and large rivers, usually occupying the warm, quiet, shallow, turbid water of bays and backwaters. It is moderately tolerant of environmental degradation. It prefers slightly warmer and more turbid water than the black crappie, but most water bodies that have white crappie also have black crappie. The white crappie eats zooplankton, aquatic insect larvae, and fish. Spawning occurs from May to June.

BLACK CRAPPIE
Pomoxis nigromaculatus   17.8–30 (max 50.2) cm

DESCRIPTION: Body deep, compressed side to side (laterally). Mouth large, upper jaw extending to middle of eye. Predorsal region (from snout to base of dorsal fin) long, arched, with a shallow dip over eye. Dorsal and anal fin bases of length equal to distance between eye and dorsal fin origin. 7–8 (sometimes 9) dorsal spines, first shorter than last. White body dominated by black blotches and mottling (less pronounced in juveniles or in turbid water bodies). Tail, dorsal, and anal fins with wavy black bands, spots.

LOOK-ALIKES: White crappie; also hybridizes with white crappie.

NOTES: The black crappie is common statewide. It inhabits lakes, backwaters, and medium to large streams and rivers, preferring the warm, quiet, deep, clear, vegetated water of bays and pools. Although a warmwater species, it can persist in cooler water than the white crappie. It is moderately tolerant of environmental degradation and eats zooplankton, aquatic insect larvae, snails, leeches, and fish. Spawning occurs from May to June and sometimes July over sand or fine gravel near vegetation.

long predorsal region (A = B)

Largemouth and Smallmouth Bass

SMALLMOUTH BASS
Micropterus dolomieu   2.3–45 (max 57.5) cm

DESCRIPTION: Mouth large, slightly upturned; upper jaw extending to mideye but never beyond eye. 2 dorsal fins moderately connected. Usually 3 dark streaks on each side of head. Brown specks that often coalesce into 8–16 vertical bars; bars *not* fused into a lateral stripe. Eye red. In juveniles, upper jaw similar to adults; vertical bars pronounced; tail brightly colored with yellow center, diffuse black band, and whitish edge.

juvenile

LOOK-ALIKES: Largemouth bass.

NOTES: The smallmouth bass is common statewide. It inhabits medium to large rivers and lakes, preferring warm, clear water and usually avoiding quiet, turbid water. The smallmouth bass is intolerant of environmental degradation. It eats mainly zooplankton, aquatic insect larvae, fish, and crayfish. Spawning occurs from May to June over gravel.

adult

22.9–47.5 (max 62.5) cm

juvenile

DESCRIPTION: Mouth very large, upturned; upper jaw reaching at least back of eye (except in juveniles). 2 dorsal fins barely connected. Streaks on head faint or absent. Broad, irregular black stripe, broken into blotches, from snout to base of tail (often faint in adults). Eye golden brown. In juveniles, upper jaw reaching middle to back of eye; prominent lateral stripe appears as series of vertical blotches; tail not brightly colored.

LOOK-ALIKES: Smallmouth bass.

adult

NOTES: The largemouth bass is common statewide. It inhabits lakes, medium to large rivers, and tributary streams, preferring warm, shallow, vegetated water. The largemouth bass is moderately tolerant of environmental degradation. It eats mainly zooplankton, crustaceans, aquatic insect larvae, and fish. Spawning occurs from May to July in shallow, vegetated areas, usually over sand or gravel.

Other Sunfishes

15–20 (max 30) cm

DESCRIPTION: Body deep, compressed side to side (laterally). Mouth large, extending beyond middle of eye. No teeth on tongue (compare with warmouth, page 246). Pectoral fins short, rounded. 5–7 (usually 6) anal fin spines. Body brown or olive with dark spots or mottling, often in horizontal rows on sides and fins. Eye usually reddish. Ear flap completely black to edge. Breeding males often darker color. Juveniles more likely to have mottling.

LOOK-ALIKES: Green, longear, and orangespotted sunfishes; warmouth.

NOTES: The rock bass is common statewide. It inhabits medium to large streams and lakes and shallow waters of the Great Lakes, preferring warm, clear water with gravel substrate and some vegetation or other forms of cover (e.g., woody debris, boulders). The rock bass is intolerant of environmental degradation. It eats mainly zooplankton, aquatic insect larvae, crayfish, and fish. Spawning occurs from May to June over sand or gravel.

GREEN SUNFISH
Lepomis cyanellus

7.5–15 (max 25) cm

DESCRIPTION: Body deep, compressed side to side (laterally). Mouth and lips large, extending to middle of eye. Pectoral fins rounded. 3 anal fin spines. Body usually solid yellow or blue green with dark mottling. Faint spots or bars. Wavy turquoise lines on cheek and opercle. Ear flap dark with light margin. Vague dark blotch usually at rear of second dorsal fin; blotch at base of anal fin. Breeding males have dark vertical bars and light margin on dorsal, anal, and tail (caudal) fins.

 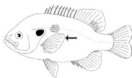

LOOK-ALIKES: Bluegill, longear, and orangespotted sunfishes, pumpkinseed, rock bass, and warmouth. Hybridizes with all of these, especially pumpkinseed, except for rock bass.

NOTES: The green sunfish is common in S. Wisconsin and uncommon in the north. It inhabits small, shallow lakes and ponds and pools of low-gradient streams and small rivers, preferring warm, shallow, quiet water, often near vegetation beds. It is very tolerant of environmental degradation, including high turbidity, siltation, and habitat modifications. It eats zooplankton, aquatic insect larvae, and snails. Spawning occurs from May to July.

PUMPKINSEED
Lepomis gibbosus

12.5–20 (max 25) cm

DESCRIPTION: Body deep, compressed side to side (laterally). Mouth small, upper jaw scarcely reaching front of eye. Pectoral fins long, pointed. 3 anal fin spines. Cheek and opercle with alternating wavy blue and orange lines. Back olive and sides yellow, with blue and yellow-orange spots; sometimes 7–10 faint vertical bars; belly orange. Ear flap dark with bright red-orange posterior dot.

LOOK-ALIKES: Bluegill; green, longear, and orangespotted sunfishes; and warmouth. Hybridizes with all of these.

NOTES: The pumpkinseed is common statewide. It inhabits lakes, ponds, impoundments, and low-gradient streams and rivers, preferring warm, shallow, quiet, vegetated or brushy water. The pumpkinseed is moderately tolerant of environmental degradation. It eats mainly aquatic insects, zooplankton, and snails. Spawning occurs from May to July in warm, shallow bays over sand or fine gravel. This species is especially likely to hybridize with other *Lepomis* species.

SUNFISHES (Centrarchidae)

WARMOUTH
Lepomis gulosus

8.9–20 (max 26.7) cm

DESCRIPTION: Body deep, compressed side to side (laterally). Mouth large, upper jaw extending to or beyond middle of eye. Teeth on tongue (compare with rock bass, page 244). Pectoral fins rounded. 3 anal fin spines. Body brown with irregular yellow blotches; belly yellow. Dark red-brown lines radiate from rear of eye. Eye red. Fins with wavy dark bands. Ear flap short, with yellow edge. Breeding males with bright colors, black pelvic fins. Juveniles without many adult markings.

LOOK-ALIKES: Bluegill; pumpkinseed; rock bass; and green, longear, and orangespotted sunfishes; hybridizes with all of these except rock bass.

NOTES: The warmouth is found sporadically statewide; it occurs at many localities but is usually uncommon. It inhabits lakes and streams, preferring quiet, turbid, vegetated water. The warmouth is moderately tolerant of environmental degradation, and it eats zooplankton, aquatic insect larvae, and fish. Spawning occurs from May to July over silt or fine gravel.

ORANGESPOTTED SUNFISH
Lepomis humilis

5–10 (max 12.5) cm

DESCRIPTION: Body small (the smallest Wisconsin sunfish), deep, compressed side to side (laterally). Mouth small, upper jaw extending to front of eye. Large sensory pores above upper lip. 3 anal fin spines. Pectoral fins short, rounded. Body light blue or gray, often with irregular orange spots, faint vertical bars, and wavy turquoise lines on cheek and opercle. Ear flap relatively long, with wide, white edge. Breeding males with bright colors, red eyes, black edges on white pelvic fins. Juveniles with faint vertical bars or blotches instead of spots.

LOOK-ALIKES: Bluegill; green and longear sunfishes; pumpkinseed; rock bass; and warmouth; hybridizes with all of these except rock bass.

NOTES: In Wisconsin the orangespotted sunfish is found only in the southern part of the state and is uncommon in wadeable streams. It primarily inhabits sloughs, backwater lakes, and shallow margins of large rivers, preferring the warm, quiet, turbid water of soft-bottomed pools and backwaters. It is moderately tolerant of environmental degradation, including siltation and low oxygen. It eats zooplankton, aquatic insect larvae, and crustaceans. Spawning occurs from May to July.

juvenile

breeding male

246

BLUEGILL
Lepomis macrochirus   **12.7–22.5 (max 30.5) cm**

DESCRIPTION: Body deep, compressed side to side (laterally). Mouth small, not extending under pupil of eye. Pectoral fins long, pointed. 3 anal fin spines. Body color dark or silvery blue: color usually pale in turbid water, darker in stained water. Faint vertical bars. Ear flap completely black—no light margin. Large diffuse black spot often at rear of second dorsal fin. Breeding males have bluish sheen, bright red-orange breast.

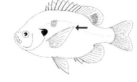

LOOK-ALIKES: Green, longear, and orangespotted sunfishes; pumpkinseed; and warmouth; hybridizes with all of these, especially pumpkinseed.

NOTES: The bluegill is abundant statewide and is one of the most popular game fishes in Wisconsin. It inhabits lakes and midsized streams to large rivers, preferring warm, clear, vegetated water. It is moderately tolerant of environmental degradation: though it can somewhat tolerate high turbidity and siltation, it is somewhat sensitive to low oxygen. It eats mainly terrestrial insects, aquatic insect larvae, and zooplankton. Spawning occurs from May to August over sand or fine gravel.

juvenile

LONGEAR SUNFISH
Lepomis megalotis   **5–12.5 (max 15) cm**

THREATENED

DESCRIPTION: Body deep, compressed side to side (laterally). Mouth small, not extending to pupil of eye. Pectoral fins short, rounded. 3 anal fin spines. Body dark with turquoise spots above, yellow to orange below. Cheek and opercle with wavy turquoise lines; fins clear to orange. Ear flap very long (adults only), often upward-slanted, black with red to yellow edge. Breeding males have bright colors and red eyes; often with orange dorsal, anal, and caudal (tail) fins; blue-black pelvic fins. Juveniles dark with yellow spots, white belly.

breeding male

LOOK-ALIKES: Bluegill, green, and orangespotted sunfishes; pumpkinseed; rock bass; and warmouth; hybridizes with all of these except rock bass.

NOTES: The longear sunfish is found in S.E. and N.W. Wisconsin, and it is rare. It inhabits streams, rivers, and occasionally lakes, preferring warm, shallow, quiet, clear, vegetated water. It is intolerant of environmental degradation, including high turbidity, siltation, and habitat degradation. It eats zooplankton, terrestrial insects, aquatic insect larvae, and crustaceans. Spawning occurs from June to July over gravel, sand, or hard mud.

juvenile

TEMPERATE BASSES (MORONIDAE)

Moronidae is a small family of six species in the Northern Hemisphere, three of which occur in Wisconsin. These are the white bass and the yellow bass, which are native, and the white perch, which is introduced. The yellow bass (*Morone mississippiensis*) is found only in larger rivers and lakes.

The temperate basses have deep bodies; large, toothy mouths; a saw-edged *preopercle* (gill-covering bone); two dorsal fins that are barely connected to each other; and a forked tail. They superficially resemble members of the sunfish family but are not closely related, and their spawning behavior greatly differs. Unlike sunfish, temperate basses do not build nests or care for their eggs and young.

WHITE PERCH
Morone americana

12.5–20 (max 34.3) cm

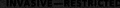
INVASIVE—RESTRICTED

DESCRIPTION: Body deep, arched, compressed side to side (laterally). No teeth on tongue. Preopercle with saw-toothed edge. 2 dorsal fins slightly connected. 3 anal fin spines; second and third spines about equal in length; 8–10 anal rays. Tail forked. Usually a solid color: pale olive, silver, or white; sometimes with a hint of mottling. Breeding males with bluish chin.

juvenile

LOOK-ALIKES: White bass and freshwater drum.

anal fin

NOTES: In Wisconsin the white perch is found in the Great Lakes and the lower reaches of their tributaries and is most common near Green Bay and Duluth. It is rare in wadeable streams. It inhabits lakes and medium to large rivers, preferring pools. The white perch is moderately tolerant of environmental degradation. It eats zooplankton, crustaceans, aquatic insect larvae, and fish. Spawning probably occurs from April to June over sand or gravel. It is perceived by many as a nuisance fish in Wisconsin, accused of eating the eggs of other fishes and possibly outcompeting them for food, although conclusive studies are lacking.

WHITE BASS
Morone chrysops   20–30 (max 47.5) cm

DESCRIPTION: Body deep, arched, compressed side to side (laterally). Teeth on tongue. Eye yellowish. Preopercle with saw-toothed edge. 2 dorsal fins may be touching but are not connected by a membrane. 3 anal fin spines, second clearly shorter than third; 11–13 (usually 12) anal rays. Tail forked. Body color silvery, with 6–7 horizontal dark stripes. Dorsal fin and tail dark gray; pectoral, pelvic, and anal fins clear to white. Breeding males sometimes with bluish chin.

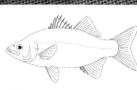

LOOK-ALIKES: White perch.

NOTES: In Wisconsin the white bass is found mainly in the southern part of the state, where it is common in large lakes and rivers. It is rarely seen in wadeable streams except during spawning. It prefers open water with moderate current and is moderately tolerant of environmental degradation. It eats zooplankton, crustaceans, aquatic insect larvae, and fish. Spawning occurs from April to June, often in tributary streams, over firm substrate or occasionally aquatic vegetation.

TROUT-PERCHES (PERCOPSIDAE)

There are only two species in the trout-perch family, and both of them are only found in North America. Wisconsin's only species is the trout-perch. This family is related to the pirate perch and to cavefishes (family Amblyopsidae).

The trout-perch's common name comes from its resemblance to both a trout and a perch: it has an adipose fin like the former, and its fin spines and mouth help it to resemble the latter. Trout-perches also generally have a large head; one to two weak spines at the anterior edge of each dorsal, pelvic, and anal fin; and small scales.

The word *Percopsidae* is from the Greek *perkē* (perch) and *ops* (similar).

	TROUT-PERCH
5–10.2 (max 15) cm	*Percopsis omiscomaycus*

DESCRIPTION: Body deep; caudal peduncle slender. Head large. Single dorsal fin, slightly sickle-shaped. Adipose fin present. Body yellow olive with rows of 7–12 dusky spots along back and sides.

LOOK-ALIKES: Ruffe and yellow perch.

NOTES: In Wisconsin the trout-perch is found mostly in the northern part of the state, where it is uncommon to common. It inhabits large rivers and lakes and their tributaries, preferring mostly clear water. The trout-perch is moderately tolerant of environmental degradation. It eats zooplankton, aquatic insect larvae, and crustaceans. Spawning occurs from April to June and possibly July, usually over sandbars in lakes or rivers.

250

Amphibians

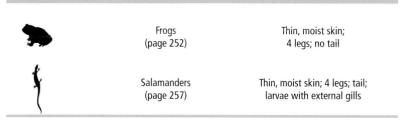

| | Frogs (page 252) | Thin, moist skin; 4 legs; no tail |
| | Salamanders (page 257) | Thin, moist skin; 4 legs; tail; larvae with external gills |

Amphibians are fascinating and important components of stream ecosystems. They help control populations of pests and provide food for predators. They are among the most visible wildlife in many areas and are often among the most beloved by people. The breeding calls of frogs and toads are harbingers of spring, and some are quite melodious.

Frogs and salamanders are the two types of amphibians found in Wisconsin. (Caecilians, a small group of legless amphibians, also belong to this class but do not occur here.) Of these, seven frogs and two salamanders may be found in and along wadeable streams.

Key Traits

Amphibians are characterized by having both aquatic and terrestrial life stages. The word *amphibian* is from the Greek *amphi* (of both kinds) and *bios* (life), referring to these two habitats. Their dual habitat needs and sensitivity to environmental degradation make them excellent indicators of the health of both upland and aquatic habitats.

Amphibians have thin, semipermeable skin that needs to remain moist at all times. This skin allows for the exchange of water and gases with the environment, including oxygen. They are *ectothermic* (cold-blooded) animals whose body temperatures reflect their surroundings. Unlike reptiles, they prefer cool, damp places because their thin skin makes them prone to desiccation (drying out) under warm and dry conditions. For this reason, many species are nocturnal (active after dark) in order to take advantage of cooler, more humid conditions. Some frogs, however, are active during the day because they live in humid, cool microclimates in forests or near water.

Like reptiles, amphibians shed their skin periodically. Shedding occurs with growth and wear but is also influenced by light, temperature, and food supply. Unlike reptiles, many amphibians eat their shed skins, presumably for the nutrients they contain.

Life Cycle and Reproduction

For several species, amphibian breeding begins shortly after spring emergence, which is triggered by spring rains or frost-out. These early-emerging, early-breeding species often engage in a mass migration from overwintering sites to their breeding wetlands. Spring migrations usually occur after dark on rainy nights. The early spring breeders often use temporary (ephemeral) ponds that have been created by snowmelt and spring rains. These temporary wetlands do not support fish, which are major predators of amphibian eggs and larvae. (Some fishes, such as minnows and sticklebacks, also outcompete amphibian larvae for food.) Other amphibians breed in late spring, often in semipermanent, fishless wetlands. And still others breed in summer, generally in permanent water where fish are present. These species occur in lower densities as a result of predation and competition with fish.

The young of all Wisconsin amphibians hatch from eggs, and all but one species begin life in water as larvae. (The eastern red-backed salamander [*Plethodon cinereus*] is completely terrestrial, laying eggs in dead wood.) Eggs and larvae are most sensitive to the effects of water quality degradation, while adult amphibians are especially sensitive to terrestrial and shoreline habitat conditions.

Overwintering

Perhaps the most amazing thing about some Wisconsin amphibians is their ability to overwinter. A few species freeze solid during the winter. In late fall or early winter, as their body temperatures drop to near 0°C (32°F), their metabolisms produce a glycol-like "antifreeze," and water migrates outside of their cells. When temperatures drop below freezing, their body fluid freezes, but the cells usually do not rupture. They cease breathing, and their entire system shuts down, including the heart. In spring they literally thaw out and resume activity.

Other amphibians burrow underground to avoid freezing or enter the water and remain submerged under the ice, where they take in oxygen through their skin to maintain life support. Many species that overwinter underwater remain only sluggishly active, although central newts and mudpuppies do remain active in the cold water.

Ecological Notes

Amphibians play very important roles in the natural communities where they live. Frogs and salamanders provide high-quality food for predators such as birds, mammals, fish, and reptiles. They are also the primary vertebrate predators of insects and other invertebrates in many freshwater environments. Grazing by tadpoles helps control the growth of algae and other aquatic plants.

Beyond their direct ecological values, amphibians also benefit humankind. Many have skin secretions that can be used for pharmaceutical purposes. Northern leopard frogs show some promise for helping us combat cancer. And amphibians provide one of the easiest venues to study and experience nature. Many a naturalist got his or her start chasing frogs at a local pond or along the lakeshore on a summer vacation, and anyone who appreciates nature can enjoy the melodic chorusing of frogs.

FROGS (ORDER ANURA)

Wisconsin is home to twelve species of frogs, including the American toad. Of these, six are found in wadeable streams.

All Wisconsin frog species breed and deposit eggs in water, usually in wetlands. Once at the breeding site, male frogs begin to call for mates. When a female selects a suitable male, he mounts and clasps the female behind her front limbs (an embrace called *amplexus*) to stimulate egg laying and then fertilizes her eggs externally as she lays them. The eggs eventually hatch into larvae, called tadpoles or polliwogs, which later metamorphose into adult frogs.

Some frog species breed in ephemeral wetlands: ponds and other areas that are filled with water briefly during the spring, then dry up as the season gets hotter. Such ponds are safe for tadpoles because they lack fish. For these species, tadpoles mature quickly (in six to eight weeks), which they must do in order to avoid running out of water before they are fully developed. Other frog species breed in more permanent wetlands. These species take longer to develop; several overwinter as tadpoles, then become mature adults the following spring.

The life spans of Wisconsin frogs vary widely: cricket frogs often live less than a year, whereas bullfrogs may live five to ten years.

Tadpoles are primarily herbivores and often play a key role in ecosystems by grazing algae. Once metamorphosis occurs, adult frogs are carnivorous, feeding exclusively on live prey such as insects, insect larvae, other invertebrates, and small vertebrates.

The order name *Anura* means "tailless," from the Greek *an* (without) and *oura* (tail).

TOADS (BUFONIDAE)

Toads have short and stout bodies, short legs, and dry skin that is bumpy or warty. Prominent *parotid glands* are located at the back of the toad's head and produce a toxic secretion that is effective at repelling most predators.

EASTERN AMERICAN TOAD
Anaxyrus americanus americanus
5–9 cm

DESCRIPTION: Skin thick, dry, rough. Parotid glands behind eyes, evident as large swellings. Back brown to reddish to olive, with scattered dark spots that each encircle 1 to 3 wart-like bumps on back. Call is a long, high-pitched, uninterrupted trill lasting up to 30 seconds; each male has a slightly different pitch.

LOOK-ALIKES: None in wadeable streams.

NOTES: The eastern American toad's thick skin allows it to retain body fluids better than most other amphibians, so it can live a greater distance from water than most frogs. It lives in a wide variety of habitats ranging from prairies to wetlands to forests. It is tolerant of urban settings, where it often persists in gardens and parks. Breeding occurs from April to July.

parotid gland

TREEFROGS (HYLIDAE)

Treefrogs have flattened and slender bodies with long legs. Most species have circular disks on their fingers and toes.

EASTERN CRICKET FROG
(Blanchard's cricket frog, northern cricket frog)
Acris crepitans crepitans
1.8–3 cm

ENDANGERED

DESCRIPTION: Tiny. Body color reddish tan to green. Often with rust-colored or green triangular mark between and behind eyes. May also have bright rust or green middorsal stripe along length of body. Skin textured, with sporadic bumps that are often darker than background color. Call resembles two ball bearings clicking together at increasing speed, then dropping off.

LOOK-ALIKES: Young adult toads—parotid glands behind eyes.

NOTES: The eastern cricket frog is exceedingly rare, although it was abundant in S. Wisconsin until the 1970s. It is found along the edges of ponds and rivers and in stream floodplains and shorelines, preferring shallow gradient mud or sand flats supporting low and sparse vegetation. An exceptional jumper, it avoids predators through a series of rapid zigzag jumps into and out of the water. Breeding occurs from May to August. This frog is Wisconsin's only endangered amphibian. The cause of its decline is uncertain, but climate change and habitat degradation and fragmentation are likely culprits.

TRUE FROGS (RANIDAE)

Frogs in the family Ranidae are known as the "true frogs." They are mainly aquatic as adults, have slender and streamlined bodies with long legs, and may or may not have webbing between the toes.

Dorsolateral and tympanic folds are helpful traits to notice on many true frogs. *Dorsolateral folds* run from behind the eye to around the midbody, and *tympanic folds* wrap around the *tympanum*, or ear membrane.

dorsolateral fold

tympanum and tympanic fold

AMERICAN BULLFROG
Lithobates catesbeianus
(formerly *Rana catesbeiana*)
14–18 cm

SPECIAL CONCERN

DESCRIPTION: Large. Skin color dark solid olive to lighter pale green with variable spotting. Distinct tympanic fold that wraps around the tympanum (ear membrane). Adult female's tympanum approximately the same size as eye. Breeding males often with bright yellow chins, tympanum twice as big as eye. Call is a deep, resonating "jug-o-rum" that carries well.

LOOK-ALIKES: Northern green frog.

NOTES: The bullfrog is a shoreline-dependent species and is highly aquatic. Because tadpoles do not metamorphose until at least their second year, the bullfrog requires permanent water habitats such as lakes. It prefers habitats with tall, undisturbed shoreline vegetation and abundant submerged and floating aquatic vegetation. A female can lay up to 20,000 eggs in large films among floating vegetation on the water's surface. Breeding occurs from May to August.

NORTHERN GREEN FROG
Lithobates clamitans melanota
6–9 cm

DESCRIPTION: Light to dark olive green or brown background color with small, irregular, dark brown spots. Spots often more numerous in juveniles. Prominent dorsolateral folds that run from behind eye to about midbody. Breeding males with bright yellow chins. Call is a low "gung-*gung*-gung," like strumming on a loose banjo string.

LOOK-ALIKES: Bullfrog and mink frog.

NOTES: Because its young often overwinter as tadpoles, the northern green frog requires permanent water, like deep marshes, large ponds, and lakes. Heavy shoreline development significantly reduces populations, primarily because of lost natural shoreline vegetation. Eggs are laid in a mass attached to floating vegetation on the water's surface. Breeding occurs from May to August.

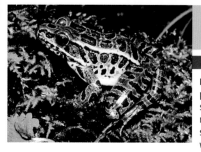

PICKEREL FROG
Lithobates palustris
4.5–8.5 cm

SPECIAL CONCERN

DESCRIPTION: Greenish brown with paired, dark brown blotches between dorsolateral folds. Undersides of thigh and groin bright golden yellow. Hind legs with rectangular dark blotches or crossbars. Call is snore-like, shorter and less broken than that of northern leopard frog, with less carrying power.

LOOK-ALIKES: Northern leopard frog.

NOTES: The adult pickerel frog prefers coldwater habitats such as springs and trout streams for living and hibernating. Breeding occurs from April to June in permanent warmwater wetlands adjacent to these coldwater streams. The warm water helps speed development of the young.

NORTHERN LEOPARD FROG
Lithobates pipiens
5–9 cm

SPECIAL CONCERN

DESCRIPTION: Green or light brown with scattered, large, rounded brown spots bordered in yellow, especially yellow on spots between dorsolateral folds. Ventral side creamy white without yellow thigh or groin markings. Call is a loud, broken snore, somewhat like a finger dragging over a well-inflated balloon.

LOOK-ALIKES: Pickerel frog.

NOTES: The northern leopard frog is found along shorelines and in bogs, largely in stagnant water; it also often forages far from water in forests, prairies, and old fields. Breeding occurs from May to June in a wide variety of wetlands, especially in fishless waters. The northern leopard frog experienced major die-offs in the early 1970s in the Upper Midwest and is still on the decline; individuals do not live as long or lay as many eggs as in the past.

MINK FROG
Lithobates septentrionalis
5–7 cm

SPECIAL CONCERN

DESCRIPTION: Color olive to brown, often with spots or mottling on back, sides, and legs. Sides of head and upper lips bright green. Dorsolateral ridges sometimes present; when present, almost always broken. Distinct, musk-like odor. Call sounds like horses' hooves trotting on a cobblestone street.

LOOK-ALIKES: Northern green frog.

NOTES: In Wisconsin the mink frog is found only in the northern part of the state. It inhabits lakes, rivers, and streams, preferring weedy areas with slow currents. It often rests on floating vegetation such as bog mats or lily pads, away from the immediate shoreline, but may also be found along shorelines. It is listed by the Wisconsin DNR as a species of special concern due to its limited range and because it is rarely encountered. Scientists surveying for frogs find it difficult to detect this species because its calling behavior is erratic; it sometimes calls for only one hour in the middle of the night. Breeding occurs from June to August; globular masses of up to 4,000 eggs are deposited in submerged vegetation.

SALAMANDERS (ORDER CAUDATA)

Salamanders are the most secretive group within Wisconsin's amphibian community. Seven species reside in Wisconsin, but most go entirely undetected by humans. Two species are found in Wisconsin streams: the common mudpuppy and the central newt.

Most adult salamanders are terrestrial and return to aquatic habitats only for breeding. The common mudpuppy, however, is exclusively aquatic, retaining its larval gills in adulthood. The central newt is another exception, having multiple potential life stages beyond the larval stage, with its changes in habitat influenced by environmental conditions. (See page 259 for a description of the central newt's complex life stages.)

Unlike frogs, salamanders remain silent during the breeding season. Some species breed in single pairs, while others breed in a mass. Almost all salamander breeding involves an elaborate courtship. The male deposits *spermatophores* (clusters of sperm cells) in front of the females. She picks these up with her *cloacal lips* located ventrally behind her rear legs and internally fertilizes her eggs. She later deposits them in appropriate habitat. Male salamanders are capable of breeding with several females. While most amphibians breed in the spring, mudpuppies and central newts breed in the fall.

Both the mudpuppy and the central newt overwinter underwater. Although many species of amphibian that overwinter underwater remain only sluggishly active in winter, both of these species remain quite active despite the cold water.

Salamanders are carnivorous throughout their lives, both as larvae and as adults. (This contrasts with frogs, which are herbivorous as tadpoles.)

Salamanders have some amazing regenerative capabilities, being able to regrow digits (toes) and even full limbs. Some salamanders, like newts, can actually regenerate eye lens tissue from other tissue that had a previously different function. Interestingly, regenerated amphibian limbs appear to resist tumor growth. Even injected tumor cells are somehow reprogrammed to become life-producing cell structures. Where one would expect a tumor to form, another appendage appears. Scientists hope to someday use this miraculous process to regenerate lost human limbs.

The order name *Caudata* comes from the Latin *cauda* (tail).

MUDPUPPIES (PROTEIDAE)

Mudpuppies are salamanders that are exclusively aquatic, not spending any life stage on land. The common mudpuppy is the only species in this family found in Wisconsin. Mudpuppies may also be called "waterdogs," especially in the southern United States.

COMMON MUDPUPPY
Necturus maculosus maculosus
30.5–40.5 cm

SPECIAL CONCERN

DESCRIPTION: Body large. Gills bushy, feather-like, deep red. Dorsal color a rusty brown or grayish with scattered dark spots. Occasionally, color a dark bluish black with fine brown speckling. Each foot with 4 toes. Tail finned.

LOOK-ALIKES: None in wadeable streams.

NOTES: The common mudpuppy is Wisconsin's largest and only totally aquatic salamander. It inhabits lakes, rivers, and sometimes streams, preferring large flat rock microhabitats, although large riprap (piled boulders) and logs may also be used. It uses eroded holes within clay sediment layers in submerged riverbanks. It eats aquatic invertebrates, small fish, and other amphibians. The mudpuppy is the only host to the state-endangered salamander mussel, which would presumably go extinct if the mudpuppy was eliminated. The rumor that mudpuppies are poisonous is false. Breeding occurs in October and November.

NEWTS (SALAMANDRIDAE)

Newts are primarily aquatic salamanders. The central newt is the only newt found in Wisconsin. Compared with other salamanders, its life history is unusual, as it is capable of producing three life phases beyond the larval stage: aquatic adult; terrestrial adult; and *eft*, a terrestrial juvenile form. It can make multiple transitions between its aquatic and terrestrial forms, adjusting to changes in environmental conditions. It appears that in Wisconsin, most newt larvae transform directly into the adult aquatic form and are only occasionally found in terrestrial forms. Drought and wet cycles seem to influence what phase or phases may occur, although there is no clear pattern. It is likely that, under drought conditions, larvae may leave the water to transform into efts, or aquatic adults may leave the water to transform into terrestrial adults. Both efts and terrestrial adults may later return to water and transform back to aquatic forms.

The central newt is one of Wisconsin's smallest salamanders.

CENTRAL NEWT
Notophthalmus viridescens louisianensis
6.5–10 cm

aquatic adult

DESCRIPTION: Body small. Aquatic adult has smooth skin; color brownish orange to light olive-colored with orange and black spots. No gills. Tail is finned. Ventral side yellowish with many black flecks. Larva is brown green in color. Tail heavily finned. Has external gills. Terrestrial adult has skin textured like medium sandpaper; color dark olive to brown above, with whitish ventral side speckled with black flecks. Tail not finned. Eft (terrestrial juvenile) is plain brown orange with tiny black flecks throughout. Tail not finned.

LOOK-ALIKES: None in wadeable streams.

NOTES: The central newt inhabits well-vegetated lakes, ponds, roadside ditches, and more permanent riparian wetlands. It may be found in wadeable backwater areas. It eats small earthworms, snails, aquatic insects, and larvae of other amphibians. Its cells have amazing regenerative properties: many of its body parts can fully regenerate when lost, including eyes, legs, and certain internal organs. Breeding occurs from September to November.

Reptiles

	Snakes (page 260)	Scaly, dry skin; no legs
	Turtles (page 263)	Scaly, dry skin; shell; legs

Reptiles can be among the most stirring stream animals to observe, whether watching turtles bask on a log or catching a glimpse of a snake darting for cover. They are also important to streams, providing food for predators and controlling populations of amphibians, invertebrates, and small rodents.

In general, reptiles are cold-blooded animals that breathe air, lay shelled eggs, and have skin that is covered in scales or *scutes* (large scales). Turtles, lizards, and snakes are all reptiles; six turtle species and two snake species are found in Wisconsin streams. The word *reptile* comes from the Latin *repere* (crawl).

SNAKES (ORDER SQUAMATA, FAMILY COLUBRIDAE)

Wisconsin has twenty snake species, of which only two are found in wadeable streams. Both of these are in the family Colubridae, a family of harmless snakes with pointed tails. (Wisconsin is home to two venomous species of snake, the eastern massasauga [*Sistrurus catenatus catenatus*] and the timber rattlesnake [*Crotalus horridus*; special concern]. Both live mainly in S.W. Wisconsin, and neither is found in streams.)

Key Traits

Snakes are characterized by their slender, legless body; dry skin; immobile eyes; and forked, flicking tongue. They have colors or patterns that help them to blend in with their natural surroundings, and a number of species undergo pattern or color changes as they mature. Color is often the easiest way to tell different species apart, but because color varies, other features can also be useful. These features include color *pattern* (as opposed to hue), body and head shape, and behavior.

A snake's skin is dry and scaly, unlike the common misconception that it is slimy. Snake skin scales are made out of keratin, the same substance as fingernails. Scales help snakes maintain internal moisture and take the wear and tear of crawling about. Scales also help snakes to crawl and climb.

Shedding of skin is triggered by a snake's growth and scale wear. Younger individuals may shed two or three times during the active season (April–October) due to rapid growth. Once maturity is reached, shedding may occur only once a year, but this differs between species and also depends on food supply and other factors. Just prior to shedding, a snake's appearance becomes dull, and its eyes appear swollen and milky. A snake's vision is impaired at this time, and it may be more irritable and aggressive when encountered. The newly developing skin can be easily damaged during this "opaque" stage, and handling should be avoided or done very gently. After shedding, the snake's markings are bright and clear, and its scales look especially glossy.

Snakes do not see well, because their eye lenses do not move or change shape. However, they have a wide field of vision and can detect movements quickly. Scales over snakes' eyes offer protection from elements in their environment.

A snake's tongue plays a vital role in its survival. Its primary purpose is to locate food. Although the tongue does not have taste buds, its moist, forked portion picks up invisible scent particles from the surrounding air. When a snake flicks its tongue at you, it is simply trying to figure out what you are.

Seasonal Behavior and Reproduction

Snakes are *ectothermic* (cold-blooded), relying on their surroundings to control their body temperatures. This helps to explain their secretive nature, especially during the summer months, when they often retreat underground, under objects, or into dense vegetation to avoid overheating during the day. Wisconsin snakes are generally active from April to October and remain dormant underground for the remaining months.

Breeding by snakes can occur at any time during the active season but often occurs in spring upon emergence from hibernation. Females lay their eggs in places where the eggs are likely to retain and gain moisture and where warm temperatures will accelerate development of the young. This is often in old tree stumps, compost piles, and even old mattresses and other debris found in fields. A notable exception to this is the eastern hog-nosed snake (*Heterodon platirhinos*; special concern), which takes up to a full day to painstakingly excavate its own nest chamber.

Egg-laying snakes in Wisconsin deposit their eggs primarily in May and June, with hatching occurring sixty to ninety days later. Live-bearing snakes, including both of the species found in streams, may give birth from late July until late September.

Feeding

All snakes are carnivores, eating animals exclusively. Both of Wisconsin's stream species feed by seizing prey with their jaws and swallowing it alive. Their inward-pointing teeth help prevent slippery or writhing prey from escaping, and powerful digestive juices start digestion as soon as the prey is swallowed. (Some other types of snakes use constriction or venom to kill prey.)

Snakes' jaws are specialized to help them eat large food items. The upper and lower jaws are made of loosely connected bones that can move away from each other as well as away from the skull during swallowing. After moving the food item into its throat, the snake constricts its body above the food item and literally pushes the prey down to its stomach. After feeding, snakes will often "yawn," an exercise to realign the jawbones to their normal position.

Ecological Notes

Snakes play very important roles in many natural communities as predator and prey. Smaller snakes are a valuable food source for small mammals and birds. They also consume large quantities of worms, insects, and small vertebrates. Medium-sized snakes are fed on heavily by birds of prey, especially by hawks. Medium and large snakes are particularly important in Wisconsin ecosystems for their rodent control.

Despite their importance, many snake populations have declined in Wisconsin due to habitat loss and fragmentation and due to persecution by humans.

COMMON WATERSNAKE
Nerodia sipedon sipedon
61–101.5 cm

DESCRIPTION: Body medium to large, robust. Color gray, brown, or tan, marked with dark brown, red brown, or black transverse blotches, which often fade with age. Underside white, with bright red half-moons interspersed irregularly with dark gray speckling.

LOOK-ALIKES: None in Wisconsin. (Water moccasin [*Agkistrodon piscivorus*]—venomous, with broad head, yellow tail tip, and often darker color; DOES NOT occur in Wisconsin.)

NOTES: The common watersnake is usually found in or close to permanent water bodies, but it prefers clean rivers, streams, and lakeshores. Its diet includes crayfish, slow-moving fish, and a variety of amphibians. It is nonvenomous but is sometimes mistaken for a water moccasin (cottonmouth) and is subsequently killed. (Water moccasins do not occur in or anywhere near Wisconsin.) It is a live-bearer, giving birth in late summer.

QUEENSNAKE
Regina septemvittata
38–61 cm

ENDANGERED

DESCRIPTION: Body medium-sized. Back brown or gray with 3 black stripes running lengthwise; sides with pale yellow stripes running lengthwise. Ventral surface cream-colored with 4 dark-colored stripes, 2 in center and 2 closer to sides.

LOOK-ALIKES: Watersnakes and gartersnakes (e.g., plains gartersnake [*Thamnophis radix*; special concern]—not found in streams).

NOTES: The queensnake requires clear streams with moderate to fast currents and rocky substrate; it often basks in shoreline vegetation. It feeds almost exclusively on freshly molted crayfish. A live-bearer, it gives birth in late summer.

TURTLES (ORDER TESTUDINES)

The word *turtle* sometimes gets confused with the words *tortoise* and *terrapin*, but all refer to turtles. In the United States, *tortoise* generally means a land-dwelling turtle, although there are land-dwelling turtles that are not tortoises. *Terrapin* usually refers to a species that is edible. There are approximately 330 turtle species worldwide, and 55 are native to the United States. Wisconsin has 11 species, of which 6 are found in wadeable streams.

Turtles are believed to have existed on earth longer than any other group of reptiles. Fossil records suggest that they were present as long as 200 million years ago, and they have changed little in structure since then. Turtles are also believed to be among the longest-living creatures, with some species easily living past one hundred years of age. Some individuals may live in excess of two hundred years.

Key Traits

The most distinctive characteristic of a turtle is its shell, which protects the turtle from predation. (Hatchlings and young turtles are especially vulnerable to predation because their shells are not entirely hardened.) The shell is made up of about sixty different bones. The top of the shell is called the *carapace*, and the bottom is the *plastron*. The turtle's ribs and backbone are fused to form the carapace. *Scutes* (large scales) cover the shell and help prevent the invasion of bacteria and fungus into the underlying bone. Scutes also contain all of the shell's patterns and colors.

A turtle's head, neck, and legs are covered with dry, scaly skin. In aquatic turtles, the scales help prevent excess water from entering the body. Turtles shed their skin, though generally not in large pieces. Some aquatic turtles also shed their scutes annually, while others, like the wood turtle, add annual growth to their shells without shedding their scutes.

Recent evidence suggests that turtles commonly vocalize underwater to communicate where visibility is poor.

Basking and Overwintering

Many aquatic turtles frequently bask on shorelines, floating logs, or other objects. Basking is important for regulating a turtle's body temperature and to aid digestion. Vitamin D from sunlight allows for the uptake of calcium from their food, a critical element for shell development in younger turtles and also necessary for producing healthy eggshells in female turtles. Basking increases a turtle's body temperature and dries the shell, inhibiting bacterial and fungal growth. Basking on logs over deep water or near dense aquatic vegetation enables turtles to retreat quickly to safety when alarmed.

Bottom-dwelling turtles, such as the musk and common snapping turtle, bask less frequently. As a result, healthy layers of moss often grow on their carapaces and help them blend into their environment. These turtles also have a much-reduced plastron, with minimal cover of their ventral area.

All of the turtles in this guide spend the winter underwater, either buried in substrate or lying fairly immobile on the stream or lake bottom. They do not hibernate but are semiactive in winter.

Breeding

Determining the sex of a turtle differs by species. Adult males usually have longer, thicker tails, with the vent located in their tails behind the back edge of the carapace. On adult females the vent is at or forward of the back edge of the carapace. In many aquatic species, such as map and softshell turtles, adult males are usually much smaller than adult females. Male Blanding's and wood turtles have concave plastrons to accommodate breeding activity.

Turtles in Wisconsin may breed at any time during their active season, but most breeding activity occurs shortly after emergence in the spring. Courtship displays are common in turtles. Male painted and map turtles use their elongated foreclaws during courtship. While swimming backward in front of a female, the male will wave his claws around the female's head and stroke her snout and chin. If the female is receptive, she sinks to the bottom, where mating takes place.

All turtles lay their eggs on land, most in a self-excavated nest. Most turtles in Wisconsin nest once a year, but some painted turtles and map turtles may nest twice in the same season. Nesting usually occurs around or after dusk, but it may also occur near dawn or during the day on cloudy or rainy days. Turtle nesting occurs from late May until early July in Wisconsin.

Once the eggs are laid, females leave them to hatch on their own, where they remain very vulnerable to predation. Egg incubation typically lasts from sixty to ninety days in Wisconsin, depending on the species, although it may take even longer in cool summers, and some nests laid late in the season may not hatch until the following spring. Incubation temperatures determine the sex of turtles in most Wisconsin species, including Blanding's, map, painted, and snapping turtles. For these species, turtle nests produce more females at high incubation temperatures and more males at lower temperatures; sometimes temperature differences between the top and bottom of a nest produce mixed sexes within the same clutch.

Turtles are generally slow to mature, especially compared to other animals, including other reptiles. Female Blanding's turtles may take from seventeen to twenty years to reach sexual maturity. Slow maturation is usually offset by the fact that turtles are naturally long-lived organisms. Their ability to live and reproduce for many decades is likely the reason turtles have survived for so long.

Feeding

Turtles generally feed on plants or on slow-moving prey such as earthworms, slugs, snails, or insect larvae. All aquatic turtles must be in water to swallow food. The Blanding's and wood turtles, being semiterrestrial, can eat on land or in water. Some aquatic species, like snappers, may occasionally seize prey on land, but they typically move into water to aid swallowing.

Turtles have well-developed senses for smelling food, and some have keen color recognition, especially for the color red. Turtles are toothless, but they have sharp, horny beaks, somewhat similar to bird beaks, that are capable of grabbing and tearing food items. They typically feed by seizing prey and swallowing it whole or by using their powerful foreclaws to tear the food into smaller portions.

Turtles tend to feed little when water temperatures are below 18°C (65°F), which means that many turtles do not feed from September through early June.

Ecological Notes

Wisconsin turtles play a significant role in many aquatic habitats. You might think of them on the one hand as the "garbage disposals" in these systems because they consume a variety of living and freshly dead animals, including fish, insects, and other aquatic life. Small turtles also serve as prey for a variety of other wildlife, including great blue herons, mink, and game fish. Turtle eggs are a delicacy for many species, including raccoons, skunks, crows, and foxes.

Turtles are often liked or even loved by people. A booming pet trade has brought them into millions of American homes over the past few decades. They have also been harvested and sold as food for humans for thousands of years.

Turtles face a multitude of conservation problems, the greatest being habitat loss due to urban sprawl, wetland drainage, road construction, and shoreline development. Riprapped shorelines (lined with rocks for stabilization) can be lethal to baby turtles that get trapped between the rocks as they make their way back to water. In order for populations of turtles to survive over the long term, large areas of contiguous habitat must be available. Our elimination of large predators has also allowed medium-sized predators to flourish, resulting in higher rates of nest predation, which can be devastating to turtle populations. Five of Wisconsin's eleven turtle species are listed as endangered, threatened, or of special concern.

SOFTSHELL TURTLES (TRIONYCHIDAE)

Softshell turtles are found in North America, Asia, Europe, and Africa, and two species are found in Wisconsin. The eastern and western spiny softshell turtles are actually two subgroups of the same species. The other Wisconsin species, the midland smooth softshell (*Apalone mutica mutica*; special concern), is not found in wadeable streams.

Softshell turtles don't often leave the relative safety of the water, but females must leave the water to excavate their nests and lay eggs. Generally, nests are found along sandbars and in areas adjacent to the rivers, streams, and lakes these turtles inhabit.

Turtles in this family are characterized by a lack of scutes on their shells; long, tubular snouts; and heavily webbed feet. Their softer, more flexible shell gives them greater mobility in water.

EASTERN AND WESTERN SPINY SOFTSHELL TURTLES
Apalone spinifera
12.5–24 cm

male

DESCRIPTION: Snout long and pointy; nostrils C-shaped. Scutes absent; carapace with row of spines along front edge. Neck long (not always observable). 2 yellow, black-bordered lines along each side of head. Juveniles and males with olive-gray carapace with small black markings often resembling thin donuts. Adult females with dark olive or tan carapace with brown and gray mottling.

LOOK-ALIKES: Midland smooth softshell turtle (*Apalone mutica mutica*)—not found in streams.

NOTES: Spiny softshell turtles can be found in large rivers, lakes, reservoirs, and streams, especially in water bodies with muddy or sandy bottoms. They spend significant amounts of time buried in the substrate in shallow water, especially at night, to remain concealed while inactive. They eat a variety of animals, including fish, invertebrates, mollusks, and carrion. Unlike smooth softshells, spiny softshells are often aggressive when seized and can inflict painful bites. They do not bite in water in natural situations.

SNAPPING TURTLES (CHELYDRIDAE)

The Chelydridae are a North and Central American family of mainly freshwater turtles. They are characterized by their defensive snapping behavior when encountered on dry land and by their long tails.

EASTERN SNAPPING TURTLE
(common snapping turtle)
Chelydra serpentina serpentina
20.5–40.5 cm (male),
18–46 cm (female)

DESCRIPTION: Head and limbs robust. Jaws large. Snout pointed; beak prominent. Neck long. Carapace with saw-toothed back edge. Tail nearly as long as carapace, with a row of jagged dorsal scales. Plastron greatly reduced—limbs very exposed from underside. Carapace color light brown to black. Plastron often yellowish-colored.

LOOK-ALIKES: Common musk turtle (*Sternotherus odoratus*)—smooth edge to rear carapace; not usually found in streams.

NOTES: The eastern snapping turtle inhabits varying habitats, especially ponds, lakes, and backwaters of rivers. It is sometimes found in streams and uses them to move between other water bodies. A predator and a scavenger, it feeds on aquatic animals and plants, consuming almost any animal it can catch. It is an important top predator in aquatic food chains. Snappers can deliver painful and potentially serious bites and should be respected when encountered. But contrary to popular belief, in water they flee from people and are not inclined to bite unless grabbed or harassed.

BOX AND WATER TURTLES (EMYDIDAE)

Emydidae is a family with nearly fifty species, all of which live in the Western Hemisphere. Eight species are found in Wisconsin, four of which are found in wadeable streams. Turtles in this family come in a variety of colors and patterns and may live either in water, on land, or both.

MIDLAND AND WESTERN PAINTED TURTLES
Chrysemys picta marginata and *C. picta bellii*
10–20.5 cm

western painted turtle

DESCRIPTION: Head and legs dark, with thin yellow stripes. Carapace flat, smooth, keelless, without serrations along rear edge. Carapace dark; plastron orange to red with center blotch. Western: Carapace usually greenish. Plastron usually light orange to reddish; blotch large, oak leaf–shaped. Midland: Stripes on head and limbs may be red, orange, or yellow. Marginal scutes on carapace strongly marked with red. Plastron usually pale yellowish orange; blotch narrow, elongated.

LOOK-ALIKES: Northern map turtle.

NOTES: Both of these turtles are subspecies of the painted turtle (*Chrysemys picta*). In Wisconsin the western painted turtle is found mainly in the extreme northwestern and western part of the state, while the midland painted turtle is found in the extreme southeast, but intergrades between the two may be found statewide. The painted turtle inhabits marshes, ponds, shallow bays of lakes, and backwaters of rivers that support dense aquatic vegetation. It eats aquatic plants, snails, crayfish, insects, and small fish. It spends a great deal of time basking on logs and on mats of floating vegetation on sunny days.

BLANDING'S TURTLE
Emydoidea blandingii
14–25.5 cm

SPECIAL CONCERN

DESCRIPTION: Shell elongated, highly domed. Carapace usually blackish, with specks or dashes of yellow. Hinge allows plastron to fold upward toward carapace, especially the front portion. Head dark brown to black, often with scattered spots or swirls of yellow. Chin brilliant yellow. Plastron yellow, with black blotches toward outer edges.

LOOK-ALIKES: Wood turtle. Ornate box turtle (*Terrapene ornata*; endangered)—chin not yellow; not found in streams.

NOTES: The Blanding's turtle prefers shallow marshy habitats with abundant submerged vegetation, although it can be found in almost any aquatic habitat. It is semiterrestrial and often moves between wetlands during the active season, making migrations of up to 2.5 km from water to nest. Largely carnivorous, it eats crayfish, snails, tadpoles, fish, insects, worms, grasses, and berries. The Blanding's turtle's numbers are declining due to low reproductive success, hatitat loss and fragmentation, and heavy road mortality among females.

WOOD TURTLE
Glyptemys insculpta
15–24 cm

THREATENED

DESCRIPTION: Scutes with sculptured growth rings. Head dark brown to blackish and unpatterned. Neck socket and leg sockets pale yellow to orangish red. Carapace medium brown, occasionally with black flecks and faint yellow rays. Plastron yellow, with black blotches toward outer edges. Hatchlings with tails slightly longer than carapace and olive green to light brown color.

LOOK-ALIKES: Blanding's turtle.

NOTES: The wood turtle is semiaquatic, preferring moderate to fast-flowing water. It spends a great deal of time in forested habitats adjacent to rivers and streams, where it feeds on berries, greens, night crawlers, worms, and other invertebrates. It sometimes pounds the ground with its front feet or plastron to mimic the vibrations of falling raindrops in order to lure earthworms out of the ground to eat. It frequently basks on land and is less observable than other riverine turtles. Females often nest communally, and their eggs are often heavily predated. The wood turtle's numbers have diminished in Wisconsin due to overcollecting, lack of reproductive success, and heavy road mortality among females.

NORTHERN MAP TURTLE
(common map turtle)
Graptemys geographica
**10–16 cm (male),
16.5–27 cm (female)**

DESCRIPTION: Head and neck olive brown with thin yellow lines running from head onto neck. Pronounced yellow spot behind each eye. Carapace olive brown, patterned with fine yellow lines resembling road map. Plastron uniformly colored yellow or creamy. Back edge of shell modestly serrated. Females with large, broad heads and jaws.

LOOK-ALIKES: Midland and western painted turtles. False map turtle (*Graptemys pseudogeographica*; special concern) and Ouachita map turtle (*G. ouachitensis*)—not found in streams.

NOTES: The northern map turtle inhabits riverside channels and backwaters, large streams, and some reservoirs. It prefers habitats with slow to moderate current, soft substrate, and abundant aquatic vegetation. Largely carnivorous, its diet includes insect larvae, carrion, crustaceans, and aquatic plants. The large jaws of females are adapted to cracking mollusk and crayfish shells.

REFERENCES

General

Integrated Taxonomic Information System (ITIS). http://www.itis.gov.
Mikel, Gina. Scientific Illustrator Website. http://www.scientificillustrator.com/.

Introduction

Schaller, F. W., and G. W. Bailey, eds. *Agricultural Management and Water Quality*. Ames: Iowa State
    University Press, 1983.
US Geological Survey National Elevation Dataset. http://ned.usgs.gov/.
USGS/WDNR Stream Natural Communities Model Data. 2007. http://dnr.wi.gov/topic/rivers/natural
    communities.html.
Wisconsin DNR Trout Stream Classification Data. 2008. http://dnr.wi.gov/topic/fishing/trout/.

Plants

Barnes, Burton V., and Warren H. Wagner, Jr. 1981. *Michigan Trees*. Ann Arbor: University of Michigan
    Press.
Boos, Thomas, Kelly Kearns, Courtney LeClair, Brenden Panke, Bryn Scrive, Bernadette Williams, and
    Olivia Witthun. 2010. *A Field Guide to Terrestrial Invasive Plants in Wisconsin*. PUB-FR-436. Madi-
    son: Bureau of Endangered Resources and Division of Forestry, Wisconsin Department of Natural
    Resources.
Borman, Susan, Robert Korth, and Jo Temte. 1997. *Through the Looking Glass . . . A Field Guide to
    Aquatic Plants.* Stevens Point: Wisconsin Lakes Partnership.
Center for Aquatic and Invasive Plants, University of Florida Institute of Food and Agricultural Sciences.
    http://plants.ifas.ufl.edu/.
Cofrin Center for Biodiversity and the University of Wisconsin Green Bay. http://www.uwgb.edu/BIO
    DIVERSITY/herbarium/.
Cooke, Sarah Spear. 1997. *A Field Guide to the Common Wetland Plants of Western Washington &
    Northwest Oregon.* Seattle, WA: Seattle Audubon Society.
Eggers, Steve D., and Donald M. Reed. 1997a. Wetland Plants and Communities of Minnesota and Wis-
    consin. US Army Corps of Engineers, Saint Paul District. Jamestown, ND: Northern Prairie Wildlife
    Research Center Online. http://www.npwrc.usgs.gov/resource/plants/mnplant/index.htm (Version
    03SEP1998).
Eggers, Steve D., and Donald M. Reed. 1997b. *Wetland Plants and Plant Communities of Minnesota &
    Wisconsin*. Saint Paul, MN: US Army Corps of Engineers, Saint Paul District.
Haack, John, and Valerie Haack. 2008. *Lake Plants You Should Know: A Visual Field Guide*. Shell Lake,
    WI: Haack Family Plant Scans.
Harris, James G., and Melinda Woolf Harris. 2001. *Plant Identification Terminology: An Illustrated Glos-
    sary*. Payson, UT: Spring Lake Publishing.
Maine Field Guide to Invasive Aquatic Plants and Their Common Native Look Alikes. 2007. Maine Cen-
    ter for Invasive Aquatic Plants, Maine Volunteer Lake Monitoring Program.

References

Pojar, Jim, and Andy MacKinnon. (1994) 2004. *Plants of the Pacific Northwest Coast: Washington, Oregon, British Columbia, and Alaska*. Edmonton, AB: Lone Pine Publishing.

Robert W. Freckmann Herbarium, University of Wisconsin–Stevens Point. Wisconsin Plants Website. http://wisplants.uwsp.edu.

Skawinski, Paul M. 2011. *Aquatic Plants of the Upper Midwest: A Photographic Field Guide to Our Underwater Forests*. Wausau, WI: P. Skawinski.

USDA, NRCS. 2010. The PLANTS Database. http://plants.usda.gov. National Plant Data Center, Baton Rouge, LA.

Washington State Department of Ecology. Non-native Freshwater Plants. http://www.ecy.wa.gov/programs/wq/plants/weeds/index.html.

Washington State Department of Ecology. An Online Version of an Aquatic Plant Identification Manual for Washington's Freshwater Plants. http://www.ecy.wa.gov/programs/wq/plants/plantid2/index.html.

Wisconsin State Herbarium. http://www.botany.wisc.edu/herbarium/.

Invertebrates

Aquatic Nuisance Species Task Force. 2007. *National Management and Control Plan for the New Zealand Mudsnail (Potamopyrgus antipodarum)*. U.S. Fish and Wildlife Service and National Oceanic and Atmospheric Administration. http://www.anstaskforce.gov.

Bouchard, R. William, Jr. 2004. *Guide to Aquatic Invertebrates of the Upper Midwest*. Saint Paul: University of Minnesota Press.

Bureau of Endangered Resources, Wisconsin Department of Natural Resources. 1999. *The Endangered and Threatened Invertebrates of Wisconsin*. PUB-ER-085-99. Madison: Bureau of Endangered Resources, Wisconsin Department of Natural Resources.

Chironomidae Research Group Volunteer Stream Monitoring Interactive Verification Program. Saint Paul: University of Minnesota. http://midge.cfans.umn.edu/vsmivp/.

Jass, Joan, Jan Annesley, and Dreux J. Watermolen. 2007. *Help Us Find Wisconsin's Freshwater Sponges*. Madison: Bureau of Science Services, Wisconsin Department of Natural Resources. Brochure.

Legler, Karl, Dorothy Legler, and Dave Westover. 2007. *Color Guide to Dragonflies of Wisconsin*. Sauk City, WI: Karl Legler.

Lillie, Richard A., Stanley W. Szczytko, and Michael A. Miller. 2003. *Macroinvertebrate Data Interpretation Guidance Manual*. PUB-SS-965. Madison: Bureau of Science Services, Wisconsin Department of Natural Resources.

McCafferty, W. Patrick, and Arwin Provonsha. (1981) 1983. *Aquatic Entomology: The Fishermen's Guide and Ecologists' Illustrated Guide to Insects and Their Relatives*. West Lafayette, IN: Purdue University.

Merritt, Richard W., and Kenneth W. Cummins. (1978) 2008. *An Introduction to the Aquatic Insects of North America*. Dubuque, IA: Kendall/Hunt Publishing Company.

Neuswanger, Jason. 2012. Troutnut.com. http://www.troutnut.com.

Society for Freshwater Science. http://www.freshwater-science.org/Index.aspx.

Voshell, J. Reese, Jr. 2002. *A Guide to Common Freshwater Invertebrates of North America*. Granville, OH: McDonald & Woodward Publishing Company.

Crayfishes

Hobbs, Horton H., III, and Joan P. Jass. 1988. *The Crayfishes & Shrimp of Wisconsin*. Milwaukee, WI: Milwaukee Public Museum.

Hobbs, Horton H., II, and Joan P. Jass. 2003. Crustaceans of Wisconsin. http://www.mpm.edu/collections/research/invertebrates/wicrayfish/. Milwaukee Public Museum.

Karstad, Aleta, and the Project Crayfish Group. 2008. Ontario Crayfish Identification Guide. http://www.pinicola.ca/crayfishontario/craydentpage.htm. Toronto Zoo & Ontario Nature, folding laminated identification guide.

Swecker, Casey D., Dr. Tom Jones, and Jay Kilian. 2008. Photographic Key to the Crayfishes of Maryland. http://www.dnr.state.md.us/irc/docs/00015708.pdf. Maryland Department of Natural Resources.

References

Mussels and Clams

Freshwater Mussels of the Upper Mississippi River. 2003. Madison: Wisconsin Department of Natural Resources.

McMurray, Stephen E., J. Scott Faiman, Andy Roberts, Bryan Simmons, and M. Christopher Barnhart. 2012. *A Guide to Missouri's Freshwater Mussels*. Jefferson City: Missouri Department of Conservation.

Mussel Monitoring Program of Wisconsin. http://www.wiatri.net/inventory/mussels/. Madison: Bureau of Endangered Resources, Wisconsin Department of Natural Resources.

Fishes

Becker, George C. 1983. *Fishes of Wisconsin*. Madison: University of Wisconsin Press.

Bosanko, Dave. 2007. *Fish of Wisconsin Field Guide.* Cambridge, MN: Adventure Publications.

Froese, R., and D. Pauly. 2012. *FishBase*. http://www.fishbase.org.

Lyons, J., P. Hanson, E. White, J. F. Kitchell, and P. Moy. 2012. Wisconsin Fish Identification Database. http://wiscfish.org.

Lyons, J., K. M. Schoephoester, J. Griffin, J. M. Stewart, and D. Fago. 2012. Wisconsin Department of Natural Resources and Wisconsin Aquatic Gap Mapping Application. http://infotrek.er.usgs.gov/fishmap.

Page, Lawrence M., and Brooks M. Burr. 1998. *Peterson's Field Guide: Freshwater Fishes.* Boston: Houghton-Mifflin.

Amphibians and Reptiles

Christoffel, Rebecca, Robert Hay, and Megan Monroe. 2002. *Turtles & Lizards of Wisconsin*. PUB-ER-104. Madison: Bureau of Endangered Resources, Wisconsin Department of Natural Resources.

Christoffel, Rebecca, Robert Hay, and Lisa Ramirez. 2008. *Snakes of Wisconsin*. PUB-ER-100. Madison: Bureau of Endangered Resources, Wisconsin Department of Natural Resources.

Christoffel, Rebecca, Robert Hay, and Michelle Wolfgram. 2001. *Amphibians of Wisconsin*. PUB-ER-105. Madison: Bureau of Endangered Resources, Wisconsin Department of Natural Resources.

Vogt, R. C. 1981. *Natural History of Amphibians and Reptiles of Wisconsin.* Milwaukee: Milwaukee Public Museum.

GLOSSARY

2-ranked (leaves): Emerging in opposite rows along the stem, creating a flattened appearance; apparent especially when viewed in cross section.

3-ranked (leaves): Emerging in 3 distinct rows along the stem; apparent especially when viewed in cross section.

abdomen: The last (most posterior) body region of insects, crayfish, and other invertebrates; the belly of fish and other vertebrates.

abundant (distribution): Describes species that are found very frequently. In this guide, the terms *abundant*, *common*, *uncommon*, and *rare* describe species from those most frequently encountered to those least frequently encountered.

acute (angle): Sharp, less than 90°.

adipose fin: A small fleshy fin without spines or rays located between the dorsal fin and tail. In Wisconsin found exclusively in 4 fish families: bullhead catfishes, smelts, trout-perches, and salmons and trouts.

alga (pl. algae): One of a group of aquatic photosynthetic organisms that range from unicellular to multicellular forms and that generally possess chlorophyll but lack true roots, stems, leaves, and reproductive structures characteristic of plants.

allelopathic (plant): Describes the ability to inhibit the growth of other plants by releasing chemicals.

alternate (leaf arrangement): Arranged singly on alternating sides of the stem, creating a zigzag appearance.

ammocoete: The larval (juvenile) stage of lampreys characterized by a lack of eyes, hooded mouth, lack of teeth, and frequent burrowing.

anadromous (fish): Living primarily in the ocean but migrating up rivers and streams to spawn. In the Great Lakes region, describes fishes that spend most of their time in the Great Lakes but breed and spawn in rivers and streams.

anal: Pertaining to the anus or, in invertebrates, to the most posterior end of the body.

anal fin: The unpaired fin on the ventral surface between the vent and tail of a fish.

annual (plant): Describes a plant that sprouts from seed, grows, reproduces, and dies within 1 growing season (as opposed to *perennial*).

annulus (pl. annuli): See *rest line*.

antenna (pl. antennae): A sensory appendage of the head, occurring in pairs.

anterior: Toward the front or head of an organism (as opposed to *posterior*). In mussels, the shorter end of the shell as measured from the umbo.

aquatic: Pertaining to life in water. In invertebrates, spending at least 1 life stage submersed in water. In plants, spending at least some part of the year with roots submersed in water or saturated soil.

areola: In crayfish, the region on the carapace that is delineated by a pair of arched grooves forming an hourglass shape. Grooves indicate the edges of the gill chamber.

arrangement (of leaves): See *leaf arrangement*.

atheridium (pl. atheridia): A male reproductive structure in lower plants such as algae.

avian: Pertaining to birds.

axil: The junction of 2 structures on a plant (e.g., the stem and the base of a leaf).

backwater: A quiet water in the floodplain adjacent to the main channel of a stream or river, such as a *slough*. Often in a marsh.

ballast: Water or other heavy material placed in a lower compartment of a boat for stability.

bar: A dark rectangular band or stripe of color on the side of an organism, such as a fish.

barbel: A thin, flexible, whisker-like projection near the mouth of a fish that is a sensory organ with the ability to taste and feel; useful for finding food.

basal: Pertaining to the base. In plants, basal leaves emerge from the plant base rather than from along the stem.

baseflow: The relatively constant flow of stream water coming from groundwater discharge.

beak: A beak-shaped protrusion, often on plant seeds or invertebrate mouths. In mussels, the raised part of the dorsal margin of the shell representing the earliest period of shell growth, also called the *umbo*.

beak cavity: In mussels, a depression or pocket on the inside of each valve leading into the beak.

beak sculpture: In mussels, the raised loops, ridges, or bumps on the umbo, often eroded away in older shells.

bicuspid (teeth): Ending in 2 points.

bivoltine: Producing 2 generations per year.

blade: The main part of a leaf; everything except for the leafstalk.

body length (or total length): In fish, the straight-line distance from the snout tip to the tail end.

bract: A small, modified leaf just below a flower. Usually leaf-like, but sometimes resembles a flower petal.

branchiostegal rays: In fish, the bones located just posterior to the gills on the ventral side (underside).

bud: See *winter bud*.

bud scar: In plants, horizontal scars on the stem where new growth has emerged from the terminal bud (stem tip) each spring. Bud scars along the stem mark annual growth, which can be used to determine the age of perennial plants.

byssal thread: See *byssus*.

byssus (or byssal thread): In mussels: In family Dressenidae, the black, thread-like hairs used to attach the shell to the substrate. In family Unionidae, the sticky, elastic thread secreted by the juvenile upon release from its host, not used for permanent attachment.

calcareous shell: The exoskeleton of a snail or mollusk, comprised primarily of calcium carbonate. Encloses, supports, and protects the soft parts of the animal.

capsule: A dry fruit that has 2 or more seeds.

carapace: In invertebrates, a hardened shield covering the head and thorax.

carnivorous: Feeding mainly on other animals; predatory.

carrion: The carcass of an animal that has died.

case-builders: Types of caddisflies that use silk excreted from salivary glands and small fragments of rocks, sand, twigs, fallen leaves, or aquatic plants to build protective shelters.

catchment: See *watershed*.

catkins: In many woody plant species, small clusters or spikes of unpetaled flowers.

caudal: Pertaining to the tail of fish or invertebrates.

caudal fin: In fish, the tail; the single fin at the posterior end.

caudal peduncle: The narrow body region of a fish between the anal fin and the tail.

caviar: Unfertilized fish eggs, particularly of sturgeon, that have been processed and salted to be eaten as a delicacy.

cephalothorax: In some invertebrates, the head and thorax united as a single body segment.

channelization: The straightening of a stream's channel to facilitate draining cropland or urban areas.

cheek: The region of a fish between the eye and the first gill cover (*preopercle*).

chelicera (pl. chelicerae): Mouthpart or fang, as on a spider.

chevron: A V-shaped marking.

chitin: A carbohydrate that is the main component of the exoskeletons in arthropods.

chlorophyll: A green pigment important to photosynthesis, which enables plants and algae to absorb energy from sunlight to produce sugars and oxygen.

circumferential scales: In fish, the scales found in rows that encircle the body just anterior to the dorsal fin.

circumoral teeth: In adult lampreys, the 3–4 large teeth located on the sides of the mouth opening.

class: The taxonomic category above order and below phylum.

closed (leaf sheath): In grasses, a leaf base wrapping around the stem, with fused margins forming an enclosed tube (as opposed to *open*).

cocoon: A silken sheath in which caddisflies pupate into winged adults.

collector/filterer: An invertebrate that eats mainly detritus and periphyton by collecting food off of the stream bottom or filtering suspended food particles out of the water.

collector/gatherer: An invertebrate that eats mainly algae, bacteria, diatoms, and detritus deposited on the streambed.

common (distribution): Describes species that are found frequently. In this guide, the terms *abundant*, *common*, *uncommon*, and *rare* describe species from those most frequently encountered to those least frequently encountered.

complete metamorphosis: In insects, a life cycle consisting of 4 stages: egg, larva, pupa, and adult. Larvae and adults look dramatically different (as opposed to *incomplete metamorphosis*).

compound (leaf): Describes a leaf that is divided into multiple leaflets that are connected to each other by stems. A compound leaf can be identified by the presence of a bud scar at the leaf base—leaflets do not have bud scars at the base.

compound eyes: Eyes made of many individual photoreceptors, common in arthropods and some annelids and mollusks.

concave: Curving inward.

conglutinate: In mussels, a mass of *glochidia* (fertilized eggs).

connectivity (in streams): The flow, pathways, and movement of water, energy, and organisms in streams.

convex: Curving outward.

cross-venation: In leaves, veins running perpendicular to the main parallel veins.

decurved: Dipping down, as in the lateral line of some fishes.

deep-bodied: Describes a fish that is tall from top to bottom; *laterally compressed*.

detritivore: Describes an organism that feeds mainly on detritus.

detritus: Decaying organic matter, including leaves, wood, etc.

diatom: A type of 1-celled algae that is microscopic and builds unique glass cases.

dimorphic: Having 2 types of form. For example, in mussels, shells are dimorphic if male and female shells differ from each other in appearance.

disk: In daisy-like flowers, the central disk of the flower-like structure; the disk is actually composed of many small disk flowers.

dissolved oxygen: Oxygen that is dissolved in water, usually derived from photosynthesis or atmospheric diffusion.

distal: Pertaining to the outermost end of a structure (away from the base).

distribution: The range of a species; the areas of the state where it has been identified.

divergent (wings): With the tips of the wing pads pointing laterally away from the body midline.

divided (leaf): Having 2 or more leaflets that arise from a common leaf base and are not separate leaves.

DNR: Department of Natural Resources.

dorsal: Referring to the top side of the body in fish and most invertebrates. In mussels, referring to the part of the shell where the hinge is located.

dorsal fin: An unpaired fin on the "top" (dorsal) side of a fish. A dorsal fin can have both soft rays and spines, only soft rays, or only spines. Some fishes, such as some perches and sunfishes, have a dorsal fin with anterior spines and posterior soft rays.

dorsoventrally: From top to bottom, used in describing body form.

doubly serrated (leaf): Having 2 sets of serrations at the leaf margin: 1 larger and, within the large serrations, a subset of smaller serrations.

drainage basin: See *watershed*.

drift (debris): See *glacial till*.

Driftless Area: In Wisconsin, the area not covered with ice during the most recent glacial period. Located in the southwestern part of the state, this area is characterized by deep, steeply sloped valleys and a large number of groundwater-fed streams.

drumming: Mating behavior exhibited by adult male stoneflies, which strike their abdomens on hard surfaces to attract females, and by adult male freshwater drums, which vibrate muscles and tendons against their swim bladder.

dun: An informal term for the *subimago* life stage of mayflies, characterized by translucent wings that are colored grayish blue (or dun).

ear flap: In fish, the extended rear edge of the most posterior gill cover (*opercle*).

ecotone: The interface between two distinctly different environments (e.g., stream and upland area).

elongate: Long.

elytron (pl. elytra): In adult beetles, the hardened forewing that covers the membranous hind wing.

emergence: The transition from the immature aquatic life stage of an insect into the terrestrial or aerial winged adult stage.

emergent (leaf, plant): Extending above the water surface.

endangered: Describes any species whose continued existence as a viable component of Wisconsin's wild animals or wild plants is determined by the state Department of Natural Resources to be in jeopardy on the basis of scientific evidence. Unless otherwise noted, species labeled "endangered" in this guide are endangered in Wisconsin but may not be endangered across their entire range. Federally endangered: Describes any species that is in danger of extinction throughout all or a significant portion of its range, other than insects determined to be pests whose protection would present a risk to humans.

ephemeral (stream): Describes a stream that flows only at certain times of the year, such as during storm events or spring runoff.

erect: Stiff, upright; not drooping.

estuarine: Related to estuaries, aquatic areas where salt and freshwater mix.

eutrophic (water): Describes water rich in organic or mineral nutrients. Eutrophication often results in increased plant and/or algae growth followed by decomposition, leading to low dissolved oxygen concentrations.

excurrent siphon: In mussels, the organ that releases waste into the water.

exoskeleton: In arthropods, the hardened external shell.

exotic: Introduced from another country or region; not native to the place where found; *introduced*.

extirpated: Locally extinct, as from a watershed or state.

family: The taxonomic category above genus and below order.

federally endangered: See *endangered*.

federally threatened: See *threatened*.

femur: In insects, the third segment of a leg (as counted from the base); often the largest segment.

filament: A slender, thread-like projection.

filter feeder: An animal that filters food from the water.

fin base: The junction where a fin attaches to the body.

finely divided (leaf): Divided into many small sections, which are often very slender.

fishery: A term often used to describe the fishing industry, including commercial and recreational catching of fish, as well as sale of fish.

fishes: Multiple species of fish (as opposed to multiple individuals of the same fish species).

flank: The side of the body.

floating leaf: A leaf that is on or held just above the water surface.

floating-leaf plant: A rooted plant that has mostly floating leaves.

floret: A small or reduced flower, for example, in grasses.

flower: The reproductive structure of a flowering plant; often with showy petals.

foot: The hard, muscular organ of a mollusk used for locomotion.

forb: An herbaceous plant that is not grass-like.

free-floating (plant): Not rooted, floating freely with the wind and currents.

frenum: A fleshy bridge partially connecting the upper lip to the snout in longnose dace, western blacknose dace, and darters.

fry: A young fish that has just hatched from an egg.

fusiform: A streamlined body shape with tapered ends, for example, in trout.

gemmules: The reproductive structures of a sponge.

genus (pl. genera): The taxonomic category above species and below family used as the first, capitalized portion of a species' scientific name.

gill cover: In fish, 1 of 2 bony plates on the head that cover the gills.

gill filaments: Narrow, pointed projections on the ends of fish and aquatic insect gills, often used in taxonomic identification of mayflies.

gill rakers: In fish, tiny finger-like projections on the inside of gill arches used to filter small food items from the water column or stream sediment.

gills: Respiratory organs used by aquatic animals to breathe dissolved oxygen in water.

glacial till: Fragmented rock and soil gathered by the leading edge of a glacier and deposited when the glacier melts.

glide: A flowing portion of a stream that has a smooth water surface and uniform depth and velocity. Sometimes called a *run*, but glides are characterized by more uniform depth than runs.

glochidia (sing. glochidium): In native mussels of Wisconsin, fertilized eggs with 2 shells, a central muscle, and rudimentary organs. Glochidia attach to the gills of a host species (usually fish) and remain there until they have matured into juveniles.

gradient: Slope, as in the slope of a stream.

habitat: The place where an organism lives.

hard water: Water that is high in mineral content, especially calcium and magnesium ions.

hatch: An informal term used to describe the mass *emergence* of insects from the water.

head: In fish, the body region anterior to the gill covers.

headwater: The origin of a stream or river; often used to describe small streams.

herb: A plant without woody parts.

herbaceous (plant): Nonwoody.

herbivorous: Feeding primarily on vegetation.

hinge: In mussels, the location where the 2 shells fit together, often held in place by a ligament, opposite of where the shell opens.

hinge line: In mussels, the line formed by the hinge relative to the umbo and the rest of the shell.

horizontal mouth: A mouth positioned at a flat, horizontal angle.

hydrology: The study of water, especially as it flows over the land's surface.

hyporheic zone: The porous subsurface area beneath and alongside a streambed, where there is mixing of shallow groundwater and surface water; this area is inhabited by young invertebrates.

imago: The adult life stage of an insect.

incised (stream): Describes streams that are deeply cut into the earth with nearly vertical streambanks. In Wisconsin, incised streams often result from deposition of eroded soil into valley bottoms, creating much taller banks than would naturally occur and disconnecting streams from their floodplains.

incomplete metamorphosis: In insects, a life cycle consisting of 3 life stages: egg, larva, and adult. Larvae resemble wingless adults (as opposed to *complete metamorphosis*).

incurrent siphon: In mussels, the organ that takes in oxygen and filters algae and other organic material from the water.

inferior mouth: A mouth positioned on the ventral surface of the head and/or pointed downward, for example, in the sucker family.

inflated: In mussels, a wider or enlarged shell or portion of a shell.

inflorescence: A cluster of flowers.

insectivorous: Feeding primarily on insects.

insects: Invertebrates with 3 segments (head, thorax, and abdomen), 3 pairs of segmented legs, antennae, and compound eyes.

intolerant (of environmental degradation): Unable to live or reproduce sustainably because of altered or degraded environmental conditions.

introduced: Describes populations found outside their natural range; *exotic*.

invasive: In the state of Wisconsin, describes any species or "variety" that is not native to Wisconsin and that causes or is likely to cause economic or environmental harm or harm to human health. Invasive species may be either *prohibited* or *restricted*.

invertebrate: An animal without a backbone.

invertivorous: Feeding primarily on invertebrates.

iridescent: Exhibiting rainbow colors.

joint: In grasses and some other plants, the swollen junction where a leaf connects to the stem; the *node*.

juvenile: A sexually immature organism.

keel: A narrow ridge. In fish, often on the ventral surface; in plants, often on the stem.

keeled: Having a narrow ridge or *keel*.

knob: In mussels, a large bump or raised protuberance on the outside of the shell; usually few in number.

labium (pl. labia): In insects, the lower lip or the mouthpart that is most posterior.

labrum: In insects, the upper lip or most anterior mouthpart (aside from paired mouthparts such as mandibles).

larva (pl. larvae): In organisms that undergo metamorphosis, the first life stage after hatching from eggs. In invertebrates that undergo *incomplete metamorphosis*, often substituted with the term *nymph*.

lateral: Pertaining to the side.

lateral line: A line of sensory pores extending from the gills to the tail of a fish.

laterally compressed: Compressed from side to side (rather than from top to bottom); *deep-bodied*.

lateral teeth: In adult lampreys, rows of small teeth radiating from the sides of the mouth opening. In mussels, the elongated teeth along the hinge line of the shell.

leaf arrangement: The placement of leaves along the stem, a useful identifying characteristic in plants. Common leaf arrangements include *opposite*, *alternate*, *whorled*, and *basal*.

leaflet: In plants, a small "leaf" that is actually part of the larger true leaf. Leaflets can be distinguished from true leaves by the presence of bud scars at the base of leaves—leaflets do not have bud scars.

leaf pack: A clump of decomposing leaves.

leaf scar: In woody plants, the mark left behind by a fallen leaf. Leaf scar shape can be useful for identification in winter.

left-handed (snail): Describes a snail with a shell that opens on the left side when the shell is positioned with the pointed end up and the opening facing the observer.

lemma: In grasses, the outer of 2 bracts that enclose the flower spikelet.

lenticel: On woody plants, raised pores that often appear as spots or lines on the bark and that assist with gas exchange between the plant and the atmosphere.

ligule: In grasses, an appendage at the junction of the leaf blade and leaf sheath.

linear (leaf): Having a long and narrow shape.

lobed (leaf): Having fingers (or lobes) that are larger than teeth and project outward from the main leaf blade.

macroalga (pl. macroalgae): A large alga resembling a plant; an alga large enough to be seen without magnification.

macroinvertebrate: An animal without a backbone that can be seen without magnification (generally larger than 0.5 mm).

macrophyte: A plant large enough to be seen without magnification; often describes aquatic plants.

mandible: In invertebrates, 1 of a pair of anterior mouth appendages, often opposable.

marginal spines: In crayfish, spines that may protrude from the sides of the rostrum where it begins to taper to a point.

medial: Along the middle plane of the body.

metamorphosis: A physical transformation to a different form. See *complete* and *incomplete metamorphosis*.

microalga (pl. microalgae): An alga too small to be seen with the naked eye.

midline: Halfway up on the sides of a fish; similar to the position of the lateral line.

midrib: The central vein of a leaf, running from the leaf base to the tip; also *midvein*.

midvein: The central vein of a leaf, running from the leaf base to the tip; also *midrib*.

molluscavore: Describes an organism that feeds on mollusks.

molting: In invertebrates, shedding the exoskeleton and forming another as part of the growth process.

Glossary

mottling: Dark, irregular blotches of color.

multivoltine: Producing 2 or more generations per year.

nacre: In mussels, the interior layer of the shell; can be variously colored, including white, pink, salmon, green, purple, pearly, or iridescent.

nape: In fish, the area between the back of the head and the dorsal fin; the *predorsal region*.

native: Describes organisms found within their natural range.

nocturnal: Primarily active at night.

node: In grasses and some other plants, the swollen junction where a leaf connects to the stem; the *joint*.

nursery log: A fallen, decomposing log that provides a rich substrate for other plants, such as mosses, herbs, and trees.

nutlet: A dry fruit with 1 seed.

nymph: In invertebrates that undergo *incomplete metamorphosis*, a larva that looks similar to the adult life stage but without wings.

oblique mouth: A mouth that is upturned at an angle 0° to 60° from the horizontal position.

oblong: Having the shape of or resembling a rounded rectangle or ellipse.

omnivorous: Feeding primarily on both animals and vegetation.

oogonia: In algae, small female sex structures.

open (leaf): In grasses, a leaf base wrapping around the stem with 1 margin overlapping the other (as opposed to *closed*).

opercle: In fish, the largest and rearmost bony plate of the gill covers. See *operculum*.

operculum (pl. opercula): In fish, the largest and rearmost bony plate of the gill covers. See *opercle*. In some gill-breathing snails, a protective, lid-like cover drawn over the shell opening when the snail retreats inside the shell.

opportunistic feeder: An organism that eats whatever is available.

opposite (leaf arrangement): Arranged in pairs along the stem, with 2 leaves opposite each other at each node.

oral disk: The circular, sucking mouths of lampreys. See *suction disk*.

order: The taxonomic category above family and below class.

organic pollution: Sewage, manure, fertilizer, sediment, and other nutrient-rich carbon-based materials that enter surface waters and feed bacteria, resulting in reduced dissolved oxygen concentrations.

origin (of fin): The most anterior (front) part of the fin base.

outlet: In a watershed, the point at which water exits the watershed, usually from a stream or river. An outlet can be an arbitrary point chosen along a stream; all land draining to the outlet is the watershed of the stream as defined by the outlet.

ovate: Egg-shaped; *ovoid*.

ovoid: Egg-shaped; *ovate*.

paired fins: Fish fins that come in pairs (i.e., pectoral fins and pelvic fins).

palatine teeth: In some fishes, small teeth growing on the palatine bones on the sides of the roof of the mouth.

palea: In grass, the inner of 2 bracts that enclose the flower spikelet.

palmate: Branching out from a single point like fingers from a palm; usually refers to leaflets or veins on a leaf.

papilla (pl. papillae): A small, round, nipple-like projection that is usually found on the lips of certain fishes, especially in the sucker family.

papillary fringe: In adult lampreys, the fringe of papillae surrounding the suction disk mouth.

papillose (papillate, papillary): To be covered in papillae, or rounded bumps.

parasitic: Living on or in a host species to obtain nutrients.

parr: Young trout and salmon with dark vertical bands on their sides.

parr marks: The dark vertical bands on the sides of young trout and salmon.

pectoral fins: In fish, the paired fins below or just behind the gill covers on the sides or ventral surface of the body.

pedipalp: In water mites and other arachnids, a pair of appendages used for grasping, feeding, locomotion, and/or reproduction.

peduncle: See *caudal peduncle.*

pelvic fins: In fish, the paired fins on the ventral surface of the body, usually between the pectoral fins and the anal fin (sometimes below or in front of the pectoral fins).

perennial (plant): Describes a plant that sprouts from seed, grows, reproduces, and dies over the course of more than 1 growing season (as opposed to *annual*).

perennial (stream): Describes a stream that flows year-round.

periostracum: In mussels, the outside layer or covering of the shell, often with distinctive coloration or patterns.

periphyton: Algae, bacteria, fungi, and other small aquatic organisms living on solid substrates in streams. Periphyton often creates a film over rocks, logs, and debris.

petiole: Leafstalk.

phloem: In plants, the part of the vascular system that carries sugars to the various parts of the plant.

phylum (pl. phyla): The taxonomic category above class and below kingdom.

phytoplankton: Tiny, free-floating, photosynthetic organisms. Microscopic algae are a type of phytoplankton.

piercer: An insect that uses a proboscis to penetrate the bodies of other animals to feed on body fluids or plant stems to feed on vascular fluids.

pioneer (species): In plants, describes a species that is typically one of the first to colonize a recently disturbed area. Pioneer species are usually fast-growing and shade-intolerant.

piscivorous: Feeding primarily on fish.

pistil: In plants, the female reproductive part of the flower, containing the ovary and a pollen-receptive tip.

pith: In plants, the spongy material in the center of certain branches or stems.

planktivore: Describes an organism that feeds mainly on plankton.

plankton: Tiny free-floating aquatic organisms.

pleopod: In crayfish, 1 of several small appendages under the abdomen (tail). A crayfish has 5 pairs of pleopods, 1 pair on each of the first abdominal segments.

plicate: In fish, especially redhorses, describes lips that are folded into pleated ridges and grooves.

pollution: Sources of degradation to water bodies such as substances or heated water entering streams due to human activities. Pollution often comes from cropland erosion or urban runoff; sediment and nutrients are the main pollutants in Wisconsin streams.

pool: A quiet, slow-moving, deep portion of a stream that has a smooth water surface; the water depth is greater and the velocity is slower than other parts of the stream.

posterior: Toward the rear or tail of an organism (as opposed to *anterior*). In mussels, toward the longer end of the shell as measured from the umbo.

posterior ridge: In mussels, the ridge on the valve running from the umbo to the posterior ventral edge.

posterior slope: In mussels, the area along the dorsal part of the shell between the posterior ridges of the valves.

postorbital distance: In fish, the distance from the posterior edge of the eye to the posterior edge of the operculum.

predator: An organism that eats mainly other animals.

predorsal region: In fish, the area between the back of the head and the dorsal fin; the *nape*.

predorsal scale: In fish, the row of scales from the dorsal fin to the head along the midline.

preopercle: In fish, the front gill cover plate; the sickle-shaped bone below and behind the eye.

prickles: In fish, small, sharp points on the skin.

primary producer: An organism that transforms energy from sunlight into biomass (e.g., a plant).

proboscis: In insects, a long, tubular mouthpart used to penetrate plants or animals to feed on internal fluids.

process: In animals, a limb or appendage.

prohibited (invasive species): In Wisconsin, describes a nonnative species that is not currently found in Wisconsin or that is present only as small infestations but that, if introduced into the state, is likely to cause significant harm. With a few exceptions, it is illegal to possess, transport, transfer, or introduce a prohibited species without a permit. See also *invasive* and *restricted*.

proleg: In invertebrates, a leg-like structure that is fleshy and unsegmented.

prothorax: The first (most anterior) segment of the thorax.

protrusable (mouth): In some fishes, for example, suckers, describes the structure of the jaws and lips that enables a fish to extend its mouth to form a tube-like shape to help capture prey.

pseudocardinal teeth: In mussels, the triangular, often serrated structures located on the anterior, dorsal part of the shell; the structures on each valve fit together to help the mussel hinge.

pubescence (in plants): Short, soft hairs.

pupa (pl. pupae): In insects that undergo complete metamorphosis, the transitional life stage between larva and adult. In this stage, larval traits are lost and adult traits are developed.

pupal: Pertaining to the life stage of a pupa; see *pupa*.

pupate: To develop into the life stage of a pupa; see *pupa*.

pustules: In mussels, bumps or small raised protuberances on the outside of the shell, often occurring in large numbers.

pustulous: In mussels, describes having the shell surface covered with pustules.

rapid: A swift-flowing portion of a stream that has deep, turbulent water flowing over large rocks and debris; a large riffle.

rare (distribution): Describes species that are found very infrequently. In this guide, the terms *abundant*, *common*, *uncommon*, and *rare* describe species from those most frequently encountered to those least frequently encountered.

ray (fin ray): One of the flexible, segmented supporting rods of a fin, often branching near the tip and usually soft. When rays are counted for identification, all rays in a fin must be counted, including the smallest.

ray (flower): A "petal" in a daisy-like flower that is actually a single, reduced flower itself.

ray (marking): A colored line. In mussels, lines located on the periostracum, radiating from or near the umbo toward the ventral margin of the shell.

reach (of stream/river): A section of a stream or river. In scientific research, a reach is the defined segment of the stream that has been selected for monitoring.

redd: A shallow depression or nest dug by trout and salmon in streambed gravel used for spawning.

rest line: In mussels, a darkened line denoting a period of slow or nongrowth, typically formed during winter. May be referred to as an *annulus*.

restricted (invasive species): In Wisconsin, describes a nonnative species that is already well established in the state and is known to cause, or have the potential to cause, significant harm. With a few exceptions, it is illegal to transport, transfer, or introduce a restricted species without a permit. See also *invasive* and *prohibited*.

rhizome: In some plants, a horizontal stem that runs underground, appearing root-like; often used for vegetative reproduction.

riffle: A shallow, fast-flowing portion of a stream where water turbulently flows over coarse gravel or larger rocks and boulders.

right-handed (snail): Describes a snail with a shell that opens on the right side when the shell is positioned with the pointed end up and the opening facing the observer.

riparian: Located along a riverbank or streambank or the shoreline of a lake.

riprap: Large rocks placed along shorelines of lakes, streams, and rivers for bank stabilization.

river continuum concept: The idea that as a river flows from its headwaters to its mouth there are predictable changes in the river's physical conditions and chemical makeup that result in predictable biological changes.

robust (body): Stout.

rosette: In plants, a circular cluster of leaves growing from a single point on the stem.

rostrum (pl. rostra): In crayfish, the nose-like tip of the carapace that projects between and in front of the eyes. In insects, a beak used for penetrating prey or plants to suck out fluids.

run: A flowing segment of a stream with a smooth water surface and significant flow velocity (i.e., not a pool). Sometimes called a *glide*, but runs are characterized by more variable depth than glides.

sac fry: A recently hatched fish, especially salmon or trout, that is attached to and feeds off a yolk sac.

saddle: In fish, a dark blotch extending over the back.

scale: In grasses and sedges, one of the small, round plates protecting the florets. In fish, one of the small, round plates protecting the skin.

scavenger: An animal that feeds on dead animals.

sclerotized: Hardened, as in the body wall of many insects.

scraper: An invertebrate that eats mainly periphyton, either by scraping it off of solid substrate or by grazing it.

sculpted: In mussels, numerous fine ridges or structures covering all or a portion of the shell.

scute: A hardened plate or scale; found on turtle shells and on sturgeons.

sedimentation: The deposition of a layer of sand, silt, or fine sediment that covers stream bottom habitat, usually due to upland erosion and/or slow water current; *siltation*.

semiaquatic: In invertebrates, spending at least 1 life stage associated with, but not submersed in, water (e.g., water striders live on the water surface).

semivoltine: Requiring more than a year for each generation to mature and reproduce.

sepal: A structure below the flower petals, usually green. Sometimes sepals appear petal-like, with the same color and structure as the petals.

serrated: Having a saw-toothed, irregular edge; see *toothed*.

seta (pl. setae): A hair-like projection. In aquatic insects, used for filter feeding.

sheath: Part of a leaf base that wraps partially or completely around the plant stem; see *open* and *closed*.

shell margin: In mussels, the edge or the circumference of the shell outline when laid flat.

shoal: A shallow, sandy place in a water body.

shoot: New plant growth, including stems, leaves, and flowers.

shredder: An invertebrate that eats mainly plant leaves by shredding them into small pieces for consumption.

side filaments: In insect larvae, lateral appendages on the abdomen that aid in dissolved oxygen uptake and are often mistaken for legs.

sieve apparatus: In the mouths of lamprey ammocoetes, the complexly branched papillae used for filtering food.

silt: Fine sediment particles with a silky texture, often suspended in turbid water or deposited on the streambed, particularly along quiet margins and pools; smaller than sand particles and larger than clay particles.

siltation: The process of a layer of silt or fine sediment covering stream bottom habitat, usually due to upland erosion and/or slow water current; *sedimentation*.

simple (leaf): See *undivided leaf*.

sinuosity: The degree to which a stream meanders; the degree to which its bends tend to curve.

siphon: In mussels, circular fleshy structures used to bring in water (*incurrent siphon*) and expel waste (*excurrent siphon*).

slough: A quiet backwater channel or depression adjacent to a large river, usually in marshy areas. See *backwater*.

snout: In fish, the region of the head in front of the eyes.

soft water: Water that is low in minerals, especially calcium and magnesium.

sp. (pl. spp.): Abbreviation for "species."

special concern: In the state of Wisconsin, describes a species about which some problem of abundance or distribution is suspected but not yet proven. The main purpose of this category is to focus attention on certain species before they become *threatened* or *endangered*.

spicule: In sponges, a tiny spike that provides structural support and defense against predators.

spike: In plants, a pointy inflorescence bearing multiple fruits or flowers, which are usually closely spaced.

spikelet: In grasses and sedges, a small cluster of florets.

spine: In fish, one of the rigid, unsegmented supporting bony structures of a fin; usually sharp at the tip.

spinner: An informal term for adult mayflies that have mated and died, and land on the water's surface with wings spread.

spinous dorsal fin: In fishes with 2 dorsal fins, the first (most anterior) dorsal fin, which is comprised of sharp-tipped spines, for example, in the sunfish family.

spinous ray: In fish, a hardened spine of fused soft fin rays.

spiracle: In invertebrates, a hole in the body wall that is used to draw in air or water.

sporadic (distribution): Describes species that are scattered across the state or a region in isolated or widely spaced occurrences.

spore: An asexual reproductive structure used by many organisms.

spp. (sing. sp.): Abbreviation for "species" (plural).

stamen: In plants, the male reproductive organ of a flower, which produces pollen.

state endangered: See *endangered*.

state threatened: See *threatened*.

stipule: In plants, an appendage at the junction of the leaf blade and the stem. Stipules have variable shapes. Some clasp the stem; they may also be fused or partly fused to leaves, or free of the leaves.

stocked: Describes game fish that have been raised in hatcheries and then released in streams or lakes as juveniles and sometimes as adults. Stocking promotes recreation and offsets high fishing pressure or low fish numbers; some stocked populations become naturally reproducing.

ssp.: Abbreviation for "subspecies."

stream margin: The wetted area along the streambanks with slower water velocity and often a silt- or sand-covered stream bottom; important habitat for many invertebrate species.

stream order: A way of defining the size of a stream, with lower numbers indicating smaller streams.

subimago: In mayflies, the subadult life stage preceding the adult, or *imago*, life stage. Subimagos have wings like adults, but the wings are translucent rather than transparent; subimagos do not have functioning reproductive organs.

submersed (leaf, plant): Growing under the water surface. Submersed plants are plants with most of their leaves underwater, though they may also have some floating leaves.

subopposite (leaf arrangement): Arranged almost in pairs along the stem, with 2 leaves nearly but not exactly opposite each other at each node.

subspecies: A taxonomic category below species, consisting of an interbreeding group that is usually geographically isolated from other members of the same species.

substrate: The stream bottom and/or rocks, sediment, wood, and other solid items that provide habitat for organisms.

subterminal mouth: In fish, a mouth that does not quite reach the front tip of the head, opening slightly ventrally; the upper jaw and snout extend beyond the lower jaw.

suction disk: The circular, sucking mouths of lampreys. See *oral disk*.

sulcus: In mussels, a shallow depression or furrow on the outside surface of the shell.

superior mouth: A mouth that is very upturned, at an angle more than 60° from the horizontal.

supraoral teeth: In adult lampreys, teeth located on the tooth plate, just above the mouth opening.

tarsus (pl. tarsi): In invertebrates, the outermost major leg segment; foot-like, usually with claws, often subdivided into 2–5 smaller segments.

taxon (pl. taxa): A group of organisms that are evolutionarily related to each other, for example, a family, genus, or species.

taxonomy: The scientific system of classifying and naming organisms according to evolutionary relationships and shared physical characteristics.

teardrop: In fish, especially darters, a dark vertical blotch under the eye.

terminal: Pertaining to the end: the distal end of a structure, or (in fish and invertebrates) the posterior end of the body.

terminal bud: In plants, the winter bud at the tip of the stem.

terminal mouth: In fish, a mouth that reaches the front tip of the head, with upper and lower jaws of equal length; can be horizontal or oblique (upturned).

terrestrial: Rooted in dry ground (plants) or living on dry ground (animals).

thoracic: Pertaining to the thorax, the body region between an insect's head and abdomen.

thoracic plate: In insects, a sclerotized and often darkened body segment used to identify various aquatic insect larvae.

thorax: In invertebrates and other animals, the second (middle) major body region, between the head and the abdomen.

threatened: Describes any species that appears likely, within the foreseeable future, on the basis of scientific evidence to become *endangered* in the state of Wisconsin. Unless otherwise noted, species labeled "threatened" in this guide are threatened in Wisconsin but may not be threatened across their entire range. Federally threatened: Describes any species that is likely to become federally endangered within the foreseeable future throughout all or a significant portion of its range.

tolerant (of environmental degradation): Able to live and reproduce sustainably in degraded environmental conditions often associated with low levels of dissolved oxygen or poor habitat quality.

toothed (leaves): Having edges with regular teeth; teeth usually have pointed tips that are small relative to the leaf size. See *serrated*.

transformer: A lamprey in the process of metamorphosis from larva (ammocoetes) to the adult life phase; the transformer phase usually lasts approximately 6 months.

transparency: Clarity of water (as opposed to *turbidity*).

transpiration: The process by which water that is absorbed by plants (usually through the roots) is released back into the atmosphere through pores in the stems and leaves.

trematode: A parasitic flatworm; trematodes often infest mussels as well as many vertebrate animals.

tributary: A stream that flows into a larger water body.

truncate: Having the end shortened or squared off.

tuber: In plants, a thickened, bulb-like structure on a root or rhizome providing food storage; also used for vegetative reproduction.

tubercle: A hardened, often pointed bump. In fish, usually one of many scattered on the head, fins, and/or scales on adult males during spawning and used to sense female sex pheromones. In mussels, a pointed, rounded, or knob-like projection on the shell.

turbid: Describes water that is cloudy (with low transparency), usually due to sediments in the water.

turbidity: Cloudiness or murkiness of water, usually due to sediments or phytoplankton in the water (as opposed to *transparency*).

turbinate: Upturned.

turion: See *winter bud*.

umbel: A cluster of flower stalks arising from a single point; all stalks have similar lengths.

umbo: In mussels, the raised part of the dorsal margin of the shell representing the earliest period of shell growth, also called the *beak*.

uncommon (distribution): Describes species that are found infrequently. In this guide, the terms *abundant*, *common*, *uncommon*, and *rare* describe species from those most frequently encountered to those least frequently encountered.

undivided leaf: Having only 1 main leaf and not divided into smaller leaflets; *simple*.

unicuspid (teeth): Ending in 1 point.

univoltine: Producing 1 generation per year.

upturned mouth: In fish, a mouth that is angled upward.

valve: In mussels, 1 of the 2 halves of the shell.

vascular plant: A plant that has roots, stems, and leaves with a transport system for water, minerals, and sugars.

vegetative (reproduction): In plants, describes asexual reproduction that occurs through growing new stems, leaves, and roots without using flowers for sexual reproduction.

veliger: A free-swimming life stage of the young of some mussel species, including the invasive zebra and quagga mussels.

venation: Patterns of veins in plant leaves and insect wings, often used in identification.

vent: A fish's ventral opening anterior to the anal fin, containing the anus and genital pore.

ventral: On the belly or underside of an animal (e.g., fish or invertebrates). In mussels, referring to the edge of the shell opposite the hinge.

ventral keel: A narrow ridge on the ventral surface of an animal, particularly in fish.

vermiculations: Worm-like, white, wavy lines, for example, on the dorsal surface of a brook trout.

voltinism: The number of generations produced by an organism per year.

wadeable stream: A stream that can be safely waded to chest level at most times of the year at most points in the stream, except in its deepest pools.

waterfowl: Water birds such as ducks and geese.

watershed: An area of land that collects water from rainfall and snowmelt.

Weberian apparatus: In fish, a small series of bones in contact with the bladder that assist in sensing pressure waves.

Glossary

whorl: In plants, a group of 3 or more leaves arising from a single point on the stem, arranged evenly around the stem. In snails, the coils of the shell.

whorled (leaf arrangement): Arising in whorls along the stem.

wing: In mussels, a flattened extension of the shell on the dorsal side, either posterior, anterior, or both.

winged: Having wings or lateral extensions that resemble wings, as in the fruits of many trees (e.g., maples) or the leafstalks of some plants (e.g., spatterdock).

winter bud: In many plants, a tightly packed, often enclosed structure of reduced leaves that survives through the winter and triggers spring growth; in aquatic plants, often called a *turion*.

xylem: In plants, the part of the vascular system that carries water upward from the roots to the various parts of the plant.

zooplankton: Tiny, free-floating, or weak-swimming crustaceans that typically inhabit ponds, lakes, and large river impoundments.

ILLUSTRATION CREDITS

There are over 1,200 illustrations in this book, and here we credit these images to the many contributors who made the book possible. In the credits listed below, each illustration in the book is assigned a code (e.g., *27a6*) to indicate its location. The first number in this code represents the page number on which the illustration appears. The letter represents the location on that page. For illustrations that appear in species or group descriptions, *a* represents the first species or group entry on the page, *b* the second, and so on; for illustrations that appear in the general introduction or chapter introductions, letters are assigned from left to right or from top to bottom. For illustrations that appear in species or group entries (most images in the book), a final code number is assigned (e.g., the *6* in the code *27a6*). This final number represents an illustration's position relative to other images in the entry and is assigned according to the following rules: 1) A final number *1* always refers to the main illustration in an entry. 2) If all illustrations in an entry are set in a single vertical column, then subsequent final numbers are assigned from top to bottom. 3) If any illustrations in an entry are set side-by-side, then subsequent final numbers are assigned clockwise beginning with *1*. 4) If clockwise labeling leaves one or more illustrations unlabeled in the center of the "clock," those illustrations' final numbers are assigned last.

Introduction

Sam Batzli, WisconsinView, Space Science and Engineering Center, University of Wisconsin–Madison: 3
Linda Deith, Wisconsin Geological and Natural History Survey: 6a
Cate Harrington, The Nature Conservancy: 8
Christina Isenring, Wisconsin Department of Natural Resources: 5
Mike Miller, Wisconsin Department of Natural Resources: iv–v, 4
Bob Queen, Wisconsin Department of Natural Resources: 11a, 11b
Matt Rehwald, 1) USGS National Digital Elevation Model, 2) Wisconsin Department of Natural
    Resources Statewide Hydropgraphy Data Layer: 6b
Matt Rehwald, USGS/WDNR Stream Natural Communities model data,
    http://dnr.wi.gov/topic/rivers/naturalcommunities.html, 2007: 7
Jerry Sullivan, Wisconsin Department of Natural Resources: 12, 13
Gervase Thompson, Wisconsin Department of Natural Resources: ii–iii
Robin L. Vannote, G. Wayne Minshall, Kenneth W. Cummins, James R. Sedell, Colbert E. Cushing, "The
    River Continuum Concept," *Canadian Journal of Fisheries and Aquatic Sciences* 37 (1980), ©
    2008 Canadian Science Publishing or its licensors: 9
David Winston, Wisconsin Department of Natural Resources: 2

Plant Photos

Derek Anderson, Freckmann Herbarium, University of Wisconsin–Stevens Point: 69a1
AQUAFIX, Inc., www.naturalake.com: 85a1
Steven J. Baskauf, http://bioimages.vanderbilt.edu: 34b1
Richard Bauer, Wisconsin Department of Natural Resources: 51b1
Bob Bierman, Freckmann Herbarium, University of Wisconsin–Stevens Point: 54a1, 61a4

Merel R. Black, Freckmann Herbarium, University of Wisconsin–Stevens Point: 30a2, 35b1, 38b1, 39a2, 39b4, 43b1, 43b5, 49a1, 50b3, 52a2, 54a5, 58a1, 60a2
Center for Aquatic and Invasive Plants, University of Florida Institute of Food and Agricultural Sciences: 65a1, 65b1, 79b2, 81a2
Peter Chen, College of DuPage: 37b1
Michael Clayton, University of Wisconsin Plant Teaching Collection: 27a3
Theodore S. Cochrane, Wisconsin State Herbarium: 42b1
Kerry Ann Dressler, Bio-Photo Services: 64a4, 81a1
Paul S. Drobot, Plant Stock Photos: 30a4, 32b1, 34b6, 35b5, 37a1, 37b2
David J. Eagan: 36b1
Eric Epstein: 59a1
Gary Fewless, Cofrin Center for Biodiversity, University of Wisconsin–Green Bay: 33a2, 35a3, 36a2, 38a2, 41b1, 43a5, 43a6, 44a3, 44b4, 45a2, 45a5, 47a2, 48a4, 49a2, 49a3, 51a1, 51a2, 51a4, 52b1, 52b3, 52b4, 53a1, 56b1, 56b4,57a4, 59b1, 61a5, 62a1, 64b5, 66a5, 66a6, 68a2, 68a3, 68a5, 68b2, 73a1, 73a2, 75b2, 76a4, 77b1, 78b2, 78b3, 80a4, 80a5, 81b1, 81b2, 82a1, 82a4, 82b1, 82b2, 82b3, 82b5, 83a2, 83a3, 83b1, 83b2, 84a1, 84a5, 84a6, 84b1, 84b4, 84b5
Fish and Game New Zealand: 86a2
Evelyn Fitzgerald: 33b1
Vanessa Fox, DePauw University: 27a4, 30b1, 30b3
Steve Garske, Great Lakes Indian Fish and Wildlife Commission: 36a1, 36a3, 36a4, 43b3, 45a1, 50b1, 50b4
Erich Haber, National Botanical Services, Ottawa, Ontario: 55a1, 55a3
Jeff Hansen, Kansas Native Plants: 27b4, 31a3, 32a3, 32a4
Steve Heiskary, Minnesota Pollution Control Agency: 85a2
Roberta Hill, Maine Volunteer Lake Monitoring Program: 61b3, 80a1
Steve Hurst, USDA-NRCS PLANTS Database: 29b6
Hugh H. Iltis, Wisconsin State Herbarium: 45b2, 58a4
Emmet Judziewicz, Freckmann Herbarium, University of Wisconsin–Stevens Point: 29a1, 41a1, 62a5
Bruce Kirchoff: 31a1
K. M. Klemow, Wilkes University: 27b1, 27b3
Joanne Kline: 70a1, 83a1
Kitty Kohout, Wisconsin Department of Natural Resources: 27a1, 27a5, 38a1, 42a1, 49a6, 75a2
Robert R. Kowal, University of Wisconsin–Madison: 34a4, 50a1, 59b2
Dave Lee: 28b2, 33b2
Ben Legler: 64a1
Rebecca MacDonald: 34b5
Maine Forest Service: 28b1, 29b1
Robert W. Freckmann, Freckmann Herbarium, University of Wisconsin–Stevens Point: 43a1, 44a4, 45b1, 46a6, 53a4, 66a1, 68a1, 70a4, 70b2, 72b2, 73a5, 74a4, 75a3, 79a1
Keir Morse, www.keiriosity.com: 28a1, 31b3, 33b3, 43b4, 48a5
Michelle Nault, Wisconsin Department of Natural Resources: 49a4
Christopher Noll: 29a4, 32b3, 38b2, 39a3, 44b1, 44b2, 52a1
Joseph G. O'Brien, US Forest Service, Bugwood.org: 28b5
Ohio Division of Forestry: 29b3, 32a1
John M. Randall, The Nature Conservancy: 36b2
Paul Redfearn, Ozarks Regional Herbarium, Missouri State University: 53a2
Matt Ritter, Cal Poly Biology Department: 34a1
Rob Routledge, Sault College, Bugwood.org: 34b2, 34b4
Hanno Schaefer: 55b1
Jeff Schardt: 79b1
Georg Schramayr: 61b1, 61b2
Erica Shelby, Arkansas Department of Environmental Quality: 86a1
Paul Skawinski: 47a3, 50a4, 51b2, 54a4, 55a2, 55b4, 56a1, 56b3, 57a1, 57a5, 58a3, 58b3, 58b5, 59b3, 59b4, 60a4, 60b1, 60b3, 61a1, 62a2, 63a1, 63a2, 64b1, 64b4, 66a4, 66b1, 67a1, 68b1, 68b3,

69a4, 70a5, 70b1, 71a1, 71a3, 71b1, 72a1, 72a2, 72b1, 73b1, 73b3, 74a1, 74a3, 74b1, 74b2, 75a1, 75b1, 76a1, 76a2, 76b1, 76b3, 77a1, 77a2, 77b2, 78a1, 78a3, 78b1, 79a2, 79a3, 80b1, 81b3, 82a3

David G. Smith, www.delawarewildflowers.org: 58b1

Stephen Solheim: 31b2, 41b5, 44a1

Janice Steifel, Freckmann Herbarium, University of Wisconsin–Stevens Point: 35a1, 39a1

Joshua Sulman, Sparganium Research Website, www.botany.wisc.edu/jsulman/jsulman.htm: 47a4

Kenneth Sytsma, Botany Department, University of Wisconsin–Madison: 29a5, 30a1, 31b1, 33a1

Matthew L. Wagner: 28a3, 28a4, 29a3, 39b1, 46a1, 47a1, 51a3, 60a1, 81b4

Richard Webb, self-employed horticulturist, Bugwood.org: 29b4

Dennis W. Woodland: 48a1, 55b2

www.ukwildflowers.com: 63b1

Plant Drawings

Center for Aquatic and Invasive Plants, University of Florida Institute of Food and Agricultural Sciences: 21g, 45a3, 45a4, 63a3, 63a4, 63a5, 63b2, 63b3, 63b4, 64a2, 64a3, 64b2, 64b3, 65a2, 65a3, 65b2, 65b3, 79b3, 79b4, 81a3, 81a4

Norman Criddle: 33a3

Norman Criddle; image courtesy of Panteek.com, *Farm Weeds of Canada*, 2nd ed. (Department of Agriculture, Canada, 1909): 41a2

Crown Copyright, courtesy of the UK Forestry Commission's Forest Research Agency: 21a

Linda Ellis, Missouri Department of Conservation: 56a2

Melinda Woolf Harris, *Plant Identification Terminology: An Illustrated Glossary*, by James G. Harris and Melinda Woolf Harris (Payson, UT: Spring Lake Publishing, 2001): 23a, 23b, 23c, 23d, 23e, 23f, 23g, 23h, 23i, 23j, 23k, 23l, 23m, 23n, 23o, 24c, 25a, 25b, 25c, 25d, 25e, 25f

Laura Line, Center for Aquatic and Invasive Plants, University of Florida Institute of Food and Agricultural Sciences: 67a2, 67a3, 67a4

South Carolina Department of Natural Resources: 22d

USDA-NRCS PLANTS Database / N.L. Britton and A. Brown, *An Illustrated Flora of the Northern United States, Canada and the British Possessions*, vol. 1 (New York: Charles Scribner's Sons, 1913): 28a2, 32a2, 34a2, 34a3, 36a5, 39a4, 42b2, 43a2, 44a2, 45b3, 46a3, 46a4, 46a5, 47a6, 48a2, 48a3, 49a5, 50a2, 50a3, 52b2, 53a3, 53a6, 55b3, 56b2, 69a2, 69a3, 70b3, 70b4, 71a2, 71b2, 71b3, 72a3, 72b3, 73a3, 73a4, 73b2, 74a2, 74b3, 75a4, 75b3, 75b4, 77a3, 77a4, 77b3, 77b4

USDA-NRCS PLANTS Database / N.L. Britton and A. Brown, *An Illustrated Flora of the Northern United States, Canada and the British Possessions*, vol. 2 (New York: Charles Scribner's Sons, 1913): 21h, 27a2, 27a6, 27b2, 27b5, 29b2, 29b5, 31b4, 33b4, 33b5, 35b3, 37a4, 38a3, 38a4, 50b2, 52a3, 52a4, 58b2, 58b4, 61b4, 61b5, 61b6, 62a3, 68a4

USDA-NRCS PLANTS Database / N.L. Britton and A. Brown, *An Illustrated Flora of the Northern United States, Canada and the British Possessions*, vol. 3 (New York: Charles Scribner's Sons, 1913): 21b, 30a3, 32b2, 34b3, 35a4, 39b3, 39b5, 51b4, 60b2, 79a4, 83b3, 83b4, 84a2, 84a3, 84a4, 84b2, 84b3

USDA-NRCS PLANTS Database / A.S. Hitchcock (rev. A. Chase), *Manual of the Grasses of the United States* (Washington, DC: USDA Miscellaneous Publication No. 200, 1950): 43a3, 49a7

USDA-NRCS PLANTS Database / USDA NRCS, *Wetland Flora: Field Office Illustrated Guide to Plant Species* (USDA Natural Resources Conservation Service): 28b3, 28b4, 29a2, 30b2, 31a2, 35a2, 35b2, 35b4, 35b6, 37a2, 37a3, 37b3, 37b4, 37b5, 38b3, 39b2, 41b2, 41b4, 42a2, 42a3, 42b3, 43b2, 45b3, 46a2, 47a5, 51b3, 52b5, 54a2, 54a3, 57a2, 57a3, 58a2, 60a3, 61a2, 61a3, 62a4, 66a2, 66a3, 66b2, 66b3, 76a3, 76b2, 78a2, 80a3, 82a2, 82b4, 83a4

Carol Watkins, *Through the Looking Glass . . . A Field Guide to Aquatic Plants*, by Susan Borman, Robert Korth, and Jo Temte (Stevens Point: Wisconsin Lakes Partnership, 1997): 21c, 21d, 21e, 21f, 22a, 22b, 22c, 22e, 24a, 24b, 41b3, 43a4, 53a5, 70a2, 70a3, 80a2, 80b2, 80b3

Invertebrate Photos

Christina Anderson, Wisconsin Department of Natural Resources: 116a3

Ettore Balocchi: 119a3

Illustration Credits

Barcode of Life Database, http://www.barcodinglife.org: 98a3
Roy J. Beckemeyer: 91a2
Amy Benson, US Geological Survey: 130a2
Donald S. Chandler, University of New Hampshire: 109b1
Stephen Cresswell: 91b3
Philip J. Emmling, Badger Fly Fishers/University of Wisconsin Sea Grant Institute: 93a1, 93a3, 94a4, 96a1, 96b4, 97a1, 97a2, 98a1, 122b1
Freshwater Gastropods of North America Project: 131b1
Joyce Gross, http://joycegross.com: 93b3
Dean C. Hansen: 120a2
Mike Higgins: 102a2
Matthew A. Hill, EcoAnalysts, Inc.: 92a1, 99a1, 126b1
James C. Hodges Jr.: 98b1
Jarmo Holopainen, University of Eastern Finland: 117a1
Connie L. Isermann, University of Wisconsin–Stevens Point: 130b1
Gabor Keresztes, xespok.net/diptera: 120a3
Karl Kjer: 97a3
Martin S. Kohl, http://mkohl1.net/FWshells.html: 130a1, 130a5, 131a1, 131c1
Kenneth A. Krieger, Heidelberg University (USA): 98b5
R. Stephen Krotzer: 101b1
Chris Lukhaup: 122a1
Richard W. Merritt: 104a2
Milwaukee Public Museum: 132a1, 132a2, 132a3
Minnesota Department of Natural Resources: 127a1
Murray-Darling Freshwater Research Centre: 93b1
Jason Neuswanger, Troutnut.com: 91a1, 91b1, 94a1, 96a4, 96b1, 97b1, 98b6, 99a3, 99b1, 101a1, 103a1, 103b1, 106a1, 106b1, 106b3, 107a1, 107b1, 107b4, 108a1, 108a3, 108b1, 108b4, 109a1, 109a3, 110a1, 110a4, 112a1, 112a3, 112b1, 112b3, 113a1, 113b1, 114a1, 114a3, 114b1, 116b1, 117b1, 119a1, 119b1, 119b4, 120a1, 120b1, 121a1, 123a1
Robert L. Newell: 96b3, 98b3, 104a1, 107a4, 113a3, 113b3, 120b3
Henry Ramsay, ramsayflies.com: 96a3, 97b3, 99b2, 106a4, 109b3
Randall Schietzelt, Harper College: 93b4
J.C. Schou, Biopix.com: 128a1
Mark Siddall: 124a1
William A. Smith, Wisconsin Department of Natural Resources: 102a1
Andrei Tanasevitch, http://www.andtan.newmail.ru: 126a1
Kenneth J. Tennessen: 101b3, 103a4, 103b5
Paul P. Tinerella, University of Minnesota Insect Collection: 116a1
Trépas: 114b3
John R. Wallace, Millersville University: 101a4

Invertebrate Drawings

Nelson Annandale, *Freshwater Sponges, Hydroids & Polyzoa* (London: Taylor and Francis, 1911): 88h
R. William Bouchard, Jr.: 87a, 87b, 87c, 87d, 87e, 87f, 87g, 87h, 88a, 88b, 88c, 88d, 88e, 88f, 88g, 91a3, 91b2, 92a2, 92a3, 93a2, 93a4, 93b2, 93b5, 94a2, 94a3, 96a2, 96a5, 96b2, 96b5, 97a4, 97b2, 98a2, 98b2, 98b4, 99a2, 99b3, 99b4, 101a2, 101a3, 101b2, 102a3, 102a4, 102a5, 103a2, 103a3, 103b2, 103b3, 103b4, 104a3, 104a4, 104a5, 104a6, 106a2, 106a3, 106b2, 107a2, 107a3, 107b2, 107b3, 108a2, 108a4, 108b2, 108b3, 109a2, 109b2, 110a2, 110a3, 112a2, 112b2, 113a2, 113b2, 114a2, 114b2, 116b2, 116b3, 116b4, 117a2, 117b2, 119a2, 119b2, 119b3, 120a4, 120a5, 120b2, 121a2, 122a2, 123a2, 124a2, 126a2, 126b2, 127a2, 128a2, 130a3, 130a4, 131a2, 131b2, 131c2
Gina Mikel, scientificillustrator.com: 122b2
Karl Scheidegger, Wisconsin Department of Natural Resources: 130b2

Illustration Credits

Crayfish Photos

Susan M. Beyler, Wisconsin Department of Natural Resources: 140a1
Chris Lukhaup: 137a1, 137b1, 138a1, 139b1
Milwaukee Public Museum: 140b1
Craig Roesler, Wisconsin Department of Natural Resources: 137b5, 138b1, 139a1

Crayfish Drawings

Horton H. Hobbs III: 134a, 134b, 137a2, 137a3, 137a4, 137b2, 137b3, 137b4, 138a2, 138a3, 138a4,
    138b2, 138b3, 138b4, 139a2, 139a3, 139a4, 139b2, 139b3, 139b4, 140b2, 140b3, 140b4
Texas Journal of Science: 140a2, 140a3, 140a4
Ward's Natural Science Establishment: 135a, 135b

Mussel and Clam Photos

Kevin Cummings, Illinois Natural History Survey: 156c1, 156c2, 157b1
Minnesota Department of Natural Resources: 146a1, 146b1, 147a1, 147b1, 147c1, 148a1, 148b1,
    148c1, 149a1, 149b1, 149c1, 150a1, 150b1, 151a1, 151b1, 151c, 152a, 152b, 152c1, 152c2,
    153a1, 153a2, 153b1, 153b2, 153c1, 154a1, 154b1, 154b2, 154c1, 155a1, 155b1, 155c1, 156a1,
    156b1, 157a1, 158a1, 158b1, 158c1, 159a1, 159a2, 159b1, 159c1, 160a1, 160a2, 160b1, 160c1,
    161a1, 161b1, 161c1, 162a1, 162b1, 164a1, 165a1, 165a2
Myriah Richerson, US Geological Survey: 163a1, 163a2

Mussel and Clam Drawings

J. Scott Faiman, Conservation Commission of the State of Missouri: 144a, 145a
Texas Parks and Wildlife Department: 142a, 143a

Fish Photos

George C. Becker, *Fishes of Wisconsin* (Madison: University of Wisconsin Press, 1983): 234b2
David Jude, School of Natural Resources and Environment, University of Michigan: 179a1
John Lyons, Wisconsin Department of Natural Resources: 171a1, 171a2, 171a4, 172a1, 172a2,
    172a3, 173a1, 173b1, 174a1, 174b1, 174b4, 175a1, 175a3, 175b1, 176a1, 177a1, 177a2, 178a1,
    178a3, 179a3, 179a4, 180a1, 181a1, 181a3, 181b1, 181b3, 183a1, 183a2, 183a4, 183a5, 183b1,
    183b2, 183b3, 183b5, 184a1, 184a2, 184a3, 184a4, 184b1, 184b2, 184b4, 184b5, 185a1, 185a5,
    185a6, 185a8, 186a1, 186a4, 186a6, 186a7, 187a1, 189a1, 189a3, 190a1, 190a2, 191a1, 192a1,
    192b1, 192b2, 193a1, 193b1, 193b3, 194a1, 194a2, 194b1, 194b2, 195a1, 195a2, 195b1, 196a1,
    196a2, 196b1, 196b2, 197a1, 197a3, 197b1, 197b3, 197b5, 198a1, 198a2, 198a3, 198b1, 198b2,
    199a1, 199a3, 199a4, 199a5, 200a1, 200a2, 201a1, 201a3, 202a1, 202a2, 202b1, 203a1, 203a3,
    203b1, 203b4, 204a1, 204a2, 204b1, 204b2, 205a1, 205a3, 205b1, 205b3, 206a1, 206a2, 206b1,
    206b2, 207a1, 207a3, 207a4, 207b1, 207b4, 208a1, 208a2, 208b1, 208b2, 209a1, 209a3, 209a4,
    210a1, 211a1, 211a3, 213a1, 213a3, 213a4, 213b1, 213b3, 213b4, 214a1, 214a2, 214a3, 214b1,
    214b2, 215a1, 215a3, 215b1, 215b3, 216a1, 216a2, 216a3, 216b1, 216b2, 217a1, 217a3, 217b1,
    217b3, 218a1, 218a2, 218b1, 219a1, 219b1, 219b3, 220a1, 220a2, 220a4, 221a1, 221a2, 221a5,
    221b1, 221b2, 221b4, 221b5, 222a1, 222a2, 224a1, 224a4, 225a1, 225a3, 225a4, 225a6, 226a1,
    226a4, 227a1, 227a3, 227a4, 228a1, 228a3, 228a4, 229a1, 229a2, 229a4, 229a5, 230a1, 231a1,
    232a1, 232a2, 233a1, 233a3, 234a1, 234b1, 235a1, 235a2, 236a1, 236a3, 237a1, 237a4, 237b1,
    237b4, 238a1, 238a2, 238a3, 238b1, 238b3, 239a1, 239a3, 239b1, 239b2, 239b5, 239b6, 240a1,
    240a2, 240a3, 240b1, 240b2, 240b4, 241a1, 241b1, 241b3, 241b4, 242a1, 243a1, 243b1, 243b3,
    243b4, 244a1, 244a2, 244a3, 244b1, 245a1, 245a3, 245b1, 245b3, 246a1, 246b1, 246b2, 246b3,
    246b4, 247a1, 247a3, 247b1, 247b3, 247b4, 248a1, 248a2, 248a3, 249a1, 250a1
Paul Peeters: 228a2, 229a3

Fish Drawings

American Society of Ichthyologists & Herpetologists: 191a2, 192a2
George C. Becker, *Fishes of Wisconsin* (Madison: University of Wisconsin Press, 1983): 168c, 171a3,
    172a4, 173a2, 173a3, 173b2, 173b3, 174a2, 174a3, 174b2, 174b3, 174b5, 175a2, 175a4, 175b2,

291

175b3, 175b4, 176a2, 177a3, 178a2, 180a2, 181a2, 181b2, 182a1, 182b2, 183a3, 183b4, 184b3, 185a4, 185a7, 186a5, 189a2, 190a3, 191a3, 192a2, 192b3, 193a2, 193b2, 194a3, 194b3, 195a3, 195b2, 195b3, 196a3, 196b3, 197a2, 197b2, 197b4, 198a4, 198b3, 199a2, 199b, 200a3, 201a2, 202a3, 202b2, 202b3, 203a2, 203b2, 203b3, 204a3, 204b3, 205a2, 205b2, 206a3, 206b3, 207a2, 207b2, 207b3, 208a3, 208b3, 209a2, 210a2, 211a2, 212a, 212b, 213a2, 213b2, 214a4, 214b3, 215a2, 215b2, 216a4, 216b3, 217a2, 217b2, 218a3, 219a2, 219b2, 220a3, 220a5, 221a3, 221a4, 221a6, 221b3, 221b6, 222a3, 224a2, 224a3, 225a2, 225a5, 226a2, 226a3, 227a2, 228a5, 229a6, 230a2, 231a2, 232a3, 233a2, 234b3, 235a3, 235a4, 236a2, 236a4, 237a2, 237a3, 237b2, 237b3, 238a4, 238a5, 238b2, 238b4, 239a2, 239a4, 239b3, 239b4, 240a4, 240b3, 240b5, 241a2, 241b2, 242a2, 243a2, 243b2, 244a4, 244b2, 245a2, 245b2, 246a2, 246b5, 247a2, 247b2, 249a2, 250a2, 166a, 166b, 166c, 166d, 166e, 166g, 166h, 167a, 167b, 167c, 167d, 167e, 167f, 167g, 167h, 167i, 167j, 167k, 167l, 167m, 168a, 168b
Donna R. Francis: 166f, 179a2
Susan Laurie-Bourque, Canadian Museum of Nature: 166i, 187a2
Le Naturaliste Canadien / La Société Provancher d'histoire naturelle du Canada, "Larvae of Eastern American Lampreys," *Le Naturaliste Canadien* 77, no. 3–4 (1950): 185a2, 185a3, 186a2, 186a3

Amphibian Photos

Dan Nedrelo: 256a1, 256c1
Ohio Division of Wildlife: 258a1, 259a1
Allen Blake Sheldon: 253a1, 254a1, 255a1, 255b1, 256b1

Amphibian Drawings

Georgine Price, Wisconsin Department of Natural Resources: 251a, 251b, 253a2, 255a, 255b

Reptile Photos

Ohio Department of Natural Resources, Division of Wildlife: 262b1
Allen Blake Sheldon: 262a1, 266a1, 267a1, 267b1, 268a1, 268b1
Wisconsin Department of Natural Resources: 265a1

Reptile Drawings

Georgine Price, Wisconsin Department of Natural Resources: 260a
Helen South, helensouth.com: 260b

INDEX

Index